Oracle DBA Mentor

Succeeding as an Oracle Database Administrator

Brian Peasland

〈IOUG〉
Independent oracle users group

Apress®

Oracle DBA Mentor: Succeeding as an Oracle Database Administrator

Brian Peasland
Fargo, ND, USA

ISBN-13 (pbk): 978-1-4842-4320-6   ISBN-13 (electronic): 978-1-4842-4321-3
https://doi.org/10.1007/978-1-4842-4321-3

Copyright © 2019 by Brian Peasland

Managing Director, Apress Media LLC: Welmoed Spahr
Acquisitions Editor: Jonathan Gennick
Development Editor: Laura Berendson
Coordinating Editor: Jill Balzano

Cover designed by eStudioCalamar

Cover image designed by Freepik (www.freepik.com)

Distributed to the book trade worldwide by Springer Science+Business Media New York, 233 Spring Street, 6th Floor, New York, NY 10013. Phone 1-800-SPRINGER, fax (201) 348-4505, e-mail orders-ny@springer-sbm.com, or visit www.springeronline.com. Apress Media, LLC is a California LLC and the sole member (owner) is Springer Science + Business Media Finance Inc (SSBM Finance Inc). SSBM Finance Inc is a **Delaware** corporation.

For information on translations, please e-mail rights@apress.com, or visit http://www.apress.com/rights-permissions.

Apress titles may be purchased in bulk for academic, corporate, or promotional use. eBook versions and licenses are also available for most titles. For more information, reference our Print and eBook Bulk Sales web page at http://www.apress.com/bulk-sales.

Any source code or other supplementary material referenced by the author in this book is available to readers on GitHub via the book's product page, located at www.apress.com/9781484243206. For more detailed information, please visit http://www.apress.com/source-code.

Printed on acid-free paper

This book is dedicated to my three boys: Chay, Jace & Jenner

Table of Contents

About the Author

Brian Peasland is a seasoned Oracle database administrator with well over 20 years working with all Oracle database versions since Oracle 7.1 was released. He is a constant contributor to the My Oracle Support and Oracle Developer communities as well as other forums. Brian has been writing for SearchOracle.com since 2001. He has B.S. and M.S. degrees, majoring in Computer Science for both. Brian is the author of *Oracle RAC Performance Tuning*.

Brian and his wife reside in Fargo, ND, where they are very busy raising their three kids and shuttling them from one sport to another. During the summer, he can often be seen on the baseball diamond, and in the winter, it's in the hockey rink.

About the Technical Reviewer

 An Oracle ACE since 2017, **Mike Donovan** currently serves as CTO for Dbvisit Software, a New Zealand–headquartered company focused solely on Oracle replication. Having worked there for the better part of a decade he has held numerous technical and customer-facing roles, developing considerable knowledge and experience in this domain, building on his technical consulting and Oracle database administration background.

Mike is an enthusiastic advocate of Oracle technologies, who also loves exploring new tools and solutions like Kafka and cloud-based offerings, and is increasingly taking on an evangelist role championing these areas of interest. Mike enjoys writing and speaking on these topics and has been fortunate to have been invited to present at user groups and conferences all over the world, such as Oracle OpenWorld, IOUG Collaborate, RMOUG Training Days, NLOUG Tech 17 and 18, and dbtech showcase (Japan), amongst others.

An avid reader and voracious learner, Mike enjoys running, listening to music, and cooking in his spare time.

Acknowledgments

I dedicated my first book, *Oracle RAC Performance Tuning*, to my late father. As I was working on that book, I was creating outlines for a few more books. One of the ideas I had was to create this book that provided mentorship advice to database administrators. There are so many books on the market that teach you a wealth of introductory information, but none of them teach you how to learn Oracle on your own other than to buy another book. I wanted this book to be about more than just the introductory information. I wanted to give the reader the tools to be able to take charge of their career and grow in the direction they desire. Oracle Real Application Clusters requires advanced skills from the DBA. Similarly, Oracle performance tuning requires advanced skills. Putting both of them together really requires you to know your craft. My first book is for the seasoned Oracle veteran, and who better to dedicate the book to than the seasoned influence in my life, my father? This book is more entry level and, as such, I have dedicated this to my three boys, Chay, Jace and Jenner. Parents have no greater role than to mentor their children to grow up to be responsible adults and be able to find their own way in this world. We cannot teach them everything they need to know to succeed in life, but we can give them the skills they need to figure things out on their own. Dedicating this book to my sons seemed natural. I mentor them through the early stages of their life, analogous to my attempts at mentoring readers on a professional level.

I would like to thank Jill Balzano and Jonathan Gennick at Apress for their hard work on this book. I would also like to thank anyone else at Apress who worked behind the scenes.

The best books have great technical reviewers keeping the author honest. Thanks to Mike Donovan for his hard work. He made me think of ideas that were not in the original manuscript, which just made the book a better product.

I want to thank anyone that reads my work, be it this book, articles I write for websites or my blog, or answers to questions on many different forums. As you will learn later in this book, I write a lot to help enhance my career. You'll have to read more to understand. If I did not have anyone to read my work, then I would not write as much, and my career growth would suffer. So, thanks for reading. It helps me out a great deal and I hope it helps you as well.

Introduction

Over the more than two decades I have been working as an Oracle database administrator, I have been both a mentor and a mentee too many times to count. This book is a collection of the things I have learned that have worked for me, as well as the advice given to me and given by me over the years. In a standard mentor/mentee relationship, both parties are in the same location, working hand in hand with face-to-face contact. Today's world often dictates the mentor/mentee relationship be more distant. We are constantly learning from others how to improve our craft, often from strangers with no formal mentorship relation. For example, we may be mentored by someone giving advice in a discussion forum. We may be mentored by reading a highly regarded Oracle professional's blog. We may even be mentored just by reading the advice someone has taken time to write down in a book, as you are about to embark on today. Thanks for reading!

This book is intended for those starting out in their career as an Oracle database administrator. Even those with a few years of experience will find helpful information here. If you want to advance to the top level of this profession, the information in this book will help you get there. I know of many database administrators that wished they had the information in this book to jumpstart their careers. Non-Oracle database administrators will still find this book useful. Except for the Oracle-specific information, the other advice in the book can be used to enhance your career. I was able to quickly and easily learn how to administer SQL Server and other database platforms by following the advice I give here.

Oracle DBA Mentor does more than teach you how to administer an Oracle database. I could have easily written a book that said, "do this, that, and the other," but then it would be like all the others on the market. The biggest differentiator of this book and anything else I have seen so far is that this book teaches you how to expand your knowledge after you are done reading. After you have learned that this, that, and the other do not solve your problem, where do you turn next? This book helps you figure it out.

I use the words "I," "you," and "we" a lot in this book. This style was chosen on purpose because I wanted you to feel as if we are in an actual mentor/mentee relationship even though I am not there in person. I am talking directly to you, the reader, as I write the words here.

Chapters 1 and 2 introduce some soft skills to help you succeed in this job. For many of us, this information is already known. Just in case, I make sure you understand the database administrator's most important role is to be the data guardian and I suggest how to interact with others over the course of your career.

In Chapters 3 through 8, we set up a testbed server, install Oracle, create a database, and implement security and backups. We need this system to be able to explore more as we read the next chapters in the book.

Chapters 9 through 12 show you how to use the Oracle database. Most books tell us the steps to connect to an Oracle database. We will see how it all works. Chapter 10 discusses the importance of testbeds and developing test cases. We created a testbed for our use and now it's time to start using it. Using a testbed is the first thing we can do to help us help ourselves in learning more about Oracle.

Chapters 13 through 16 are the meat of the book. This is where you learn the different avenues for getting answers to questions not found in all of the Oracle books you could ever buy. As you will discover, I strongly recommend you read the Oracle documentation, as most of your answers are written there. Chapter 13 helps unlock the voluminous documentation set. Chapter 14 explores the data dictionary, Chapter 15 explains My Oracle Support, and Chapter 16 examines the benefits of social media.

Chapters 17 through 19 help us maintain a database system once we have it set up. We explore how to apply patches in Chapter 17. We discuss how to upgrade a database in Chapter 18. Chapter 19 covers capacity planning.

Chapters 20 and 21 conclude the book. These are overviews of the Oracle architecture and advanced options, respectively. So much more could be written here. The idea is that you learn some of the high-level concepts so that when you need the information in the future, you already have an introduction.

PART I

Initial Setup

CHAPTER 1

Introduction

If you have grabbed a copy of this book, you most likely have landed (or are hoping to land) a job as an Oracle database administrator (DBA) and are looking for assistance on the next steps in your career. There are plenty of books on the market that will relate tons of technical information on how the Oracle database works. I have many such books in my library. Those books provide a wealth of useful information and are great resources.

As the title of this book indicates, it is intended to serve as a mentor to you in your career as a DBA. A mentor is often there to work hand in hand with the mentee, guiding their career. I cannot be there by your side, so I figured the next best thing to do is to write down the advice and insights I have imparted to others over the years. I want this book to feel more personal than a typical computer book, more like any other mentor/mentee relationship, so I use words like "I" and "we" often. This book will most likely be one of many mentors you will have in your career. Many entry-level database administrators work alongside a senior-level DBA, who is their primary mentor. This book should supplement your primary mentor's guidance. You will also receive advice from other Oracle professionals you encounter, who will impact your career growth without being an official mentor.

What makes this book that you are reading different is that its aim is to teach you how to find the answers that are not in the other books on this topic. What happens if you need more information? Where do you turn? The most common answer is to look in the Oracle documentation, and that is a great response. Too often, people are afraid to use the Oracle documentation because it is vast and complex. In Chapter 13 of this book I will teach you how to leverage the documentation to your advantage. Unfortunately, the Oracle documentation is not always complete, so where do you go next? This book will give you pointers on how to proceed when the information is not readily available.

Sometimes the best resource for the answers you seek is within yourself. One of the most common types of questions I get from many entry-level Oracle DBAs is something along the lines of "Can I do *X* in Oracle?" If you've asked that question, then the answer is

© Brian Peasland 2019
B. Peasland, *Oracle DBA Mentor*, https://doi.org/10.1007/978-1-4842-4321-3_1

clearly "No!" because it indicates you haven't even tried. During the course of this book, we will build a system where we can create answers to many of our own questions. While building this system, we will cover many best practices. If you follow the advice in this book, not only will you have a testbed to work with, but you will have confidence that the Oracle systems you are creating and administering will be able to handle many of the different needs required from the system.

This book is not highly technical. It is meant to be used in the beginning of your database administration career. Some might call this a *junior DBA* level. Intermediate-level DBAs may also find some useful information in here as well. If you are a senior-level DBA, you likely know most of the information presented in this book. However, I have found that too many senior DBAs have had to learn this information the hard way and wish someone would have given them the knowledge presented in this book earlier in their careers (which was part of my motivation to write this book). This book is just a start on your career-long journey. No one becomes a great DBA overnight. You've probably met some great DBAs in your career already. How did they get to such lofty status? Through hard work and constant learning. I've been an Oracle DBA for over 20 years and I'm still learning new things all the time. It is the challenge of solving complex database problems and learning how to leverage the database engine's features that is the most rewarding aspect of this career for many of the top-level database administrators I have met.

Much of what is in this book stems from things I have learned from the many DBAs that have mentored me through the years, but sadly I lacked a true hands-on mentor in my early days. I was the only DBA at my first job in this field, so there was no one to mentor me. Most of my "mentors" have never even met me and probably don't even know my name or that they helped my career. But during my career I've taken tips and tidbits from many different people and used those to formulate the basis of what you will be reading here.

Now comes my first bit of advice to help you grow your career: give as much as you get. It sounds simple, right? However, giving takes time, energy, and discipline and, as such, people typically do not share enough of their knowledge as they could. One of the secrets I've learned over the years is that the act of sharing my knowledge with others teaches me as much as I teach them. When you must formulate your thoughts, especially in written form, something happens in the brain where you learn the material better than had you not written anything. Most of knowledge sharing in the Oracle community is done in written form through books, blog posts, white papers, and forums.

Tip   Share your knowledge. You will learn just as much as you teach.

While this book is Oracle focused, you can use these same principles and techniques for working with other database systems. For example, in Chapter 13 we will spend time learning about the Oracle documentation. If you are a SQL Server DBA, you just need to convert this knowledge to Microsoft's Books Online. While this book covers Oracle-related forums, there are many for SQL Server as well. The advice is the same, and you just need to convert it to work for the other database engine.

It is highly likely that in your career you will be asked to work with multiple database platforms. In my current job, I work primarily with Oracle but also SQL Server and MongoDB. I have worked with PostgreSQL, MySQL, and DB2 over the years. Whenever I work with a new database system, I try to figure out how I do a task in Oracle and then see how the other database engine does the same thing. For example, all database engines have some form of transaction logging. In Oracle, it is the online redo log. In SQL Server, it is called the transaction log. Both engines have the same capability. It is how they implement that functionality that differs.

Becoming a DBA

Typically, there are two career paths to becoming a database administrator. In general, the junior-level database administrator was either an application developer or a system administrator (SysAdmin) prior to working as a DBA. Application developers that become DBAs normally have experience working on database-centric applications and have already been exposed to tables, queries, and other database activities. Former system administrators understand the operating system, disk subsystems, and basic networking skills, all of which are essential for a database administrator to understand. No matter which of these two paths the DBA traveled before embarking on their database career, they most likely demonstrated a high degree of skill before being promoted to fill a junior-level DBA position in their company. Sometimes, the DBA will work on database-related projects in their organization without being an official database administrator. They may take this job experience and parlay that into an entry-level DBA position at another company. While possible, it is more rare for someone to obtain a DBA position without having been a developer or SysAdmin in the past. Those who start as a DBA without coming from one of these two paths typically focused on database systems in college.

I've often told people that the database engine sits between the application and the server. As such, it makes sense to hire junior-level DBAs from one end or the other. Ideally, the candidate would have experience in both servers and application development, but that is often harder to find.

It can be difficult to obtain your first database administrator job. For starters, the job is technically complex, but that is also one of the reasons it can be very exciting. In addition to understanding how the database engine works, the DBA needs to have good knowledge of system administration and application development, as already discussed. The DBA also needs to understand networking and storage, and possess a thorough grasp of IT security. Today's DBA should have experience with cloud technologies. One of the challenges facing database administrators is the breadth of knowledge required to be good at this job. But this also is very appealing to many DBAs—the job never gets dull because there is so much to learn and so many different areas to explore. The variety, complexity, and chance to explore new features are attractive qualities of the job to many different people.

Another stumbling block to landing that first DBA job is the importance of the data within a company. Data is an organizational asset. It needs to be protected yet made available to support the business. Many companies are reluctant to trust individuals with little experience to manage, maintain, and secure one of the most important pieces of their IT infrastructure. We will discuss this further in the section "Data Guardian" later in this chapter.

So how do you land that first DBA job? For most people, you begin your career in either system administration or application development, as mentioned earlier. If you started as a SysAdmin, then learn as much as you can about networking and storage and IT security. If you began as an application developer, then take the time to understand as much as you can about creating good database applications. Learn the ins and outs of table design, formulating SQL statements, and how to get the best application performance by leveraging the proper database features like indexes, materialized views, and more.

Next, try to focus your career with a slant in the database direction. Talk to your manager about your desire to learn more about database administration. Volunteer for small database-related projects, even if they are out of scope for your traditional duties. As you will learn later in this book, you can download the Oracle database, install it on a test system, and begin playing with the product. There is nothing stopping you from building your Oracle database knowledge and experience right now! At some point in your career, you will likely build other skills, both soft and technical, relevant to the DBA role.

Once you've had a chance to test the waters on a few DBA tasks, start keeping an eye out for junior-level DBA job openings. Many times, if your manager knows of your interest, they may be willing to take a chance on you, as a good employee, to grow your career in your desired direction. A good manager understands the value in keeping good employees happy, even if it means the employees have to replace their skillset as they move to another position within the company.

Not all managers are willing to help their employees grow their career paths. Another stumbling block may simply be the lack of opportunities within your current company. In this case, managers cannot simply create a job opening just because an employee wants to change positions. If either of these situations applies to you, it may be time to look for employment outside your current company. At the end of the day, it is up to you to move your career forward. You may desire to move forward with your current company or you may have to decide to make a bigger change if your company cannot help you fulfill your career aspirations.

If you are interviewing for a new position at some other company, you will inevitably be asked a question like "Where do you see yourself in five years?" This is your chance to tell the prospective new employer of your desire to work your way toward a DBA position. Seize the day! Make it plain and let your intentions be known. Some companies may determine that you are not a good fit for them based on this answer, but many others will, as they understand the value of engaged and enthusiastic employees. From my own experience, I'd rather work for a company that takes an interest in helping me advance my career in my desired direction than to obtain a job where I see no future career growth. Too many people are stuck in jobs they hate. I'd rather have a career that gives me satisfaction doing work that is challenging and rewarding. Ultimately, you have to look inside yourself to find out what motivates and excites you. For me, that is being a DBA. I cannot imagine working a different job. Since you're reading this book, you may feel the same. No matter which avenue you choose to get to that first DBA job, good luck to you!

Typical Day of the DBA

The title of this section is a bit of a misnomer, because a typical data doesn't exist for the DBA. Sure, every DBA I've talked to starts their day by getting a copy of coffee or other morning beverage and then checking their e-mail for anything that requires immediate attention, but after that, the day is likely to be anything but typical. The variety is appealing to many DBAs because they are not *stuck* doing the same thing day after day.

Most database administrators do have a similar portfolio of duties and responsibilities, such as:

- Checking backup job status

- Securing databases

- Creating new databases

- Creating new database objects

- Making sure the data is up and running

- Tuning database performance

- Designing databases

- Planning database capacity

- Working closely with other IT staff and application developers

- Participating in an on-call rotation

- Installing software

- Performing extract, transform, and load (ETL) activities

- Troubleshooting

This is not an exhaustive list by any means, and the DBA will likely have other duties as well. Many times, you will not work actively on an assigned duty for a long period of time. For example, I only perform capacity planning activities a few times each year, but checking the backup job status is a daily function. There are ebbs and flows, and *seasonal* variation, all of which keeps things interesting.

DBA duties will vary from company to company as well. Different organizations have tailored the position for their own needs and purposes. For example, I worked at one company that used only third-party software applications. In this context the DBA was responsible for working with the application vendor to provide database services for the software. At another company I was required to work closely with the application developers and assist them in writing SQL statements. Both jobs gave me a DBA title, but the nature of the work was considerably different.

The Data Guardian

I alluded to it in the previous section, but mastering this topic is vitally important to your success as a database administrator. The DBA is the company's *data guardian*. However, when I ask fellow DBAs what they consider their most important duties, the typical reply is "backups." My reply to the most important duty of a DBA question is "to protect the data." Backups are just one component of the overall mission of protecting the data.

Data is a valuable asset. Companies like Google and Facebook give you their products for free. Have you ever wondered why? The simple answer is that they make money off data you generate for them. What you search for and who you follow generate data points that build a profile of you, the user. Those data points are then used in a variety of ways. Google and Facebook, for example, can generate targeted advertisements for other companies with these profiles. They can sell the data to third parties.

Even if your company is not in the business of buying or selling data, the data in their databases is still a valuable corporate asset. A company that sells products may want to learn more about its customers. In college, I learned about a famous case where a grocery store mined data on their customers' buying patterns and discovered that beer and diapers were sold together in high frequency on the weekends. The grocery store surmised that the father was sent to the store to get diapers for the baby and bought some beer to take home as well. The grocery chain started putting beer and diapers next to each other at the end of an aisle and increased sales on both. Learning about their customers is one way companies leverage their data assets.

Even if you do not think your company's data is valuable, hackers certainly do. Hackers will try all sorts of methods to obtain access to your company's data. The company invests a large amount of money for hardware, licenses, and salaries to store data and make it available to the business. Yet as Data Guardians, we cannot allow unrestricted access to this data. To do so could potentially jeopardize business operations. We simply cannot have anyone and everyone making changes to the data. For example, a company that sells sporting goods has data showing the inventory of the products they sell. If the company has ten baseball bats in stock, then the database should reflect that fact. If someone nefariously or accidently changes the data to reflect there are zero bats in the inventory, then customers won't be able to order the product and the company will lose potential sales. Conversely, if someone changes the data to indicate there are 100 baseball bats in the inventory, then the sales system may try to sell 90 bats that do not exist, leading to upset customers when these orders are not able to be fulfilled. Having upset customers leads to lost sales in the future, and this must be avoided. This sporting goods company needs an accurate inventory of their products reflected in their databases.

Many database systems today also store information that has value in its own right, due to its sensitive nature, such as *personally identifiable information* (PII). PII is data that can be used to identify a specific individual, such as name and birth date, tax identification numbers, credit card numbers, and more. Any PII in the database needs to be encrypted so that should a hacker obtain access to the database, they cannot get any value from this data.

Failure to protect data is bad for business on many levels, as we know from the many headlines of yet another data breach in recent times. For example, in 2013, Target Corporation suffered a well-known data breach, and this reportedly cost the company over $300 million! Yahoo suffered a data breach to over 3 billion accounts in 2013-2014. When Yahoo was purchased by Verizon, the sale price was estimated to be $350 million less than it would have been had the breach not occurred. It is estimated that 60% of small companies that suffer a data breach go out of business.

I've always taken the approach that as a DBA, I am my company's data guardian. The DBA needs to be the one that is always thinking about protecting the data. This means ensuring that only those that have a legitimate business need are able to access the data, and only those with appropriate authority to modify data can do so. We restrict access to the data as much as possible. The DBA is constantly being asked to provide access to data to new avenues within the business. As companies learn to leverage their data as an asset, they are exploring new ways to use that data to drive revenues. Not only will data be used in new and exciting ways, the DBA may need to give business units just what they need, and no more, to protect the data. The DBA may also need to cleanse data before another business unit gains access.

Data protection is much more than just backups. The DBA needs to make sure database engines have the most up-to-date security patches applied. The DBA grants and revokes privileges in the database. The DBA needs to be familiar with SQL injection and other database hacking techniques. The DBA needs to learn how to encrypt data in the database as well as how to protect the encryption keys. Hopefully, this section has convinced you that the most important job of the DBA is not backups. Rather, the DBA must be adept at all aspects of data protection. The DBA needs to be the data guardian.

Moving On

As stated earlier, this book is different than others because it not only focuses on technical information necessary to become a successful Oracle database administrator, but also gives you advice on how to learn things you won't find in any books. This book can help serve as one of the many mentors you will use to advance your database administrator career. I have designed this book to not only help you learn more about administering Oracle databases, but also to help you discover how to learn things you will not find in other books, even the Oracle documentation.

The next chapter does not have what you might consider to be technical information. Rather, it focuses on the soft skills necessary to perform work as a database administrator. Please do not skip this chapter because it still contains very important information.

.

CHAPTER 2

Working As a DBA

The previous chapter I went over the career path to becoming a database administrator as well as the general duties and responsbilities of the DBA, including their role as the Data Guardian. In this chapter, we will spend time discussing how to work as a database administrator. The information in this chapter is not technical in nature and can be used by non-Oracle DBAs as well. Rather, this chapter will focus on the soft skills all good database administrators should possess. Much of the information in this chapter can be used outside of the DBA role and applied to other positions in the organization as well.

The Rude DBA

Depending on whom you ask, the database administrator is usually a well-respected profession in the IT world. As we discussed in the previous chapter, the DBA usually comes from either an application development or system administration background. It is more rare for someone to become a database administrator straight out of college. Typically, the DBA worked up to the position and demonstrated a high degree of skill to get there.

When you are working as a DBA, try to remember that you not only represent yourself and your organization, but you also represent this profession. I've always thought of the database administrator as being one of the top positions of the IT career ladder. As such, you will interact with many people inside your organization. If you follow the advice in future chapters, you will interact with many people in the world-wide Oracle community. Representing yourself in a positive manner will have greater impact on your lifelong career than if you are demonstrating poor behavior. Sadly, I've come across too many DBAs in this world who are always grumpy and obstructionists to others, traits not exclusive to DBAs. As an example, a DBA refuses to grant privileges or create new databases regardless of the business need and without giving an explanation. I've heard too many stories about the DBA being a jerk and being hard to work with.

© Brian Peasland 2019
B. Peasland, *Oracle DBA Mentor*, https://doi.org/10.1007/978-1-4842-4321-3_2

There could be many reasons why some DBAs have this attitude, but please do not be this type of DBA. If you get a request for a privilege or a new database and you know the request should not be satisfied, instead of refusing the request in some rude manner, a better approach is to figure out what the requestor really needs and how you can help them do their job. Do not respond "Your request is denied" but rather "Sorry, but satisfying that request as you have outlined it will cause other problems. Can we do it another way so that you can do your job but my concerns are still met?"

Tip   Don't be the rude DBA. Be the helpful one.

I've always been of the unsubstantiated opinion that the rude DBA is a small part of the reason for the rise of the schema-less databases that have become very popular today. Application developers have stated that these databases, like MongoDB, are great because they can install and set them up and begin coding without ever having to get assistance from the DBA. My counterpoint is that by avoiding the DBA, developers miss many other aspects of database administration the DBA normally thinks about. A few of those aspects relate to database security and a proven backup and recovery implementation. The application developer is not used to being the data guardian, a concept we talked about in the previous chapter. In Chapter 7, we will discuss how a DBA should think of recovery before backups, a viewpoint that most application developers do not even consider. In 2017, over 25,000 unsecured MongoDB databases were hit with ransomware[1]. It's not that MongoDB is an insecure database platform. Rather, these deployments had weak passwords and default usernames. The DBA was bypassed, security was never given a thought, and companies paid the price. Had DBAs been involved in these projects, the databases likely would have been secured because a good DBA thinks about these things. I wonder how many of the companies with those 25,000+ MongoDB installations now wish their DBA was in charge of their database platform.

This example is not meant as an indictment of MongoDB. It's a great product and I currently manage a few MongoDB databases. Out of the box, MongoDB, Oracle, and other database platforms are not secure. It is the database administrator's job to lock things down no matter which database platform is being deployed. The point of the

---

[1]https://www.zdnet.com/article/mongodb-ransacking-starts-again-hackers-ransom-26000-unsecured-instances/

example is that people try to avoid rude DBAs and will find workarounds that lack security and other controls essential to good data governance.

Tip   The rude DBA is a liability. The helpful DBA is an asset.

Being helpful doesn't mean the DBA needs to do whatever a coworker requests. There are many times I will deny a request. Any time I deny a request, I do so with politeness and a follow-up on how to get the requestor back to work. The requestor needs to get their job done. They know something in the database is currently blocking them from completing their task. Most requestors I have met are not as knowledgeable as the database administrator as to how to properly get past their database roadblock. This is where the DBA must help formulate the request into something that satisfies both parties.

Multiplatform Work

Today's DBA usually has to work with a variety of database platforms. It is rare for a database administrator to focus solely on one database platform. Early in my career as a DBA, I was hired to work at a company that only used Oracle database systems. Our small team of DBAs worked day in and day out with Oracle. One day, our manager told us that SQL Server was coming into the shop and one of us would need to get up to speed on the product. I jumped at the opportunity. I was surprised I didn't have a fight on my hands deciding which DBA on the team would manage this new product. While my primary expertise lies with Oracle, since that day, I have never had a job where I did not have to manage both Oracle and SQL Server. On that day, I knew that being able to manage multiple platforms would be good for my future career prospects. I have found that it is more beneficial to my career growth to be able to work successfully with multiple database platforms. After I learned SQL Server in addition to Oracle, I did not stop there. I continued to learn more about other database products, especially as new ones were introduced to the community.

Over the years, I've worked on many different database engines: Oracle, SQL Server, MongoDB, MySQL, PostgreSQL, and DB2, to name a few. Today's database administrator is being asked to do the same. Many times, you will be asked to support different database platforms due to third-party software deployments. One product works on Oracle and another product only supports SQL Server, as an example. With the rise of NoSQL databases, you may find that your trusted relational databases are not an appropriate solution to satisfy ever-increasing volumes of data. As such, your career will more than likely have you working on multiple database platforms. So how do you do it? How do you work with all these products that can be so different from each other?

I learned in my first SQL Server administration class how I needed to approach the new system. Prior to my DBA career, I made the personal choice to attend college and obtain a degree in computer science, with a focus on database systems. In college, I learned the theory of how database systems should work. I studied normal forms, properties of transactions, relational database theory, and so much more. I never gave it much more thought as I learned to be an Oracle DBA. Sitting there in my first class on SQL Server, the instructor was talking about creating tables in a SQL Server database. My thoughts started to center on how in Oracle we create the table in a tablespace and a database is composed of multiple tablespaces, but SQL Server is a bit different. Then I remembered how one of my professors in college talked about the database engine having the responsibility of abstracting the storage from the database design. That's when it occurred to me that I should rely on the relational database theory I was taught in college and that all I needed to do was to figure out how each database platform implemented the theory. The next day of the SQL Server administration class, we were going to be discussing backup and recovery. I knew how this worked in Oracle. I remembered from my college days that database systems have a transaction journal and that a backup plus the journal lets me recover my data to a point in time. From an Oracle perspective, that transaction journal is the online and archived redo logs. I learned in class that SQL Server keeps a transaction log for each database. My foundation in how database systems work in general, from my college courses, let me easily spot how Oracle implements the details, as I was now in the workforce. Working on a new platform, I immediately knew I needed to just figure out how that system implemented the transaction journal, after which I was off and running.

Tip   If you know the general database theory, encountering a different platform means you just need to know how the platform implements the theory.

For me, those college days are a distant memory. Database systems have changed so much since then. Database vendors are constantly implementing new features, like materialized views, that I never learned about in college. Oracle introduced materialized views and I've used them to successfully improve application performance in certain situations. One day I needed to do something with SQL Server and I thought materialized views would be a good fit if I could just figure out how SQL Server implements that feature. In those cases, when I know which feature to leverage in Oracle and want to implement it in another database engine, I do a simple web search with the Oracle feature and other platform name. A quick web search for "SQL Server materialized view" led me quickly to a Microsoft feature called indexed views—different name but very close to the same feature. I then searched for "SQL Server indexed views" and was off and running with the other platform. It works both ways. If you come from a SQL Server background and have to work on Oracle, searching for "Oracle indexed views" will quickly lead you to the materialized view feature name.

After I know which feature in the new database engine promises to give me the functionality I seek, I then turn to the product's official documentation to learn more.

Tip   If you know the feature on one platform and want to find a similar feature on a different platform, perform a web search for "*other_platform feature_name*" and you can quickly figure out which feature is similar on the other platform.

So long as you know what feature you use on one platform to do the job, it normally doesn't take long to find out the similar feature's name on another database platform. This allows you to quickly perform tasks on a platform that you may not be familiar with.

Another tip is to search for "*old_platform* for the *new_platform* DBA." This will provide guides to help you translate from one platform you already know to another one you are starting to work with. For example, you could search for "Oracle for the SQL Server DBA" or vice versa. When working with a new database platform on which I need to get up to speed quickly, I often perform a similar search. It doesn't take too long for me to find a "cheat sheet" (or several). The cheat sheet quickly clues me in to the terminology I need for the new database engine. However, you should only use the results as a guide. Use the product's official documentation for the best source of information. All too often I find a cheat sheet written by someone who knows one database engine well and only has a cursory knowledge of the other product, and they often miss some very important information. For example, when contrasting and comparing Oracle's "database" to a SQL Server "database," it is common for cheat sheets to fail to explain clearly that the term "database" means two different things in the two different platforms. A cheat sheet typically devotes one sentence to highlight the differences when a full paragraph is needed to explain more accurately the differences. Therefore, you should refer to the official documentation to learn more.

Lastly, having a good foundation in database theory is not essential but it does help. Oracle is a relational database. As such, the Oracle DBA should learn Dr. Edgar F. Codd's relational theory as well as the work of Christopher J. Date. Codd and Date are the pioneers of the relational database that we use today. As I alluded to earlier, if you know the theory of how the engine is supposed to work, then you can easily focus on how the engine implements that theory.

Let me illustrate the point with a car example. Would you take your Toyota to a mechanic that only knows how to fix a Chevy 5.7L engine? I would rather take my vehicle to a mechanic that knows the principals of how a combustion engine is supposed to work. Gas is mixed with oxygen and moved into a cylinder. A spark ignites the gas fuel mixture, which pushes a piston that causes the engine to move. A Toyota sedan might have fuel injection instead of the old-fashioned carburetors. That Chevy 5.7L mechanic will not know anything about fuel injection. But the mechanic that understands the foundations of how combustion engines work knows that fuel injection is a different method of delivering the fuel and oxygen to the cylinder.

Back to relational database engines, the manufacturers try to adhere to many of Codd's and Date's theoretical foundations. As I have said before, if you know the theory behind how it is supposed to work, all you need to do is figure out how a particular vendor implemented that detail. This makes working with different database platforms much easier. Even if you work with only one database platform, a good foundation on database theory will help your career. Sadly, too many colleges these days are focusing on giving their students "employable skills," which means they teach the specifics of the top industry needs and gloss over the theoretical foundations. Do not get me wrong. Employable skills are great. But I have seen too many colleges focus on Oracle and totally skip the work of Codd and Date. The student graduates and easily finds a job as an Oracle DBA, armed with the knowledge they learned from that institution. The college and the student are both happy. Then the student advances through their career and is asked to work on MySQL. Too bad for the student they are only a Chevy 5.7L engine mechanic. The student was never given a proper foundation in database theory and likely will have a hard time adjusting to the different database platform.

Take a retrospective look at your own educational background. If you did not receive a proper education in database theory, take some time to invest in yourself by learning more about the theory of how it *should* work. Then apply that theory to the databases you manage to see how it *actually* works.

Typical DBA Answers

It seems when someone asks a question to the database administrator, I have observed that there are a few answers that are often given that seem to fall into these three categories:

- Yes, I can do that.

- No, I cannot do that.

- It depends.

The first answer is one that everyone loves to hear. They asked you for something and you are going to satisfy their request.

The middle answer is the one everyone hates to hear. Earlier in this chapter, I described the rude DBA. It is often this answer that starts to define the rude DBA, the one that is difficult to work with. As was stated previously, if this is the answer you need to provide to someone, find a gentler way to say it and make sure you strive to provide them some assistance so that they can get back to performing their job. On those occasions where you need to say "No," always provide a solid reason why the request cannot be satisfied. If you can explain why you denied the request, you will not be thought of as the rude DBA. Be prepared to defend your request at a later date. The requestor will inevitably say to someone that they cannot do their job because your denial is getting in the way. Management may come to you and ask why you denied the request. You need to have a good, solid, factual basis for the denial. No one likes to hear "No" but sometimes it needs to be said.

Which brings me to the final answer, which is every database administrator's favorite response. "It depends." What often happens is someone comes to the DBA with a request but has left out crucial details the DBA needs to know. The DBA needs to perform some investigative work to learn more. For whatever reason, decisions in database systems are often a balancing act. Add something on one side of the scales and the other side is impacted, and vice versa. For example, an application developer asks "Will adding an index to this table help my performance?" The answer is, predictably, "It depends." If the

SELECT statement uses the index, it may well complete faster. But on the other side of the scale is INSERT performance, which can be negatively impacted if too many indexes are created on a table. Even the first part of the answer depends on details that have yet to be defined. An index does not necessarily help SELECT performance. The number of rows in the table and how many rows need to be returned are crucial details missing from the question. Sometimes what looks like a simple request on the surface requires more analysis before a proper answer can be given.

Whenever giving the "It depends" answer, it is usually a good idea to ask probing questions to help provide the best possible answer. The requestor often does not know which details they need to provide to obtain the correct answer. If the requestor knew enough to provide these details, they would be knowledgeable enough to answer their own question. They are coming to the DBA for assistance and, many times, the DBA needs to lead them by the hand, so to speak. If the DBA still needs to give an "It depends" answer, the DBA should explain the trade-offs so the requestor has the best information possible.

Know Your Audience

As a database administrator, you are the organization's best resource for anything related to the database. The DBA needs to be able to communicate with people from many different areas of the company. The successful DBA is one that can change their vocabulary depending on the audience. How you talk to the CEO and CIO will differ from how you talk to other IT staff, which in turn will differ from how you talk to other database administrators. For example, if you are talking to IT management and start throwing around terms like *buffer cache* or *shared pool*, you will be talking over their heads and they won't be able to follow what you say. Instead, use the term *cache*. Most IT management understands what a cache is. When discussing the same topic with the CEO, who many not know what cache means, use the term *database memory* and they will probably have a better idea. However, if you use the term *cache* when talking with another Oracle DBA, they will ask "Which one?" The DBA is well versed in the different functions of the shared pool and buffer cache, so you can be more specific. Understanding your audience and how to quickly provide terms they can understand will make you a more effective communicator. Table 2-1 illustrates how you might change your terminology depending on whom you are talking to.

Table 2-1. *Audience Database Translations*

Talking to DBAs	Talking to IT Staff	Talking to non-IT People
Buffer cache	Cache	Database memory
View	View	Stored query
Instance	Database	Database
Redo logs	Transaction logs	Transactions journal
Table	Table	Table
Index	Index	Index
Tablespace	Data files	Database

Table 2-1 is definitely not an exclusive list but it does give you an idea of how to choose words depending on the audience. Most people who interact with databases get the idea of a *table* or an *index*, so a DBA usually can use those words no matter who the audience is composed of. However, as a DBA, you really need to focus on the body language of non-IT people when talking to them. There are a lot of non-IT people who work with databases and get some basic concepts like tables and indexes and even transactions. As you are talking to them, watch how they are responding to your terminology. You may have simplified your words and still be talking over their heads. If they struggle with the term *table*, say something like "A table is like how data is arranged in an Excel spreadsheet with columns and rows." Most people have worked with Excel or similar and can then get the concept. If they are struggling with the concept of a transaction, give them an example of withdrawing or transferring funds from their bank account. Try your best to keep a cool head. Do not get frustrated if you have to take extra time when talking with someone who does not understand database technology. Analyze if you are accurately getting your point across and be prepared to provide even more background information. Be prepared to be their mentor, if you will.

In the case of Oracle memory structures like the shared pool, we would refer to that structure by its name when talking with another Oracle DBA, but would change it to *cache* for IT staff and *database memory* for non-IT people, as we already discussed. Oracle DBAs refer to connecting to the *instance* when conversing with each other, but to everyone else, it's just the *database*.

If the audience's skill level is unknown, it is best to start talking as if they are in the non-IT category. Make the database-related terms as simple as possible. During your discussions, listen to the words they say. Many times, the terms they use can clue you in to how you need to change your vocabulary to fit their skill level and communicate more effectively. When fielding a request for database service, the first thing the DBA should do is listen to the details of the request. Remember that not everyone speaks the same terminology as the DBA. Do not dismiss their request right away. They may not understand how to properly ask for what they need because they do not understand how to speak your language. This is one avenue the rude DBA really needs to focus on for improvement.

Moving On

This chapter discussed different facets of how you should work and interact with others during the course of your database administration career. The chapter did not contain any technical content, but that is going to change as you turn the page. In this chapter we discussed the importance of not being a rude database administrator and the need to investigate further when someone submits a request to you. We went over the notion that different people you will interact with come from different audiences and that it is up to you to use the proper terminology based on the audience. We also addressed the fact that today's DBA often needs to work with different platforms. A good foundation in database theory can help the DBA navigate from one database platform to another.

In this book you will build some best practices for managing an Oracle database as well as learn more about the product. Before we can begin, we need a place to practice Oracle techniques. In the next chapter you will set up a virtual machine on your workstation or laptop so that you have a place to learn and explore.

CHAPTER 3

Creating Our Server

This chapter is the first in the book to introduce some technical content. Every database administrator needs a place to experiment with ideas, try out new features, and verify changes work as expected. The DBA needs a non-production environment because as they do work for the first time, they may break something. We do not want things to break in production. Ideally, when we are making a change in production, the change is well understood, rehearsed, and there are no surprises. Getting to such a point often requires multiple attempts. Production databases should never be treated as a playground.

Many organizations provide non-production areas for the DBA and for other IT personnel. In an ideal world, these non-production workspaces match the production environment as closely as possible. But what do you do if your company does not have any non-production environment for you to use? What if you just need a simple database, mostly empty, to test out a few concepts?

Virtualization technologies have changed life for the better for IT staff. Today's container environments, like Docker and Kubernetes, and cloud technologies are making similar improvements for IT infrastructure. This chapter will show you how to create a Linux virtual machine on which you will install and create an Oracle database. Chapter 10 will discuss the importance of testbeds and building test cases. What you build in the next few chapters will provide you with such a testbed.

Even if your company provides non-production areas for your use, you may still find it beneficial to create simple testbeds on your workstation or laptop. We often think of non-production databases for our development and testing efforts as we produce and verify changes, respectively. I have often said that while these are non-production, they are production for someone. If you take down a development database in the middle of the day, application developers cannot work. If you take down a test database in the middle of the day, the quality assurance team cannot validate the changes. The database administrator needs their own personal work area where they can experiment with

© Brian Peasland 2019
B. Peasland, *Oracle DBA Mentor*, https://doi.org/10.1007/978-1-4842-4321-3_3

changes and new features. They need to have complete control over this environment, and if they make a mess of things, they are only hurting themselves. Providing a testbed server also lets the database administrator run databases on different operating systems, which they may need for their environment.

Downloading VirtualBox

For this chapter, we will use Oracle VM VirtualBox to manage the virtual machines (VMs). There are other virtual hypervisors that you could certainly use, such as VMware Fusion or Microsoft Hyper-V. I chose VirtualBox for this book because it is free and because many Oracle professionals use the product. Due to its widespread use, you can find many helpful resources for running Oracle on VirtualBox.

To download VirtualBox, point your web browser to `www.virtualbox.org` and, on the main screen, click the big Download VirtualBox button to display the latest and greatest version of this product. Figure 3-1 shows an example of the button to look for and was the latest and greatest version when this chapter was written.

Figure 3-1. *VirtualBox Download button*

VirtualBox is available for multiple platforms, including Windows, macOS, and Linux. After you click the Download button, you will be taken to a page to download the product for your platform. This chapter will show you how to create a testbed server running Oracle on Linux with VirtualBox on a Windows desktop or laptop, but the instructions are very similar on other platforms as well. On the download page, I'm going to click the "Windows hosts" link. Select your preferred platform and the download will begin. Once the download is complete, run the installation software. On Windows, this is as simple as double-clicking the .exe file that was downloaded. The wizard walks you through the installation steps. You can accept the default values supplied by the wizard. At one point, there is a warning that the installation process will temporarily reset your machine's network connections, so make sure it is a good time to do so before clicking the Yes button. An example of this warning is shown in Figure 3-2.

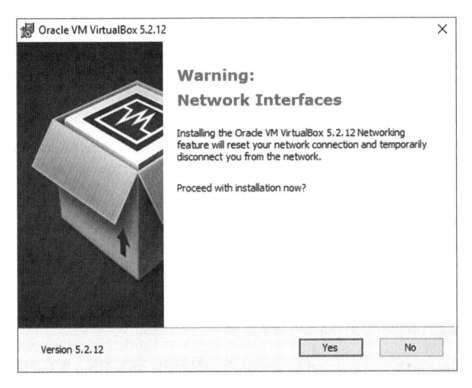

Figure 3-2. *VirtualBox installation network warning*

That was easy. VirtualBox is now installed.

Downloading Oracle Linux

The next step is to download the Oracle Linux operating system. We could run Oracle on Windows or another certified operating system. I chose Linux for this book because it is widely used. If you can run Oracle on Linux, you also have the knowledge to run it on any of the supported Unix variants. Also, Oracle Linux is free to download and use; if you want support for the OS, you will need a maintenance contract.

Point the web browser to http://otn.oracle.com, which is now called the Oracle Developer Network (previously the Oracle Technology Network hence 'otn' in the URL). On the left side of the page is a section titled Essential Links. Click the Software Downloads link in that section. In Figure 3-3, we can see the Software Downloads link is the second item in the list.

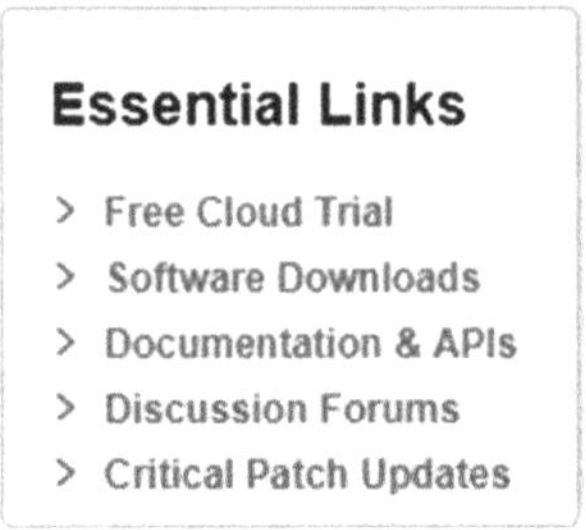

Essential Links

> Free Cloud Trial
> Software Downloads
> Documentation & APIs
> Discussion Forums
> Critical Patch Updates

Figure 3-3. *OTN Essential Links*

On the next page, scroll down to the section titled IT Infrastructure. Click on the link in that section titled Oracle Linux and Oracle Enterprise Kernel. You can see the link as the first item in Figure 3-4.

Servers and Storage Systems

- Oracle Linux and Oracle Enterprise Kernel
- Solaris 10
- Solaris 11

- Oracle VM Server
- Oracle Flash Storage System and Pillar Axiom Plug-ins

Figure 3-4. *Oracle Linux download link*

Clicking the Oracle Linux and Enterprise Kernel link shown in Figure 3-4 will take you to the Oracle Software Delivery Cloud website. If you have an Oracle Single Sign-On account, like one used for My Oracle Support, then click the Sign In button and enter your credentials. If you do not have an account, click the New User link and create a free account. Figure 3-5 shows the Sign In button and the New User registration links.

Oracle Software Delivery Cloud

Welcome to the Oracle Software Delivery Cloud.

Here you can download Oracle software products. If you have questions regarding the download process, please see our Frequently Asked Questions.

Sign In

Forgot User ID / Password?

New User? Register Here

Figure 3-5. *Oracle Software Delivery Cloud sign-in screen*

On the next screen, enter "Oracle Linux" in the search box and click the Search button. The results displayed will have the latest and greatest version of the OS as the top link, as you can see in Figure 3-6.

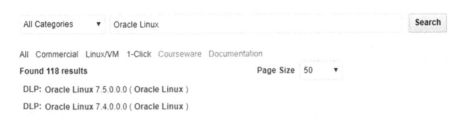

Figure 3-6. *Oracle Linux search results*

At the time of writing, Oracle Linux 7.5 is the latest version, so I will click that link. Click the link for whichever version is the latest at the time you are reading this. Clicking the link adds this software to the cart. Next, click the cart icon, an example of which is shown in Figure 3-7.

Figure 3-7. *Download cart icon*

The next page shows the contents of your cart, which should only contain the one product. Clicking the Continue button takes you to the Oracle Standard Terms and Restrictions page. After reading the terms, check the box to agree to the terms and click the Continue button.

The download page lets you download the entire Oracle Linux product suite. This is much more than we need for this book. We just need the OS, which at the time of writing is titled "Oracle Linux Release 7 Update 5 for x86 (64 bit)" and is the last item in the list, as shown in Figure 3-8.

☑ V975367-01.iso   Oracle Linux Release 7 Update 5 for x86 (64 bit), 4.1 GB

Figure 3-8. *Linux download ISO file*

Click the file name to start the download. At the time of writing, that file name is V975367-01.iso. Depending on when you try to download the OS, the version and file name may be different. Once the software has been downloaded to your system, you can begin to create the virtual machine.

Creating the Server

To begin creating our testbed server, simply start the VirtualBox program. In Figure 3-9, you can see that I already have two virtual machines created, one for testing Oracle 12.2 new features and another for playing around with Oracle Multitenant. Your VirtualBox Manager may not show any virtual machines if this is your first attempt at creating one.

Figure 3-9. *Oracle VM VirtualBox Manager*

Most likely, you do not have any VMs created as of yet. Click the New button to create your first VM. In the dialog box, you need to give your virtual machine a meaningful name and select the operating system type and version. An example of this is shown in Figure 3-10.

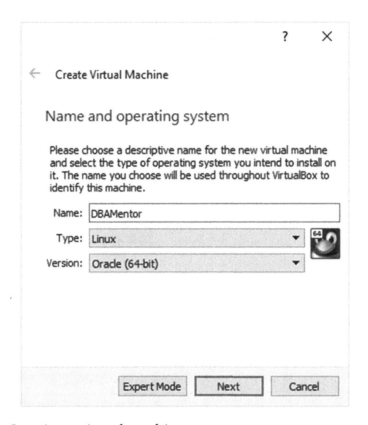

Figure 3-10. *Creating a virtual machine*

I named this VM after the book title, but you can provide any name you desire. The OS type is Linux and the version is Oracle (64-bit). Then click Next.

The next step is to allocate memory to this virtual machine. You'll want to allocate at least 4GB of memory. This memory comes from your workstation or laptop, a.k.a the *host*, so make sure your workstation or laptop has at least 8GB of RAM. Every Oracle version has different memory requirements. The version we will be installing in this book necessitates a 4GB operating system. If you use less memory, Oracle will be sluggish or may not perform at all. Your workstation or laptop needs enough memory to run the VM as well as any other applications you have open. If your host has more than 8GB of RAM, you can certainly allocate additional memory to the VM, but there is little benefit for the testbed we are creating. The memory size can be seen in Figure 3-11. Click Next.

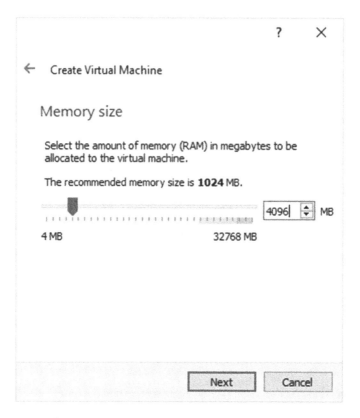

Figure 3-11. *Setting the memory size*

On the next screen, make sure "Create a virtual hard disk now" is selected and click the Create button. On the screen after that, confirm that the virtual hard disk type is VDI and then click Next. The virtual hard disk can either be a fixed size or dynamically created. The benefit to a dynamically created disk is that the file used to simulate the hard disk will start off small and grow as needed, up to a maximum size. The fixed-size option will allocate up to the max size right away. I typically use the dynamic allocation, but you can choose the other option as well. Click Next.

On the next screen, shown in Figure 3-12, provide a file name and a disk size. I typically keep the file name the same as the VM name. You can click the icon to the right of the file name to choose a non-default location for the disk file. For this machine, we'll create a 60GB disk. We will need this amount to have enough space for installing the operating system, installing the Oracle software, and creating our first database. Click the Create button.

Figure 3-12. *Creating the virtual hard disk*

Before we start the virtual machine, let's change a few other settings VirtualBox did not prompt us for. In the VirtualBox Manager, click the virtual machine and then click the Settings button (the yellow gear icon). You can see that the DBAMentor VM is selected, in blue, in Figure 3-13.

Figure 3-13. *Accessing the VM settings*

31

On the Settings page, select Network in the navigation pane on the left. Make sure the Adapter 1 tab is selected, as shown in Figure 3-14. Then make sure the Enable Network Adaptor box is selected and the Attached To menu has NAT chosen. The NAT network adapter lets the virtual machine connect to the outside world.

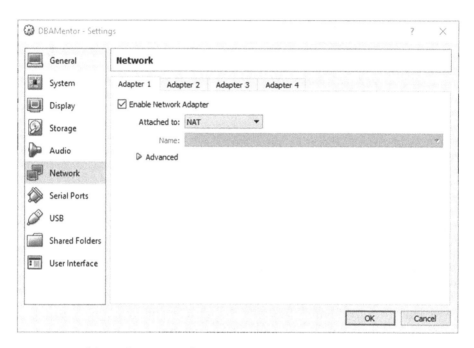

Figure 3-14. *Enabling the network adapter*

We will also want a second network adapter so that the tools on our workstation or laptop can connect to the Oracle database inside the virtual machine. Select the Adapter 2 tab. Make sure the Enable Network Adapter box is selected. For the Attached To option, choose Host-only Adapter, as shown in Figure 3-15.

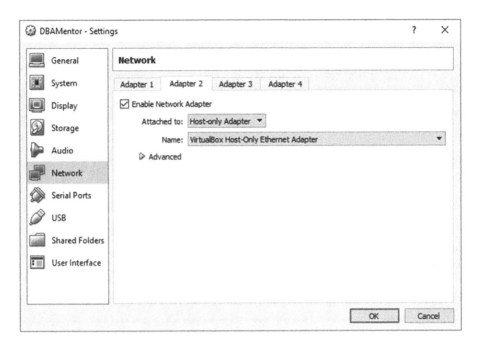

Figure 3-15. *Choosing Host-Only Adapter*

We're also going to add a shared folder so that we can easily pass files back and forth between our host workstation and the virtual machine. In the Settings panel, select Shared Folders in the navigation pane. Click the icon that looks like a folder with a green plus sign. This will pop up a dialog box. I am going to map the C:\temp directory on my workstation to the C_temp mount point on my Linux guest and make this auto-mount every time I start the VM. You can map the shared folder to any location on the host's hard drive. Because I am mapping the shared folder to C:\temp, I am obviously running VirtualBox on Windows. If you are running on macOS or Linux, your folder will be a different location. My settings are shown in Figure 3-16.

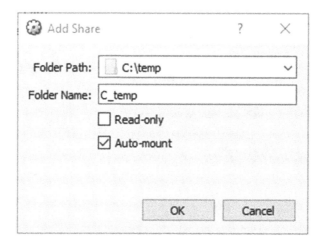

Figure 3-16. *Shared folder definition*

After I click OK, the settings look like the screen shown in Figure 3-17.

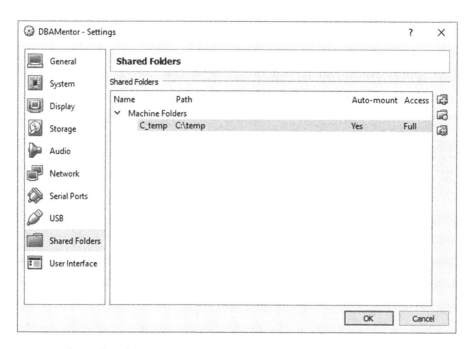

Figure 3-17. *Shared Folders settings*

Click OK to accept the current settings. We are now ready to power on our virtual machine. In the VirtualBox Manager, click the VM and click the green Start button. The virtual machine does not have an operating system yet, so VirtualBox asks us to point to one. Click the folder icon and navigate to the ISO file you downloaded for Oracle Linux and then click the Start button. In Figure 3-18, we can see the V975367-01.iso file I downloaded at the time of writing.

Figure 3-18. *ISO location*

When the red Oracle Linux screen appears, press the I key and then press Enter to boot. If you wait 60 seconds, VirtualBox will test the media and then boot on its own.

Oracle Linux has started and wants to learn some information so that it can complete its configuration. The first page asks you to select which language you prefer during the installation process, as shown in Figure 3-19. Select the language and click the Continue button.

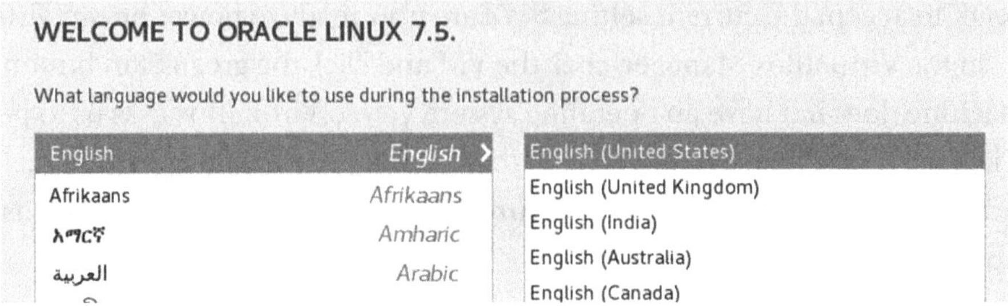

WELCOME TO ORACLE LINUX 7.5.

What language would you like to use during the installation process?

English	English ❯	English (United States)
Afrikaans	Afrikaans	English (United Kingdom)
አማርኛ	Amharic	English (India)
العربية	Arabic	English (Australia)
		English (Canada)

Figure 3-19. *Language selection for the installation process*

On the Installation Summary screen, you can change the date and time, the keyboard, and other items. Make sure those setting are correct for your environment. Figure 3-20 shows the Software Selection button. Click that button.

SOFTWARE SELECTION
Minimal Install

Figure 3-20. *Software Selection button*

The icon is saying a minimal installation will be performed but we want to make sure we have a bit more. I always select the Server with GUI radio button on the left side and check the Performance Tools and System Administration Tools check boxes on the right side. The Oracle Universal Installer is a GUI-based tool. Having a server with a GUI gives us the infrastructure we need to install Oracle. We can install Oracle without a GUI environment, but having it there makes the job easier, as we will see in Chapter 5. Click on the icon in Figure 3-29 to see the Software Selection screen, which should look like Figure 3-21. Make sure Server with GUI is selected as well as the two add-ons. Click Done to complete the selection.

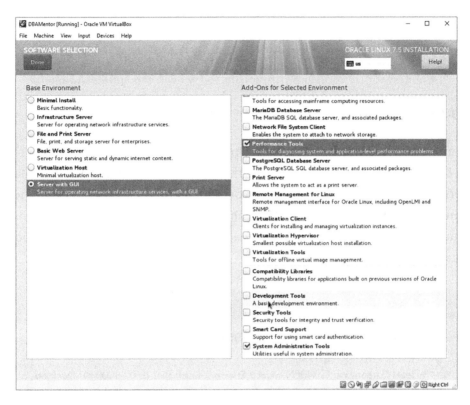

Figure 3-21. *Software Selection screen*

Back on the Installation Summary screen, the Installation Destination button has red text, as shown in Figure 3-22, which means it needs our attention. Click the button to modify the installation destination.

Figure 3-22. *Installation Destination button*

Make sure the radio button to automatically configure partitioning is selected. Then click the Done button. If you want more manual control, you can manually configure partitioning of the virtual machine's hard disk. Since this is our first virtual machine, we will let VirtualBox do the work for us. On the Installation Destination screen, the storage options should look like Figure 3-23.

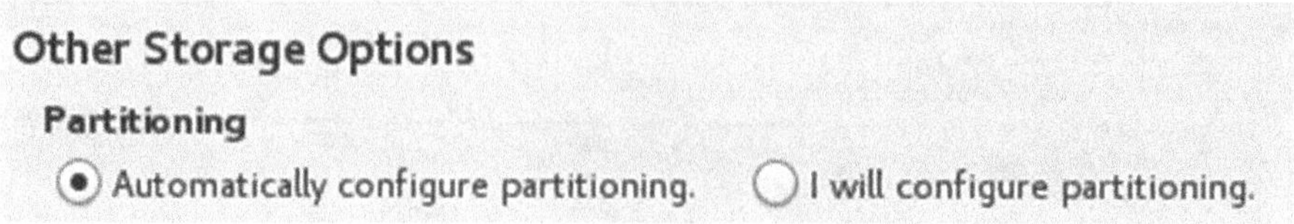

Other Storage Options

Partitioning

◉ Automatically configure partitioning.   ○ I will configure partitioning.

Figure 3-23. *Storage options*

One more item needs to be addressed. On the Installation Summary screen, click the Network & Hostname button. On the Network and Hostname screen, there should be two Ethernet adapters shown in the list. (If you remember, we defined a second network adapter in the step shown in Figure 3-15.) The two network adapters will be given adapter names. In Figure 3-24, the adapter names are enp0s3 and enp0s8. Your adapter names may be slightly different.

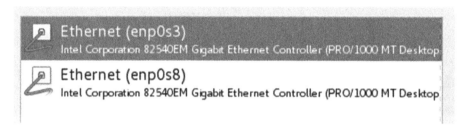

Ethernet (enp0s3)
Intel Corporation 82540EM Gigabit Ethernet Controller (PRO/1000 MT Desktop)

Ethernet (enp0s8)
Intel Corporation 82540EM Gigabit Ethernet Controller (PRO/1000 MT Desktop)

Figure 3-24. *Ethernet adapters*

For the first adapter listed, make sure the button on the right is set to On, as shown in Figure 3-25. It defaults to Off and we want the operating system to start both adapters automatically. Click the button to change its value. Then select the other network adapter and make sure it is set to On as well.

Figure 3-25. *Ethernet adapters turned on*

At the bottom of the Network and Hostname screen, you can optionally give this machine a hostname and click the Apply button. In Figure 3-26, I have named this machine dbamentor.localdomain. You can give this machine any name that makes sense to you.

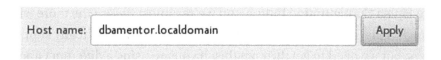

Figure 3-26. *Naming the host*

The network configuration is complete. Click the Done button. Back on the Installation Summary page, click the Begin Installation button.

While the installation proceeds in the background, click the button to set the root password, shown in Figure 3-27. Setting the root password is as simple as entering the password twice in the dialog box and press the Done button to confirm your selection.

Figure 3-27. *Root Password button*

Next to the Root Password button is a button to create a user. It currently says "No user will be created." You can create a user at this time, or when the OS reboots it will prompt you to create a user. Just do not create a user named oracle. In a later chapter, we will create an oracle user when we install the software. If we create the user now, it may be created incorrectly.

After the installation of the OS is complete, a button will appear that enables you to reboot the machine. Click the button to reboot. After the reboot is complete, we only have a few more steps. One is to accept the license. Click the button shown in Figure 3-28 to read the license agreement. Check the box indicating you accept the terms and click Done.

Figure 3-28. *License Acceptance*

Click the Finish Configuration button and we're almost there. One more wizard to walk through. This final wizard seems very redundant as we've already supplied these answers, but we need to get through this. If you are using a different Oracle Linux version, the wizard steps may vary slightly from what I encounter, but the following information will help you get through the installation.

The first page of the wizard asks me to confirm my language and then click Next. I then confirm my keyboard setting and click Next. The next screen asks me for my location preferences, which I confirm and click Next. On the next screen I supply the time zone information and click Next. The subsequent screen asks for some online accounts, and I just click the Skip button. I am then asked for my name and to define my userid. When you get to this step, enter dummy values because we will create our account for the Oracle software later. After I define the user, the next screen asks for the password, which I supply and click Next. I am now done with the wizard and I can click the button to start using Oracle Linux. If you have completed all of these steps, you should see a confirmation screen like Figure 3-29.

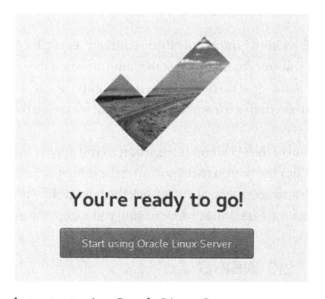

Figure 3-29. *Ready to start using Oracle Linux Server*

After clicking the button to start using the server, I am signed in to a Gnome interface with the userid I supplied in the wizard.

The virtual machine setup is complete. On the top menu, I choose Machine ➤ ACPI Shutdown to close it down for now. We'll return to this virtual machine later in the book.

Moving On

In this chapter we set up a virtual machine for our use later in the book. We will use this VM as a testbed for learning more about Oracle. In Chapter 10, we will discuss testbeds in more detail. However, you are probably getting a sense of why they are important after reading this chapter. If you look back at Figure 3-9, you can see my workstation already had two testbeds, one for learning new features of Oracle 12.2 and another for exploring the Multitenant option. Now that you know how to set up a server with VirtualBox, you can begin using VMs to test out a myriad of possibilities, some not even related to databases.

With VirtualBox, it is possible to clone VMs so that you do not have to repeat these steps for other testbeds. Cloning an existing VM means you can create a new testbed much faster.

Before we can install Oracle, we need to discuss file layouts, the subject of the next chapter. The easiest thing to do would be to place all files in a singular location. However, that would be the easiest route just for installing Oracle and creating our first database. Future maintenance will be harder. The next chapter will focus on planning a foundation for success for the future needs of our Oracle database.

CHAPTER 4

Disk Layouts

Before we can install the Oracle database software for the first time, we need to plan our disk layout strategy. This chapter will start by discussing Oracle's Optimal Flexible Architecture (OFA) and then give some general guidelines regarding where to create your database on disk.

As I stated earlier in this book, we will see some best practices as we work through the material. This chapter is filled with best practices. If you are setting up Oracle in a production environment, you will want to follow the best practices as much as possible. For simple testbeds, it may be more desirable to just place your files on a big disk drive and not give this chapter much thought. Many times, we want to spin up a testbed as quickly as possible even though we know it is not production ready. Also, if you are using prebuilt VirtualBox images, or even Oracle on Docker or other containers, the disk layout has already been decided for you.

As we will discuss in this chapter, OFA is a set of guidelines for placing Oracle files on disk and there are always times to deviate from the standard practices. I have been to many sites where OFA was followed to the letter and to other sites where OFA was not given any thought, let alone implemented on database servers. No matter what path you choose, make things consistent across the entire enterprise. It is time consuming for the database administrator to work on one database server and look for files in one location, and then shift their work to another database server and have to hunt for files because they are in a completely different location. Keeping your files in the same locations across all database servers will save time and reduce human error should a database administrator accidentally remove files or directories they did not think were part of an Oracle environment. When setting up my Oracle databases, I follow the OFA guidelines as much as possible, even for development and test environments. For testbeds where I am the only user, I often just place the files on disk in any fashion.

Tip   Keep your file locations consistent across the enterprise.

© Brian Peasland 2019
B. Peasland, *Oracle DBA Mentor*, https://doi.org/10.1007/978-1-4842-4321-3_4

While the OFA guidelines offer specific locations on disk, you may be tempted to use another location. For file locations, I would recommend that you follow the OFA guidelines as much as possible for anything other than your personal testbed. There may be some time in the future where your organization hires an Oracle consultant to come in and assist you with your work. The consultant most likely knows the OFA guidelines and will expect to find files in a specific location. If you use a different location, the consultant will waste valuable time learning your enterprise configuration. Since consultants charge by the hour, this wasted time will incur additional costs to the organization. Similarly, there may come a time in the future where your organization hires another DBA to add to your team. If this DBA has prior experience, they will likely be familiar with the OFA guidelines. Sticking to the OFA guidelines will help consultants or new DBAs get up to speed quicker in your environment. For example, I was called in to help with a database problem for an Oracle system I had never seen before. The database administrator who was in charge of this system, but was unavailable at that current time, did not follow OFA guidelines. Because of this, it took me longer to find the alert log and other trace files I needed to resolve the issue, which in turn led to a longer time to resolve the problem.

Optimal Flexible Architecture

Optimal Flexible Architecture (OFA) is a set of guidelines that Oracle Corporation provides to help us define where to place the files for Oracle on disk. These include the database's files, the Oracle software files, and any trace files, all of which are discussed in this section.

Keep in mind that OFA offers guidelines, not rules. You do not have to follow them. For a quick and simple setup of Oracle, usually for a personal testbed, you may ignore these guidelines. If you do plan on using your Oracle installation for development, testing, or production purposes, then follow the OFA guidelines as a best practice.

ORACLE_BASE

Before we can install any Oracle software, we need to have a base location. This location is called the Oracle Base, and many times on Unix and Linux environments, the $ORACLE_BASE environment variable is explicitly defined to this location. The OFA guidelines suggests that ORACLE_BASE be located at /u01/app/oracle on Unix and Linux machines. On Windows, ORACLE_BASE is often located in the C:\oracle directory.

As stated, this is just a guideline and you can have ORACLE_BASE in any other location, but this book will assume the guidelines are followed unless otherwise noted.

More accurately, the OFA guidelines recommend that ORACLE_BASE be located in */disk_unit/*app/*owner*. It is very common for the disk unit to be /u01, but you may also see /u02, /u03, and so on. In days past, it was common for storage administrators to mount the differently numbered disk units. With today's storage area networks and network file systems, /u01 is common and the others are more rare. Your storage admin may use different disk unit naming conventions like /disk1 and /disk2. Just ask your storage admin to be consistent. On Windows machines, the disk is mounted as a drive letter, so you may see ORACLE_BASE in D:\app\oracle or E:\app\oracle, but many sites shorten this to D:\oracle or E:\oracle, respectively. No matter which convention you use, be consistent.

The Oracle Base is the root of the Oracle software and its log files. The Oracle database software will be installed in a subdirectory of the base. Oracle keeps an internal inventory of the Oracle software and its patches in $ORACLE_BASE/oraInventory. Oracle database files can be a subdirectory of the base as well.

Remember that in Chapter 3 we set up a Linux server with Oracle's VirtualBox. As such, this book will mostly talk about Linux environments. If you will be working with Oracle on Windows servers, the translation is very similar. On Windows machines, the environment variable is named %ORACLE_BASE% and often points to C:\oracle or D:\oracle.

ORACLE_HOME

It is possible to have more than one Oracle database on a single server, each with a different Oracle version. The biggest, but not sole, benefit of OFA today is to help facilitate different Oracle versions on the same server. With OFA, you can easily install the Oracle 11.2.0.4, 12.1.0.2, and 12.2.0.1 versions and have no conflicts.

Oracle handles each version independently by installing it in its own home directory, called $ORACLE_HOME (%ORACLE_HOME% on Windows). The OFA guidelines place $ORACLE_HOME in a folder with a naming scheme similar to $ORACLE_BASE/product/*version*/*type*, where *version* denotes the Oracle version installed and where *type* is typically *dbhome_X* for database software, *client_X* for Oracle Client software, or *grid_X* for Oracle's Grid Infrastructure. Here are some examples of ORACLE_HOME directories:

/u01/app/oracle/product/11.2.0/dbhome_1

/u01/app/oracle/product/11.2.0/dbhome_2

/u01/app/oracle/product/12.1.0/dbhome_1

/u01/app/oracle/product/12.1.0/dbhome_2

Those examples illustrate one of the problems I have always had with this OFA guideline, and is one of the places I deviate from OFA just a bit. Take a look at the first two examples. Both say version 11.2.0 and one is type dbhome_1 and the other is type dbhome_2, so we do have an idea that both directories contain Oracle database software for the 11.2.0 version. My issue is that Oracle database versions are denoted with three decimal points but the OFA guidelines only use two. If I told you one of those paths was for Oracle 11.2.0.3 and the other was for 11.2.0.4, you would have no idea which one was which just by looking at the directory structure. This applies similarly to the last two examples. Which one is for Oracle 12.1.0.1 and which for 12.1.0.2? You cannot tell.

This is where I always break slightly from the guidelines. I add one more decimal point and explicitly state the full Oracle version in the path. So my Oracle home directories would look like this:

/u01/app/oracle/product/11.2.0.3/dbhome_1

/u01/app/oracle/product/11.2.0.4/dbhome_1

/u01/app/oracle/product/12.1.0.2/dbhome_1

/u01/app/oracle/product/12.1.0.1/dbhome_1

With the full versions in the directory path, the type is always dbhome_1, provided that the same version is only installed once. I have often dropped the type and been left with these simpler path names:

/u01/app/oracle/product/11.2.0.3

/u01/app/oracle/product/11.2.0.4

/u01/app/oracle/product/12.1.0.1

/u01/app/oracle/product/12.1.0.2

Leaving off the type is optional. I leave off the type just to make the Oracle home directory path a bit shorter. You will find yourself typing the path many times throughout the day. Whatever you do, just be consistent across the enterprise. If you are working on a larger database team, everyone will need to know and understand the convention in use for your organization.

With different Oracle home directories, we can easily prepare for future upgrades. For example, suppose I want to upgrade my existing databases to the 12.2.0.1 version. I install the new version in /u01/app/oracle/product/12.2.0.1 and the Oracle software is in its own home, free of conflicts from the other versions. As I upgrade databases to the newer version, the older versions may become unused and I can remove them.

In some cases, an organization may have a requirement that some Oracle software needs to be owned by a different user. This is called *separation of duties*. It is very common to have the Grid Infrastructure owned by the "grid" user and the Oracle database software owned by the "oracle" user on a Linux machine. The separation of credentials is important for organizations that have one team responsible for the cluster software, Grid Infrastructure, and another team responsible for the database software. By having different owners of the two software components, we can ensure each team can manage only their component without access to the other. OFA helps us because each ORACLE_HOME directory is self-contained for that software type and for that version.

Database Administration Files

There are many files the database administrator needs that are outside the software installation directories. Many of the admin files are located in $ORACLE_BASE/admin. Table 4-1 shows subdirectories of this location.

Table 4-1. *Admin File Directories*

Directory	Contents
/u01/app/oracle/admin/audit	Audit trail records
/u01/app/oracle/admin/create	Scripts to create the database
/u01/app/oracle/admin/dpdump	Data Pump file location
/u01/app/oracle/admin/scripts	DBA scripts

Diagnostic Files

We will delve into diagnostic files in more detail in Chapter 12, but for now, it is important to know where the files are located. Diagnostic files are located in the $ORACLE_BASE/diag directory. The next subdirectory is the type of diagnostic files. For our case, we are interested in the diagnostic files for the database, so we will look in $ORACLE_BASE/diag/rdbms. Subdirectories exist for diagnostic files for the Oracle Listener, client software, and more. In the rdbms subdirectory, our files will be found in $ORACLE_BASE/diag/rdbms/*db_name*/*instance_name*. If you are not running Oracle Real Application Clusters (RAC), the instance name will be the same as the database name. An example of the location might be:

> $ORACLE_BASE/diag/rdbms/orcl/orcl

Our database name is orcl in the example above.

Database Files

The OFA guidelines suggest that we store database files in $ORACLE_BASE/oradata/*db_name* as a starting point. If your database is for anything other than a testbed, the disk for ORACLE_BASE may not be large enough to store all of the files. It is very common for the DBA to separate database files to different disk locations, for a number of reasons. They may need multiple disk units because one disk unit is not large enough. They may want multiple disk units so that highly active database files can be segregated to reduce disk contention.

If more than one disk is being used, they are typically mounted to the Unix or Linux server similar to the following example:

> /u01/app/oracle/oradata/orcl/data01

> /u01/app/oracle/oradata/orcl/data02

The database name is orcl in the example above. It should be noted that data01 and data02 are different disk units with different mount points. On Unix/Linux, they look to be subdirectories off the same disk, but they are not. Your organization may use a different directory structure for the Oracle disk, which is perfectly acceptable. Again, just be consistent across the enterprise.

Working with the storage administrator, the DBA may decide to put online redo logs on their own disk to help out with performance. Online redo logs are write-intensive files, especially for databases that have a high transaction rate. Moving online redo logs to their own disk units is commonly done to spread out the disk I/O demands. They may be placed on a mount point similar to

> /u01/app/oracle/oradata/orcl/redo01

Similarly, archived redo log files may be placed on its own mount point like this:

/u01/app/oracle/oradata/orcl/arch

On Windows systems, we use different drive letters. I often continue with this convention, even on Windows servers. I could have my two data disks as

D:\oracle\oradata\orcl

E:\oracle\oradata\orcl

And my online and archived redo logs in

F:\oracle\oradata\orcl

G:\oracle\oradata\orcl

But it's hard to know which is which. So I'll include one more subdirectory just to make it more clear:

D:\oracle\oradata\orcl\data01

E:\oracle\oradata\orcl\data02

F:\oracle\oradata\orcl\redo01

G:\oracle\oradata\orcl\arch

Now I can easily tell what type of files I want on which disk device just by inspecting the directory path. The extra subdirectory does nothing to help administration of the database and its files other than to self-document the purpose of the drive. You can certainly create your own naming convention, but again, keep consistent across the enterprise.

There is one more OFA guideline pertaining to database files, and that addresses the name of the file itself. The OFA guideline suggests that we name control files control*XX*.ctl, name online redo logs redo*XX*.log, and name database files tablespace_name*XX*.dbf, where *XX* is a sequential number. So, for example, I might have three control files with names control01.ctl, control02.ctl, and control03.ctl. Online redo logs would be named redo01.log, redo02.log, and redo03.log. Database files for the SYSTEM and SYSAUX tablespaces are usually named system01.dbf and sysaux01.dbf respectively. An application data tablespace with multiple files might have files named app_data01.dbf and app_data02.dbf as an example.

While OFA provides guidelines for naming the database's files, Oracle Managed Files (OMF) changes things a bit. With OMF, the DBA simply provides a disk location for data files and, optionally, another disk location for online redo log files. The DBA denotes these locations with the DB_CREATE_FILE_DEST and DB_CREATE_ONLINE_LOG_DEST_n parameters. After that, the database handles the details for the DBA. The database will name control files with a convention like ora_%u.ctl, where %u is a unique code. Data files are named with the convention ora_%t_%u.dbf, where %t is the tablespace name. OMF works great for testbeds. However, I rarely use OMF for production databases because the DB_CREATE_FILE_DEST parameter can only specify one disk location.

There are many DBAs that will not use the .log extension on online redo logs and will ignore the OFA guideline. Their reason is that some system administrator may come across the file and think it's a simple log file filled with text and remove it to free up some disk space, not knowing that this is a critical file to the database and that its deletion can cause the database to crash. Instead, these DBAs will use redo*XX*.orl. Just so long as they are consistent across their enterprise, they won't have any issues.

Full Picture

In the next two chapters, we'll be installing the Oracle database software on our Linux machine and creating our first database. Now that we're at the end of this chapter, we have a better idea of where things will be placed on our server. Table 4-2 shows the locations of our files on our testbed that we will use throughout the remainder of this book.

Table 4-2. *Directory Structure*

Directory Path	Contents
/u01/app/oracle	ORACLE_BASE
/u01/app/oracle/oraInventory	Oracle Inventory
/u01/app/oracle/product/12.2.0.1	ORACLE_HOME
/u01/app/oracle/admin	Admin files
/u01/app/oracle/diag/rdbms/orcl/orcl	Diagnostic files
/u01/app/oracle/oradata/orcl	Database files

If you have problems remembering where certain files are located, use Table 4-2 as your reference.

If I were using a Windows server, all of the /u01/app/oracle paths would be translated to C:\oracle.

Moving On

This chapter introduced you to Cisco Optimal Flexible Architecture (OFA) and a few of its guidelines. Knowing where to find certain files on disk is important to the DBA. Following these guidelines makes it easier to find files and reduces the chances of human error when someone mistakenly deletes a file because they were unaware of what it was. Again, whatever convention you use, even if you deviate from the OFA guidelines, keep it consistent across the enterprise.

The next chapter will focus on downloading the Oracle database software and installing it on our server. We will install in the ORACLE_HOME directory noted in Table 4-2. In Chapter 6, we will create our first database. By the end of the next two chapters, the entire file structure noted in Table 4-2 will be populated with files.

CHAPTER 5

Installing Oracle

In Chapter 3, we created our server that we will use throughout this book. In Chapter 4, we discussed different areas of our file system. If you recall, when Oracle is installed, two directories are created called the Oracle Base and the Oracle Home. This chapter will focus on installing Oracle for the first time, using the base and home directories. In Chapter 6, we will create our first database.

This chapter will show how to install the Oracle Database 12c Release 2 (12.2) version on our testbed. If you are using a different Oracle version, you can use this chapter as a guide. If your version is slightly lower or higher than 12.2, then most of this chapter will match. The farther away from 12.2 you get, the more differences you may see.

Accessing the Installation Guide

The Oracle documentation contains many answers to questions you may have. The documentation set that is relevant to this chapter is called the *Oracle Database Installation Guide*. This document is a must-read for anyone installing Oracle. Like all documentation from Oracle, there is an updated guide for each specific version. At the time of writing, Oracle 12.2 is the most current version available for on-premises deployments. Before I installed Oracle 12.2 for the first time, I made it a point to read that version's *Installation Guide*. Once the next version, Oracle Database 18c, is released for on-premises installations, I will read that version of the *Installation Guide*. Most of it will be information I already know, so it doesn't take too long to read the next version's documentation. However, I still read the latest *Installation Guide* because it may contain a few new pieces of information. For example, the new version may change the amount of minimum memory needed to support an Oracle database. If you do not read the new version's *Installation Guide*, you may experience installation issues because you do not have enough memory. A preface to the *Installation Guide* contains a summary of the changes for the new release and is always worth reading.

B. Peasland, *Oracle DBA Mentor*, https://doi.org/10.1007/978-1-4842-4321-3_5

Tip   Always read the current version of the documentation set. It may contain new information that wasn't in your older version.

Oracle documentation, for all Oracle products, is accessible from the Oracle Help Center, located at `https://docs.oracle.com`. Click the Database button, shown in Figure 5-1, to access the database documentation.

Database
Oracle databases lead the world
delivering innovative solutions

Figure 5-1. *Database documentation button*

On the main Database Documentation page, we can see different database documentation sets. We are interested in the Oracle Database documentation set, so click that button, which is shown in Figure 5-2.

Figure 5-2. *Oracle Database documentation button*

The next page defaults to the latest and greatest documentation version, which at the time of writing is the Oracle Database 18c documentation. However, this book is written for Oracle 12.2, so in the drop-down menu located under Oracle Database, select the Oracle 12.2 version, as shown in Figure 5-3.

Figure 5-3. *Database version selection*

If you are working with a different Oracle version, you can choose that from the drop-down list. After you choose the version of interest, the documentation links below the drop-down menu will change to match that version.

In the section labeled Topics, click the Install and Upgrade link. You should see installation guides for different platforms such as AIX, Solaris, Windows, and Linux. We created our server (in Chapter 3) with the Oracle Linux operating system, so choose the *Database Installation Guide for Linux* by clicking either the HTML or PDF link to suit your preference, as you can see in Figure 5-4.

Database Installation Guide for Linux

HTML ⎹ PDF

Figure 5-4. *Database Installation Guide for Linux links*

Please take some time to familiarize yourself with the *Installation Guide*'s contents. It's not a bad idea to skim this document, at a minimum, before proceeding with the rest of this chapter. This chapter will not cover everything in that guide. If you do not read this guide before proceeding, make sure to read it at some future date. Chapters 1 through 7 are the most important to read. You can read either Chapter 8 or 9 if you are using a file system or Automated Storage Manager (ASM), respectively. Chapter 11 walks you through how to install the software, which we will cover in this chapter.

Many of your questions are answered in this guide. Which exact version of Linux can I use? How much memory and disk space does my server need? What are the steps to install Oracle software? Even the Optimal Flexible Architecture we discussed in Chapter 4 has an appendix devoted to it in this guide.

Downloading Oracle Database Software

Before we can install the Oracle database software, we need to download it from some location. If you have a valid support contract with Oracle, you can download from `https://edelivery.oracle.com`. Oracle also lets you download from its Oracle Technology Network at `https://otn.oracle.com`. The Technology Network requires you to have an Oracle account, but setting that up is free. Sign in to the Technology Network and then, in the Essential Links section, click Software Downloads. On the next page, scroll down a bit until you see the Database section. Click the Database 12c Enterprise/Standard Editions link, an example of which you can see in Figure 5-5.

Database

- Database 18c Client
- Database 12c Enterprise/Standard Editions
  Including: Client, Grid Infrastructure,
  Examples, Gateways, more

- ILM Assistant
- Instant Client
- MySQL
- NoSQL Database

Figure 5-5. *Developer Network Database download link*

On the next page, there is an Accept License Agreement radio button that you must select to accept the license terms. None of the download links will work until you accept the license agreement. In Figure 5-6 you can see a link to the OTN License Agreement and the radio button to accept that license.

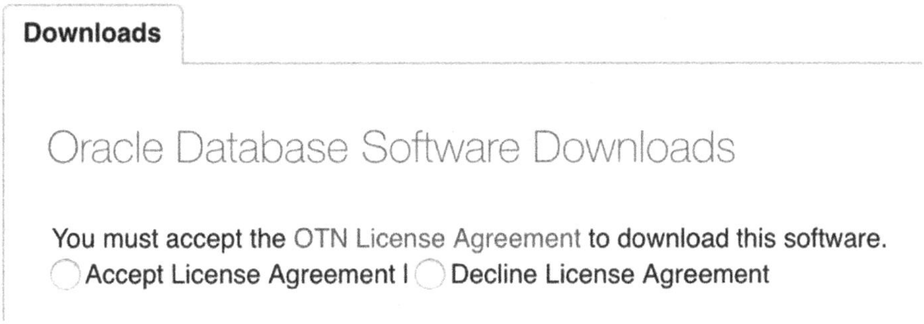

Downloads

Oracle Database Software Downloads

You must accept the OTN License Agreement to download this software.
○ Accept License Agreement I ○ Decline License Agreement

Figure 5-6. *OTN License Agreement link and acceptance*

Make sure you click the OTN License Agreement link and read the license! You cannot use this software for any database that you need to license. You cannot use it for production databases or for any part of your business. What you can do is use it for simple testbeds, as we will be doing in this book.

After you click the radio button to accept the license agreement, scroll down until you see the Oracle Database 12c Release 2 section. Click the link named File 1 next to the Linux operating system. If you are working on a different operating system, you can see the ones available to you in that same section. File 1 is the database software. If you need other software, click the See All link, which takes you to a page where you can download the Database Client, Grid Infrastructure, Database Gateways, and Example schemas. We are only interested in the database RDBMS software, so download the file named linuxx64_12201_database.zip onto your workstation.

Getting the Server Ready

Before we can perform the actual install, we need to perform a few minor tasks. If your virtual machine is not running, start it from VirtualBox and log in as the root superuser. When the virtual machine first starts up, it asks who to log in as, but root is not listed. Click the Not Listed link and enter root for the username and provide the password. Once signed in, go to Applications ➤ Favorites and start the Terminal application.

This is our command window. In this window, type "yum search oracle-rdbms". Yum is a Linux utility that can be used to easily download and install operating system packages. Our command will search for any packages in the yum repository that contain the string "oracle-rdbms" in its name. We can see the search results in Listing 5-1.

Listing 5-1. Yum Search Results

```
[root@dbamentor ~]# yum search oracle-rdbms
Loaded plugins: refresh-packagekit, security
public_ol6_UEKR3_latest                                | 1.2 kB      00:00
public_ol6_latest                                      | 1.4 kB      00:00
========================= N/S Matched: oracle-rdbms =========================
oracle-rdbms-server-11gR2-preinstall.x86_64 : Sets the system for Oracle single
     ...: instance and Real Application Cluster install for Oracle Linux 7
oracle-rdbms-server-12cR1-preinstall.x86_64 : Sets the system for Oracle single
     ...: instance and Real Application Cluster install for Oracle Linux 7

  Name and summary matches only, use "search all" for everything.
```

There should be two results, a preinstall file for 11gR2 and another for 12cR1. Even though we are installing Oracle 12cR2, the 12cR1 preinstall file works just fine. If you see other versions, install the one that most closely matches the Oracle version you are installing.

Much of the operating system setup defined in the *Oracle Database Installation Guide* will be handled for us by installing this file on our server. The preinstall file is only available for the Linux operating system. Other operating systems need to be configured manually following the steps in the *Installation Guide*.

In the command window, install the file as follows:

```
yum install oracle-rdbms-server-12cR1-preinstall.x86_64
```

You will be prompted to verify that it is ok to proceed. Press 'y' and hit the Enter key to proceed. Similarly, answer 'y' for any other prompts that may come up.

In order to get the Oracle database software file we downloaded (in the prior section) onto the database testbed server, we need to use the file share between the virtual machine and our host that we set up in Chapter 3 (refer to Figure 3-16). Just in case you skipped that part, go to VirtualBox Manager, click the VM, and then click the Settings button. Next, click the Shared Folders icon. Click the blue folder icon with a green plus sign so that you can add a shared folder. On my MacBook laptop, I defined the folder path to my user's desktop. On the Linux side, this will be seen as HostDesktop. I made sure to check the Auto-mount option, as shown in Figure 5-7.

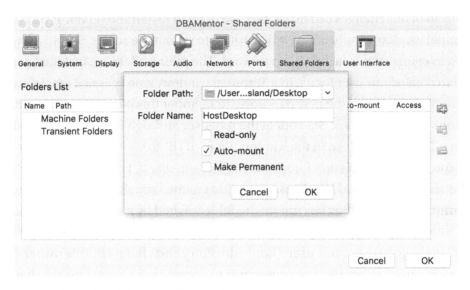

Figure 5-7. *Shared Folders configuration*

For security purposes, you can optionally select to make this mount read-only on the Linux VM side. That way, the virtual machine cannot make changes to the host's files in that directory.

Before the shared folders will work, we need to set up Guest Additions, extra components for the operating system that Virtual Box needs to extend the functionality of the OS in a virtual machine. Not only will Guest Additions let us access shared folders, it will allow us to copy and paste between the virtual machine and the host environment. Guest Additions will also let us move our mouse more easily between the VM and the host.

Before we can install Guest Additions, we need to install some kernel source code. That can be done with the following command:

```
yum install kernel-uek-devel-$(uname -r)
```

This command instructs yum to install a package. The package's name will depend on your current Linux version. The "uname -r" portion is returning that OS version.

With that package installed, reboot your VM. Sign back in as root and select Insert Guest Additions CD Image from the Devices menu of your virtual machine's window. You will be prompted to run the software, so click OK. When the installation is complete, press Enter to close the window.

Before all of our changes can take effect, we need to restart the server. Type "reboot" in a Terminal window (Applications ➤ Favorites) to reboot the server. Sign in as root. We now need to change the "oracle" user password. The preinstall file we installed earlier in this section created our user for us. In a Terminal window, type "passwd oracle" and you will be prompted twice for the new password. Remember this password, as you will be using it throughout this book. Sign out of the root user and sign in as the oracle user.

Open a Terminal window. In the window, type "df –h" to see the mounted disk devices. You should see an entry for something like /media/sf_HostDesktop. The "sf" stands for *shared folder*, and HostDesktop is what I named my shared folder in Figure 5-7.

Unfortunately, VirtualBox has the shared folder owned by root. In our Terminal window, enter "su" to log in as root. Enter the root password when prompted. We'll copy the installation file to the oracle user's home directory and change the file ownership so that oracle can take control. The commands to accomplish copying the database software download to the virtual machine are in Listing 5-2.

Listing 5-2. Copying DB Software to VM

```
cd /media/sf_HostDesktop
cp linuxx64_12201_database.zip /home/oracle/.
chown oracle:oinstall /home/oracle/linuxx64_12201_database.zip
exit
```

That last command exits the root user and you should be returned back to the oracle user. We will now unzip our download file:

```
unzip /home/oracle/linuxx64_12201_database.zip
```

We are now ready to begin our installation.

Installing Oracle

In the old days, Oracle Corporation had to create a different installer for each platform. The Java programming language came to the rescue with its "write once, run anywhere" philosophy. The installer for Oracle software is now written in Java and is the same program no matter which platform you are using. Oracle now calls this the Oracle Universal Installer (OUI). Not only was this beneficial to Oracle Corporation, but it is also beneficial to you because you only have to learn how to use one install utility.

We install the database software by launching the OUI. We simply change our directory to the location where we unzipped the software and execute the program as shown in Listing 5-3.

Listing 5-3. Starting the OUI

```
cd /home/oracle/database
./runInstaller
```

The OUI starts. The first screen is to check for security updates, shown in Figure 5-8. For now, we'll leave those fields blank and click the Next button. We will tackle patching the database software with security updates in a future chapter.

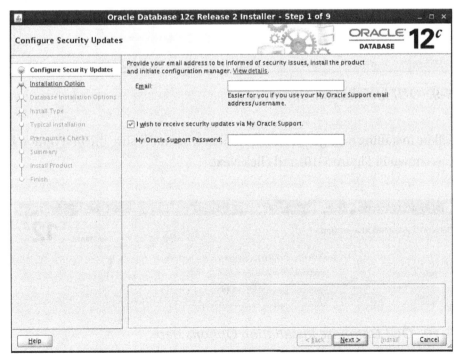

Figure 5-8. *OUI Configure Security Updates step*

After clicking the Next button, you will be asked to confirm that you wish to remain uninformed of security updates. Click the Yes button.

On the next screen, shown in Figure 5-9, we are going to select the option to install the database software only. We do not have any databases on this server to upgrade and we will tackle creating a database in the next chapter. Click the Next button.

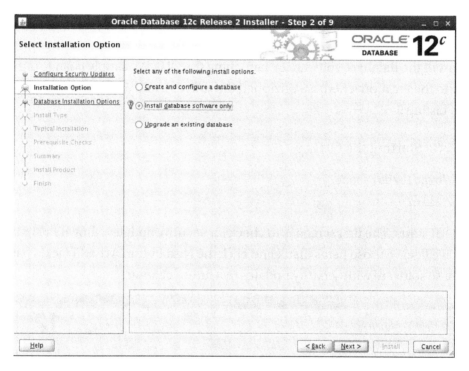

Figure 5-9. *OUI Installation Option step*

We will be installing a single-instance database, so make sure the first option is selected, as shown in Figure 5-10, and click Next.

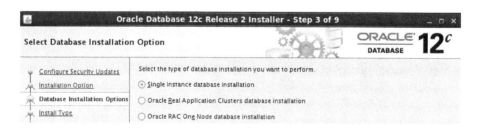

Figure 5-10. *OUI Database Installation Options step*

The OUI is capable of handling both Enterprise Edition and Standard Edition. I typically want all of the features available to me, so I'm going to select Enterprise Edition and click Next. You can see this choice in Figure 5-11.

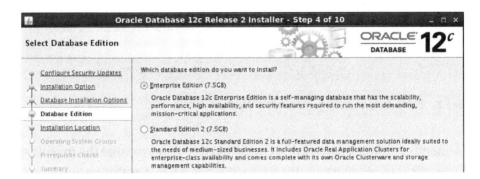

Figure 5-11. *OUI Database Edition step*

On the next screen, we now know enough to fill in the blanks. Remember that the previous chapter defined the Oracle base directory and the Oracle home. This screen is where we tell the OUI the locations of those two directories. But first we need to create the Oracle base directory. Start a command window and issue the commands in Listing 5-4.

Listing 5-4. Creating Oracle Base Directory

```
su      (enter the root password when prompted)
mkdir -p /u01/app/oracle
chown -R oracle:oinstall /u01
exit
```

Then fill out the boxes as shown in the example in Figure 5-12. The first box is the location of the Oracle base, often referred to by the $ORACLE_BASE environment variable. The second box, while not as obvious, is the location of the Oracle home, often referred to by the $ORACLE_HOME environment variable. Click Next to continue.

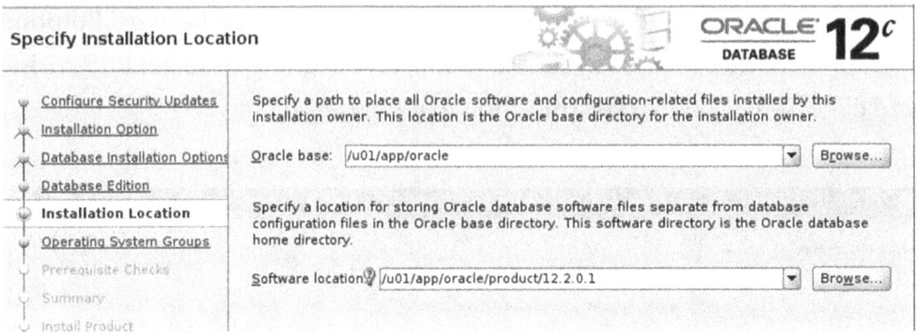

Figure 5-12. *OUI Installation Location step*

Also remember from Chapter 4 that Oracle needs a place to store the inventory
of the Oracle software products on this server. We refer to this as the oraInventory
directory. The OUI will automatically populate this value. In Figure 5-13, we can see the
oraInventory directory is one level up from the Oracle base shown in Figure 5-12. This is
common practice. The OUI may give us a warning message when we click Next, which
we will acknowledge.

We also have the option of specifying the operating system group that will be able to
modify the inventory. The default of oinstall is sufficient, as can be seen in Figure 5-13.
Click the Next button.

Figure 5-13. *OUI Create Inventory step*

On the next screen, we are asked to specify different operating system groups for
different functionality. If we were concerned about separation of duties, we might have
different people in our organization that are responsible for the database backups, in
which case we would not want those staff members to have other functionality, so we

could choose their group differently from the rest in this screen. Since this is a testbed and we will be the only ones accessing it, the default dba group is sufficient. It is very common to see Oracle installed with just the dba group in use, as shown in Figure 5-14. Click the Next button.

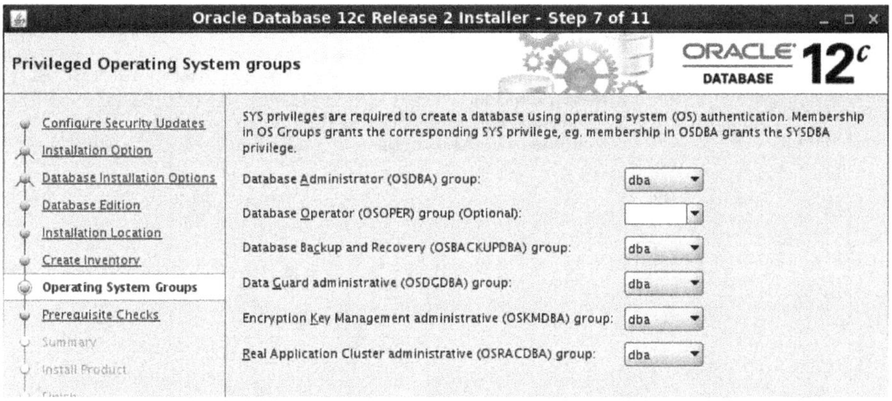

Figure 5-14. *OUI OS Groups step*

The next screen walks through some prerequisite checks. The OUI verifies that your server is set up correctly before installing the software. If there is something amiss, the OUI will let you know. You should remediate any findings before proceeding past that screen; otherwise, you may have issues to fix at a later date. When I installed the software, the OUI did not find any issues, so the OUI automatically advanced to the Summary screen, shown in Figure 5-15.

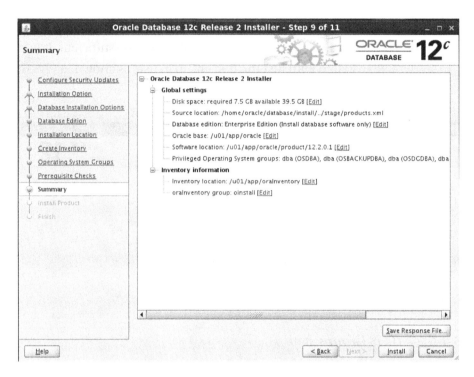

Figure 5-15. *OUI Summary*

Everything is ready to go. We have answered all of the wizard's questions and all that is left is to click the Install button. At the bottom right of the wizard in Figure 5-15, you can see a button labeled Save Response File. The OUI has asked you a series of questions and you provided answers. You can save your answers, your responses to these questions, in a file. This is useful when you want to install the Oracle database software multiple times. Instead of walking through the wizard, you can launch the OUI and point it to the response file and the OUI will skip all of these screens.

We can monitor the installation progress on the next screen. We can see that the OUI will be copying files to the Oracle home directory. After the files have been copied, the OUI will recompile the software, also called linking the binaries. At the very end, we will be asked to execute two scripts as the root user. We can see an example of the install progress in Figure 5-16.

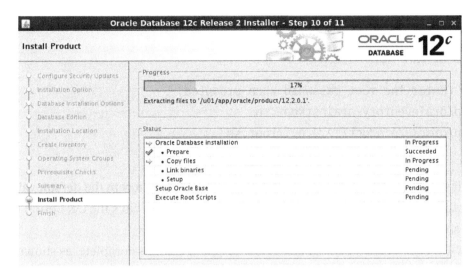

Figure 5-16. *OUI installation progress*

Once the OUI has reached the last step, it will pop up a window similar to Figure 5-17. This window asks us to run two scripts as a root user.

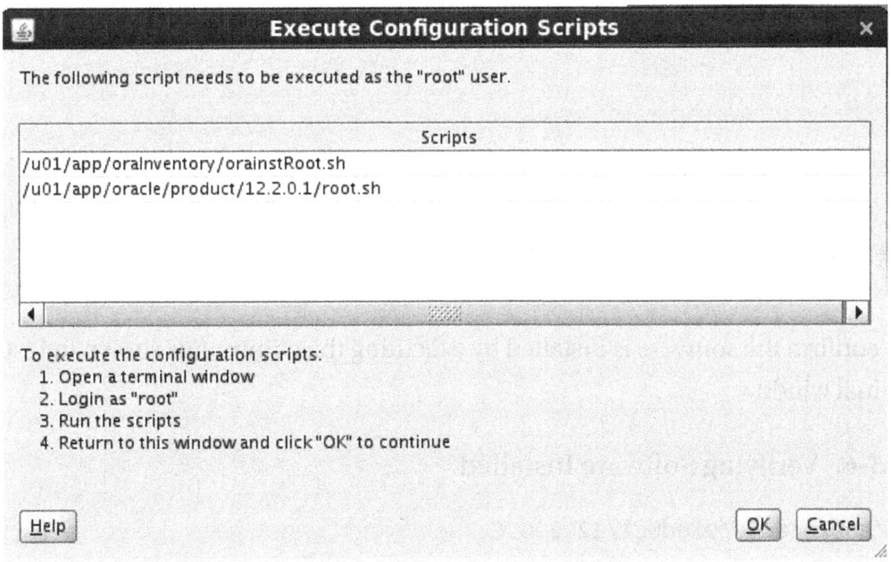

Figure 5-17. *OUI Execute Configuration Scripts screen*

In a Terminal window, perform the commands shown in Listing 5-5.

Listing 5-5. Run Root Scripts

```
su      (enter the root password when prompted)
/u01/app/oraInventory/orainstRoot.sh
/u01/app/oracle/product/12.2.0.1/root.sh
exit
```

The last script will have a few prompts to answer. Simply accept the default values by pressing the Enter key. Once the root scripts have completed, click the OK button in the window shown in Figure 5-17.

The OUI then gives us confirmation that our installation is complete, as shown in Figure 5-18. Click the Close button.

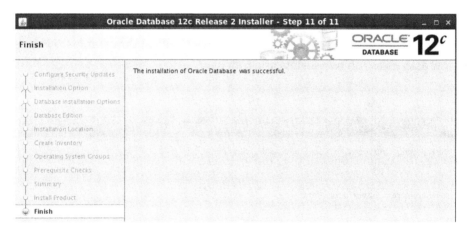

Figure 5-18. *OUI Finish screen*

Let's confirm the software is installed by executing the commands shown in Listing 5-6 in a terminal window.

Listing 5-6. Verifying Software Installed

```
cd /u01/app/oracle/product/12.2.0.1
ls -l
```

We should see a number of directories present in our Oracle home.

Moving On

The Oracle database software is now installed on our testbed. We could not proceed directly to this chapter because we needed the information in Chapter 4 to be able to answer some of the Oracle Universal Installer's questions. For most of the wizard's prompts, we simply accepted the default values.

Now that we have the software installed, we will create our first database in the next chapter. We will walk through another Java-based wizard, the Database Configuration Assistant, and create the database we will use in our testbed.

CHAPTER 6

Creating Our Database

In the previous chapter, we installed the Oracle database software on our testbed server. In this chapter, we will create our first Oracle database and have a fully functional system where we can practice and learn Oracle.

The Oracle Universal Installer does have an option where you can install and create a database in unison. In this book, we will perform the actions separately, install the software then create the database. You are encouraged to create another virtual machine at a later date and test out installing and creating the database at the same time. You may find this option to be a time saver.

Creating the Database

Oracle includes a wizard called the Database Configuration Assistant (DBCA) to walk us through the database creation steps. Like most of the wizards and like the Oracle Universal Installer we used in Chapter 5, the DBCA is written in Java so it functions the same no matter which platform you are on. You can create an Oracle database manually, but the DBCA automates the process and reduces your chances of human errors. Always use the DBCA unless you have a specific need that requires you to create the database manually.

If your virtual machine is not running, start it. Then log in as the oracle user. Start a command line window, Terminal, from Applications ➤ System Tools. Before we can start the DBCA, we need to set up our environment with the commands in Listing 6-1. Type these two export commands in your Terminal window.

Listing 6-1. Setting the Environment Variables

```
export ORACLE_HOME=/u01/app/oracle/product/12.2.0.1
export PATH=$ORACLE_HOME/bin:$PATH
```

© Brian Peasland 2019
B. Peasland, *Oracle DBA Mentor*, https://doi.org/10.1007/978-1-4842-4321-3_6

The first command sets an environment variable pointing to our Oracle home directory. The second command modifies the PATH environment variable. If you do not tell the operating system were to find the utility, it will search its predefined path looking for it. We add the bin subdirectory of the Oracle home to the path. If you are running on other Unix variants, you may need to add other environment variables like LD_LIBRARY_PATH. On Windows platforms, this is unnecessary as the OUI defined these for us when the software was installed. With the environment variables defined, type "dbca" in the Terminal window and press the Enter key. After a short period of time, the DBCA starts. The initial DBCA screen is shown in Figure 6-1.

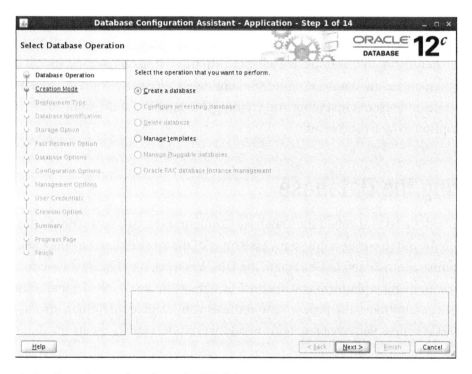

Figure 6-1. *Creating a database in DBCA*

At this point, we only have two options. We will select the option to create the database.

As you can see in Figure 6-1, the DBCA does more than just create Oracle databases. It can also be used to configure an existing database, delete databases, and so much more. Because this system does not have any databases running, those options are not available to us. The DBCA does come with some predefined templates to simply administration, but for our purposes, we will walk through all the options. After making sure the option to create the database is selected, click Next. The DBCA will advance to the Creation Mode screen shown in Figure 6-2.

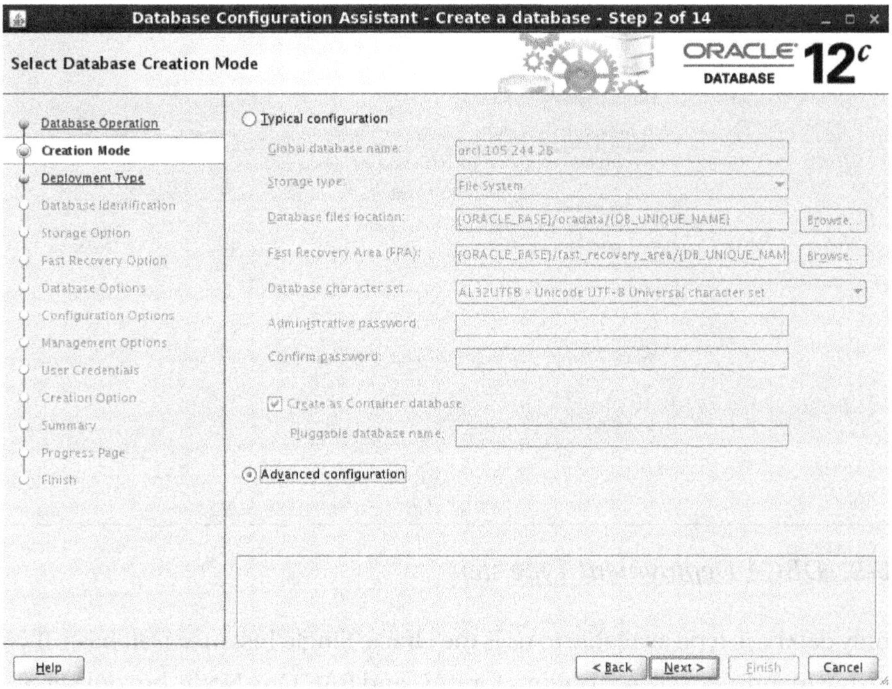

Figure 6-2. *DBCA Creation Mode step*

In an effort to make things easier for the database administrator, Oracle has provided a short outline with some typical configuration items. If the Typical Configuration option is chosen, the DBCA skips a number of steps. Instead, we will choose the Advanced Configuration option and walk through each of the steps to learn more about this process. Click Next to advance to the Database Deployment Type screen shown in Figure 6-3.

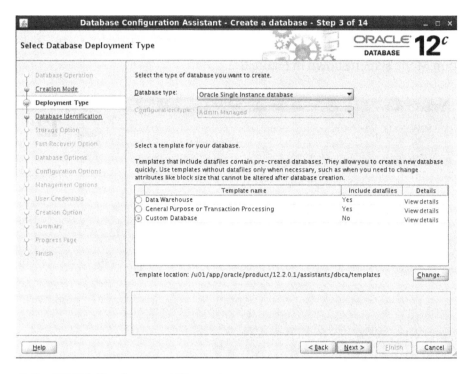

Figure 6-3. *DBCA Deployment Type step*

The only database type available to us is the Oracle Single Instance Database. If you pull down that menu, you will see options for RAC and RAC One Node, but our server is not configured for those choices. The rest of this screen asks us to choose a template. Notice that the first two templates include the data files. If you choose any of these templates, the DBCA will run much faster because it is not creating a database. Instead, it is copying files that already exist in the Oracle home directory of a database that has been pre-created. These templates work very well for creating a testbed database, but never use them for production. Your production database will be getting features and configurations you may not want.

Tip   Always choose the Custom Database option when creating production databases.

In this chapter we are creating a database for a testbed, but we also want to see how the rest of the wizard behaves so that we can learn from the questions it asks. Choose the Custom Database template and click Next. The DBCA will advance to the Database Identification screen shown in Figure 6-4. The image in Figure 6-4 is a portion of the entire screen.

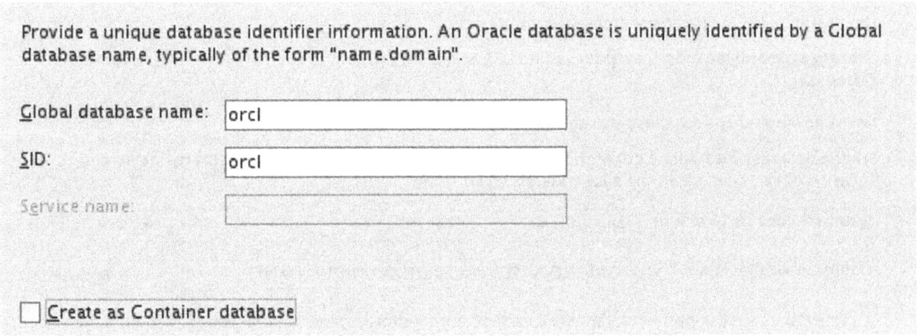

Provide a unique database identifier information. An Oracle database is uniquely identified by a Global database name, typically of the form "name.domain".

Global database name: `orcl`

SID: `orcl`

Service name:

☐ Create as Container database

Figure 6-4. *DBCA Database Identification step*

We will name this database orcl, which is shorthand for Oracle. As you progress through your database career, you will find that others commonly create a testbed database with this name. If you do not like this database name, you are free to choose one of your own.

Never use this name for production. Instead, give production databases a meaningful name. I typically include a one-letter designation indicating if the database is for production (P), development (D), or test (T). For example, if our production database will support our financial applications, I might name it FINP. The development and test databases for this application might be named FIND and FINT respectively. Now I can easily identify not only the main application using the database, but also its intent.

I've also created databases named TEST for some of my testbeds. When working with a new version, I might create a database with the version number in its name, for example ORCL122 for an Oracle 12.2 database. I never use the version number in its name for anything other than a testbed because the database will likely be upgraded at some point in the future and then the name becomes erroneous.

You are limited to eight characters for the database name. If you use P, D, and T to designate the type as outlined above, then that leaves seven characters to denote the application or other such usage. Whatever you use, make it meaningful and keep it consistent across the enterprise.

In the DBCA, make sure both the Global Database Name and SID fields are set to orcl. Make sure the Create As Container Database option is not selected. You will have to uncheck this box as it is selected by default. When you create a container database, you will be using the Oracle Multitenant option. Multitenant is certainly worthy of exploring at a later date, but for now we will not use that option. Click the Next button to arrive at the Storage Option screen, partially shown in Figure 6-5.

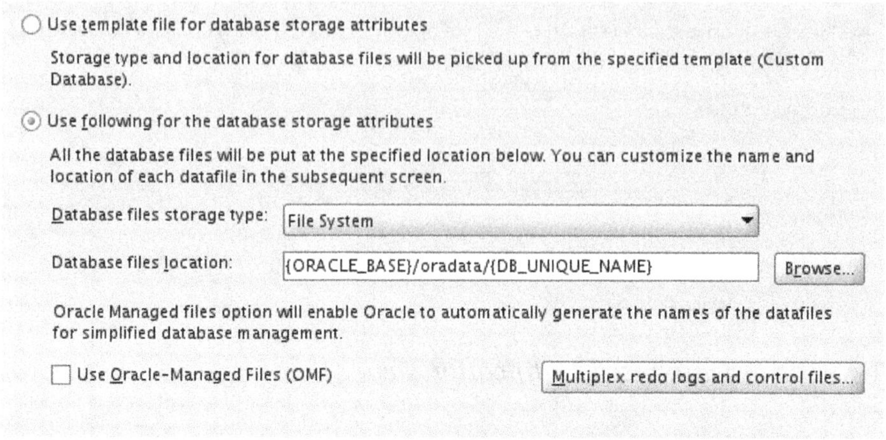

○ Use template file for database storage attributes

Storage type and location for database files will be picked up from the specified template (Custom Database).

◉ Use following for the database storage attributes

All the database files will be put at the specified location below. You can customize the name and location of each datafile in the subsequent screen.

Database files storage type: [File System   ▾]

Database files location: [{ORACLE_BASE}/oradata/{DB_UNIQUE_NAME}   ] [Browse...]

Oracle Managed files option will enable Oracle to automatically generate the names of the datafiles for simplified database management.

☐ Use Oracle-Managed Files (OMF)   [Multiplex redo logs and control files...]

Figure 6-5. *DBCA Storage Option step*

We now need to tell the DBCA where to put the database's files. Select the second radio button as shown in Figure 6-5. We will use a traditional file system instead of Oracle's ASM. The default location is sufficient. Click the Next button to advance to the Fast Recovery Option screen shown, a portion of which is shown in Figure 6-6.

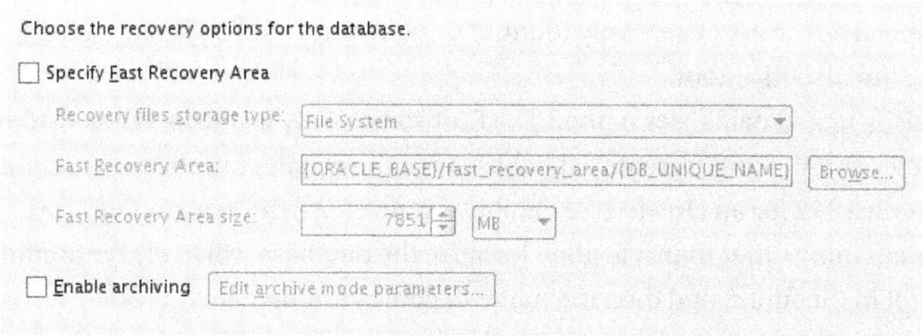

Choose the recovery options for the database.

☐ Specify Fast Recovery Area

Recovery files storage type: [File System   ▾]

Fast Recovery Area: [{ORACLE_BASE}/fast_recovery_area/{DB_UNIQUE_NAME}] [Browse...]

Fast Recovery Area size: [7851 ⬍] [MB ▾]

☐ Enable archiving [Edit archive mode parameters...]

Figure 6-6. *DBCA Fast Recovery Option step*

As Figure 6-6 shows, we have the option of defining a Fast Recovery Area. This option lets us define a location where Oracle can write backup files and transaction logs. For now, we will leave those options unchecked and click the Next button. The DBCA will advance to the Network Configuration screen, the relevant portion shown in Figure 6-7.

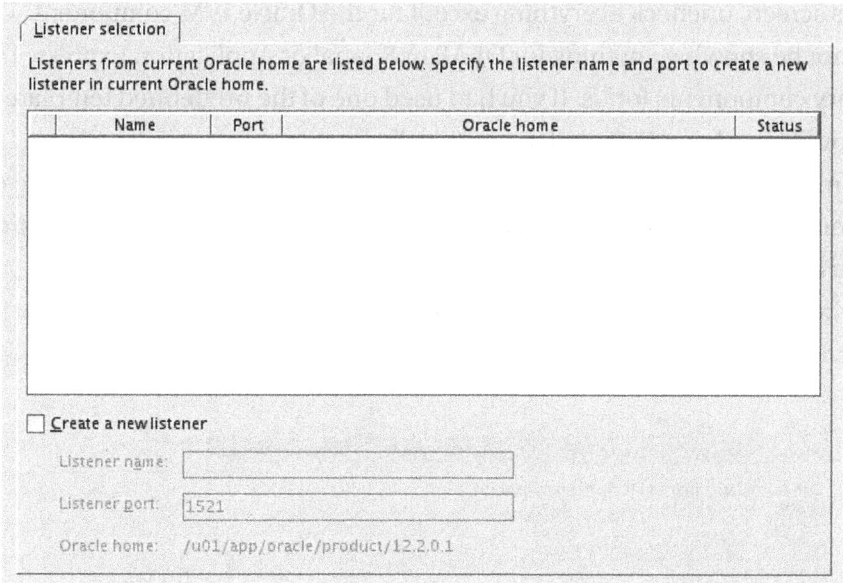

Figure 6-7. *DBCA Network Configuration step*

We do have the option of creating a Listener at this point in the DBCA. We will skip this section by simply clicking the Next button. It is easy to create a Listener, as will be shown later in this chapter. After clicking the Next button, the DBCA will advance to the Database Options screen, most of which is shown in Figure 6-8.

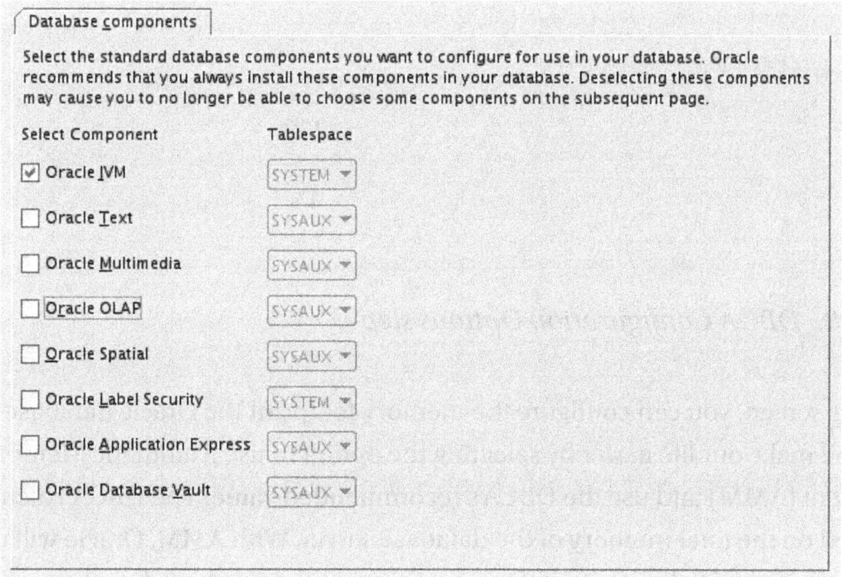

Figure 6-8. *DBCA Database Options step*

On this screen, uncheck everything except for the Oracle JVM component. This book will not be showing anything for OLAP or Spatial or Application Express. These are unnecessary components for us. If you had used one of the predefined templates, these options would have been included automatically for you.

There may certainly be times when you want to test out and play with those extra options. You now know how to create a testbed database and include those options should you desire.

After clicking the Next button, the DBCA will advance to the Configuration Options screen as we can see most of it in Figure 6-9.

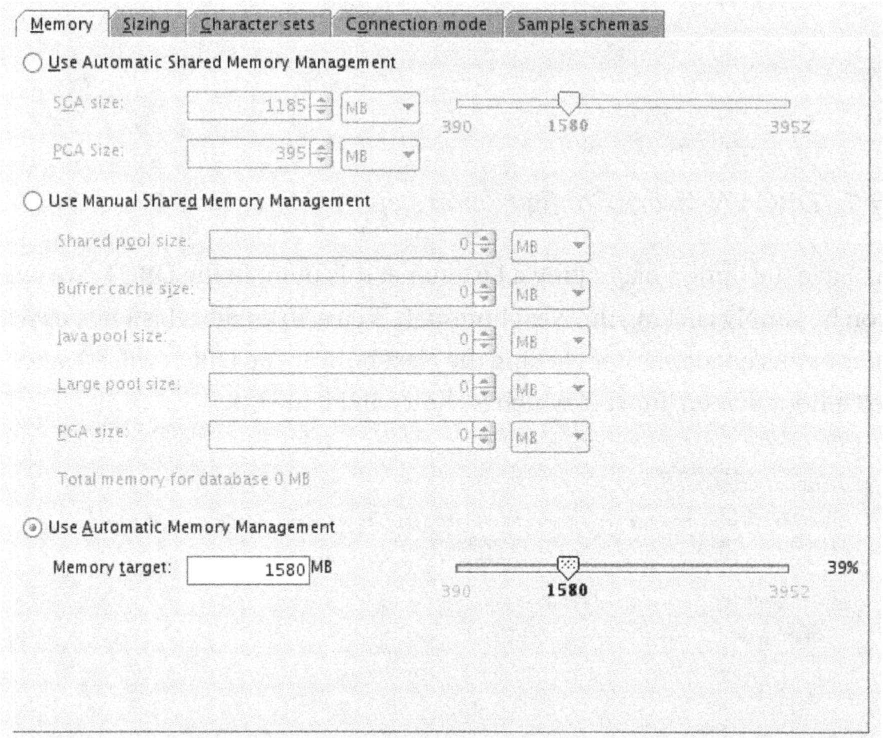

Figure 6-9. *DBCA Configuration Options step*

On this screen, you can configure the memory footprint the Oracle database will use. We will make our life easier by selecting the option to use Automatic Memory Management (AMM) and use the DBCA's recommended value. The DBCA calculates this value based on the total memory of the database server. With AMM, Oracle will decide how much memory to allocate to different memory structures based on the workload, thus simplifying the administration tasks. However, for production purposes, the recommended options are rarely a good choice and the DBA must arrive at better values. The other tabs let us control other configuration items. It is a good idea for you to just click each of those to see what they contain, but for now we will accept the default values and click Next to arrive at the Management Options, partially shown in Figure 6-10.

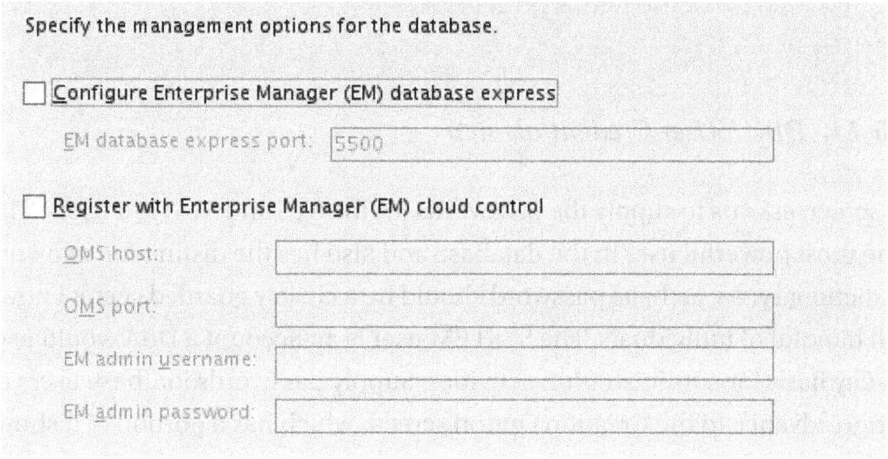

Figure 6-10. *DBCA Management Options step*

This screen asks us to configure different management options. We have three choices. We can use Enterprise Manager (EM) Database Express, Enterprise Manager Cloud Control, or nothing. We will configure this database with none of the EM options by unselecting any check boxes. Both EM options are web-based graphical management tools of the database. The difference is that EM Database Express is for just this one database, whereas EM Cloud Control is a centralized platform capable of managing all of the Oracle databases in your enterprise. In this book we will use neither of these tools, although Chapter 11 will provide an overview for those that are interested in learning more. Uncheck the boxes and click Next and the DBCA will advance to the User Credentials screen, a portion of which is shown in Figure 6-11.

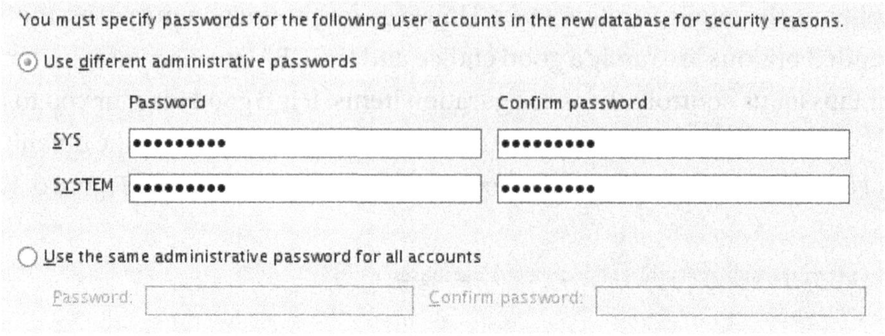

Figure 6-11. *DBCA User Credentials step*

This screen asks us to supply the passwords for the SYS and SYSTEM users. The SYS user is the most powerful user in the database and also has the distinction of owning the data dictionary. As such, its password should be a closely guarded secret known to a small handful of individuals. The SYSTEM user is an account a DBA would use on a day-to-day basis for administration activities. Supply passwords for these users and click Next to advance to the Creation Option screen, which has a portion of it shown in Figure 6-12.

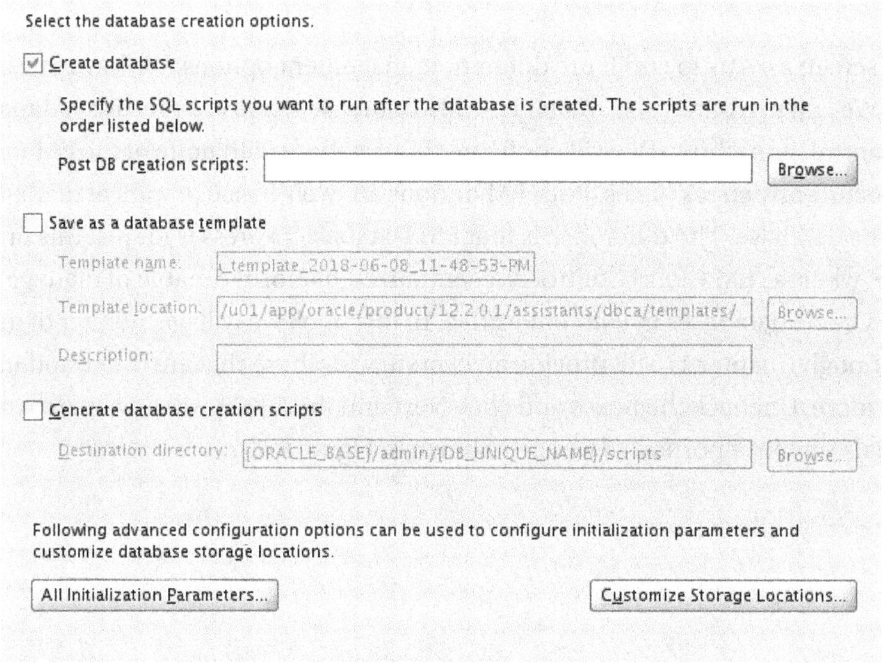

Figure 6-12. *DBCA Creation Option step*

By the time we reach the screen in Figure 6-12, we have provided everything the DBCA needs to know to create the database. Now the DBCA wants to know how to proceed. We could save the collection of all of our settings as its own template to speed up database creation in the future, just like the option of saving a response file when installing Oracle covered in Chapter 5. We could have the DBCA create scripts to create this database at a later date. For now, we will make sure the Create Database box is checked. After all, this option is the point of the entire chapter. Click Next and the DBCA will show us a summary of our options, a section of which can be seen in Figure 6-13.

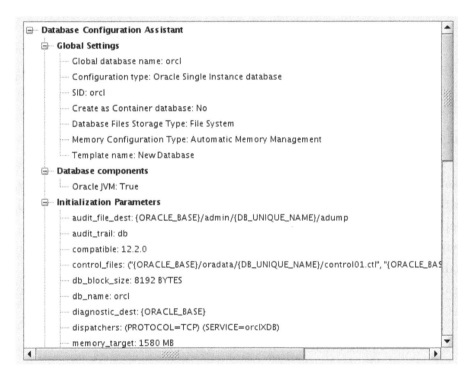

Figure 6-13. *DBCA Summary*

We are finally presented with a Summary screen. This gives us a chance to review all of the settings we have defined to the DBCA. If something looks amiss, we can click the Back button appropriately to make changes to the answers we have previously supplied. Once we are satisfied, we click the Finish button and the DBCA will go to work. Figure 6-14 shows the a section of the Progress screen of the DBCA creating the database.

Progress
Database "orcl" creation in progress...

16%

Steps	Status
✓ Creating and starting Oracle instance	Finished
✓ Creating database files	Finished
⏱ Creating data dictionary views	In Progress
Adding Oracle JVM	
Completing Database Creation	
Executing Post Configuration Actions	

DBCA Log Location:/u01/app/oracle/cfgtoollogs/dbca/orcl/trace.log_2018-06-08_11-48-53-PM
Alert Log Location:/u01/app/oracle/diag/rdbms/orcl/orcl/trace/alert_orcl.log

Figure 6-14. *DBCA Progress screen*

We can watch the DBCA as it works through various steps. It will start the Oracle instance, then create the database's files and the data dictionary. The list of steps in this screen depends on the answers we supplied to the DBCA.

If anything goes wrong with creating the database, the first place to look is in the file noted as the DBCA Log Location.

Once the database has been created, the DBCA will show one final screen, the Creation Complete panel, partially shown in Figure 6-15.

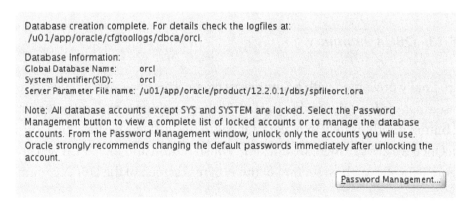

Database creation complete. For details check the logfiles at:
 /u01/app/oracle/cfgtoollogs/dbca/orcl.

Database Information:
Global Database Name: orcl
System Identifier(SID):   orcl
Server Parameter File name: /u01/app/oracle/product/12.2.0.1/dbs/spfileorcl.ora

Note: All database accounts except SYS and SYSTEM are locked. Select the Password
Management button to view a complete list of locked accounts or to manage the database
accounts. From the Password Management window, unlock only the accounts you will use.
Oracle strongly recommends changing the default passwords immediately after unlocking the
account.

Password Management...

Figure 6-15. *DBCA DB creation complete*

Click the Close button to exit the utility. Our database has now been created and is ready for use.

Starting the Oracle Listener

If we want users to be able to connect from outside the database server, we need to have an Oracle Listener running. The Listener's job is to broker incoming connection requests. If you recall from Figure 6-7 earlier in this chapter, we declined to create a Listener when the database was created. We really do not have to create a Listener. Instead, we just start it up.

Being that this is not a production-ready server and it is only our testbed, we have to perform a simple task before we can start the Listener. Our testbed will not be known by any server name on our network and thus will not be registered in the network's DNS server. To get around this, we have to add our hostname to the virtual machine's /etc/ hosts file. On the server, open a Terminal window. Since we are signed on as the oracle user, we type "su" to connect as root and supply the root password. Then issue the command in Listing 6-2.

Listing 6-2. Adding Hosts Entry

```
echo "127.0.0.1 dbamentor dbamentor.localdomain" >> /etc/hosts
```

The command above will add our hostname to the list. Type "exit" to leave the root prompt. Back at the oracle prompt, issue

```
lsnrctl start
```

This will start the Listener, on the default port, which is normally sufficient. Wait a few minutes and check the status of the Listener. We can see the lsnrctl status command and its output in Listing 6-3.

Listing 6-3. Listener Status

```
[oracle@dbamentor ~]$ lsnrctl status

LSNRCTL for Linux: Version 12.2.0.1.0 - Production on 10-JUN-2018 23:34:03

Copyright (c) 1991, 2016, Oracle.  All rights reserved.
```

```
Connecting to (ADDRESS=(PROTOCOL=tcp)(HOST=)(PORT=1521))
STATUS of the LISTENER
------------------------
Alias                    LISTENER
Version                  TNSLSNR for Linux: Version 12.2.0.1.0 - Production
Start Date               10-JUN-2018 23:29:22
Uptime                   0 days 0 hr. 4 min. 40 sec
Trace Level              off
Security                 ON: Local OS Authentication
SNMP                     OFF
Listener Log File        /u01/app/oracle/diag/tnslsnr/dbamentor/listener/
                            alert/log.xml
Listening Endpoints Summary...
  (DESCRIPTION=(ADDRESS=(PROTOCOL=tcp)(HOST=dbamentor)(PORT=1521)))
Services Summary...
Service "orcl" has 1 instance(s).
  Instance "orcl", status READY, has 1 handler(s) for this service...
Service "orclXDB" has 1 instance(s).
  Instance "orcl", status READY, has 1 handler(s) for this service...
The command completed successfully
```

We can see from the output that our database has contacted the Listener and is now ready for incoming connections. The instance "orcl" has a status of READY in the output above.

Issuing Our First Queries

Now that our database is running, let's issue a few queries. First, we need to set our environment to be able to connect to that database. Oracle includes a script to help us. In a Terminal window, type ". oraenv" (make sure to include a space between the dot and oraenv). The script will ask us which database we want and we reply "orcl" as shown in Listing 6-4.

Listing 6-4. Setting Our Environment

```
[oracle@dbamentor ~]$ . oraenv
ORACLE_SID = [oracle] ? orcl
The Oracle base has been set to /u01/app/oracle
```

If we had multiple Oracle databases running on this server, we could use this method to change which database we want to interact with. The oraenv script uses the /etc/oratab file to know the Oracle home directory for our database. If we look in that file, there is only one non-comment row in it:

```
orcl:/u01/app/oracle/product/12.2.0.1:N
```

When we replied orcl, the oraenv script determined the Oracle home directory was /u01/app/oracle/product/12.2.0.1 by reading this file.

Now with the environment set, we can fire up SQL*Plus and connect to the database. Type "sqlplus system" at the command prompt and provide the user's password when requested. Once connected, let's verify we are connected to our database by asking for its name, as shown in Listing 6-5.

Listing 6-5. Database Name

```
SQL> select name from v$database;

NAME
---------
ORCL
```

Next, we'll ask for the instance name in Listing 6-6.

Listing 6-6. Instance Name

```
SQL> select instance_name,status from v$instance;

INSTANCE_NAME       STATUS
---------------                 ------------
orcl                OPEN
```

The instance name matches the database's name and this is expected. If this were an Oracle RAC database, the instance name would have a number appended to the database name, such as orcl1.

One last thing we will do in this chapter is to shut down the instance and then start it back up again. Our current user, SYSTEM, does not have the appropriate privileges for these actions, so we will connect as SYS. Since we are local to the database server, we can just connect with "/ as sysdba" as shown in Listing 6-7. This connects us to the SYS user without requiring a password.

Listing 6-7. Shutdown and Startup

```
SQL> connect / as sysdba
Connected.
SQL> shutdown immediate
Database closed.
Database dismounted.
ORACLE instance shut down.
SQL> startup
ORACLE instance started.

Total System Global Area 1660944384 bytes
Fixed Size                   8621376 bytes
Variable Size             1056965312 bytes
Database Buffers           587202560 bytes
Redo Buffers                 8155136 bytes
Database mounted.
Database opened.
```

Every time we shut down the virtual machine, we will want to shut down the Oracle instance first. Every time we start the virtual machine, we will want to start the Listener and the Oracle instance.

On Windows, the service created by the DBCA will handle shutdown/startup automatically for you. On Linux and Unix, you can use dbshut and dbstart scripts in $ORACLE_HOME/bin to help automate the shutdown and startup respectively. However, in testbeds I rarely use these because I tend to break my databases when I am trying out new things. My personal preference is to avoid starting a broken database when I start the virtual machine. Your opinion may be different so you may choose to automate the startup and shutdown in your testbed.

Moving On

In this chapter, we created our first database. This chapter completes the initial setup of our testbed. We even ran a few queries against the database to ensure it was up and running just fine.

   In the next chapter, we will learn some basics on how to back up the database. Remember that we want to be the data guardian and protect the database. Backup and recovery is one of our first lines of defense.

PART II

Using Oracle Database

## CHAPTER 7

Recovery and Backup

So far in this book, we have created our virtual machine, installed the Oracle database software, and created our first database. Now that we have things up and running, we need to start by protecting our database. Remember from Chapter 1 that the database administrator is the data guardian. It is your responsibility to protect the data and ensure it is safe. This chapter and the one that follows are vital for the data guardian. In this chapter, we will discuss Oracle backup and recovery. In the next chapter, we will discuss database security.

Recovery Before Backups

I see it most every day. Database administrators discuss backup and recovery in the wrong order. I see questions like, "What is the best way to back up my database?"; "How can I back up a very large database?"; "What is Oracle's preferred backup utility?"; "Should I perform incremental backups?" Every one of these questions is discussing backups without any discussion of recovery. Even the term *backup and recovery* is out of order in my opinion. Every person learning to be a database administrator would be better off if the term were *recovery and backup* because that's the order we need to think about things.

Tip   Define your recovery requirements before designing your backup solution.

Thinking about the recovery requirements before backups is one of my biggest topics I have been a champion of throughout my career. I now see other database administrators following suit and a small cadre of us are starting to change attitudes. As a reader of this book, you are now part of the movement to discuss recovery before backups.

© Brian Peasland 2019
B. Peasland, *Oracle DBA Mentor*, https://doi.org/10.1007/978-1-4842-4321-3_7

Backups serve one purpose and one purpose only: to be able to get the database operational and back in business and help recover after a failure. It is not the action of taking backups that is important. It is the action of restoring and recovering from a failure that is the vital task. Too many database administrators implement a backup solution first and then either hope it will let them restore from failures or blindly trust it will work for them going forward. In both cases, the database administrator has made a critical error in judgment. Readers of this book will go forward knowing they have to understand their recovery requirements before implementing a backup solution. Please help spread the word that it is recovery requirements that drive the backup solution, not the other way around.

Most Oracle database administrators will tell you to use Oracle Recovery Manager (RMAN) to back up and restore your databases. They'll tell you to perform full backups weekly or monthly and, if your database is large or has a high transactional volume, to perform incremental backups in between. On the surface, this seems like good advice and may be sufficient for a very large majority of your needs. What if your management tells you that you need to ensure your database is back up and running in less than an hour and your database is 100 terabytes in size? RMAN is going to have a difficult time restoring such a large database in such a short timeframe. This is not meant as a knock against RMAN. RMAN is a great product and, if it all possible, you should use it. RMAN is Oracle's preferred backup and recovery utility. Just like any utility, there are pros and cons to using it. Sometimes, your recovery requirements dictate the use of a different tool. Instead of thinking about which tool you will be using for backup and recovery, let's first define the recovery requirements.

Recovery Requirements

Before designing a backup solution, document your recovery requirements. This will often require the database administrator to work closely with their management, who in turn may need to work closely with the organization. Remember from Chapter 2 that we covered knowing your audience and considered a few techniques on how to communicate with people from different skill sets. Gathering recovery requirements is where your communication skills come in handy.

The recovery requirements need to be documented and used to craft a service-level agreement (SLA). The SLA should include what is known in the industry as the recovery time objective (RTO), a measure of how quickly your database needs to be up and running after a failure. Your recovery requirements also need to indicate the level of acceptable data loss, called the recovery point objective (RPO), usually denoted as a period of time. Do I need to recover every transaction, in which case the RPO is zero? Or can the organization afford to lose one week's worth of data or something in between? The DBA needs to know these two metrics to be able to design a backup strategy that lets them meet the SLA requirements.

The lower the RTO or the data loss, RPO, the more expensive the solution will be to implement. For example, if your organization can afford seven days of downtime and can lose one month's worth of data, then you can write backups to offsite tape media on a monthly basis. You will have plenty of time to bring that tape back to your data center and restore your database. If your requirement is zero data loss and your database must be operational in five minutes, then RMAN or disk-based snapshots are not going to help you. You would need to implement Data Guard and have a transactionally consistent copy of your database in another data center. The first scenario is cheaper and easier to implement. The second scenario is much costlier.

The organization is paying for the disaster recovery solution you need to implement. Since they have to pay for what you design as the DBA, it is incumbent that you and the organization have a solid understanding of the expectations from all parties. This is why the SLA is so important.

The SLA is more than just a document so that all parties understand the expectations. It is also a contract between the database administrator and the business. If the DBA is not implementing a backup and recovery strategy that meets the SLA, the DBA should be terminated from the organization. If the organization is not paying for the resources required to meet the SLA, the DBA should document such so they are not liable when they cannot meet the terms in the agreement.

Tip   Work with management to implement a service-level agreement for recovery of the company's databases.

The SLA should include the following items for each and every database in the enterprise:

- Recovery time objective, the time within which it must be operational

- Recovery point objective, the acceptable amount of data loss

- A list of disaster scenarios, such as fire, flood, hurricane, tornado, or human error, applicable to the data center(s) that house the database.

- How much downtime is acceptable to back up the database, if any

- Any special needs for this database

Production databases often have much different SLA terms than non-production databases. Many DBAs only create an SLA for production databases, but your non-production databases should have an SLA as well. Development and test databases can often withstand much longer outages and lose much more data, and it needs to be documented as such. Remember that while your organization's end users rely on your production database, your dev and test databases are considered production for someone as well, typically internal staff. If your development database is down, application developers may not be able to work. If the test database is down, quality assurance staff may be unable to work.

Today's IT infrastructure can help facilitate meeting non-production SLA requirements. For example, with cloud computing, it is easy to throw away a broken development test database and spin up another one, however you may experience total data loss. With Oracle Multitenant, you can clone databases for different purposes. For example, I have a weekly golden image, which is a copy of production mounted up in an Oracle Multitenant database. All development and test databases are cloned from these golden images. Should a development database become too broken to use, we simply destroy it and re-clone from a golden image. The whole point of this paragraph is that technology changes can help meet SLA requirements. Cloud, Multitenant, virtualization, and containers are newer technologies that can assist the DBA.

Once the SLA has been created and all parties have signed off on the document, the database administrator needs to go through it and design a recovery test plan. The recovery test plan ensures that everything in the SLA is accounted for and that the DBA has verified disaster can be mitigated as required. The recovery test plan is a checklist of items that must be met, according to the SLA.

Notice that in this section, we only discuss the recovery half. We never think about backups during the analysis of our recovery requirements. The SLA should never have anything in it about backups, only recovery. If your SLA says to use any specific backup methodology, strike that term from the document. I've seen too many SLAs that say, for example, to perform full backups weekly with incremental backups daily—that language does not belong in the SLA. The SLA should never constrain the backup solution. Rather, it should help craft the backup solution. After testing, the DBA may discover the backup solution does not meet the SLA's recovery requirements, so the DBA may need to employ another backup solution. This is easier to do if the backup solution is not in the SLA.

Tip   Only after the SLA is complete can the backup solution be created.

Now that the database administrator knows the scenarios they need to recover from, how quickly, and with the maximum acceptable data loss, the DBA is finally able to design a backup solution. The Oracle DBA may very well find that using RMAN for full backups once a week and incremental backups daily is sufficient. The DBA may also find that they need to implement more than one backup solution. For example, the DBA may be required to be able to refresh a schema in development on a periodic basis. This requirement would fall under the "special needs" mentioned in the final bullet point in the previous list. The DBA may opt for RMAN backups to fulfill most of the recovery requirements, but also leverage database exports for this special requirement. Or, the DBA may decide to use RMAN backups in a Multitenant environment that creates clones for development databases.

After the backup solution has been designed and implemented, it is vital for the database administrator to test recovery against all of the requirements. The DBA should use the recovery test plan, derived from the SLA, to ensure the SLA terms are covered. If a recovery requirement cannot be met, the DBA will need to figure out how to handle that requirement. Does the existing backup solution need to be modified to handle that extra requirement while handling all the rest? Or does the DBA need to implement another tool to meet that requirement?

The database administrator should review the SLA with management on a yearly basis. All parties need to ensure the terms of the agreement still hold for the upcoming year. Things change over time, and what was valid when the SLA was created may no longer be valid.

The DBA should also practice the recovery test plan on a yearly basis, at a minimum. This ensures that technology changes over the past year will not impact the ability to meet the SLA. The annual recovery testing should verify that each and every SLA requirement is still being met. If the DBA has their recovery requirements checklist mentioned above, they can use it here. Performing regular recovery tests also keeps the DBA's skills up to date. One of the worst feelings as a DBA is to have everyone waiting for the DBA to return a production database back into service and not be able to remember what to do. An annual review is essential. Ideally, the review should be performed biannually or even quarterly. If your company is audited due to business or regulatory requirements, multiple recovery tests will be needed.

Tip   At least yearly, review the SLA and exercise the recovery test plan.

Backup and Recovery Documentation

Oracle has documented how to perform backup and recovery in the *Database Backup and Recovery User's Guide*. Every Oracle database administrator should read this guide from front to back at least twice. To access the *Database Backup and Recovery User's Guide*, point a web browser to `https://docs.oracle.com` and click the Database button. Then click the Oracle Database button, click the drop-down menu, and select your database's version. Each version typically introduces changes and provides new features for backup and recovery. It is important for the Oracle DBA to read this document when a new version is introduced. With your version selected, click the Administration link in the Topics section. If you scroll down a bit, you will see a section titled Backup and Recovery. This section should contain two manuals, the *Database Backup and Recovery Reference* and the *Database Backup and Recovery User's Guide*. This chapter will cover both the Oracle 12.2 and 18c versions of the database.

The *Database Backup and Recovery Reference* contains all the details on the RMAN backup commands. You will come across many examples of RMAN commands. On occasion, the example may come close to what you want to do but be a bit different. The *Backup and Recovery Reference* details what each command can do and lists all of its options. Take time to familiarize yourself with this manual. The idea is not to know everything in the manual but to have an idea of what it contains. Some day in the future you may need to find something in this manual.

The *Database Backup and Recovery User's Guide* is the main one to read. This document contains a lot of information on how to use Oracle's utilities to back up and recover your databases, including RMAN, Flashback Database, and user-managed backup and recovery.

All readers of this book are strongly encouraged to read the *Backup and Recovery User's Guide*. This chapter will not cover nearly as much information as what Oracle provides in that guide. Not only will you learn things when you read that manual, but pay attention to what is in there and where it is located. Take note of the Table of Contents to learn how the document is organized. Like all of the Oracle documentation, you will need to refer to it at some later date.

Early on in the *Backup and Recovery User's Guide*, you may spot a statement that people who have not read this book may not think twice about. In Chapter 1 of the *Backup and Recovery User's Guide*, it states "As a backup administrator, your primary job is making and monitoring backups for data protection." Readers of this book know that the primary job is to get our database up and running and recover from a failure. Backups are not your primary job; recovering from failures is. Backups are a means to that end.

Backup Types

Oracle databases have two different classifications when talking about backup types. The first classification is the "temperature" of the backups. The second classification is the management type of the backup.

Hot and Cold Backups

Backups are either *hot* backups or *cold* backups. The temperature is used to denote if the database is open and available for business (hot) while the backup is performed or is down (cold) while the backup is taken. In today's 24×7 world, cold backups are very rare for production databases. Cold backups are great because they are the easiest to implement and the easiest to recover from. However, with the demand for constant availability, we often need to rely on hot backups.

A database consists of files on disks. When backing up a database, a copy of that file is written to a backup destination. The bigger the files and the bigger the database, the longer it takes to complete the backup. The problem with a database is that it is a living, breathing entity. Transactions are continually occurring and modifying the database's data files. After the backup has started, but before it has yet to complete, a transaction may modify files that are already backed up, and modify files that have yet to be backed up. This will result in an inconsistent backup. One mechanism we have available to handle this is to stop all transactions, meaning perform a cold backup. With a cold backup, we know that all the files are transactionally consistent with a specific point in time.

If we need to perform hot backups, we need another mechanism to be able to resolve any transaction inconsistencies that occurred while the data files were being copied to the backup destination. In Oracle, hot backups require us to configure the database for archivelog mode. In archivelog mode, the Oracle database will maintain copies of the transaction logs in a special location on disk. We perform a hot backup. When recovering the database from that hot backup, Oracle uses the transactions in the log files to resolve any inconsistencies. Hot backups let us protect our database while keeping it open for business, but it comes at the cost of maintaining transaction logs.

RMAN and User-Managed Backups

There are two management types for Oracle backups. We can either let Recovery Manager govern the process or we can leave it up to the user. Both types are documented in the *Database Backup and Recovery User's Guide*.

In the old days, the database administrator always managed backup and subsequent recovery operations. When a disaster occurred, the DBA needed to analyze the problem, assess what to restore, and perform the proper steps to get the database open for business. Losing a control file required the DBA to perform a different action than the action required after losing a data file. The DBA needed to be well versed in the various disaster scenarios and the appropriate recovery steps.

The database administrator was responsible for writing their own backup scripts. Once the DBA wrote a backup script that worked for most situations, the DBA used it as much as possible to back up many different databases. Hot and cold backup scripts were completely different. If the database was in archivelog mode, the DBA needed another script to manage the archivelog destination so that it would not fill up.

The DBA needed to pay attention to every detail of both backup and recovery. As such, there was a high chance of human error in the process. It would be terrible to find out there was a human error in the backup script at the time when you needed to recover from a disaster. User-managed backup and recovery is a time-consuming, fragile activity.

Oracle Corporation introduced Recovery Manager with the Oracle 8.0 version. With RMAN, the database administrator was relieved of having to know all of the details. RMAN figures everything out for you. With RMAN, recovery from a lost control file or a lost data file is the same. You tell RMAN to restore everything. RMAN figures out what went wrong and puts the pieces back together for you. If you use Enterprise Manager and have it schedule a backup of your database, it will run RMAN commands behind the scenes for you. RMAN has grown and matured over the years since its introduction and has many features you may enjoy. Hopefully, you can see why RMAN is Oracle's preferred backup and recovery utility.

With RMAN available, is there ever a need for user-managed backups anymore? Many database administrators will tell you to always use RMAN, but I still find use for user-managed backups on occasion. The two places I implement user-managed backups are for a quick and easy backup of a small testbed database, and for backing up very large databases that can leverage hardware-based disk snapshot capabilities.

Later in this chapter, we will perform a user-managed backup of our testbed database we created in the previous chapter. The process is super simple and very intuitive, and you do not have to remember any RMAN commands.

All of this may sound like I am against RMAN, which I am not. RMAN is an excellent utility and I would recommend using it so long as it meets your recovery requirements. What I am against is when people say to use RMAN, or that it is a preferred backup tool, when they have no knowledge of the exact recovery requirements that need to be satisfied.

Remember that recovery requirements define the backup solution. If my requirement is to be able to restore a 200TB database in under ten minutes, good luck doing that with RMAN. The utility simply cannot perform backups or restores that fast for such a large database. But many disk subsystems let storage administrators take snapshots of the files on disk. We can have a user-managed backup strategy where the database is put in backup mode, the snapshot is taken, and backup mode is ended. The entire process can be completed in a few minutes. To restore, we shut down the database and have the storage administrator revert to a good snapshot. Even for a 200TB database, this process can be completed in minutes. The database administrator will have to write the backup scripts, and work with the storage administrator, and both need to handle all the details. However, some recovery requirements dictate a solution that RMAN cannot handle. RMAN can handle almost all recovery requirements, but not every one of them. Document those recovery requirements, then choose the backup tool.

Logical Backups

Too many database administrators rely solely on *logical backups* for their databases, which for most cases is an incorrect backup solution, as this section discusses. Logical backups can meet some recovery requirements. However, they rarely meet recovery requirements for production databases.

What is a logical backup? It is one taken with an export utility like Data Pump's expdp. RMAN and user-managed backups are *physical backups* because they make a duplicate copy of the data files to a backup destination. At the time the backup is taken, the database's file and what is in the backup destination are identical. Over time, the database's file will change and diverge from the backup copy. I should note that physical backups with RMAN often work at the data block level, which is smaller than the file level. This technical difference does not change the differences between logical and physical backups.

A logical backup reads the contents of a table and writes the table's data to a dump file. The dump file does not resemble any of the database's files. Rather, the dump file contains the structure of the table and the data itself. The biggest difference between a physical backup and a logical backup is that one can never roll forward any changes since the logical backup was taken. With a physical backup, you can restore the database and, if you have the transaction logs, you can bring the database to a later point then when the backup was taken, called *rolling forward*. Rolling forward reduces or even eliminats any data loss. Because a logical backup cannot be rolled forward, it can suffer from significant amounts of data loss depending on how old it is and how much has changed since the logical backup was performed.

All too often, I will hear junior-level database administrators ask questions about recovering their database from a failure, and the initial response is to ask for more details about how the database was backed up. The DBA needing the assistance responds that they use Data Pump for their backups. It is at this point that I know this database administrator has given little thought about their recovery requirements. They simply implemented a backup solution they thought would cover their needs, and nine times out of ten, they learn a hard lesson. This is not to say that logical backups are bad. They do serve a purpose, but logical backups are rarely the only backup option for a production database.

Logical backups are well suited for copying data from one database to another. RMAN can do this to some degree as well. With Data Pump, I can export just one schema and import into another database. I can export a set of tables as well. Logical backups can also be used when taking a snapshot in time of the data. I will often use Data Pump when I need to preserve a schema's contents, normally right before I destroy the entire schema. I'll copy the dump files to tape media or some other offsite storage. Years later when someone says they need the data, it can be difficult to restore a user-managed or RMAN backup because I need the same exact database version in use when the backup was taken. Data Pump from an older version can be imported into a newer

Oracle version without issues. Logical backups serve a purpose. Physical backups serve a purpose. The database administrator needs to learn the differences and how each one impacts their ability to recover. The DBA would then leverage the most appropriate method.

Restore and Recovery

We often use the terms *restore* and *recover* interchangeably to mean the same thing. In Oracle terms, they have distinctly different meanings. It is important to note the differences.

When you *restore* an Oracle database, you are simply placing the database's files back on disk. The restore phase copies the files from the backup location to the server somewhere Oracle can access it. Usually, we try to restore to the same exact location, but if we lose that disk device, we may need to restore the files to a different location on the server.

Remember that the database is a living and breathing entity. Transactions are constantly making changes to the data. The *recovery* phase will ensure that all committed transactions have their changes written to the data files and that any uncommitted transactions are rolled back. No matter if you perform a hot or cold backup, the recovery phase is still needed.

Our Cold Backup

Now that we have created our testbed database, it's time to back it up. Because this is a testbed, I may break things while I'm trying out new concepts. It would be nice to be able to get back to a known state. This database does not have any production purposes and I can lose all of the data inside. After all, it's just a testbed. I have no need for any quick recovery, so my RTO can be quite large. Now that I know my simplistic recovery requirements, I can design my backup strategy. For my testbeds, I often take a cold, user-managed backup of the database.

When performing a user-managed backup of the database, we need to back up the control files, the online redo logs, and the data files. The control files contain the master directory of where all the other files are located. The online redo logs contain the transaction log. The data files contain the data in the database. We can query V$CONTROLFILE, V$LOGFILE, and V$DATAFILE to learn the names and locations of these files. Listing 7-1 shows basic queries to learn the locations of these files.

Listing 7-1. Files for Cold Backup

```
SQL> select name from v$controlfile;

NAME
--------------------------------------------------------------------------------
/u01/app/oracle/oradata/orcl/control01.ctl
/u01/app/oracle/oradata/orcl/control02.ctl

SQL> select member from v$logfile;

MEMBER
--------------------------------------------------------------------------------
/u01/app/oracle/oradata/orcl/redo01.log
/u01/app/oracle/oradata/orcl/redo02.log
/u01/app/oracle/oradata/orcl/redo03.log

SQL> select name from v$datafile;

NAME
--------------------------------------------------------------------------------
/u01/app/oracle/oradata/orcl/system01.dbf
/u01/app/oracle/oradata/orcl/sysaux01.dbf
/u01/app/oracle/oradata/orcl/undotbs01.dbf
/u01/app/oracle/oradata/orcl/users01.dbf
```

Because this is a testbed, all the files are in the same location. Let's create a backup directory, shut down the instance, back up the database, then start up the instance. We can do this without leaving SQL*Plus by preceding all host commands with an exclamation point. Listing 7-2 shows the steps to perform a cold backup.

Listing 7-2. Cold Backup

```
SQL> !mkdir /u01/app/oracle/oradata/db_backup

SQL> shutdown immediate
Database closed.
Database dismounted.
ORACLE instance shut down.
SQL> !cp /u01/app/oracle/oradata/orcl/* /u01/app/oracle/oradata/db_backup/.
```

```
SQL> startup
ORACLE instance started.

Total System Global Area 1660944384 bytes
Fixed Size                   8621376 bytes
Variable Size             1056965312 bytes
Database Buffers           587202560 bytes
Redo Buffers                 8155136 bytes
Database mounted.
Database opened.
```

Our backup is complete. No matter what kind of damage we do to our test database, we can always revert to the day this backup was taken. As shown in Listing 7-2, the cold backup was pretty simple for our testbed. We created a backup destination, shut down the instance, copied the files to the backup destination, and then started the instance.

To recover from a failure, all we need to do is shut down the instance, copy the files back, and start it up again. It's really that simple, which is why I like user-managed cold backups for testbeds. User-managed cold backups are easy to understand and easy to perform for this testbed. If your database is more complex and files are in different locations, the backup and recovery can be more complex.

Let's shut down the instance and remove a data file, then try to start the instance. We are simulating the loss of a data file. The data file may be lost because a human accidentally deleted it or because the disk has a bad spot where the file was located. Listing 7-3 shows what happens when we try to start the instance that has a missing database file.

Listing 7-3. Simulating Loss of a Data File

```
SQL> shutdown immediate
Database closed.
Database dismounted.
ORACLE instance shut down.
SQL> !rm /u01/app/oracle/oradata/orcl/users01.dbf

SQL> startup
ORACLE instance started.
```

```
Total System Global Area 1660944384 bytes
Fixed Size                  8621376 bytes
Variable Size            1056965312 bytes
Database Buffers          587202560 bytes
Redo Buffers                8155136 bytes
Database mounted.
ORA-01157: cannot identify/lock data file 4 - see DBWR trace file
ORA-01110: data file 4: '/u01/app/oracle/oradata/orcl/users01.dbf'
```

The file was lost for some reason. When the instance started, it was not able to find the file so it gave us the ORA-1157 error. To get things back up and running, we will shut down and abort the instance, restore our files, and start things up. We can see the steps in Listing 7-4.

Listing 7-4. Recovering from a Lost Data File

```
SQL> shutdown abort
ORACLE instance shut down.
SQL> !cp /u01/app/oracle/oradata/db_backup/* /u01/app/oracle/oradata/orcl/.

SQL> startup
ORACLE instance started.

Total System Global Area 1660944384 bytes
Fixed Size                  8621376 bytes
Variable Size            1056965312 bytes
Database Buffers          587202560 bytes
Redo Buffers                8155136 bytes
Database mounted.
Database opened.
```

The last line in the listing shows the database is now open for business.

At this point, we can now start to play "what if" games and really start to learn more about the Oracle database. We have our testbed and we can play around with things as much as we want. In a later chapter, we will discuss testbeds and test cases in more detail, but we can do a little here as well. You are encouraged to spend some time finding the answers to these questions:

What if I lost a control file?

What if I lost an online redo log file?

What if I restored just the lost file without restoring the entire database?

Develop a curiosity for asking these types of questions. When you have a question in your mind, go to your testbed and see what happens. If you totally screw things up, you can always restore from your cold backup. Remember that books like this won't teach you everything, so ask questions to learn more.

Archivelog Mode

As I mentioned earlier in this chapter, if you want to perform hot backups, you will need to configure your database for archivelog mode. When a transaction occurs, Oracle will write the transaction's changes in the online redo logs. When the transaction is complete, Oracle will write a marker indicating if the transaction committed or was rolled back. There are only a few online redo log groups in an Oracle database. If you look back at Listing 7-1, you'll see that our testbed database has three online redo log groups. Oracle will write to the first one and then move on to the second, then on to the third. When the third online redo log group is full, Oracle will go back to the first group and overwrite its contents. Because the online redo logs are used in this circular fashion, we lose the transaction history over time.

Most Oracle databases have between three and five online redo log groups. A good rule of thumb is to make the online redo log groups large enough so that we use three to four groups per hour. This means we will be overwriting the transaction logs every hour.

To save our transaction history, we need to have Oracle archive the online redo logs. Hence, we turn on archivelog mode. Once Oracle switches to the next online redo log group, it will archive the previous group. To turn on archivelog mode, we will define the archive destination. We then shut down the instance, start it in mount mode, and start archivelog mode. Finally, we open the database for business. This process does require downtime, so you may have to perform this during a maintenance window. The steps to configure the database for archivelog mode are shown in Listing 7-5.

Listing 7-5. Archivelog Mode

```
SQL> !mkdir /u01/app/oracle/oradata/arch

SQL> alter system set log_archive_dest_1='location=/u01/app/oracle/oradata/
arch/' scope=spfile;

System altered.

SQL> shutdown immediate
Database closed.
Database dismounted.
ORACLE instance shut down.
SQL> startup mount
ORACLE instance started.

Total System Global Area 1660944384 bytes
Fixed Size                   8621376 bytes
Variable Size             1056965312 bytes
Database Buffers           587202560 bytes
Redo Buffers                 8155136 bytes
Database mounted.
SQL> alter database archivelog;

Database altered.

SQL> alter database open;

Database altered.

SQL> archive log list;
Database log mode              Archive Mode
Automatic archival             Enabled
Archive destination            /u01/app/oracle/oradata/arch/
Oldest online log sequence     15
Next log sequence to archive   17
Current log sequence           17
```

The last command in Listing 7-5 shows that archivelog mode is enabled.

With the database in archivelog mode, our transactions are kept safe from being overwritten in the online redo logs. We can restore from a previous backup and roll forward using the archived redo logs. You will need to back up the archived redo logs as well. At a bare minimum, you should keep enough archived redo logs on the database server to cover the time period since the last backup of the database. If you perform a weekly full backup, you should keep seven days' worth of archived redo logs on disk. However, you should be backing up those archived redo logs so the database server's disk is not the only place they are stored.

It should be noted that there is a cost to enabling archivelog mode. When archivelog mode is turned on, Oracle will need to read the online redo log once it fills and copy it to the archivelog destination. This will require additional resources to be used on your database server, namely CPU and disk I/O. Normally, the benefits outweigh the costs, but the database administrator does need to be aware.

If we do not manage the archivelog destination, it will eventually fill up. When it fills up and Oracle cannot archive any redo logs, the transactions in the database will come to a screeching halt. For my testbed, I typically remove all archived redo logs older than one day with an RMAN command similar to that shown in Listing 7-6.

Listing 7-6. Cleaning Up Archived Redo Logs

```
[oracle@dbamentor ~]$ rman

Recovery Manager: Release 12.2.0.1.0 - Production on Tue Jun 19 13:10:46 2018

Copyright (c) 1982, 2017, Oracle and/or its affiliates. All rights reserved.

RMAN> connect target /

connected to target database: ORCL (DBID=1506090724)

RMAN> run { delete archivelog all completed before 'sysdate-1'; }

using target database control file instead of recovery catalog
allocated channel: ORA_DISK_1
channel ORA_DISK_1: SID=63 device type=DISK
List of Archived Log Copies for database with db_unique_name ORCL
=====================================================================
```

```
Key    Thrd Seq     S Low Time
------ ---- ------- - ---------
1      1    17      A 18-JUN-18
       Name: /u01/app/oracle/oradata/arch/1_17_978309988.dbf

2      1    18      A 19-JUN-18
       Name: /u01/app/oracle/oradata/arch/1_18_978309988.dbf

3      1    19      A 19-JUN-18
       Name: /u01/app/oracle/oradata/arch/1_19_978309988.dbf

4      1    20      A 19-JUN-18
       Name: /u01/app/oracle/oradata/arch/1_20_978309988.dbf

5      1    21      A 19-JUN-18
       Name: /u01/app/oracle/oradata/arch/1_21_978309988.dbf

Do you really want to delete the above objects (enter YES or NO)? YES
deleted archived log
archived log file name=/u01/app/oracle/oradata/arch/1_17_978309988.dbf
RECID=1 STAMP=979218471
deleted archived log
archived log file name=/u01/app/oracle/oradata/arch/1_18_978309988.dbf
RECID=2 STAMP=979218632
deleted archived log
archived log file name=/u01/app/oracle/oradata/arch/1_19_978309988.dbf
RECID=3 STAMP=979218638
deleted archived log
archived log file name=/u01/app/oracle/oradata/arch/1_20_978309988.dbf
RECID=4 STAMP=979218638
deleted archived log
archived log file name=/u01/app/oracle/oradata/arch/1_21_978309988.dbf
RECID=5 STAMP=979218641
Deleted 5 objects
```

RMAN has found all archived redo logs older than 24 hours and removed them from the destination. However, this is only good for a testbed. For normal operations, you will want RMAN or some other routine to back up your archived redo logs as well as the rest of your database. Then have RMAN or the other routine remove any archived redo logs that have been backed up. This way, you have your backups, plus the transactions, and can minimize your data loss should you need to restore.

Many database administrators make it a point to always put production databases in archivelog mode. I will deviate from that convention for large data warehouses that can easily re-create the lost data and where I can afford the downtime for a cold backup. Some database administrators also want their test databases in archivelog mode. The reasoning is that the act of archiving transactions does impart a certain amount of overhead on the database. In some cases, this can cause performance issues. If we roll our changes into the test database first, we have a good chance of catching any performance issues before that change hits production and we can figure out how to handle it so that production users are not negatively impacted.

Our Hot Backup

Now that our testbed database is in archivelog mode, we can perform a hot backup. This time, we'll use RMAN to perform the backup. First, we will configure RMAN so that it knows where to create the backups. In Listing 7-7, we will invoke the RMAN utility and configure the backup destination.

Listing 7-7. RMAN Configuration

```
[oracle@dbamentor ~]$ rman

Recovery Manager: Release 12.2.0.1.0 - Production on Tue Jun 19 13:18:06 2018

Copyright (c) 1982, 2017, Oracle and/or its affiliates. All rights reserved.

RMAN> connect target /

connected to target database: ORCL (DBID=1506090724)

RMAN> configure default device type to disk;

using target database control file instead of recovery catalog
new RMAN configuration parameters:
```

```
CONFIGURE DEFAULT DEVICE TYPE TO DISK;
new RMAN configuration parameters are successfully stored

RMAN> configure controlfile autobackup on;

new RMAN configuration parameters:
CONFIGURE CONTROLFILE AUTOBACKUP ON;
new RMAN configuration parameters are successfully stored

RMAN> configure channel device type disk format
'/u01/app/oracle/oradata/db_backup/backup%d_%u_%s_%p';

new RMAN configuration parameters:
CONFIGURE CHANNEL DEVICE TYPE DISK FORMAT
'/u01/app/oracle/oradata/db_backup/backup%d_%u_%s_%p';
new RMAN configuration parameters are successfully stored
```

We instructed RMAN to write the backups to disk. We want the control file to be backed up automatically. The last command specifies the disk location and the file name format. This configuration can be overridden easily in your RMAN scripts. Backing up to disk is very common due to its speed. I try to write backups to disk set aside just for that purpose. If the backup needs to be written to tape, another job will copy the backup from disk to tape. If the backup needs to be sent offsite, I will use a tool like rsync or robocopy. RMAN also has the ability to write directly to tape media if you choose.

With the defaults set, our RMAN command to back up the database becomes that much easier. In Listing 7-8, we can see the backup is one simple command to back up the database plus the archived redo logs.

Listing 7-8. RMAN Hot Backup

```
RMAN> run { backup database plus archivelog; }

Starting backup at 19-JUN-18
current log archived
using target database control file instead of recovery catalog
allocated channel: ORA_DISK_1
channel ORA_DISK_1: SID=71 device type=DISK
channel ORA_DISK_1: starting archived log backup set
channel ORA_DISK_1: specifying archived log(s) in backup set
```

```
input archived log thread=1 sequence=22 RECID=6 STAMP=979219448
input archived log thread=1 sequence=23 RECID=7 STAMP=979219451
input archived log thread=1 sequence=24 RECID=8 STAMP=979219492
channel ORA_DISK_1: starting piece 1 at 19-JUN-18
channel ORA_DISK_1: finished piece 1 at 19-JUN-18
piece handle=/u01/app/oracle/oradata/db_backup/backupORCL_1kt5rd15_52_1
tag=TAG20180619T132453 comment=NONE
channel ORA_DISK_1: backup set complete, elapsed time: 00:00:01
Finished backup at 19-JUN-18

Starting backup at 19-JUN-18
using channel ORA_DISK_1
channel ORA_DISK_1: starting full datafile backup set
channel ORA_DISK_1: specifying datafile(s) in backup set
input datafile file number=00001 name=/u01/app/oracle/oradata/orcl/system01.dbf
input datafile file number=00002 name=/u01/app/oracle/oradata/orcl/sysaux01.dbf
input datafile file number=00003 name=/u01/app/oracle/oradata/orcl/undotbs01.dbf
input datafile file number=00004 name=/u01/app/oracle/oradata/orcl/users01.dbf
channel ORA_DISK_1: starting piece 1 at 19-JUN-18
channel ORA_DISK_1: finished piece 1 at 19-JUN-18
piece handle=/u01/app/oracle/oradata/db_backup/backupORCL_1lt5rd16_53_1
tag=TAG20180619T132454 comment=NONE
channel ORA_DISK_1: backup set complete, elapsed time: 00:00:15
Finished backup at 19-JUN-18

Starting backup at 19-JUN-18
current log archived
using channel ORA_DISK_1
channel ORA_DISK_1: starting archived log backup set
channel ORA_DISK_1: specifying archived log(s) in backup set
input archived log thread=1 sequence=25 RECID=9 STAMP=979219509
channel ORA_DISK_1: starting piece 1 at 19-JUN-18
channel ORA_DISK_1: finished piece 1 at 19-JUN-18
piece handle=/u01/app/oracle/oradata/db_backup/backupORCL_1mt5rd1l_54_1
tag=TAG20180619T132509 comment=NONE
channel ORA_DISK_1: backup set complete, elapsed time: 00:00:01
Finished backup at 19-JUN-18
```

```
Starting Control File and SPFILE Autobackup at 19-JUN-18
piece handle=/u01/app/oracle/product/12.2.0.1/dbs/c-1506090724-20180619-00
comment=NONE
Finished Control File and SPFILE Autobackup at 19-JUN-18
```

The RMAN command is simply "backup database plus archivelog". One command covers it all. If you read through the RMAN output, you can see RMAN is reading our database's files and even backs up the archived redo log. At the end, RMAN backs up the control file and the parameter file.

Our testbed is of little value if we do not test something out. So let's run the same test we did before. I shutdown the instance and then removed the users01.dbf data file simulating the loss of a file. Now I'll use RMAN for my restore. It will figure out what is missing and get it all back in order. Remember the earlier discussion of the differences between restore and recovery? Those differences are important now because we first need to tell RMAN to restore the database, then apply recovery. In Listing 7-9, the order of operations is to start the instance in mount mode, restore the database, recover the database, then open it for business.

Listing 7-9. RMAN Recovery from Missing Data File

```
[oracle@dbamentor orcl]$ rman

Recovery Manager: Release 12.2.0.1.0 - Production on Tue Jun 19 13:29:38 2018

Copyright (c) 1982, 2017, Oracle and/or its affiliates.  All rights reserved.

RMAN> connect target /

connected to target database (not started)

RMAN> run {
2> startup mount;
3> restore database;
4> recover database;
5> alter database open;
6> }

Oracle instance started
database mounted
```

```
Total System Global Area     1660944384 bytes

Fixed Size                     8621376 bytes
Variable Size               1056965312 bytes
Database Buffers             587202560 bytes
Redo Buffers                   8155136 bytes

Starting restore at 19-JUN-18
using target database control file instead of recovery catalog
allocated channel: ORA_DISK_1
channel ORA_DISK_1: SID=34 device type=DISK

channel ORA_DISK_1: starting datafile backup set restore
channel ORA_DISK_1: specifying datafile(s) to restore from backup set
channel ORA_DISK_1: restoring datafile 00001 to /u01/app/oracle/oradata/
                    orcl/system01.dbf
channel ORA_DISK_1: restoring datafile 00002 to /u01/app/oracle/oradata/
                    orcl/sysaux01.dbf
channel ORA_DISK_1: restoring datafile 00003 to /u01/app/oracle/oradata/
                    orcl/undotbs01.dbf
channel ORA_DISK_1: restoring datafile 00004 to /u01/app/oracle/oradata/
                    orcl/users01.dbf
channel ORA_DISK_1: reading from backup piece /u01/app/oracle/oradata/
                    db_backup/backupORCL_1lt5rd16_53_1
channel ORA_DISK_1: piece handle=/u01/app/oracle/oradata/db_backup/
                    backupORCL_1lt5rd16_53_1 tag=TAG20180619T132454
channel ORA_DISK_1: restored backup piece 1
channel ORA_DISK_1: restore complete, elapsed time: 00:00:15
Finished restore at 19-JUN-18

Starting recover at 19-JUN-18
using channel ORA_DISK_1

starting media recovery
media recovery complete, elapsed time: 00:00:00

Finished recover at 19-JUN-18

Statement processed
```

RMAN figures it all out for us and gets things back in order in a short period of time.

RMAN has a ton of features, and there is so much more to learn. Again, it is very important for you to read the *Database Backup and Recovery User's Guide* to learn all of the things that RMAN can do. There is simply too much to cover in this chapter.

Moving On

This chapter is probably different than what you may have been expecting when you saw the chapter title. I could have written this chapter like so many other books: "Here are the steps to backup your database. Here are the steps to restore your database." The point of this book is to make you think beyond the procedural steps, because that is the only real way to grow your database administrator career. In this chapter, we did ask the question of determining how to get the database operational after the loss of a data file. We asked the question of what happens when you lose a control file or an online redo log. Hopefully, you'll go back and experiment some more. The worst that can happen is you totally make a mess of your test database and cannot get it operational again, but that's okay because you know how to restore from that cold backup and get up and running again.

This chapter started by laying out a convincing argument that the DBA should tackle recovery requirements before even thinking about backups. A service-level agreement should be put in place and a testing document derived. Only then is the backup solution designed and subsequently tested to ensure it meets all requirements. I encourage you to be part of the growing army of database professionals that espouses recovery requirements before backups.

The chapter then laid a foundation for understanding the different types of backups and when they are used. We performed both hot and cold backups in our testbed using RMAN and user-managed commands, respectively. We didn't stop there, but experimented just a little bit because this is how we learn. Never stop asking questions and never stop experimenting. What other questions have you thought of while reading this chapter that we did not cover? Write those questions down and see if you can figure out the answers.

The next chapter focuses on database security. If we lock down our database and make sure to protect it with backups that are specifically tailored to meet our requirements, we have gone a long way toward becoming the data guardians our companies need us to be.

CHAPTER 8

Security

In the previous chapter, we took our first steps to ensuring that we can be a good data guardian. We learned about recovery and backup. The data guardian needs to safeguard the data and be able to provide access to the data after a disaster.

This chapter rounds out the data guardian's duties and to include protecting the data from unauthorized access. This chapter focuses on database security. With today's data breaches, it is vital that all database administrators ensure their databases are secure from unauthorized access.

Accessing the Security Guide

Oracle provides many documents to help you learn about all aspects of Oracle database security. Point your web browser to `https://docs.oracle.com` and click the Database button. Then click the Oracle Database button. In the drop-down menu, select the 12.2 database version. By now, you should be familiar with getting to the Oracle documentation for your version as we have already visited many guides in the Oracle documentation set.

In the Topics section, click the Security link. You should see the two most important books, the *Oracle Database 2 Day + Security Guide* and, right below that, the *Database Security Guide*.

Tip As you read this book, make sure you are becoming familiar with the Oracle documentation.

Oracle presents a number of these "2 Day" guides on a variety of topics to get you up to speed quickly on the topic. After you've read the *2 Day + Security Guide*, the regular *Security Guide* gives you a deeper dive into the topics.

© Brian Peasland 2019
B. Peasland, *Oracle DBA Mentor*, https://doi.org/10.1007/978-1-4842-4321-3_8

Remember that as you read the Oracle documentation, it is not important to memorize every detail. Instead, try to remember what the book contains. Skim the book if needed and make sure to go over the Table of Contents. Later in your career, you will know where to look for the answers you seek.

As a reminder, it is not vital to read the Oracle documentation mentioned in each chapter of this book immediately. You can certainly read this book first, then visit the Oracle documentation later. But please take time to read the Oracle documentation at some point.

Default Users

Oracle provides many default user accounts when you create an Oracle database. You have been introduced to both the SYS and SYSTEM users earlier in this book. Some of the users that Oracle creates for you depend on if you have installed certain options. The DBA_USERS view contains a column named ORACLE_MAINTAINED that shows if the user is supplied by Oracle. We can see the Oracle-maintained users in the output from Listing 8-1. Depending on your version and the options installed, you may have more or fewer users than what Listing 8-1 shows.

Listing 8-1. Oracle-Maintained Users

```
SQL> select username,account_status
  2  from dba_users where oracle_maintained='Y'
  3  order by username;

USERNAME                 ACCOUNT_STATUS
------------------------ --------------------------------
ANONYMOUS                EXPIRED & LOCKED
APPQOSSYS                EXPIRED & LOCKED
AUDSYS                   EXPIRED & LOCKED
DBSFWUSER                EXPIRED & LOCKED
DBSNMP                   EXPIRED & LOCKED
DIP                      EXPIRED & LOCKED
GGSYS                    EXPIRED & LOCKED
GSMADMIN_INTERNAL        EXPIRED & LOCKED
GSMCATUSER               EXPIRED & LOCKED
GSMUSER                  EXPIRED & LOCKED
OJVMSYS                  EXPIRED & LOCKED
```

```
ORACLE_OCM                  EXPIRED & LOCKED
OUTLN                       EXPIRED & LOCKED
REMOTE_SCHEDULER_AGENT      EXPIRED & LOCKED
SYS                         OPEN
SYS$UMF                     EXPIRED & LOCKED
SYSBACKUP                   EXPIRED & LOCKED
SYSDG                       EXPIRED & LOCKED
SYSKM                       EXPIRED & LOCKED
SYSRAC                      EXPIRED & LOCKED
SYSTEM                      OPEN
WMSYS                       EXPIRED & LOCKED
XDB                         EXPIRED & LOCKED
XS$NULL                     EXPIRED & LOCKED
```

In today's Oracle versions, the Oracle-maintained users are locked so that no one can access the database with any of those users. Out of the box, the only two users that are unlocked are SYS and SYSTEM. Do not unlock any of the other users unless you have a specific need to do so. For the most part, you will never need to connect directly to those users, and keeping them locked will keep your system more secure. Most of the Oracle-maintained users are to serve as schemas for database options. For example, XDB is used to support XML in the database. Since you are not a database option, you do not need to connect to that user. You are a database administrator. As such, later in this chapter, you will create your own DBA account and lock SYSTEM.

Password Profile

Today's IT practitioner knows that a good password is vital to ensuring systems are secure. Passwords like password, 123456, and qwerty are just inviting hackers to use your account. Surely you have signed on to some computer system and tried to define a password for your account and you've received feedback that the password must be more than eight characters, contain a mixture of upper- and lowercase letters, and include numbers and special characters. In this section, you will learn how to create a password verification function to enforce similar rules. Before we can begin, we will need to copy an Oracle-supplied file to our home directory. We do not want to modify this file directly but instead work only on a copy of the file. In Listing 8-2, we copy the catpvf.sql script to our Linux home directory on the testbed server.

Listing 8-2. Copy Security File

```
[oracle@dbamentor ~]$ cp $ORACLE_HOME/rdbms/admin/catpvf.sql $HOME/.
```

The catpvf.sql script contains a password verification function. If you used the Database Creation Assistant (DBCA) to create the database, as described in Chapter 6, Oracle has already run these scripts against the database.

Open the catpvf.sql script in a text editor. If you scroll through this file, you will see that the first thing it does is create a function named ora_complexity_check. This function checks to see if the password contains upper- and lowercase letters, numbers, and special characters. It also checks to make sure the password is long enough. If any of these checks fails, the function raises an error.

Later in this same script is the code to create the function ora12_verify_function. This is the actual password verification function called whenever a user is created or its password has been changed. Examining this code shows that the function ensures the password does not contain the username, or the username reversed. It ensures the password does not contain the server name. We can also see the call to ora_complexity_check in Listing 8-3.

Listing 8-3. Call to ora_complexity_check

```
IF NOT ora_complexity_check(password, chars => 8, letter => 1, digit => 1,
                            special => 1) THEN
     RETURN(FALSE);
```

Out of the box, Oracle will check that the password has at least eight characters and at least one letter, one digit, and one special character. Many security experts will say that good passwords should be at least 12 characters in length. In this file let's change the 8 to a 12. Let's also require that the passwords contain at least two letters, two digits, and two special characters by changing those parameters in Listing 8-3. Then save the file.

The password verification function must be owned by the SYS user. Start SQL*Plus and connect as the SYS user and then execute the script we just modified. We can see an example of this in Listing 8-4.

Listing 8-4. Modifying the Password Verify Function

```
sqlplus sys as sysdba

SQL*Plus: Release 12.2.0.1.0 Production on Thu Jul 5 13:34:05 2018
```

Enter password:

Connected to:
Oracle Database 12c Enterprise Edition Release 12.2.0.1.0 - 64bit
Production

SQL> @catpvf.sql

The output will scroll by and, if we've modified the file correctly, no errors will be raised.

You are not limited to just one password verification function. You can have different verifications for different classifications of users. For example, you may want your administrative users to have much more restrictive passwords than those of regular users. We will see in the next section how to define the password verification function a user is forced to use for password validation.

Now that the password verification function has been modified, we can test it by changing the SYSTEM's password to something we know will not pass the test. In Listing 8-5, we first try to change the password to just "password" and then to a password that does not contain special characters.

Listing 8-5. Bad Password Attempts

```
SQL> alter user system identified by password;
alter user system identified by password
*
ERROR at line 1:
ORA-28003: password verification for the specified password failed
ORA-20001: Password length less than 12

SQL> alter user system identified by thisis12char;
alter user system identified by thisis12char
*
ERROR at line 1:
ORA-28003: password verification for the specified password failed
ORA-20026: Password must contain at least 2 special character(s)
```

Each time, the passwords did not pass the verification function and meaningful messages were given.

Security Profiles

Oracle lets us control a user's security through a *profile*. An Oracle database can have many profiles in use to support different classifications of users. I typically have two profiles defined in the databases I manage, the DEFAULT profile and a profile for administrative users. End users will receive the DEFAULT profile and admins the other profile. You can certainly add other profiles as you see fit. When profiles first became available, I never used the DEFAULT profile. However, I was burned too many times creating a user account and neglecting to denote the proper profile and then I had a user account with bad security settings. Over time, I shifted to giving end users the DEFAULT profile. Whatever you do, just make sure you are consistent across your enterprise.

The DEFAULT profile is created out of the box and you cannot remove it. If you create a new user and do not denote the profile to use, the user will receive the DEFAULT profile. In a text editor, open the file $ORACLE_HOME/rdbms/admin/utlpwdmg.sql and examine its contents. We will not be changing this file, just looking at it to gain an understanding of how Oracle has set up our database when created with the DBCA.

Tip   If you create a database manually, you will have to set up your security controls manually as well.

In the utlpwdmg.sql script, you can see the DEFAULT profile has been defined with the limits shown in Listing 8-6.

Listing 8-6. DEFAULT Profile Definition

```
ALTER PROFILE DEFAULT LIMIT
PASSWORD_LIFE_TIME 180
PASSWORD_GRACE_TIME 7
PASSWORD_REUSE_TIME UNLIMITED
PASSWORD_REUSE_MAX  UNLIMITED
FAILED_LOGIN_ATTEMPTS 10
PASSWORD_LOCK_TIME 1
INACTIVE_ACCOUNT_TIME UNLIMITED
PASSWORD_VERIFY_FUNCTION ora12c_verify_function;
```

A profile is a set of limitations on the account. We can see in Listing 8-6 that the profile is limited to a PASSWORD_LIFE_TIME of 180 days and a PASSWORD_GRACE_TIME of 7 days. So what do all of these limits mean? Table 8-1 shows the profile limit definitions for securing our Oracle database.

Table 8-1. *Profile Parameter Descriptions*

Profile Parameter	Definition
FAILED_LOGIN_ATTEMPTS	Specifies the number of consecutive login failures before Oracle will automatically lock the account.
PASSWORD_LIFE_TIME	Specifies the number of days the password can be used. After these number of days pass, the password must be changed.
PASSWORD_REUSE_TIME	Specifies the number of days before a password can be reused. For example, you may say that a password cannot be used until 365 days have passed.
PASSWORD_REUSE_MAX	Specifies the number of times you must change the password before it can be reused. For example, you may not reuse a password until you have changed it four times.
PASSWORD_LOCK_TIME	Specifies the number of days an account will remain locked if Oracle automatically locked the account due to FAILED_LOGIN_ATTEMPTS. Normally this is value less than 1.
PASSWORD_GRACE_TIME	Specifies the number of days the password can be expired but still used. For example, if you set PASSWORD_LIFE_TIME to 90 days and PASSWORD_GRACE_TIME to 7 days, the user really has 97 days to change their password. After the grace time has expired, the account is locked.
INACTIVE_ACCOUNT_TIME	Specifies the number of days of inactivity before the account is automatically locked. For example, this is useful when you want to lock accounts if the user does not log in for 365 days.
PASSWORD_VERIFY_FUNCTION	Defines the password verification function in use by the profile. This parameter is how we can leverage different password verification functions depending on the user classification.

If you specify the PASSWORD_REUSE_TIME, you must also specify the PASSWORD_REUSE_MAX, and vice versa.

As noted in Table 8-1, the PASSWORD_LOCK_TIME is specified in days. In practice we rarely lock the account for an entire day, so this value is often less than 1. It is common to see the account locked for 10 minutes. There are 24 hours in a day and each hour is 60 minutes. To compute the value of 10 minutes expressed as one day, we would perform a simple calculation like 10/(24*60), which is about 0.00694. Now I don't know about you, but I have a challenging time remembering that 0.00694 of a day equals 10 minutes. Therefore, in Listing 8-7, I'll be specifying the formula 10/(24*60) instead of 0.00694 to denote 10 minutes, which makes the limit a bit easier to decipher.

The first thing I do in production databases to lock down the security is to modify the DEFAULT profile. My corporate policies dictate that users must change their passwords every 90 days and they cannot reuse a password they've used any time in the last two years. We want Oracle to lock the account on five invalid login attempts and leave it locked for 10 minutes. We also lock accounts that have not been used in the past year. With those definitions, I can now issue the command in Listing 8-7 to modify the DEFAULT profile's settings.

Listing 8-7. Improving the DEFAULT Profile

```
ALTER PROFILE DEFAULT LIMIT
PASSWORD_LIFE_TIME 90
PASSWORD_GRACE_TIME 7
PASSWORD_REUSE_TIME 730
PASSWORD_REUSE_MAX  8
FAILED_LOGIN_ATTEMPTS 5
PASSWORD_LOCK_TIME 10/(24*60)
INACTIVE_ACCOUNT_TIME 365
PASSWORD_VERIFY_FUNCTION ora12c_verify_function;
```

As promised, I used the formula to define 10 minutes for the lock time parameter, PASSWORD_LOCK_TIME. Again, I often find it easier to determine that I meant 10 minutes from seeing the formula rather than 0.00694. However, if we query the data dictionary for our profile's password limits, we see that the lock time is expressed as a number, as shown in Listing 8-8.

Listing 8-8. Querying the Profile Limits

```
SQL> select resource_name,limit from dba_profiles
  2  where profile='DEFAULT'
  3  and resource_type='PASSWORD';

RESOURCE_NAME                    LIMIT
------------------------------   ------------------------------
FAILED_LOGIN_ATTEMPTS            5
PASSWORD_LIFE_TIME               90
PASSWORD_REUSE_TIME              730
PASSWORD_REUSE_MAX               8
PASSWORD_VERIFY_FUNCTION         ORA12C_VERIFY_FUNCTION
PASSWORD_LOCK_TIME               .0069
PASSWORD_GRACE_TIME              7
INACTIVE_ACCOUNT_TIME            365
```

Next, I'll create a profile for our admin users. This profile is more restrictive than for end users due to the increased role of the account. For admins, we want them to change passwords every 60 days. Their account should be locked after three invalid login attempts and stay locked for 20 minutes. After I create the profile, I will modify the SYS and SYSTEM users to use that profile. Listing 8-9 shows the profile creation and the user modifications.

Listing 8-9. Admin Profile

```
SQL> create profile admin_profile
  2  limit failed_login_attempts 3
  3  password_life_time 60
  4  password_verify_function ora12c_verify_function
  5  password_lock_time 20/(24*60)
  6  inactive_account_time 90;

Profile created.

SQL> alter user sys profile admin_profile;

User altered.

SQL> alter user system profile admin_profile;
```

User altered.

```
SQL> select username,profile from dba_users
  2  where username in ('SYS','SYSTEM');

USERNAME                 PROFILE
------------------------ ---------------
SYS                      ADMIN_PROFILE
SYSTEM                   ADMIN_PROFILE
```

The profile was created. The users were modified. Lastly, the users were verified that they had the proper profile.

Now that we have the admin profile in place, we can create our DBA user. It is a bad security practice to share the same account among multiple people, especially for administrative accounts. Unfortunately, I find that all too often, too many sites share the SYSTEM account with their DBA team. Each DBA should have their own unique account. In Listing 8-10, I will create my DBA account with the ADMIN_PROFILE, grant it the ability to create a session in the database, and give it the DBA role. Lastly, I will lock the SYSTEM account.

Listing 8-10. Creating a DBA User

```
SQL> create user peasland identified by MyPassword31$$ profile admin_profile;

User created.

SQL> grant create session to peasland;

Grant succeeded.

SQL> grant dba to peasland;

Grant succeeded.

SQL> alter user system account lock;

User altered.

SQL> connect peasland/MyPassword31$$
Connected.
```

Being that these commands are in a book, you can rest assured the password I used in Listing 8-10 is one that I would never use for any of my real accounts.

Tip   Create your own DBA account and lock SYSTEM.

Auditing

So far in this chapter, we've locked down database security a bit. What happens if someone does break into the database? What happens if someone who has been granted access to the database decides to misuse the privilege? We need to put measures into place that let us perform some forensic analysis to help track down security issues. We will leverage Oracle's auditing mechanisms for these purposes.

Prior to Oracle Database 12c, the DBA had to turn on auditing and then tell Oracle precisely which events to write to the audit trail. Oracle 12c introduced Unified Auditing to help simplify the process. You can still perform the traditional auditing in 12c. You can even perform traditional auditing and Unified Auditing at the same time, which Oracle calls *mixed mode auditing*.

To start auditing, you must perform two steps. First, you turn on the ability to generate audit trail records. Second, you tell Oracle what to audit. In my career, I've seen people forgot either one of these steps. The DBA will turn on auditing and then complain that Oracle is not writing anything to the audit trail, unaware that they need to perform the second step. The other common complaint I've seen is that the DBA will tell Oracle what to audit and still nothing is written to the audit trail because they forgot to turn on auditing. The first step only needs to be performed once. The second step may be performed multiple times.

Tip   Auditing is a two-step process. Turn on auditing. Tell Oracle what to audit.

If you used the Oracle 12c DBCA utility to create your database, auditing will be turned on by default. If auditing is not turned on, you can do so by issuing the commands in Listing 8-11.

Listing 8-11. Turn On Auditing

```
SQL> connect / as sysdba
Connected.
SQL> alter system set audit_trail=db scope=spfile;

System altered.

SQL> shutdown immediate
Database closed.
Database dismounted.
ORACLE instance shut down.
SQL> startup
ORACLE instance started.

Total System Global Area 4294967296 bytes
Fixed Size                   8628936 bytes
Variable Size              939525432 bytes
Database Buffers          3338665984 bytes
Redo Buffers                 8146944 bytes
Database mounted.
Database opened.
```

Because the instance was restarted, the steps in Listing 8-11 will require downtime and may need to be performed during a maintenance window.

Now that auditing is turned on, we will use two Unified Auditing policies. The first policy is named ORA_LOGON_FAILURES and will generate records in the audit trail whenever someone cannot authenticate properly to the Oracle database. The second policy is called ORA_ACCOUNT_MGMT and will generate records in the audit trail whenever an admin creates, modifies, and drops users. Oracle's Unified Auditing provides these policies out of the box because they are typical audited activities. In Listing 8-12, I told Oracle to start auditing those two policies. I had to reconnect before Unified Auditing would capture my activities. I then created a test user. Lastly, I queried the audit trail to show the activity was captured.

Listing 8-12. Auditing Actions

```
SQL> audit policy ora_logon_failures;

Audit succeeded.

SQL> audit policy ora_account_mgmt;

Audit succeeded.

SQL> connect peasland
Enter password:

SQL> create user test_user identified by h3r$passw0rd$;

User created.

SQL> select dbusername,event_timestamp,sql_text from unified_audit_trail
  2  where sql_text like 'create user%';

DBUSERNAME EVENT_TIMESTAMP                 SQL_TEXT
---------- ----------------------------- ------------------------------------
SYS        05-JUL-18 03.14.05.874100 PM   create user test_user identified by *
```

There is so much more to auditing. The two Unified Auditing policies I turned on in Listing 8-12 are the ones I use the most. However, you are encouraged to go through the *Oracle Security Guide* to learn more and see if there are other policies that are beneficial to your situation. This section was meant to show you how to start auditing important actions as well as give you an idea of what auditing is and does.

Additional Security Topics

An entire book could be written on Oracle database security. The topic is that vast. There simply is not enough room in this chapter to discuss everything related to database security. The rest of this chapter will provide a high-level discussion of security topics that you may need to explore later in your career. Hopefully, when you come across a security consideration for your database, you can refer to this section so that you may know where to explore to get the job done.

System Privileges

Oracle provides many system privileges out of the box. The ability to create a session and connect to the database is an example we have already seen in this chapter. Examples of other system privileges include the ability to create a table and the ability to create or drop users.

Object Privileges

Once a user has created objects in the database, such as tables or views, they may desire to give other users the ability to interact with those objects. A common example is to let another user see the contents of a table but not modify the data. The owner of the table would grant the ability to SELECT from the table. Executing another user's stored procedure requires another object privilege.

Roles

With these diverse types of privileges, it is often desirable to give the same classifications of users the same privileges. Earlier in this chapter, I created a DBA user. After I was done, the user was granted 237 different system privileges, in my Oracle 12.2 database. Yet the example in this chapter showed only one grant being issued. That user was granted the DBA role. You can grant multiple privileges to a role, and then when you grant the role to another user, that user inherits all that role's privileges. Roles exist for one reason only and that is to make granting of multiple privileges easier on the administrator. If the administrator had to remember all 237 system privileges that make up the DBA role in Oracle 12.2, they would be assured of missing some of them. By granting the privileges to a role, the administrator only needs to remember the role name and grant the role instead.

One oddity of the Oracle database is that roles do not work inside stored procedures, functions, and packages. If a user creates one of these objects and encounters permissions issues, the DBA should verify the object owner has been granted direct permissions on the object and not through a role.

Transparent Data Encryption

Transparent Data Encryption (TDE) is an Oracle option to encrypt the Oracle database's contents at rest. The data is encrypted within the data files on disk. The benefit is that this encryption is transparent to the end user and the applications, hence its name.

Too many people erroneously think that TDE means their database is encrypted from prying eyes, and that is not the case. Any user that can access the database and has the appropriate privileges can view the data in that object in unencrypted form.

The biggest benefit to Transparent Data Encryption is to encrypt your database backups. With TDE, you can be assured if someone gets a hold of your backup, perhaps from its offsite location, the data is encrypted so long as the backup does not also contain the database's wallet, which stores the encryption key. Just remember that once the database is open for business, anyone with access to the database can see the data in unencrypted form, transparently.

Transparent Data Encryption does require your organization to license the Oracle Advanced Security option. This option is not included in the Enterprise Edition (EE) license. You cannot use TDE with Standard Edition even if you want to license it. You must be using EE instead.

DBMS_CRYPTO

If you want to keep data safe from prying eyes, even when the database is open, your best bet would be to leverage the DBMS_CRYPTO supplied package. There is no additional license for this, but it is not transparent to the application. The application must leverage this package whenever it wants to view the encrypted data. The application must call this package to store the data in encrypted form.

Virtual Private Database

The Virtual Private Database (VPD), an Enterprise Edition feature, lets each user access the same table but allows each user to see only the data they are allowed to see. For example, you may have a table of EMPLOYEES. An employee can only see their record in this table. Managers can see their own record as well as the records of any employees that report to them. Someone in the Human Resources department may be able to see all employees in this table. VPD uses application contexts to define the records someone can see in the VPD-enabled table. Once the application context is defined, the users can only see the data they are allowed to see. In this manner, the data in a table is private to their classification.

Network Encryption

Oracle will transmit the data over the network in clear text. This may be cause for concern for some organizations. Oracle does provide the ability to encrypt data as it flows over the network. Like Transparent Data Encryption, this feature does have an extra cost with the Advanced Security option, an Oracle Enterprise Edition extra cost option.

Stronger Authentication

For some organizations, simple passwords are not enough. Oracle does provide the ability to leverage Kerberos or RADIUS for authentication. Organizations can also leverage LDAP authentication for organizations that choose to do so.

Moving On

This chapter helped us harden our database by improving its security. We configured a password verification function and then leveraged profiles to implement our security controls. This chapter and Chapter 7 have set us up to be a better data guardians for our corporate databases by outlining how to safeguard the data with backups and better security.

Remember that the topic of database security is broad and could not be covered sufficiently in one chapter of this book. It is vital that you read more about the subject, particularly the Oracle guides referenced in this chapter, to learn how to protect the data in your databases.

Up to this point, we have set up our testbed system and then made sure we have set it up for the future. The next few chapters will be a bit of a departure as we move more into how to use an Oracle database. In the next chapter, we will discuss how to connect to an Oracle database. Users rarely connect to the database from the database server itself. There are many ways to connect to a running Oracle instance, as we will soon see.

## CHAPTER 9

Connecting to Oracle

After the last few chapters, we now have an operational Oracle database in our virtual machine. If you have been following the advice in the previous chapters, you have implemented some best practices. Hopefully, you have also been reading some of the Oracle documentation that has previously been discussed.

In this chapter, we will discuss how to connect to a running Oracle instance. After all, what good is storing data in a database system if you cannot access it? In this chapter, we will discuss different methods for connecting to Oracle. All of the previous examples in this book required the application, usually SQL*Plus, to be on the same machine as the database. End-user applications are rarely running on the database server, so they need connectivity to the Oracle instance.

Local Connections

Oracle databases run on a machine somewhere on a network. This machine could be one in your organization's data center or it could exist in a cloud environment. If you can access this machine, you can make a local connection to the database. The term "local" means your database application will be on the same machine as the database.

In this section, our database application will be SQL*Plus. We have already seen a few examples of making a local connection with SQL*Plus earlier in this book. In our testbed system we have created, open a Terminal window. The testbed only has one Oracle database, but it is possible to have multiple Oracle instances on the server, potentially with different versions. Before we can connect to a local Oracle instance, we need to set up our environment so that the SQL*Plus connection knows which instance to connect to. We do that by changing our environment variables. First, we'll define the instance we want to connect to, called the System Identifer (SID). Next, we'll define the Oracle home directory. Lastly, we will add the Oracle home's bin subdirectory to our

© Brian Peasland 2019
B. Peasland, *Oracle DBA Mentor*, https://doi.org/10.1007/978-1-4842-4321-3_9

PATH so that we can just type the executable name, like "sqlplus", and it will be found. Setting the environment variables is shown in Listing 9-1.

Listing 9-1. Setting Environment for Local Connection

```
[oracle@oracle122 ~]$ export ORACLE_SID=orcl
[oracle@oracle122 ~]$ export ORACLE_HOME=/u01/app/oracle/product/12.2.0.1
[oracle@oracle122 ~]$ export PATH=$ORACLE_HOME/bin:$PATH
```

Those three commands are all we need for Oracle on Linux operating systems. On Unix platforms, you may have other environment variables. On Windows, the Database Configuration Assistant (DBCA) set up the environment variables when we installed and created the Oracle database. With our environment variables properly defined, we can make our local connection and issue a simple query to the database, as shown in Listing 9-2.

Listing 9-2. Local Connection

```
[oracle@oracle122 ~]$ sqlplus peasland

SQL*Plus: Release 12.2.0.1.0 Production on Mon Jul 9 14:12:05 2018

Copyright (c) 1982, 2016, Oracle.  All rights reserved.

Enter password:
Last Successful login time: Mon Jul 09 2018 14:12:00 -05:00

Connected to:
Oracle Database 12c Enterprise Edition Release 12.2.0.1.0 - 64bit
Production

SQL> select instance_name from v$instance;

INSTANCE_NAME
----------------
orcl
```

Notice that the connection used the DBA account I created in Chapter 8. The simple query confirmed that I was connected to the proper Oracle instance on this machine.

Oracle does provide a shortcut to setting up your environment variables. In our Linux terminal window, type ". oraenv" (a period followed by a space followed by the word oraenv). This will ask you which database you want to work with and then set your environment variables for you. In Listing 9-3, I use oraenv to set the environment for the orcl database.

Listing 9-3. Sourcing oraenv

```
[oracle@oracle122 ~]$ . oraenv
ORACLE_SID = [orcl] ? orcl
The Oracle base has been set to /u01/app/oracle
```

Remember that we manually defined the Oracle home directory. So how does Oracle know where the home directory is for this database? The answer lies in the /etc/oratab file, which is created when you run the root scripts after installing the database software. Initially, the file only has comments in it. When using the DBCA to create the database, the utility will add an entry in this file. Let's look at its contents now in Listing 9-4.

Listing 9-4. Oratab File

```
[oracle@oracle122 ~]$ cat /etc/oratab
#

# This file is used by ORACLE utilities.  It is created by root.sh
# and updated by either Database Configuration Assistant while creating
# a database or ASM Configuration Assistant while creating ASM instance.

# A colon, ':', is used as the field terminator.  A new line terminates
# the entry.  Lines beginning with a pound sign, '#', are comments.
#
# Entries are of the form:
#   $ORACLE_SID:$ORACLE_HOME:<N|Y>:
#
# The first and second fields are the system identifier and home
# directory of the database respectively.  The third field indicates
# to the dbstart utility that the database should , "Y", or should not,
# "N", be brought up at system boot time.
#
```

```
# Multiple entries with the same $ORACLE_SID are not allowed.
#
#
orcl:/u01/app/oracle/product/12.2.0.1:N
```

Most of the file consists of comments, but look at the last line of this file. It shows that for the ORACLE_SID named orcl, the Oracle home directory is /u01/app/oracle/product/12.2.0.1. When you use oraenv to set your environment, it looks in this file to find the Oracle home. From there, it can set your environment variables properly. If you use the DBCA to create the database, that utility will automatically populate the oratab file. If you use the Database Upgrade Assistant (DBUA) to upgrade to a new Oracle version, the DBUA will automatically modify this file for you. If you manually create or upgrade databases, you will have to manually modify this file. The last part of that line is either Y or N, a flag that tells the Oracle-supplied startup and shutdown utilities whether or not to handle this database. If the flag is set to Y, those utilities will start up and shut down the Oracle instance for that database whenever they are run.

This file is not present on Windows systems. Oracle uses the Windows registry to point to the Oracle home directories for each database on that server. Startup and shutdown is automated through Windows services and appropriate registry entries.

Processes and Bequeath

What happens under the covers when we create that local connection? To understand what happens, we need to take a bit of a step back. Starting an Oracle instance allocates memory and creates many processes on the database server. These processes all perform the work the Oracle database engine needs. Later in this book, we will dive deeper into these background processes to support an Oracle instance.

When an application connects to an Oracle instance, Oracle created a process on the database server dedicated to that user's session. This is called a *dedicated server process*. The application talks to the dedicated server process and the dedicated server process talks to the Oracle instance. Applications do not communicate with the instance directly. Figure 9-1 shows the workflow.

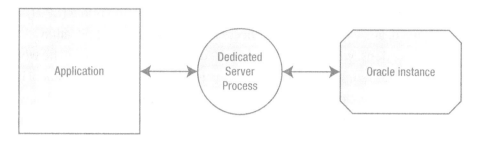

Figure 9-1. *Dedicated server process*

In our case, the application is SQL*Plus. SQL*Plus is the application's name, but sqlplus is the executable file we call to run that application. SQL*Plus talks to a dedicated server process that was created for us when we connected to the instance. In Listing 9-5, we will find out our process identifier for our current session and then look at the processes running on the server.

Listing 9-5. Local Processes

```
SQL> select spid from v$process
  2  where addr in (select paddr from v$session
  3                   where username='PEASLAND');

SPID
------------------------
7080

SQL> !ps -ef|grep 7080
oracle    7080  7069  0 14:37 ?        00:00:00 oracleorcl
(DESCRIPTION=(LOCAL=YES)(ADDRESS=(PROTOCOL=beq)))
SQL> !ps -ef|grep 7069
oracle    7069  2752  0 14:37 pts/0    00:00:00 sqlplus
oracle    7080  7069  0 14:37 ?        00:00:00 oracleorcl
(DESCRIPTION=(LOCAL=YES)(ADDRESS=(PROTOCOL=beq)))
```

From the output above, we can see from the V$PROCESS view that our dedicated server process has a server process identifier (SPID) of 7080. Using the ps command and filtering with grep, we can see a process named oracleorcl running on the server. This is our dedicated server process. Let's examine the rest of that line. Notice that it says LOCAL=YES and PROTOCOL=BEQ. This information is letting us know the dedicated server process is for a local connection and it is using the Bequeath communication protocol. We can also see that the process 7080 has a parent process with Server Process Identifier (SPID) 7069. If we use ps and grep again, we can see that process 7069 is our sqlplus application.

For local connections, you will often see the Bequeath protocol in use. The word *bequeath* means to pass something on to someone else. In this case, the protocol is simply passing the connection right to the dedicated server process. Bequeath always uses a dedicated server process and never involves an Oracle Listener, which will be discussed in the next section.

Each dedicated server process requires a certain amount of memory and other overhead on the database server. When the Internet exploded and more and more users started accessing data from a database, it became clear that the dedicated server process architecture would reach some limitations. Oracle Corporation created the *shared server process* architecture where the process on the server would be shared by multiple applications, as can be seen in Figure 9-2.

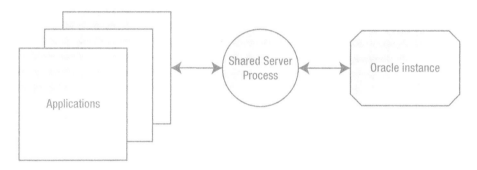

Figure 9-2. *Shared server process*

With this architecture, the number of server processes can be significantly reduced. However, we rarely see these used in practice today. Today we have application and web server connection pooling. We have Java connection pooling. All of these reduce the number of database connections. As such, today's Oracle DBA does not often need to implement the shared server architecture. I mention it here just so that you know it exists and have a basic understanding of what it means. Someday you may find that it is the proper architecture for your system.

We've seen how applications local to the database server connect to an Oracle instance. The next logical step is to discuss how applications on another machine, remote from the database server, make their connections to the instance. In practice, the application is almost never on the database server. Typically, the only application used locally to the database is SQL*Plus in the DBA's hands. End users run their applications on their desktop or interact with a web server or some other application server. Those connection requests all go through the Oracle Listener, the subject of the next section.

There is one more final note when discussing processes for Oracle databases. On Unix and Linux systems, these all appear as individual processes running on the server. On Windows systems, these are threads in the same process. One cannot easily see threads in a Windows process, which does make running Oracle on Windows a bit harder to work with from time to time.

Oracle Listener

The Listener's job is simple. Listen for incoming connection requests (hence its name), make the connection happen, and then get out of the way. Too many people erroneously think that the Listener is involved for every network communication between the application and the database, and that is not true. Once the connection has been established, the Listener is no longer needed for that session.

Tip   The Listener is only involved in brokering the connection request.

The Listener is another process on the database server. It listens for incoming connection requests on a specific port. The connection request indicates that the application wishes to connect to a specific Oracle instance on that server. If the Listener knows about that instance, the Listener will instruct the instance to start a server process, dedicated or shared. The server process and the application start talking with each other and the Listener exits the picture.

By default, the Listener uses port 1521. At one time, port 1526 was another default port for some platforms. The Listener can be configured to use a different port, but there is little reason to do so. Moving the Listener to a different port does not help make any Oracle database more secure as today's port scanning tools can quickly determine which port the Listener is really using. Additionally, if the Listener is running on a non-default port, the database administrator needs to manually configure the LOCAL_LISTENER parameter so that the instance can find the Listener.

Let's check the status of a Listener on a database server. The command to check the status is lsnrctl status, as shown in Listing 9-6.

Listing 9-6.   Listener Status

```
[oracle@oracle122 ~]$ lsnrctl status

LSNRCTL for Linux: Version 12.2.0.1.0 - Production on 09-JUL-2018 22:48:36

Copyright (c) 1991, 2016, Oracle.  All rights reserved.

Connecting to (ADDRESS=(PROTOCOL=tcp)(HOST=)(PORT=1521))
STATUS of the LISTENER
------------------------
Alias                     LISTENER
Version                   TNSLSNR for Linux: Version 12.2.0.1.0 - Production
Start Date                09-JUL-2018 13:44:41
Uptime                    0 days 9 hr. 3 min. 55 sec
Trace Level               off
Security                  ON: Local OS Authentication
SNMP                      OFF
Listener Log File         /u01/app/oracle/diag/tnslsnr/oracle122/listener/
                          alert/log.xml
Listening Endpoints Summary...
  (DESCRIPTION=(ADDRESS=(PROTOCOL=tcp)(HOST=dbamentor)(PORT=1521)))
The listener supports no services
The command completed successfully
```

There are a few things to note from the output above. We can easily see the Listener's start date and uptime. This output also shows us the location of the Listener's log file in case we need to troubleshoot its operations. Now take note of the Listening Endpoints Summary section. There are three important pieces to know from this section. One, the Listener is working with the TCP network protocol. Two, the Listener is running on the host dbamentor, our testbed. Third, the Listener is using port 1521.

Tip   The important Listener configuration information is the protocol, the host, and the port.

Those three pieces are where things often go wrong, as we will see later in this chapter.

The line below the port shows that the Listener currently supports no services. The reason there are no services at this time is that there are no Oracle instances running on the server. After starting the Oracle instance, we can check the status again, shown in Listing 9-7.

Listing 9-7. Listener with Services

```
[oracle@oracle122 ~]$ lsnrctl status

LSNRCTL for Linux: Version 12.2.0.1.0 - Production on 09-JUL-2018 23:01:00

Copyright (c) 1991, 2016, Oracle.  All rights reserved.

Connecting to (ADDRESS=(PROTOCOL=tcp)(HOST=)(PORT=1521))
STATUS of the LISTENER
---------------------
Alias                     LISTENER
Version                   TNSLSNR for Linux: Version 12.2.0.1.0 - Production
Start Date                09-JUL-2018 13:44:41
Uptime                    0 days 9 hr. 16 min. 18 sec
Trace Level               off
Security                  ON: Local OS Authentication
SNMP                      OFF
Listener Log File         /u01/app/oracle/diag/tnslsnr/oracle122/listener/
                          alert/log.xml
Listening Endpoints Summary...
  (DESCRIPTION=(ADDRESS=(PROTOCOL=tcp)(HOST=dbamentor)(PORT=1521)))
Services Summary...
Service "orcl" has 1 instance(s).
  Instance "orcl", status READY, has 1 handler(s) for this service...
Service "orclXDB" has 1 instance(s).
  Instance "orcl", status READY, has 1 handler(s) for this service...
The command completed successfully
```

This time, we can see two services, orcl and orclXDB. Whenever an instance starts and registers itself with the Listener, there will be at least two services running. The first service matches the database name. The second service is for Oracle XML database processing. We now have the four important pieces of information we need to establish a connection, the network protocol, the hostname, the port, and the service.

As you might expect, we can stop and start the Listener with the lsnrctl utility. An example is shown in Listing 9-8.

Listing 9-8. Listener Stop and Start

```
[oracle@oracle122 ~]$ lsnrctl stop

LSNRCTL for Linux: Version 12.2.0.1.0 - Production on 09-JUL-2018 23:07:10

Copyright (c) 1991, 2016, Oracle.  All rights reserved.

Connecting to (ADDRESS=(PROTOCOL=tcp)(HOST=)(PORT=1521))
The command completed successfully

[oracle@oracle122 ~]$ lsnrctl start

LSNRCTL for Linux: Version 12.2.0.1.0 - Production on 09-JUL-2018 23:07:13

Copyright (c) 1991, 2016, Oracle.  All rights reserved.

Starting /u01/app/oracle/product/12.2.0.1/bin/tnslsnr: please wait...

TNSLSNR for Linux: Version 12.2.0.1.0 - Production
Log messages written to /u01/app/oracle/diag/tnslsnr/oracle122/listener/
alert/log.xml
Listening on: (DESCRIPTION=(ADDRESS=(PROTOCOL=tcp)(HOST=dbamentor)
(PORT=1521)))

Connecting to (ADDRESS=(PROTOCOL=tcp)(HOST=)(PORT=1521))
STATUS of the LISTENER
------------------------
Alias                    LISTENER
Version                  TNSLSNR for Linux: Version 12.2.0.1.0 - Production
Start Date               09-JUL-2018 23:07:13
Uptime                   0 days 0 hr. 0 min. 0 sec
Trace Level              off
```

```
Security                    ON: Local OS Authentication
SNMP                        OFF
Listener Log File           /u01/app/oracle/diag/tnslsnr/oracle122/listener/
                            alert/log.xml
Listening Endpoints Summary...
  (DESCRIPTION=(ADDRESS=(PROTOCOL=tcp)(HOST=localhost)(PORT=1521)))
The listener supports no services
The command completed successfully
```

On startup, the Listener initially does not support any services. It can take up to five minutes for the instance to register with the Listener.

Oracle Client

When the Oracle database software is installed on a server, it contains all the executables and library files needed to support the database engine. The Oracle database software also contains Oracle's network stack so that the Oracle instance can communicate with remote applications.

When an application on a workstation needs to interact with Oracle, it must have some sort of network capabilities on its end. The application sends its request to the Oracle network stack on the application's machine, sometimes called the client machine. The Oracle network stack forwards the request to the operating system's network stack. The OS sends the request along the network, typically TCP/IP based. Once the request hits the database server, the server's OS sends it to the Oracle network stack and on to the Oracle instance.

For workstations and application servers, Oracle has provided the Oracle Client software. Oracle Client contains all of the same Oracle network stack as well as some utilities like SQL*Plus. It is very common to install Oracle Client software before installing any application that will access the Oracle database. However, it is not a requirement to do so. Some applications do not need Oracle Client because they provide their own networking capabilities. As a side note, Oracle Corporation does provide the Oracle Instant Client software which is a scaled down version of Oracle Client.

Oracle Client is much smaller than the database software. We rarely need the database's full capabilities on the client side of the architecture, so having a smaller footprint is ideal. Oracle Client can be obtained on the Oracle Technology Network in the same location as the database software.

In the early days of Oracle, the Oracle part of the network stack was called the Transparent Network Substrate (TNS). Later on, it was renamed to SQL*Net. Today, the network stack is simply called Oracle Net. The original TNS abbreviation can still be found, as we can see in the next section.

TNSNAMES

In the "Oracle Listener" section earlier in the chapter, you learned that the Listener brokers connection requests. Recall that to make a successful connection, we need to know the network protocol, the host, the port, and the service name. Those four pieces of information can be a lot to remember every time we want to make a connection to Oracle. Thankfully, we can create an alias, a shortcut, and use one name to define all four critical pieces of information.

The $ORACLE_HOME/network/admin directory may contain a file named tnsnames.ora. This is the location of our aliases. In Oracle speak, we often call these *TNS aliases*. If the tnsnames.ora file does not exist, it's only because we have yet to create it. We can create one with any text editor. A sample entry looks like Listing 9-9.

Listing 9-9. TNSNAMES Alias

```
tnsaliasX =
  (DESCRIPTION =
    (ADDRESS_LIST =
      (ADDRESS = (PROTOCOL = TCP)(HOST = localhost)(PORT = 1521))
    )
    (CONNECT_DATA =
      (SERVICE_NAME = orcl)
    )
  )
```

In Listing 9-9, the alias name is tnsaliasX. The alias can be whatever we choose. Remember those four important pieces of information? We can see them in the alias definition. The protocol (TCP), host (localhost), port (1521), and service name (orcl) are all present. Now all we have to remember is the alias name and we can use it to connect to our database. In Listing 9-9, the alias was created on the database server, so the host is just localhost. You can create a TNS alias just like this on your testbed to simulate non-local connections, as we will in this chapter. If this alias were created on a workstation in Oracle Client's network/admin directory, the host value would point to a specific database host.

A tnsnames.ora file can certainly contain multiple aliases to support multiple applications. I typically name the alias something meaningful. The example in Listing 9-9 is not very meaningful because tnsaliasX could suggest just about anything. A more meaningful alias might be hr_prod, which we could easily discern is for the production Human Resources database. Try to stay away from generic aliases like prod or dev because sooner or later you will have more than one production or development database and then you won't know which one the alias is referring to.

I'll change my alias to be dbamentor for this book. We can test the alias with the tnsping utility, as shown in Listing 9-10.

Listing 9-10. TNSPING Utility

```
oracle@oracle122 admin]$ tnsping dbamentor

TNS Ping Utility for Linux: Version 12.2.0.1.0 - Production on 09-JUL-2018
23:53:24

Copyright (c) 1997, 2016, Oracle.  All rights reserved.

Used parameter files:

Used TNSNAMES adapter to resolve the alias
Attempting to contact (DESCRIPTION = (ADDRESS_LIST = (ADDRESS =
(PROTOCOL = TCP)(HOST = localhost)(PORT = 1521))) (CONNECT_DATA =
(SERVICE_NAME = orcl)))
OK (60 msec)
```

The tnsping utility looks up the supplied TNS alias and attempts to resolve it to the protocol, host, port, and service name. The last line of output simply says OK. This utility is used to confirm that an Oracle Listener is running on that host, using that port, and can handle that service name. Basically, tnsping verifies the database's Listener has the same four components. Tnsping does not perform any other checks. Tnsping cannot be used to verify that an Oracle instance is running on that machine.

Now that we have a TNS alias defined, we can use it to make a remote connection to an Oracle instance. With SQL*Plus, we simply put the TNS alias after the username with the @ symbol separating the two. This symbol is how SQL*Plus knows where the

TNS alias starts in the supplied information. The example in Listing 9-11 connects to a database using the TNS alias.

Listing 9-11. SQL*Plus with TNS Alias

```
[oracle@oracle122 admin]$ sqlplus peasland@dbamentor

SQL*Plus: Release 12.2.0.1.0 Production on Mon Jul 9 23:57:28 2018

Copyright (c) 1982, 2016, Oracle.  All rights reserved.

Enter password:
Last Successful login time: Mon Jul 09 2018 14:37:40 -05:00

Connected to:
Oracle Database 12c Enterprise Edition Release 12.2.0.1.0 - 64bit
Production

SQL> select spid from v$process
  2   where addr in (select paddr from v$session
  3                  where username='PEASLAND');

SPID
------------------------
15206

SQL> !ps -ef|grep 15206
oracle    15206    1  0 Jul09 ?        00:00:00 oracleorcl (LOCAL=NO)
```

After the connection was established, we ran the same SQL statement from Listing 9-5 earlier in this chapter to find the dedicated server process for our connection. Notice that this is not a LOCAL connection any more. Remember that this session was launched from the database server itself, so it technically is a local connection. However, this connection did not use the Bequeath protocol. It used TCP instead. As such, it appears to Oracle as a remote, non-local connection.

The important items to remember are that remote connections need to know the network protocol, the host, the port, and the service name. We can use TNS aliases to ease the burden on our memories having to recall all that information.

Common TNS Errors

If a connection request fails, Oracle will provide an error message. For many people, the error messages can be a bit confusing. By reading this chapter, you are already well on your way to understanding how to resolve the most common errors because you know the four important pieces: protocol, host, port, and service. There is a good chance that one (or more) of those pieces is defined incorrectly. In Listing 9-12, we can see the tnsping utility has received the TNS-12545 error.

Listing 9-12. TNS-12545 Error

```
[oracle@oracle122 admin]$ tnsping dbamentor

TNS Ping Utility for Linux: Version 12.2.0.1.0 - Production on 10-JUL-2018
00:06:22

Copyright (c) 1997, 2016, Oracle.  All rights reserved.

Used parameter files:

Used TNSNAMES adapter to resolve the alias
Attempting to contact (DESCRIPTION = (ADDRESS_LIST = (ADDRESS =
(PROTOCOL = TCP)(HOST = loclhost)(PORT = 1521))) (CONNECT_DATA =
(SERVICE_NAME = orcl)))
TNS-12545: Connect failed because target host or object does not exist
```

If you read the error message carefully, you can see the clue as to the root cause of the problem. The "target host" does not exist. Look at the rest of the output where the host is defined. Notice that "localhost" is missing the letter *a*. A simple typo caused this problem. Correcting the host in the TNS alias resolved the issue. Now let's look at the next example in Listing 9-13.

Listing 9-13. TNS-12541 Error

```
oracle@oracle122 admin]$ tnsping dbamentor

TNS Ping Utility for Linux: Version 12.2.0.1.0 - Production on 10-JUL-2018
00:10:58

Copyright (c) 1997, 2016, Oracle.  All rights reserved.
```

Used parameter files:

Used TNSNAMES adapter to resolve the alias
Attempting to contact (DESCRIPTION = (ADDRESS_LIST = (ADDRESS =
(PROTOCOL = TCP)(HOST = localhost)(PORT = 15211))) (CONNECT_DATA =
(SERVICE_NAME = orcl)))
TNS-12541: TNS:no listener

This time, the error message is stating that there is no Listener running. The database administrator checks the Listener and verifies that it is up and running. Do you see the problem from the output above? Remember that a Listener runs on a specific machine listening on a specific port. The port was defined wrong. The port should be 1521, not 15211.

This is a good place to have a quick discussion about ports. We know the Listener uses a specific port, typically 1521. Firewalls need to allow access to this port if we want to connect to the Oracle instance. What is less obvious is that each server process, dedicated or shared, has its own port assigned to it, in a wide range. Opening up access to port 1521 through the firewall may not be sufficient. Work with your network team if you suspect the firewall is stopping connections from being made. If you are running Oracle in a cloud environment, work with your cloud provider.

In the next example in Listing 9-14, we will specify an incorrect value for the service name and try to make a connection with SQL*Plus.

Listing 9-14. ORA-12514 Error

[oracle@oracle122 admin]$ sqlplus peasland@dbamentor

SQL*Plus: Release 12.2.0.1.0 Production on Tue Jul 10 00:14:31 2018

Copyright (c) 1982, 2016, Oracle. All rights reserved.

Enter password:
ERROR:
ORA-12514: TNS:listener does not currently know of service requested in
connect
descriptor

The ORA-12514 error is telling us that the Listener was contacted on that host and port but it does not know anything about the service name we supplied. In this case, the database administrator will need to examine the TNS alias to determine what service name was specified. Then compare to the "lsnrctl status" output to ensure the service name is there. Typically, there is a mismatch in the SERVICE_NAME for the TNS alias.

The last example also brings up one other point. Notice that this time the error number started with ORA, not TNS. When dealing with TNS errors, you may see the Oracle code interchange the prefix, but the number will stay the same. So ORA-12514 and TNS-12514 are the same exact error.

EZ Connect

The TNS alias can make your life easier because you do not have to remember nor type in the protocol, host, port, and service name. The TNS alias can make your life more difficult when you need to connect to a remote database a few times but not often. With the TNS alias, you must open the tnsnames.ora file with a text editor, add the appropriate alias, then save the file. Finally, you can use the TNS alias in your connection. If this is the only time you will be connecting to that database, you would have to remember to edit the tnsnames.ora file once more to remove that alias.

Oracle Database 10g made life a little easier by introducing the EZ Connect method. With EZ Connect, you can specify the host, port, and service name where you would traditionally enter the TNS alias. EZ Connect always assumes the protocol is TCP, so if you need a different network protocol, you are stuck with defining a TNS alias.

With SQL*Plus, the "@tnsalias" construct is used to define the remote database to connect to. EZ Connect has the form @//*hostname:port/service*. If you omit the port, EZ Connect assumes the default port, 1521. The EZ Connect format provides three pieces of the required information: hostname, port, and service. And we know that EZ Connect only uses the TCP protocol, so that is the fourth and final piece of information.

The example in Listing 9-15 shows connecting with EZ Connect.

Listing 9-15. EZ Connect with SQL*Plus

```
[oracle@oracle122 ~]$ sqlplus peasland/password@//localhost:1521/orcl

SQL*Plus: Release 12.2.0.1.0 Production on Tue Jul 10 08:53:23 2018

Copyright (c) 1982, 2016, Oracle.  All rights reserved.

Last Successful login time: Tue Jul 10 2018 08:53:16 -05:00
```

```
Connected to:
Oracle Database 12c Enterprise Edition Release 12.2.0.1.0 - 64bit Production

SQL>
```

When using EZ Connect with SQL*Plus, you must include the username and password before the @ symbol. If you omit the password, you will receive an error.

Not all applications support EZ Connect. Oracle-supplied utilities like SQL*Plus will accept EZ Connect but many third-party applications will not. Typically, a third-party application connects to the same database all the time, so the lack of EZ Connect support is not a big deal because we would define a TNS alias for the application.

ODBC

Open Database Computing (ODBC) has been around for a very long time. Its sole purpose is to connect an application to a database of some sort. ODBC is a software driver that helps make the database connection independent of the database system in use.

Have you ever supported an application that the vendor told you can use either Oracle or SQL Server? The vendor might offer support for other database engines as well. The vendor typically does not write two different versions of its software, one for SQL Server and one for Oracle. Instead, the vendor opens a database-independent connection using ODBC. The application code is largely the same no matter which database is in use. Not all SQL statements are the same. A SQL statement issued against an Oracle database may perform differently than the same SQL statement issued against SQL Server. Good application vendors will have slightly different code paths depending on the database engine in use. However, the calls to the database are the same because of ODBC. This helps speed up application development.

On the application's machine, someone must have an Oracle ODBC driver installed for that application to connect to Oracle. It must have a SQL Server ODBC driver installed to connect to SQL Server, and so on.

On Windows systems, you can see the installed drivers with the ODBC Data Source Administrator utility. On a Windows 10 workstation, type "ODBC" in the search box (bottom left of the screen) and Windows will find the utility for you. There are two utilities, one for 32-bit and one for 64-bit. Applications that are compiled as 32-bit apps will use 32-bit ODBC drivers. Applications that are compiled as 64-bit will use 64-bit ODBC drivers.

In Figure 9-3, we can see the 32-bit ODBC Data Source Administrator. Clicking the Drivers tab displays the installed drivers. You might have to scroll down a bit to see ones for Oracle.

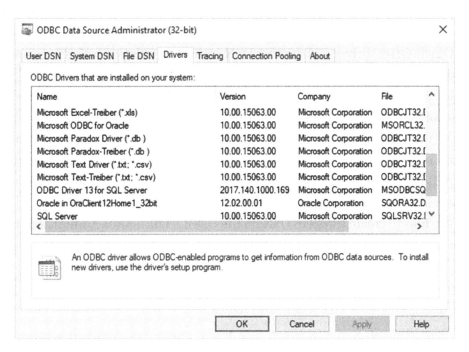

Figure 9-3. *ODBC drivers in Windows 10*

Windows normally includes many preinstalled ODBC drivers. You can see the Microsoft ODBC for Oracle driver in the list. You can also see the ODBC Driver 13 for SQL Server and SQL Server in the list.

Tip   Never use the Microsoft ODBC for Oracle driver. The ODBC driver supplied by Oracle works much better.

Toward the end of that list, you can see the driver named Oracle in OraClient12Home1_32bit, which is the Oracle ODBC driver installed when Oracle Client was installed on that machine. If you want to use ODBC for your application to connect to an Oracle database, save yourself the future headache and install Oracle Client with the ODBC driver. Other ODBC drivers may say they work with Oracle, but I've run into too many issues, especially with performance, to use anything other than Oracle's ODBC drivers.

Before you can use ODBC, you must create a Data Source Name (DSN). The application specifies a username, password, and DSN to connect to the database. If you are creating a DSN for a third-party application, the vendor may tell you what the DSN needs to be named. Otherwise, you can use any name you choose. The DSN is created for a specific ODBC driver. For example, you may have one DSN named hr_orcl_dev that uses the Oracle ODBC driver and another DSN named hr_mysql_dev that uses a MySQL ODBC driver. It is these DSNs that point to the ODBC driver to use.

There are two types of DSNs: user DSN and system DSN. The difference is the scope of visibility of the DSN. A user DSN can be used only by the user that created it. A system DSN can be used by any user of the system. If your workstation is only used by one person, then it does not matter which DSN type you configure. If your workstation is used by multiple people, then the choice can be important. Do you want others to use this same DSN? If so, then create a system DSN; otherwise, create a user DSN.

Let's see how to create a system DSN. In the ODBC Data Source Administrator, click the System DSN tab, shown in Figure 9-4. Then click the Add button to create a system DSN.

Figure 9-4. *System DSN tab in ODBC Data Source Administrator*

The Data Source Window will ask you which driver to use for this DSN. Select the Oracle driver, as shown in Figure 9-5, and click the Finish button.

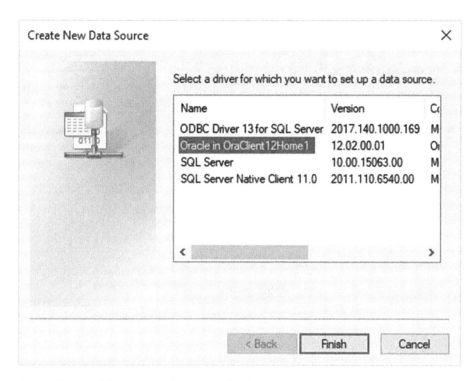

Figure 9-5. *Create New Data Source window*

Even though you clicked a button named Finish, you are not yet done. This pops up another window, shown in Figure 9-6, in which you provide the Data Source Name. As previously stated, a third-party application vendor may be expecting a specific name. You can enter an optional description if you choose. In the next field, you will need to specify the TNS alias. As shown in Figure 9-6, I created an alias named hrdev1 in my tnsnames.ora configure file to point to the correct Oracle instance. You can enter in a username as well. Third-party applications may specify the username in code.

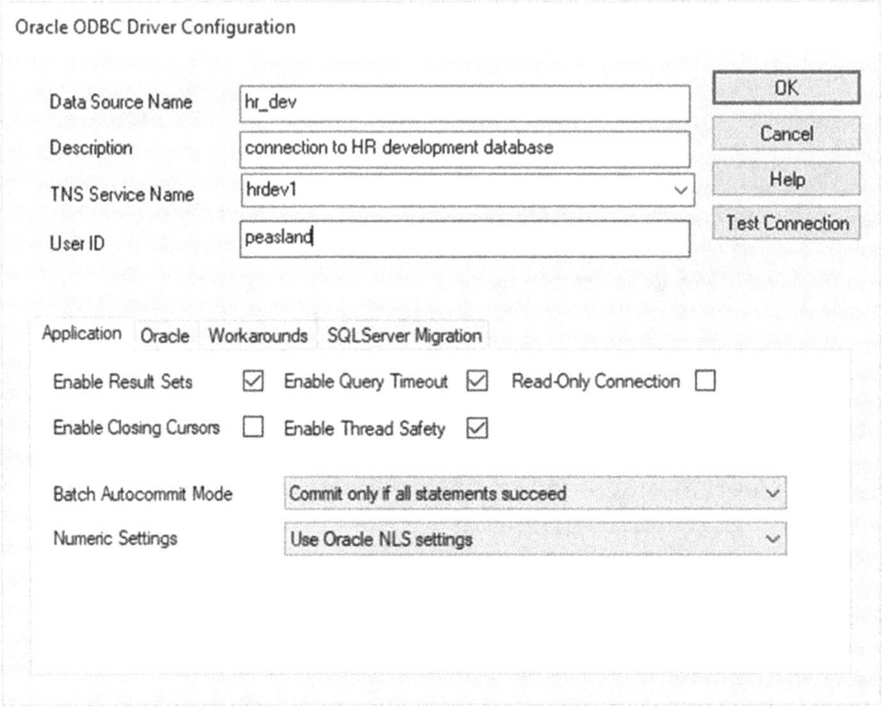

Figure 9-6. *Driver configuration*

Typically, the rest of the information in the Application, Oracle, Workarounds, and SQLServer Migration tabs can be ignored. The default values are normally sufficient. When everything looks ready, click the Test Connection button. You will receive another window asking for the username and password. If you specified a username in the DSN definition, this value will automatically be filled in for you. The window will look like Figure 9-7.

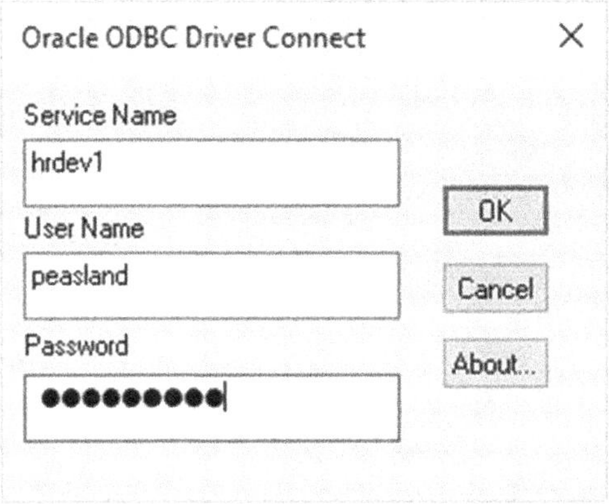

Figure 9-7. *ODBC Driver Connect*

Click the OK button to test the connection. If everything is set up correctly, you will receive another window, shown in Figure 9-8, indicating a successful connection.

Figure 9-8. *ODBC successful connection*

If there is an error, that final window will give you an error message that you will have to resolve. Otherwise, click OK to close the windows and return to the ODBC Data Source Administrator utility. The System DSN tab should show the DSN that was created.

You are not limited to using ODBC for applications. It may be useful for coding scripts that connect to a database. One popular scripting language in use today is Python. The example in Listing 9-16 shows Python code to create an ODBC connection to an Oracle DSN. Python uses the pyodbc library if you want to use ODBC.

Listing 9-16. Python ODBC Example

```
import pyodbc
cnxn = pyodbc.connect("DSN=HRDEV1")
```

If this same Python code needs to connect to SQL Server, the call to pyodbc.connect just needs to be changed to the appropriate DSN.

JDBC

ODBC was has been around since the early 1990s. Shortly after its introduction, Sun Microsystems developed the Java programming language with its "write once, run anywhere" philosophy.

To facilitate Java programs connecting to databases, Sun Microsystems released the Java Database Connectivity (JDBC) code in 1997. JDBC is very similar to ODBC but it is Java-specific whereas ODBC can be used by a variety of programming languages.

There are two types of JDBC drivers, *thin* and *thick*. Thin JDBC drivers are great because you do not need to install anything. Simply place the Java archive file (.jar) somewhere on the system where the Java program can access it. Nothing else needs to be installed. The thick driver requires you to install the full Oracle Client software. In reality, there are four types of JDBC drivers, but Type 1 and Type 2 are called thick drivers.

The rule of thumb is to use thin drivers wherever you can because deployment is so much easier. Otherwise, use thick drivers. If you are running a third-party application, the vendor will tell you which JDBC drivers to use. Just like ODBC drivers, use your database vendor's drivers as much as possible. If the application is connecting to an Oracle database, then use Oracle's JDBC drivers.

The example in Listing 9-17 shows Java code to define a JDBC connection to an Oracle database using the thin JDBC driver.

Listing 9-17. Thin JDBC Driver Example

```
String url = "jdbc:oracle:thin:username/password@//myhost:1521/orcl";
```

Moving On

This chapter has discussed various methods to connect to an Oracle database. You must be able to make such a connection to access any data contained therein. We discussed the role of the Listener and the four critical pieces of information: protocol, hostname, port, and service name. It is very common for connection errors to be caused by one of those pieces being specified incorrectly. Other common connection errors could be caused by the Listener or Oracle instance being down, or ports being blocked.

Most of the examples in this book will continue to use SQL*Plus locally on the database server. In a future chapter, we will introduce other tools to interact with your Oracle database.

It took nine chapters to get here, but we now have our testbed up and running, and we know how to connect to the Oracle instance there. In the next chapter, we will be discussing test cases and testbeds. We will explore the power of experimentation and how to learn from failures. We needed a place to experiment and learn more about Oracle. We are finally ready to shift our focus in that area.

CHAPTER 10

Test Cases

With an operational database built in our virtual machine, it's time to start playing around. The first nine chapters got us to this point where we can get to the real reason for this book, learning more about the Oracle database.

This chapter is devoted to test cases and testbeds. In this chapter, we will explore why we need testbeds and how we can create test cases to learn and to make sure we know what we are doing. As we will see in this chapter, test cases are a great way to learn and explore more about the Oracle database.

Failure

Never be afraid to fail. This is age-old advice that applies for anyone, even a database administrator. There is a less-than-obvious implicit statement at the end of that advice, which is to learn from your failures.

Failure alone does nothing. You failed. It is only when you examine what went wrong and subsequently determine a better course of action that you can succeed. It is said that you learn more from failure than from success, so do not be afraid to fail. Get excited! You are about to learn something new and grow your career. Not only will you learn from failure, but you will gain confidence in your skills and knowledge. After you have achieved success, you will have confidence that you can succeed again and know that you can figure it out should you fail again.

The major reason I wanted to write this chapter is because I see too many questions on Oracle forums asking something like "Can I create a primary key without using an index?" or "Can I create a foreign key to a table but reference something other than the primary key?" In my head, a little voice immediately responds, "No, you cannot, because you have not tried." It sounds a little rude, which is why I never provide this answer, but it is the truth. In Chapter 15, we will discuss using Oracle forums to grow your career. For now, understand that any question that starts with "can I" means you have immediately failed because you have not tried.

© Brian Peasland 2019
B. Peasland, *Oracle DBA Mentor*, https://doi.org/10.1007/978-1-4842-4321-3_10

Tip   Never ask "Can I *X*?" Try first.

What's the lesson to learn from that initial failure? It should be obvious that one needs to try. An initial attempt is always warranted. You may find that you succeed your first try. If you ask someone "Can I *X*?" and then go and try it and find out you could all along, you have wasted everyone's time asking them when you could have done the work yourself.

Almost everyone has tried something and failed. They look at what went wrong and decide to try again with a different approach. They fail again. That didn't work so the next way to analyze the situation is to determine if the new approach is leading them closer to their desired goal. If they feel this is a step closer to their preferred solution, they determine what the next step should be. If the approach is not proceeding in the needed direction, a different approach may be warranted.

You will find many times throughout your career that your attempts and subsequent actions are leading you down the wrong path. In the course of failing, learning, trying again, and failing again, you may often find that you are getting no closer to a solution. This is part of the learning process. Each of these attempts will make you a better database professional, but only if you learn from the failures.

As you backtrack trying to figure out where you went down the wrong path, you may go back to previous attempts to ascertain if a different path was needed from that point. We may have to go back to much earlier attempts. Everyone has been part of the ultimate failure where everything we try goes wrong and we must revert to the proverbial "square one" and start from the beginning.

Success

The opposite of failure is success. Success is what everyone strives for with every task they perform. If you are making a cup of coffee to start your day, you want a successful outcome. If you are tying your shoe, you want a successful outcome. If you are designing a database system, you want a successful outcome.

The best way to achieve success is to define the criteria for success. How do you know when your task has reached a successful conclusion? I know my task to make a morning cup of coffee is successful when I am drinking the beverage and my brain says, "that tastes great." Success for the task of tying a shoe is defined when the laces are fastened so they keep the shoe in place and stay that way for a sufficient period of time. If the laces appear to be tied and five steps later they come undone, the task of tying the shoes was not a success.

How about designing a database system? How do you define success? The database is up and running. Tables are populated with data. End users can access the data. Is that success? In some cases, it might be a successful outcome. However, if performance is slow and the system cannot scale to meet the demands of a larger user base, one might consider the system to be a failure.

The more accurately you can define success criteria, the higher your chances of achieving a successful outcome. Success criteria needs to be signed off by all of the stakeholders so that everyone has a solid understanding of what the project needs to accomplish to be a success. A database administrator may stand up a new database system and think they have done an excellent job and have achieved success. The DBA's manager may then look at the system and say that it is a dismal failure. They have different success criteria for this system. One person is happy and the other is anything but happy. In order for the implementation of the system to be a success, all stakeholders need to understand what that means. Clear communication and defining the expectations are key to success.

Once the success criteria has been met, the project is completed. Over time, people may evaluate the solution and decide they want new success criteria. A new project is created to achieve this new objective. It is very common in the IT business to deploy a solution and then have the overall vision change in the future. A database system that was working just fine and met its initial success criteria now needs to be modified to support the changing needs of the organization.

Tip   Make sure you know your success criteria.

Every test case shown in this chapter will have defined success criteria. Without the criteria, we will not know when to stop working on the test case. Even well-intentioned people may attempt to redefine the success criteria during the life of the project. This is called *scope creep* and can significantly impact the project's ability to achieve success within the previously defined constraints, especially on the project timeline.

Testbeds

The virtual machine we have built in this book is one of our testbeds. Every Oracle database administrator needs a testbed to practice and figure out how things work. Production environments are poor testbeds. We should test things out elsewhere and then implement the change in production only after we know exactly what we are doing.

Tip   Never make any change in production unless you know exactly what you are doing.

Remember that the DBA is the data guardian. It would be a foolish DBA that attempts something for the first time in production only to watch their action destroy the database or make it unavailable to end users.

Most IT practitioners are familiar with development (dev), test, and production platforms. Application code is created and modified in the dev environment first. Once the changes are known and working to solve the task, the changes are rolled into the test environment. Quality Analysis (QA) teams verify that the changes achieved the desired result without breaking previously existing functionality. Once testing has completed successfully, the change is rolled into production.

The database administrator needs a place to perform their work. Some organizations insist on having their DBA perform their work in the same environment in which application developers work. The problem is that DBAs can break things and the result may be a database that is no longer operational. If the DBA breaks the database, developers and QA staff may not be able to perform their work. End users will not notice that a dev or test database is down. But your developers and QA staff certainly will. Your dev and test databases can be thought of as "production" for developers and QA. Do not use dev and test databases to try out your DBA tasks because you risk impacting dev and QA work.

Tip   Dev and test databases are production for someone, just not your application end users.

The database administrator needs their own platform to work on. They need a testbed of their own. Today's virtualization and cloud technologies make it even easier for the DBA to get their hands on their own testbed. This book has shown how easy it is to create an Oracle on Linux testbed using VirtualBox. The DBA may have multiple testbeds. For example, the DBA may have an Oracle 12.2 testbed, as we have created in this book, and then create another one just for the purpose of testing an upgrade from 12.2 to the 18c version. After their upgrade testing is complete, the DBA may no longer need that testbed, in which case it can be destroyed.

Snapshots

Virtualization technologies make it easy create a point-in-time snapshot of the current state of the system. Should the database administrator subsequently break everything, they can revert to the snapshot and be back up and running as if they never changed anything. Some virtual machine hypervisors let you take a snapshot of the system while it is up and running, whereas others require the virtual machine to be off.

In the Oracle VM VirtualBox Manager, single-click the virtual machine we created for this book. Then click the drop-down arrow for the Machine Tools icon, shown in Figure 10-1, and choose Snapshots.

Figure 10-1. *VirtualBox Machine Tools icon*

You should see that no snapshots have been taken as of yet. Click the Take button to take your first snapshot. VirtualBox will give you a dialog box, shown in Figure 10-2, where you can define a name and description of the snapshot.

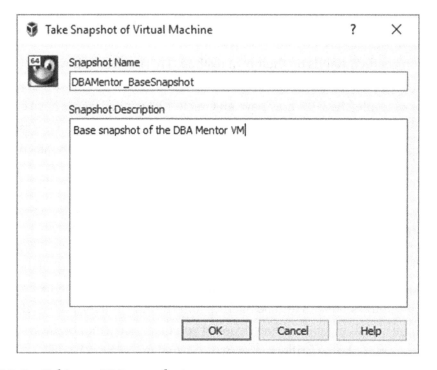

Figure 10-2. *Taking a VM snapshot*

You can enter any snapshot name or description that makes it easier to understand more about that specific snapshot. For example, you might take a snapshot before a database upgrade and name the snapshot "pre-upgrade snapshot."

When taking a snapshot of a VM with an Oracle database, make sure the database is not running; otherwise, a cold backup of the database will be taken. This assumes the database's storage is part of the virtual machine. If the storage is external to the VM, you will need to handle the backup of the database in a different manner, most likely using techniques discussed in Chapter 7.

In the VirtualBox Manager, we can see our snapshot. Figure 10-3 shows the snapshot and that the current state of the system is a child of that snapshot.

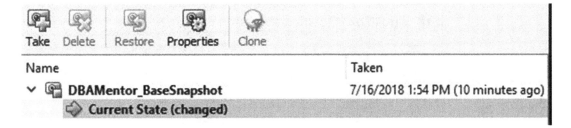

Figure 10-3. *VM snapshot in VirtualBox Manager*

We can also see the date and time the snapshot was taken. In Figure 10-4, we have a snapshot as a child of an existing snapshot.

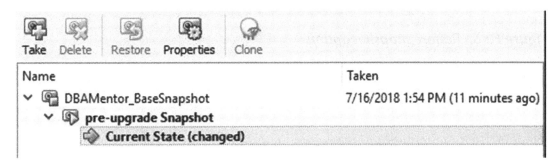

Figure 10-4. *Multiple snapshots*

To restore a previous snapshot, shut down the virtual machine. Select the snapshot to restore and click the Restore button. A dialog box asks you to confirm the restore. You are given the option of creating a snapshot of the current machine first so that you can get back to this state, as shown in Figure 10-5.

Figure 10-5. *Restore snapshot option*

With the restore operation complete, we can see the restore snapshot. Note that the current state is now a child of the snapshot we restored to in Figure 10-6.

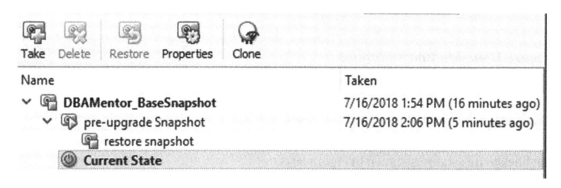

Figure 10-6. *Snapshot restored*

Snapshots are a great way to let you revert to a known, hopefully good state. Each snapshot takes a certain amount of disk space. If you take too many snapshots, you may start to feel some disk space pressure. It is a good idea to delete any snapshots you no longer need.

LiveSQL

Oracle has provided a testbed for our use they call LiveSQL. This testbed is a web-based query tool interacting with a real Oracle database. Anyone can access LiveSQL by pointing their web browser to `http://livesql.oracle.com` and start playing around. In the upper right corner, click the Sign In link and use the same Oracle credentials to access the Oracle Technology Network or My Oracle Support. On the left side, click the SQL Worksheet item, as shown in Figure 10-7.

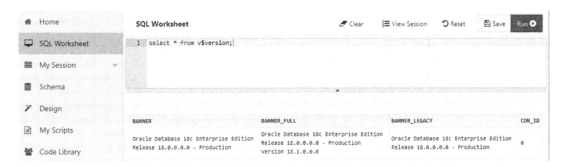

Figure 10-7. *LiveSQL*

At the time this chapter was written, Oracle 18c was available only in the cloud, which is why we did not use that version for our testbed. As you can see in Figure 10-7, LiveSQL uses the latest and greatest version of Oracle. LiveSQL is a great way to use a new version that has not yet been released for on-premises use and begin testing out new features. As this book was being edited, LiveSQL now uses the 19c version which is not available for on-premise installation.

To enter any query, type it into the SQL Worksheet and then click the Run button. You can enter any valid SQL statement, even creating tables and populating them with data. Figure 10-8 shows a table with some test data loaded into my LiveSQL schema.

SQL Worksheet   ✐ Clear

```
1  select * From emp;
```

```
EMPNO  ENAME   JOB        MGR   HIREDATE   SAL   COMM  DEPTNO

7839   KING    PRESIDENT  -     17-NOV-81  5000  -     10

7698   BLAKE   MANAGER    7839  01-MAY-81  2850  -     30

7782   CLARK   MANAGER    7839  09-JUN-81  2450  -     10

7566   JONES   MANAGER    7839  02-APR-81  2975  -     20

7788   SCOTT   ANALYST    7566  19-APR-87  3000  -     20

7902   FORD    ANALYST    7566  03-DEC-81  3000  -     20

7369   SMITH   CLERK      7902  17-DEC-80  800   -     20

7499   ALLEN   SALESMAN   7698  20-FEB-81  1600  300   30

7521   WARD    SALESMAN   7698  22-FEB-81  1250  500   30

7654   MARTIN  SALESMAN   7698  28-SEP-81  1250  1400  30

7844   TURNER  SALESMAN   7698  08-SEP-81  1500  0     30

7876   ADAMS   CLERK      7788  23-MAY-87  1100  -     20

7900   JAMES   CLERK      7698  03-DEC-81  950   -     30

7934   MILLER  CLERK      7782  23-JAN-82  1300  -     10

Download CSV
14 rows selected.
```

Figure 10-8. *LiveSQL Emp table*

You can also store scripts in your LiveSQL account for future recall.

LiveSQL is not to be used for production purposes but it serves as a great testbed, especially for those that do not have access to the latest and greatest Oracle version. LiveSQL also is a great testbed when you do not want to spend the time spinning up a virtual machine, installing Oracle, and creating a database. That being said, LiveSQL is not a great testbed for practicing database restores or other tasks where you need access to the database server.

Test Cases

It is now time to build some test cases. As said earlier in this chapter, we need to be able to learn from our failures. Test cases provide us the ability to put our task into action, analyze what went wrong, and go from there.

To write a test case, we need to have a specific task in mind. The task should be as specific as possible. If the task is too generic, we will not be able to accurately define the success criteria. A good test case should specify the inputs and the outputs and any restrictions on the execution. For example, a test case on learning to ride a bicycle may indicate that the input is a two-wheel bike. The output is being able to use the pedals to propel the bike 20 feet without falling. The restrictions are that you cannot place your feet on the ground to stop from falling.

Let's go back to one of the questions posed earlier in this chapter: "Can I create a primary key without using an index?" The success criteria is when we know the answer to the question. Can we have a primary key (PK) without using an index? Our input will be a table we create. The output will be the answer to the question. To begin with, we will verify the schema has zero objects in it, then create a table and create the primary key constraint on the table, as can be seen in Listing 10-1.

Listing 10-1. Primary Key Test Case

```
SQL> select count(*) from user_objects;

  COUNT(*)
----------
         0

SQL> create table pk_test_table (id number);

Table created.

SQL> alter table pk_test_table add constraint pk_constraint primary key (id);

Table altered.

SQL> select count(*) from user_objects;

  COUNT(*)
----------
         2
```

```
SQL> select object_name,object_type from user_objects;

OBJECT_NAME            OBJECT_TYP
-------------------- ----------
PK_CONSTRAINT          INDEX
PK_TEST_TABLE          TABLE
```

The test case started with zero objects in the user's schema. We created a very simple table and then added a primary key constraint. There are now two objects in the user's schema, the table and an index Oracle created for us. The index's name is the same as the primary key constraint name.

Notice that this table was very simple. Test cases can often use very simple objects to prove or disprove the task at hand.

Tip   Keep your test cases as simple as possible to avoid adding extra complications to the analysis.

So far, we have not answered the question of whether we can have a primary key constraint without an index. When we created the primary key constraint, Oracle automatically created the index for us. To answer the question, we must determine if we can now drop the index, shown in Listing 10-2.

Listing 10-2. Dropping the PK Index

```
SQL> drop index pk_constraint;
drop index pk_constraint
         *
ERROR at line 1:
ORA-02429: cannot drop index used for enforcement of unique/primary key
```

When we attempt to drop the index, Oracle raises the ORA-02429 error and the operation fails. We now have an answer to our question. We cannot have a primary key constraint without an associated index. Since we now have an answer to the question, the success criteria for this task is now complete. We may not like the answer, but we have the answer nonetheless.

Now let's tackle the other question posed earlier in this chapter: "Can I create a foreign key to a table but reference something other than the primary key?" For our inputs, we'll need a table with two columns, one column that serves as the primary key and another column that is not part of the primary key constraint. We will need another table that attempts to create the foreign key (FK) constraint to the non-PK column of the parent table. Our success criteria is when we know our answer to the question.

We will also drop the table we used in the previous test case. It is a good idea to clean up the objects used for test cases. In Listing 10-3, the old test table is dropped. A parent table is created with a primary key constraint. A child table is created.

Listing 10-3. FK Test Case Setup

```
SQL> drop table pk_test_table;

Table dropped.

SQL> create table parent_tbl (pk_id number, other_id number);

Table created.

SQL> alter table parent_tbl add constraint parent_tbl_pk primary key (pk_id);

Table altered.

SQL> create table child_tbl (id number);

Table created.

SQL> alter table child_tbl add constraint parent_child_fk
  2  foreign key (id) references parent_tbl(pk_id);

Table altered.

SQL> alter table child_tbl drop constraint parent_child_fk;

Table altered.
```

In the code above, we created a new table to serve as our parent and defined a primary key constraint on this table. We created a child table. Finally, we created a foreign key constraint from the child to the parent using the PK column just to prove such a constraint could be created. However, since this constraint is not answering our question, the constraint was dropped. In Listing 10-4, let's attempt to create the foreign key constraint to the parent table's non-PK column.

Listing 10-4. Adding FK Constraint Failure

```
SQL> alter table child_tbl add constraint parent_child_fk
  2  foreign key (id) references parent_tbl(other_id);
foreign key (id) references parent_tbl(other_id)
                                       *
ERROR at line 2:
ORA-02270: no matching unique or primary key for this column-list
```

We received another Oracle error. ORA-02270 says that Oracle could not find a unique or a primary key for the column in the parent table. Remember that failure means we have a learning opportunity here. The error message is indicating that we need to be referencing either a primary key or a unique constraint in the parent table. A table can have only one primary key constraint, so let's add a unique constraint to the other column in the parent table and try to add the foreign key constraint again, shown in Listing 10-5.

Listing 10-5. Adding FK Constraint Success

```
SQL> alter table parent_tbl add constraint parent_unique unique (other_id);

Table altered.

SQL> alter table child_tbl add constraint parent_child_fk
  2  foreign key (id) references parent_tbl(other_id);

Table altered.
```

This time we are successful. We have answered our initial question. We can add a foreign key constraint to a table but reference something other than the parent's primary key. We also learned something else in our failure. The foreign key constraint can reference the parent's primary key or some other unique constraint.

Before Listing 10-5, I noted that a table can have only one primary key constraint. Is that true? It should be very easy for you to create a test table with a primary key constraint. Then try to add another PK constraint to the table. Does it succeed or does it generate an error? Use test cases to challenge what we all assume to be true. Just because

I said a table can have only one primary key constraint does not make it true. Test it out for yourself.

Let's clean up from our simple test case and drop the two tables we created, starting with the parent table in Listing 10-6.

Listing 10-6. Dropping the Parent Table

```
SQL> drop table parent_tbl;
drop table parent_tbl
            *
ERROR at line 1:
ORA-02449: unique/primary keys in table referenced by foreign keys
```

We have encountered another error. This error is telling us that we cannot drop the parent table because another table is referencing the parent. Let's drop the child table first and then the parent table, shown in Listing 10-7.

Listing 10-7. Drop Tables in Correct Order

```
SQL> drop table child_tbl;

Table dropped.

SQL> drop table parent_tbl;

Table dropped.
```

Sometimes, when working with a test case, we will learn something we did not set out to discover. In our case, we learned we needed to drop the child table first, then drop the parent table.

Tip   Keep your eyes open. Test cases may teach you unexpected facts.

Test cases do more than just answer questions. They let you explore. Test cases are a fantastic way to teach yourself more about the Oracle database. These lessons often occur when you play "what if" games. For example, you may be playing around with Oracle partitioning on your testbed and you create a partitioned table as shown in Listing 10-8.

Listing 10-8. Partitioned Table Test Case

```
SQL> create table product_sales (
  2  transaction_id number,
  3  product_id number,
  4  qty_sold number,
  5  transaction_date date)
  6  partition by range (transaction_date)
  7  ( partition product_sales_2018q1
  8      values less than (to_date('04-01-2018','MM-DD-YYYY'))
          tablespace users,
  9    partition product_sales_2018q2
 10      values less than (to_date('07-01-2018','MM-DD-YYYY'))
          tablespace users,
 11    partition product_sales_2018q3
 12      values less than (to_date('10-01-2018','MM-DD-YYYY'))
          tablespace users,
 13    partition product_sales_2018q4
 14      values less than (to_date('01-01-2019','MM-DD-YYYY'))
          tablespace users
 15  );

Table created.
```

Playing What-If Games

When playing around with partitioned tables, you are likely to experiment with adding and dropping partitions and creating partitioned indexes. In dropping a partition from the table, you might ask yourself, "What if I try to restore the dropped partition from the recycle bin?" This question may not have been in your initial test case, but by playing "what if" games, you are bound to learn more. In Listing 10-9, we explore this very question.

Listing 10-9. Recovering a Dropped Partition

```
SQL> alter table product_sales drop partition product_sales_2018q1;

Table altered.

SQL> select object_name,original_name from recyclebin;

no rows selected
```

In the code above, the partition was dropped. Querying the recycle bin, we see that it is empty. This answers one question. You cannot restore a dropped partition from the recycle bin. What if we dropped the table? The table is made up of multiple partitions, and when we dropped a partition, it was not in the recycle bin. Let's play around in Listing 10-10 and find out.

Listing 10-10. Recovering a Dropped Partitioned Table

```
SQL> drop table product_sales;

Table dropped.
SQL>  select object_name,original_name,type from recyclebin;

OBJECT_NAME                      ORIGINAL_NAME               TYPE
-----------------------------    ------------------------    ----------------
BIN$cSQeOfrrEVLgVQAAAAAAAQ==$0 PRODUCT_SALES                 Table Partition
BIN$cSQeOfrrEVLgVQAAAAAAAQ==$0 PRODUCT_SALES                 Table Partition
BIN$cSQeOfrrEVLgVQAAAAAAAQ==$0 PRODUCT_SALES                 Table Partition
BIN$cSQeOfrrEVLgVQAAAAAAAQ==$0 PRODUCT_SALES                 TABLE
SQL>  flashback table product_sales to before drop;

Flashback complete.
```

We can see the table and its three partitions in the recycle bin and we could use the FLASHBACK command to recover the table. The lesson to be learned from this test case is that you cannot restore a partitioned table that was dropped, but you can restore a dropped partitioned table. Just by playing these "what if" games in our testbed, we could learn quite a lot about how Oracle's partitioned tables work.

Never be afraid to create your own test cases to either prove or disprove your theories about the Oracle database engine. The more test cases you create, the better you will get at making them. Test cases are an essential learning tool for the Oracle database administrator.

In Chapter 16, we will discuss blogging to help grow your database career. Test cases are great for blogging material. Many Oracle bloggers will want to illustrate a point and generate a simple test case to show what they want to convey. Another good way to use test cases in blogs is to show what you have learned to others.

Sample Schemas

It can take a bit of effort to create tables and populate them with data, which is one excuse people give for not building their own test cases. Oracle includes a number of sample schemas for your use. Before we dive into those, a little history may be in order.

In the early days of the Oracle database, the software developers creating the database engine needed a way to test out certain concepts. They needed testbed data as much as you do! One of those early employees was a gentleman by the name of Bruce Scott. He created a schema using his last name, SCOTT. He needed a few tables, so he created one for employees, called EMP, and one for departments, DEPT, all for a fictitious company. Armed with these two tables, he would do simple SQL statements to show how Oracle worked. This worked well enough that the Oracle distribution started including a script to create the SCOTT account. The script set the password to TIGER, which was the name of his daughter's cat. Today, you can still see people refer to scott/tiger and scott.emp, referring to this account and one of its tables.

Starting with Oracle9*i*, Oracle began shipping other sample schemas, HR for a fictitious Human Resources system and OE for a fictitious Order Entry schema. The HR schema is largely a replacement of SCOTT/TIGER. Today, the sample schemas can be found on the Oracle Developer Network in the same place you downloaded the Oracle database software. Scroll down the list of files for the database software until you find the Examples file. You can unzip this on your database server and follow the instructions to create sample schemas for your use.

If the sample schemas do not meet your needs, another Oracle employee, Dominic Giles, has created a Data Generator utility. You can find this at `www.dominicgiles.com/datagenerator.html` if you are interested. While this product was created by an Oracle employee, it is not a full-fledged Oracle Corporation product. Data Generator is a great way to create large volumes of semi-random data for test cases.

Moving On

Remember that the goal of this book is not to give you answers to all your questions. This book strives to teach you how to learn answers to questions on your own. In previous chapters, we have touched on a few books in the Oracle documentation set. Hopefully you have been getting some good exposure to the documentation. In this chapter, we introduced another powerful toolset to help you learn more about the Oracle database, the testbed and test cases.

Never be afraid to experiment. When experimenting, you will fail and that is okay. It is by examining failures and determining what went wrong, and how we can get it right, that we learn so much. We learn very little from success. Ask any database administrator you admire how often they fail and they will certainly respond with "all the time."

In the next chapter, we move on to a few tools you will use in managing Oracle databases. We have already been using one of these tools, SQL*Plus, and we will see more of these tools as well.

PART III

Learning Oracle Database

CHAPTER 11

Tools

In this chapter, we will explore a few of the tools at our disposal to help manage the Oracle database. We have already been using one of the tools, SQL*Plus. We will explore that tool more fully as well as a few others.

The Oracle database administrator needs to know which tools to leverage for the job, no different than a carpenter or a mechanic. The right tool for the right job can make your life simpler. Just like you would use a hammer to pound in a nail, you would use the Database Configuration Assistant to create a database.

I could write a chapter devoted to each of the tools discussed here. To keep it brief, this chapter will provide an overview of the tool and discuss what you will use it for. As with anything in the Oracle world, there is much to learn about the tool at a later date.

Connecting to Our Database

Earlier in this book, we created a virtual machine and built an Oracle database for our testbed. We can always use a Terminal window within the VM and use SQL*Plus, as we have been, but it would be nice if we could connect tools from our workstation to the Oracle instance inside that VM.

Recall that when we created the virtual machine in Chapter 3, we defined two network adapters. One of those is a NAT adapter, which lets the VM go to the outside world and download updates and more. The other network adapter we defined as "host-only," and this is the adapter we will connect through. In a Terminal window on the VM, type "ip addr"; this command will show us the IP addresses for each network device. On my virtual machine, the IP addresses are shown in Listing 11-1. Your VM may have slightly different addresses, so take note of your specific settings.

© Brian Peasland 2019
B. Peasland, *Oracle DBA Mentor*, https://doi.org/10.1007/978-1-4842-4321-3_11

Listing 11-1. VM IP Address

```
[oracle@oracle122 ~]$ ip addr
1: lo: <LOOPBACK,UP,LOWER_UP> mtu 65536 qdisc noqueue state UNKNOWN
    link/loopback 00:00:00:00:00:00 brd 00:00:00:00:00:00
    inet 127.0.0.1/8 scope host lo
       valid_lft forever preferred_lft forever
    inet6 ::1/128 scope host
       valid_lft forever preferred_lft forever
2: enp0s3: <BROADCAST,MULTICAST,UP,LOWER_UP> mtu 1500 qdisc pfifo_fast
state UP qlen 1000
    link/ether 08:00:27:6f:30:32 brd ff:ff:ff:ff:ff:ff
    inet 10.0.2.15/24 brd 10.0.2.255 scope global dynamic enp0s3
       valid_lft 75838sec preferred_lft 75838sec
    inet6 fe80::d629:df95:c55b:252c/64 scope link
       valid_lft forever preferred_lft forever
3: enp0s8: <BROADCAST,MULTICAST,UP,LOWER_UP> mtu 1500 qdisc pfifo_fast
state UP qlen 1000
    link/ether 08:00:27:d6:0e:5c brd ff:ff:ff:ff:ff:ff
    inet 192.168.56.101/24 brd 192.168.56.255 scope global dynamic enp0s8
       valid_lft 712sec preferred_lft 712sec
    inet6 fe80::777e:9533:78fd:6446/64 scope link
       valid_lft forever preferred_lft forever
```

We are looking for two IP addresses, one that starts with 10.0 and the other that starts with 192.168. The former is for our NAT adapter and the latter is for our host-only adapter, the one that we care about the most for this chapter. In my output, the IP address is 192.168.56.101, but yours may differ slightly. My virtual machine is running on a Windows workstation, so I'm going to start a command window, CMD. On a Mac, you would start a Terminal window. When troubleshooting network connectivity, the first thing people often ask is "Can you ping it?" Listing 11-2 provides the answer for my VM.

Listing 11-2. Ping the VM

```
C:\Users\bpeasland\Desktop>ping 192.168.56.101 -n 3

Pinging 192.168.56.101 with 32 bytes of data:
Reply from 192.168.56.101: bytes=32 time<1ms TTL=64
```

```
Reply from 192.168.56.101: bytes=32 time<1ms TTL=64
Reply from 192.168.56.101: bytes=32 time<1ms TTL=64

Ping statistics for 192.168.56.101:
    Packets: Sent = 3, Received = 3, Lost = 0 (0% loss),
Approximate round trip times in milli-seconds:
    Minimum = 0ms, Maximum = 0ms, Average = 0ms
```

From my workstation, the virtual machine could be successfully pinged. If you are having problems with this, check your IP address again. There may be multiple ones that start with 192.168, so you may have to try each. Also check the virtual machine's settings to ensure one of the network adapters is created as host-only.

The problem with the virtual machine's current configuration is that the IP address can change each time the VM starts. To make this more permanent, in the Linux VM, go to Applications ➤ System Tools ➤ Settings. Next, click the Network icon. You should see a window similar to Figure 11-1.

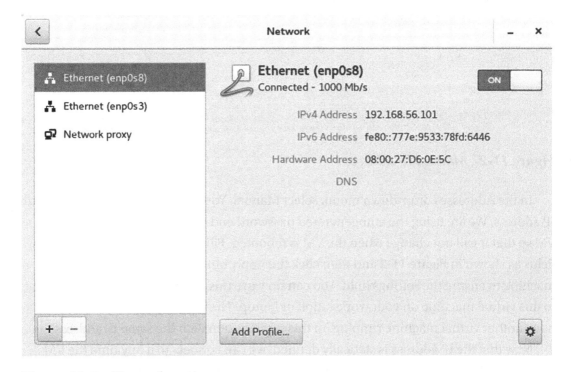

Figure 11-1. *Network settings*

Select the adapter (enp0s8) and make sure the IPv4 address starts with 192.168. You may have to select the other Ethernet adapter if the address is incorrect. In the lower-right corner, click the gear icon to change this adapter's settings. A dialog box similar to Figure 11-2 will come up.

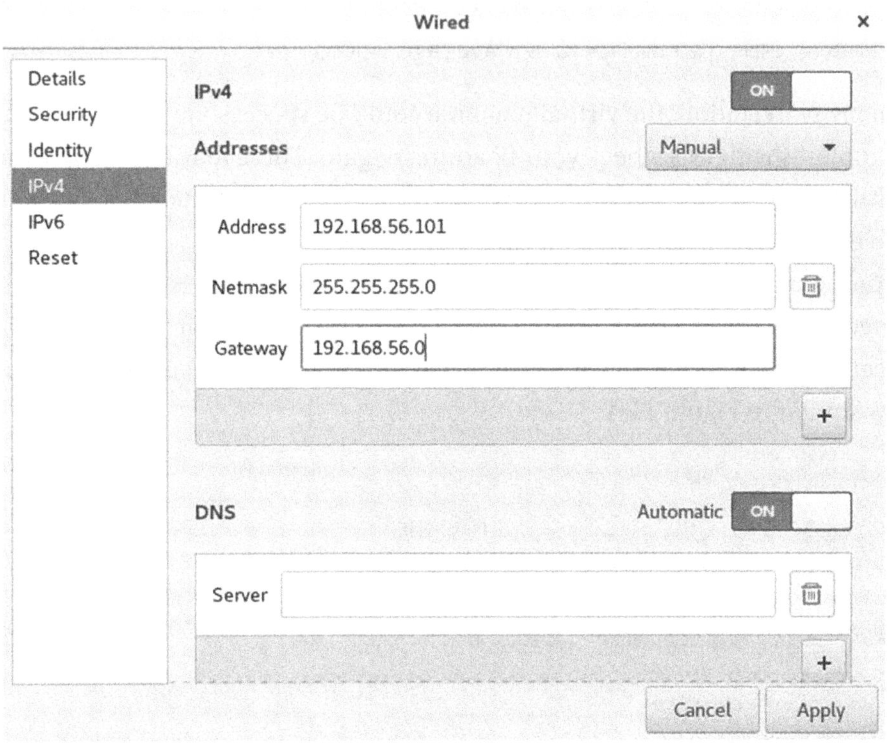

Figure 11-2. *Manual IP address*

In the Addresses drop-down menu, select Manual. You will now be able to enter your IP address. We are using the autogenerated password and making it permanent for this VM so that it will not change when the VM is rebooted. Fill in the Netmask and Gateway fields as shown in Figure 11-2 and then click the Apply button. Reboot the virtual machine to ensure the settings hold. You can now use this IP address to always connect to this virtual machine on your workstation or laptop. The only impact would be if you had another virtual machine running on this same system with the same IP address.

Now that the IP address is statically defined, we can connect to it any time the VM is up and running. However, working with IP addresses is cumbersome and we do not want to involve the network team to create an alias in DNS. To help ourselves out, we will modify our local "hosts" file. On Windows, use Explorer to navigate to the C:\Windows\System32\drivers\etc directory and open the file named hosts in any text editor. One Mac platforms, the hosts file is in the /etc directory. Toward the end of the file, add a line similar to the last entry in Listing 11-3.

Listing 11-3. Hosts Entry

```
# localhost name resolution is handled within DNS itself.
#       127.0.0.1        localhost
#       ::1              localhost
192.168.56.101       dbamentor
```

The last line of the output is my new entry to the hosts file. It contains my IP address and whatever alias I want to use to refer to this machine. I am using the alias dbamentor. Save the file, and then ping with that alias, as shown in Listing 11-4.

Listing 11-4. Ping with Hosts Alias

```
C:\Users\bpeasland\Desktop>ping dbamentor -n 3

Pinging dbamentor [192.168.56.101] with 32 bytes of data:
Reply from 192.168.56.101: bytes=32 time<1ms TTL=64
Reply from 192.168.56.101: bytes=32 time<1ms TTL=64
Reply from 192.168.56.101: bytes=32 time<1ms TTL=64

Ping statistics for 192.168.56.101:
    Packets: Sent = 3, Received = 3, Lost = 0 (0% loss),
Approximate round trip times in milli-seconds:
    Minimum = 0ms, Maximum = 0ms, Average = 0ms
```

I can now use this alias any time I want to connect to the virtual machine. This will be much easier to remember than an IP address.

If I am running the virtual machine on a Mac platform, then I can use the Terminal window to establish a Secure Shell (SSH) session to the machine. On Windows, I need an SSH client. I often use PuTTY or MobaXterm. Both are free utilities you can find by doing a simple Google search. No matter which you use, see if you can establish an SSH session to the machine. Listing 11-5 shows how I connected with MobaXterm.

Listing 11-5. SSH from MobaXterm

```
[bpeasland.winworkstation] ➤ ssh oracle@dbamentor
Warning: Permanently added 'dbamentor' (RSA) to the list of known hosts.
oracle@dbamentor's password:
Last login: Tue Jul 24 14:35:22 2018 from 192.168.56.1
/usr/bin/xauth:  file /home/oracle/.Xauthority does not exist
[oracle@dbamentor ~]$ hostname
dbamentor.localdomain
```

The hostname command at the end of the listing shows us that we did in fact connect to our virtual machine.

Now that we have established connectivity from our host operating system, we can use any utilities installed on the host to connect to the virtual machine and the database running inside it.

SQL*Plus

Many examples in this book have already used SQL*Plus, a command-line utility to start and stop an Oracle instance and to issue SQL statements to the database. There are other query tools, as we will see in this chapter, but SQL*Plus is always available. SQL*Plus is installed when we install the database software. At the very least, we can establish an SSH connection to the database server and then use SQL*Plus. Because SQL*Plus is a command-line utility, even a text-based SSH session will be sufficient.

Tip   Learn how to use SQL*Plus. It is always available to you.

If you install the Oracle Client software on your workstation, SQL*Plus is included there as well. You would have to set up a TNS alias, as shown in Chapter 9, to connect to a database on any other machine.

SQL*Plus is Oracle's standard for "if it works". Any query tool is just an application that submits SQL statements to the database and displays the results. There have been many times that a service request has been filed with Oracle Support where it looks like the Oracle database is not returning the correct results in some other query tool. The person who filed the service request gives Oracle the SQL statement and some sample data and shows how the result set returned from the database looks incorrect. If you ever run into this situation, Oracle will always ask you to reproduce the issue in SQL*Plus. If it works in SQL*Plus, then it is a problem with the query tool, not the database engine. If the SQL statement produces the wrong results in SQL*Plus, then Oracle Support needs to address the problem and help with a resolution.

SQL*Plus has many features that people may not be aware of. You can save your SQL statement to a text file. You can run a file that contains SQL statements to script out multiple actions. SQL*Plus can even generate formatted reports.

One hidden feature in SQL*Plus that many people are not aware of is the ability to edit your command. SQL*Plus keeps the current command in a buffer. Consider the example in Listing 11-6 where the database administrator attempted to create a tablespace, but an error occurred. It should be obvious that the DBA specified the tablespace's size twice in lines 3 and 4.

Listing 11-6. Incorrect SQL*Plus Command

```
SQL> create tablespace apps_ts
  2  datafile '/u01/app/oracle/oradata/orcl/apps_ts01.dbf'
  3  size 5g
  4  size 10g
  5  extent management local auto;
size 10g
*
ERROR at line 4:
ORA-02180: invalid option for CREATE TABLESPACE
```

The DBA wants to remove line 4 from this command without having to retype the SQL statement anew. The DBA can type the lowercase letter l to list the contents of the buffer, as shown in Listing 11-7.

Listing 11-7. Listing the SQL*Plus Buffer

```
SQL> l
  1  create tablespace apps_ts
  2  datafile '/u01/app/oracle/oradata/orcl/apps_ts01.dbf'
  3  size 5g
  4  size 10g
  5* extent management local auto
```

Notice the last line has an asterisk in it. The line with the asterisk is the current line. If we want to remove line 4, we need to make that the current line and then issue the command to delete that line. We simply type the line number of interest and hit the Enter key and then type "del" to remove our current line. Once the line has been removed, we can type the forward slash to execute the contents of the buffer, all shown in Listing 11-8.

Listing 11-8. Deleting a Line in the SQL*Plus Buffer

```
SQL> 4
  4* size 10g
SQL> del
SQL> l
  1  create tablespace apps_ts
  2  datafile '/u01/app/oracle/oradata/orcl/apps_ts01.dbf'
  3  size 5g
  4* extent management local auto
SQL> /
extent management local auto
                          *
ERROR at line 4:
ORA-02180: invalid option for CREATE TABLESPACE
```

When the contents of the buffer was listed, we can see the line with "size 10g" was removed. When the statement was executed again, another error was raised. The problem is that Oracle does not like the keyword *auto*. It should be *autoallocate* instead. We can see from the asterisk that our current line is the one with the error. We can change the word in the current line and re-execute the command, shown in Listing 11-9.

Listing 11-9. Changing Text in SQL*Plus Buffer

```
SQL> c /auto/autoallocate
  4* extent management local autoallocate
SQL> /

Tablespace created.
```

The c command will change, or perform a text substitution in the current line. The first character is your delimiter. In Listing 11-9, the delimiter is the forward slash, but you can choose any character, especially if the text you are trying to change contains the forward slash. After the delimiter is the text to change, followed by the delimiter again, then followed by the corrected text. Once auto is changed to autoallocate, the next forward slash executes the contents of the buffer and the tablespace is created successfully.

This buffer in SQL*Plus helps the DBA who needs to keep an eye on things over time. Type the command and see the output. Then after a period of time, just type the forward slash to execute the buffer again. In the example in Listing 11-10, the DBA needed to know the count of current sessions in the instance and watch the count change over time. Instead of typing in the command repeatedly, the DBA just pressed the forward slash for the next execution.

Listing 11-10. Multiple Buffer Executions in SQL*Plus

```
SQL> select count(*) as num_sessions from v$session where username is not null;

NUM_SESSIONS
------------
         507

SQL> /

NUM_SESSIONS
------------
         517

SQL> /

NUM_SESSIONS
------------
         500
```

If the DBA will need to run this statement in the future, the DBA may desire to save it to a script. The save command will write the contents of the buffer to a file. It is common practice to use the .sql file extension for SQL scripts. If the path is not specified, the file will be saved in the local directory. The @ symbol is used to tell SQL*Plus to load the contents of that file into the buffer and execute it. In Listing 11-11, we can see the contents of the buffer. We save that SQL statement to a file and then execute the file as a script.

Listing 11-11. Saving Buffer in SQL*Plus

```
SQL> l
  1* select count(*) as num_sessions from v$session where username is not null
SQL> save num_sessions.sql
Created file num_sessions.sql
SQL> @num_sessions.sql

NUM_SESSIONS
------------
         514
```

SQL*Plus is a valuable tool for the Oracle DBA. It is always available to you, and once you learn to leverage the power of its buffer as we have seen in the previous examples, you will find it to be a much better tool than just some command-line interaction with the database engine.

SQL Developer

Although SQL*Plus is a great command-line tool, we typically live in a GUI world. Think of SQL Developer as SQL*Plus in GUI form. The main goal of the SQL Developer product team at Oracle is to make your life easier. The tool works great for Oracle application developers and database administrators alike. The best part is that SQL Developer is free to use.

When you install the Oracle database software on the server, it includes a copy of SQL Developer. This copy is guaranteed to be out of date, so you should download the latest and greatest version. Point your web browser to `http://otn.oracle.com` and then click Software Downloads in the Essential Links section, just like you did when downloading the Oracle database software. On the next screen, SQL Developer is listed under Developer Tools even though it is not strictly a software development product. Click SQL Developer, and you will be taken to the download screen. You need click the radio button to accept the license agreement. If asked to authenticate, use the same Oracle Single Sign-On credentials you used to download the RDBMS software. I always download the version that includes the Java Development Kit (JDK) if I am downloading for Windows. For other platforms, you must supply the JDK.

The download is a zip file. There is no installation. Just unzip the file to a directory somewhere. In the software's folder, you will see the sqldeveloper executable. Run that file and SQL Developer will start. Earlier in this chapter, we made sure we had the ability to connect tools on our workstation to the database in our VM testbed. We will do that with SQL Developer in this section.

If this is the first time you have started SQL Developer, you should see a Start Page. This page contains an Overview Video link as well as links to many tutorials and demonstrations. The Start Page only lists three tutorials and demos, but there is a link to many more online. I highly recommend spending time with these as they will explain so much more about the SQL Developer capabilities than this book can. The Start Page also contains a link to the SQL Developer documentation.

Before you can interact with a database, you need to create a connection. In the Connections tab, shown in Figure 11-3, you can see I have three folders to better organize my connections.

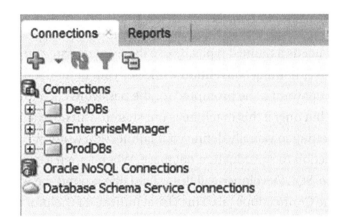

Figure 11-3. *Connections in SQL Developer*

Click the green plus sign icon to create a new database connection. A screen will pop up where you will need to fill in all the relevant details, shown in Figure 11-4.

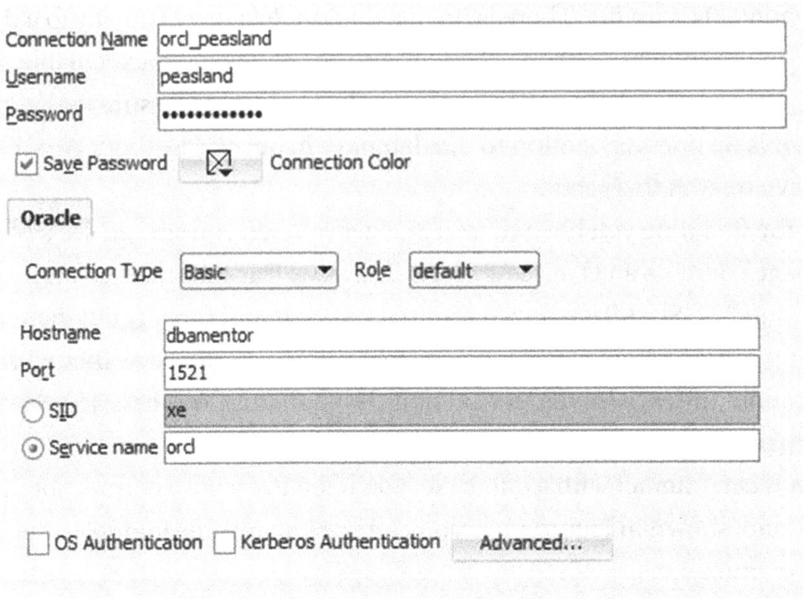

Figure 11-4. *SQL Developer connection details*

The connection needs a name. I typically use the form *dbname_username*, but you are free to use whatever naming convention works for you. Enter the username and password. If you do not want to be prompted for the password each time, check the Save Password box, but only if this machine is not shared with others. You can use the Connection Color setting to visually define your connection window. I typically choose red if this is a connection to a production database. When I open a connection to the production database, SQL Developer will draw a red line around the window. The name will also be red in the Connections tab. This visual indicator is helpful to warn me to be careful because my actions are in production and not dev or test.

In the example in Figure 11-4, I chose the Basic connection type. If you have Oracle Client installed, and have defined a TNS alias, you can change the Connection Type to TNS and then choose the alias. Since my connection is Basic, I have to supply the hostname, the port, and the service name. Once you have entered all of the information, click the Test button. If you have an error, it may be due to a firewall running on the VM. As the root user in our testbed VM, issue the following commands in Listing 11-12 in a Terminal window to disable the firewall.

Listing 11-12. Disable Linux Firewall

```
systemctl stop firewalld
systemctl disable firewalld
```

After the connection has been successfully tested, click the Save button. Double-clicking the connection will open it and bring up a worksheet. We can type in any SQL statement and click the green play button (or press Ctrl-Enter) to run the statement, an example of which is shown in Figure 11-5.

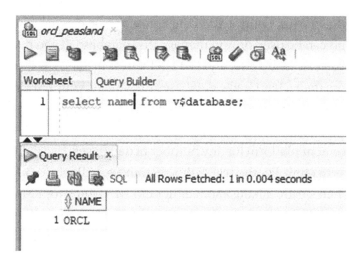

Figure 11-5. *Running a SQL statement in SQL Developer*

Multiple statements can be executed, one after the other, by clicking the Run Script button (or pressing F5). The Run Script button is next to the green play button. It looks like a page of text with the green play arrow in the bottom left corner.

Results can be sorted by any column in the Query Result window. If you want to save the results from being overwritten with the next statement execution, click the red push-pin icon. The next statement execution will be displayed in a different result tab.

The Oracle product manager for SQL Developer is Jeff Smith. He maintains a blog at www.thatjeffsmith.com and I highly recommend you bookmark this page. New versions are announced on this blog. Every time a new version comes out, you can find blog posts discussing the new features and even see them in action.

I find myself using SQL Developer more and more every day. This product is one of the more useful tools Oracle has produced. Like any valuable tool, it just makes my job easier. Take some time to spend learning how to leverage this tool.

Oracle Enterprise Manager

Included in your Oracle database license is the Oracle Enterprise Manager (EM) product. When Enterprise Manager was first created, it was a Java-based application the DBA ran on their workstation. They could connect it to an Oracle database and point and click their way through many administration tasks. As with any product, EM has matured over time. Today's EM product is now web-based and runs either the database server or some other centralized machine.

Enterprise Manager comes in two forms, either Enterprise Manager Database Express or Enterprise Manager Cloud Control. EM DB Express can be created when you create an Oracle database and can be used only to manage that database. If you need to manage a second database, you can set up a second EM DB Express instance. It should be obvious that if you have more than a few Oracle databases to manage, your EM DB Express instances will start to grow in number. Each has a different URL, so more databases means more EM DB Express URLs to bookmark. EM Cloud Control (EM CC) is a centralized management platform for any number of databases. Use EM CC if your Oracle infrastructure starts to grow. For the rest of this section, we will refer to just Enterprise Manager or EM, when we are talking about either EM DB Express or EM CC.

Enterprise Manager lets you manage your Oracle database. For example, you can see details about your tablespaces and create new ones, delete old ones, or add data files. We can see a number of tablespaces in EM in Figure 11-6.

Tablespaces

Object Type: Tablespace

Search
Select an object type and optionally enter an object name to filter the data that is displayed in your results set.
Object Name [ ] Go
By default, the search returns all uppercase matches beginning with the string you entered. To run an exact or case-sensitive match, double quote the search string. You can use the wildcard symbol (%) in a double quoted string.

Selection Mode Single ▼

Edit View Delete Actions Add Datafile ▼ Go

Select	Name ▲	Available Space Used (%)	Allocated Space Used (%)	Auto Extend	Allocated Size (GB)	Space Used (GB)	Allocated Free Space (GB)	Status	Datafiles	Type	Extent Management	Segment Management
◉	BI_2013	0.00	0.05	YES	2.000	0.001	1.999	✓	1	PERMANENT	LOCAL	AUTO
◯	BI_2014	0.00	0.05	YES	2.000	0.001	1.999	✓	1	PERMANENT	LOCAL	AUTO
◯	BI_2015	0.00	0.05	YES	2.000	0.001	1.999	✓	1	PERMANENT	LOCAL	AUTO
◯	BI_2016	0.00	0.05	YES	2.000	0.001	1.999	✓	1	PERMANENT	LOCAL	AUTO
◯	BI_DATA	98.24	98.24	NO	60.000	58.945	1.055	✓	2	PERMANENT	LOCAL	AUTO
◯	SYSAUX	3.98	90.57	YES	1.406	1.274	0.133	✓	1	PERMANENT	LOCAL	AUTO
◯	SYSTEM	2.09	98.00	YES	0.684	0.670	0.014	✓	1	PERMANENT	LOCAL	MANUAL
◯	TEMP	0.03	0.03	NO	19.531	0.006	19.525	✓	1	TEMPORARY	LOCAL	MANUAL
◯	UNDOTBS1	0.01	0.02	YES	20.000	0.004	19.996	✓	1	UNDO	LOCAL	MANUAL
◯	USERS	0.00	27.50	YES	0.005	0.001	0.004	✓	1	PERMANENT	LOCAL	AUTO

Create

Figure 11-6. *EM tablespaces*

Enterprise Manager can monitor your databases and, if it spots something wrong, it can page or e-mail the database administrator to let them know there is an issue that needs their attention. If desired, the DBA can create a fix-up job so that the next time EM spots the issue, it can automatically take corrective action.

One of the downsides to Enterprise Manager is that it makes it too easy to violate your license agreements. For example, if you are managing a database with EM and you go to the Performance home page, you can get a nice-looking chart showing the current performance of the Oracle instance. An example is shown in Figure 11-7.

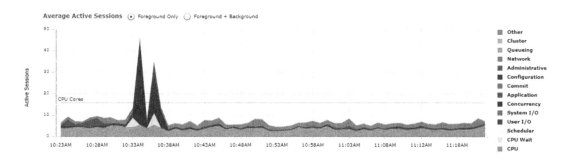

Figure 11-7. *EM Performance page*

Nowhere on this screen does it tell you that to access the page, you need to be licensed for the optional Diagnostics Pack. If you are on the Performance home page, you can go to Setup ➤ Management Packs ➤ Packs for this Page and determine which optional packs you need to license to use that page. You can see in Figure 11-8 that this page requires the Diagnostics Pack to be licensed.

Figure 11-8. *Management Packs for this Page screen*

However, if you are not licensed for this optional product, by now it is too late. Once you hit the page, Oracle will write an entry to a database table indicating that you have used this optional product. If you are audited by Oracle, they will discover you have used a product the organization has not paid for.

To stop unintended pack usage, go to Setup ➤ Management Packs ➤ Management Pack Access. On that page, uncheck the boxes for the products you are not licensed to use. It would be better if EM asked before using one of these pages to validate you are licensed for the product, but it does not do so.

Showing the SQL

Enterprise Manager is an excellent product, especially for newer database administrators that need to point and click their way to completing administration tasks. Like most administration tools, the interface removes the intricate details from you. The tools asks you a few questions, and with a click of the button, the task is complete. Unfortunately, the database administrator does not learn as much living by the point-and-click nature of any GUI tool.

In the example in Figure 11-9, the database administrator is creating a new tablespace. All that is needed is to click the OK button and the task is complete.

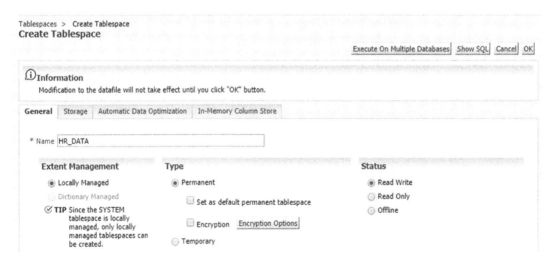

Figure 11-9. *EM Create Tablespace screen*

Instead of clicking the OK button, you can click the Show SQL button and Enterprise Manager will show you the exact SQL statement, similar to Figure 11-10.

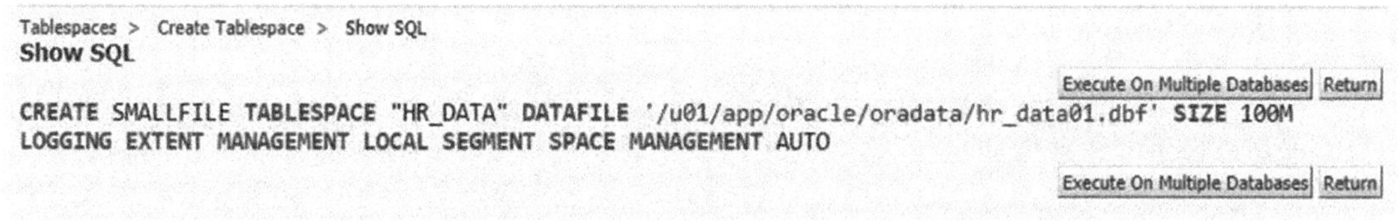

Tablespaces > Create Tablespace > Show SQL
Show SQL

Execute On Multiple Databases Return

CREATE SMALLFILE TABLESPACE "HR_DATA" DATAFILE '/u01/app/oracle/oradata/hr_data01.dbf' SIZE 100M
LOGGING EXTENT MANAGEMENT LOCAL SEGMENT SPACE MANAGEMENT AUTO

Execute On Multiple Databases Return

Figure 11-10. *EM Show SQL screen*

Many tools have the ability to show you the SQL statement they will be issuing on your behalf. The GUI tools cannot do any magic. All they are doing is asking you questions and formulating SQL statements based on how you fill in the blanks. The tool then submits the SQL statement to the database engine and waits for a reply. All of this is done behind the scenes for you.

Using this Show SQL button is a great way to learn more about the SQL statements and how they work. For example, if I click the Return button shown in Figure 11-10 and then check the box to make this a bigfile tablespace, I can then see the newly formed SQL statement and figure out what has changed.

Tip   Use the Show SQL button, or similar, to see what the tool is doing for you behind the scenes.

The next time you use Enterprise Manager, or a similar tool, spend some time determining what SQL statement the tool is issuing for you. Then experiment with changing a few options to analyze the impact to that SQL statement. In this way, you are letting the tool teach you more about SQL statements as they pertain to the task at hand.

You can create a tablespace in SQL Developer as well. To see the SQL statement that SQL Developer is sending to the database, click the DDL tab, shown in Figure 11-11.

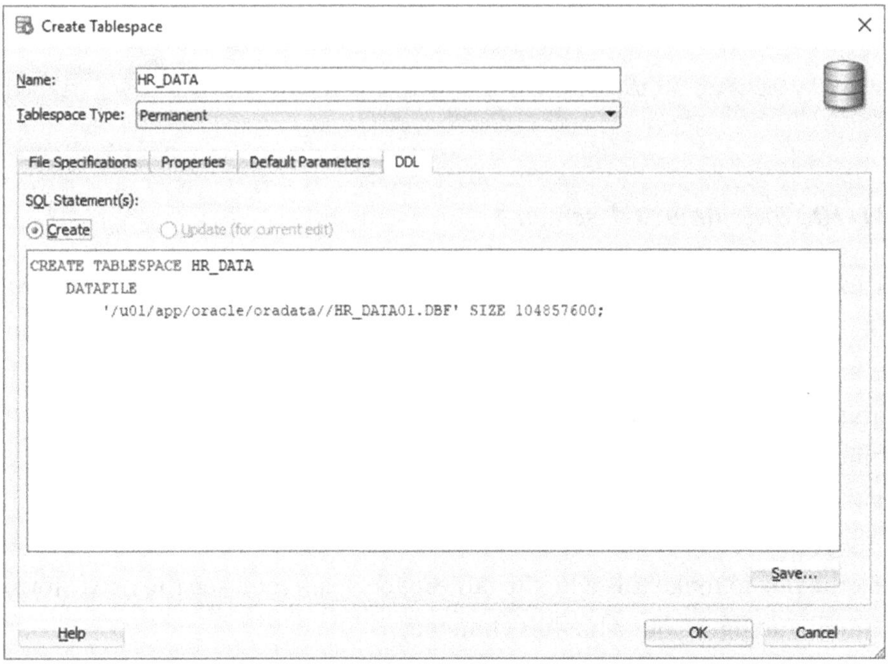

Figure 11-11. *SQL Developer DDL tab*

Experimentation with finding the exact SQL statement the tool is sending to the database is a great way to learn more about database administration.

I will also use this "show SQL" feature to help craft my SQL statement. If I'm having problems getting the syntax right and need some help, I'll walk through the tool's wizard and then see where I went wrong. I am not forced to run this statement through the tool. I can copy and paste the SQL statement into SQL*Plus or SQL Developer.

The tools will only do what the tools were designed to do. You will run into a few occasions where the tool does the majority of what you want but not the rest. You can obtain the SQL statement from the tool and then copy over to SQL Developer. From there, you can fill in the rest and be on your way. If the tool cannot complete the exact task, see if the tool can give you a start by showing you the SQL of what it can do.

Database Configuration Assistant

In Chapter 6, we used the Database Configuration Assistant (DBCA) to create our first Oracle database. The DBCA can perform other tasks as well, such as deleting a database, managing DBCA templates, and configuring an existing database, as can be seen in Figure 11-12.

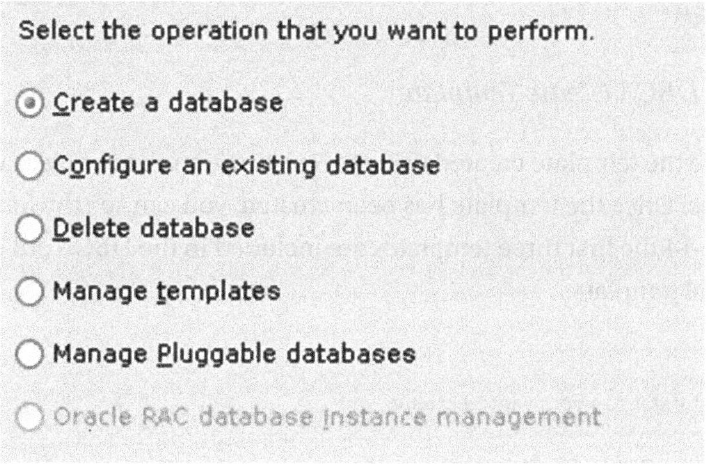

Figure 11-12. *DBCA operations*

Configuring an existing database can be used to add or remove optional components such as Oracle Text, Oracle Multimedia, Oracle Spatial, etc.

When you created an Oracle database, the DBCA walked you through a series of questions. You do have the option of saving those answers as a template so that creating future databases is not only easier, but follows your standards. If you select the option to Manage Templates, the DBCA will ask if you want to create one or delete one, similar to Figure 11-13.

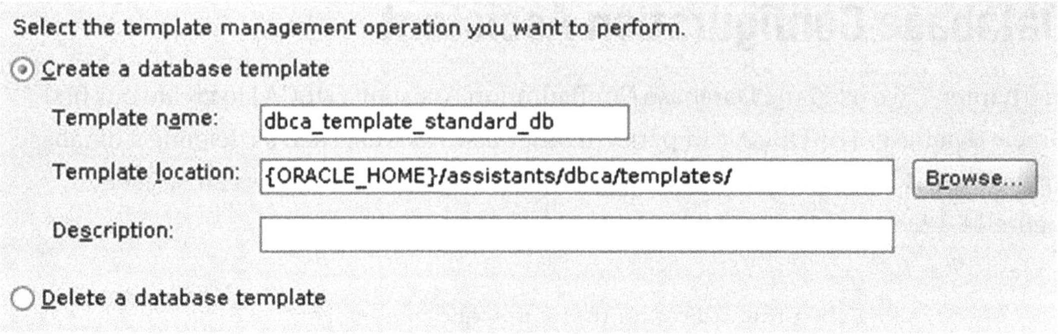

Select the template management operation you want to perform.

⦿ Create a database template

    Template name: dbca_template_standard_db

    Template location: {ORACLE_HOME}/assistants/dbca/templates/   Browse...

    Description:

○ Delete a database template

Figure 11-13. *DBCA Create Template*

You can have the template created using an existing template or by examining an existing database. Once the template has been created, you can see the template in the list. In Figure 11-14 the first three templates are included in the DBCA out of the box, but I created the final template.

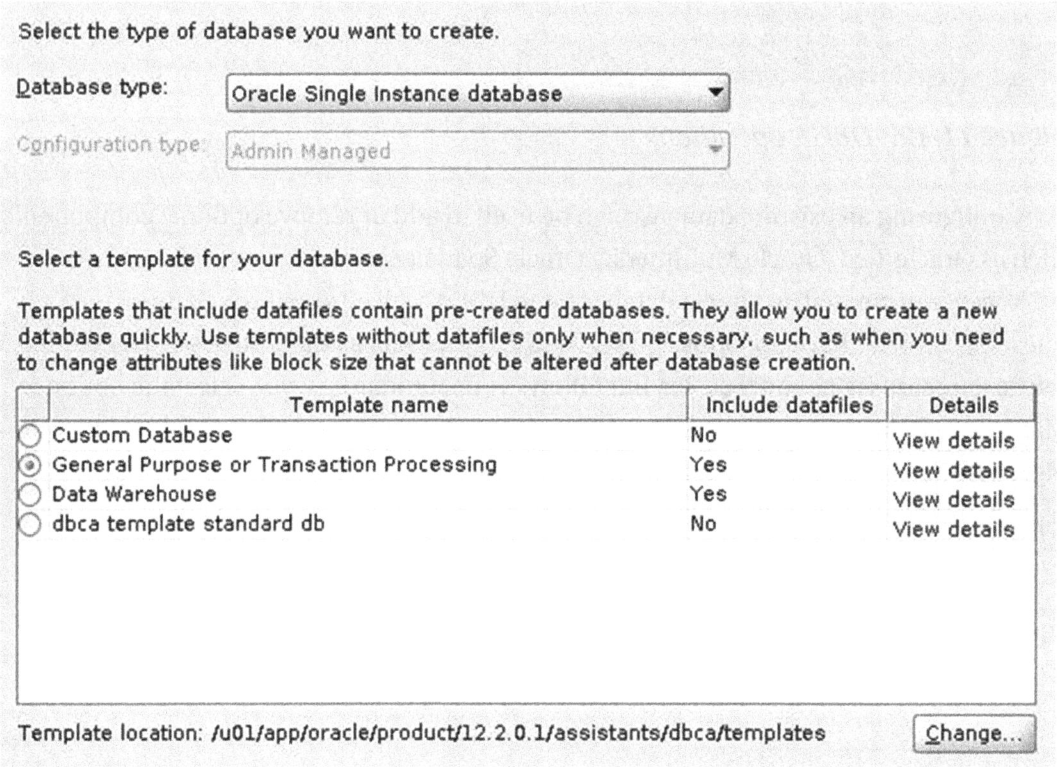

Select the type of database you want to create.

Database type: Oracle Single Instance database

Configuration type: Admin Managed

Select a template for your database.

Templates that include datafiles contain pre-created databases. They allow you to create a new database quickly. Use templates without datafiles only when necessary, such as when you need to change attributes like block size that cannot be altered after database creation.

Template name	Include datafiles	Details
○ Custom Database	No	View details
⦿ General Purpose or Transaction Processing	Yes	View details
○ Data Warehouse	Yes	View details
○ dbca template standard db	No	View details

Template location: /u01/app/oracle/product/12.2.0.1/assistants/dbca/templates   Change...

Figure 11-14. *DBCA template selection*

Network Configuration Assistant

Oracle includes a Network Configuration Assistant (NETCA) to help configure the network components of the Oracle database. The NETCA is used to configure the Listener and any LDAP authentication for the Oracle database.

In Chapter 9, we created a TNS alias by manually editing the tnsnames.ora configuration file. Most Oracle database administrators edit tnsnames.ora by hand with any text editor. The Network Configuration Assistant can also be used to modify the tnsnames.ora configuration file.

After launching the NETCA, the utility should look like Figure 11-15. Chose Local Net Service Name Configuration and click Next.

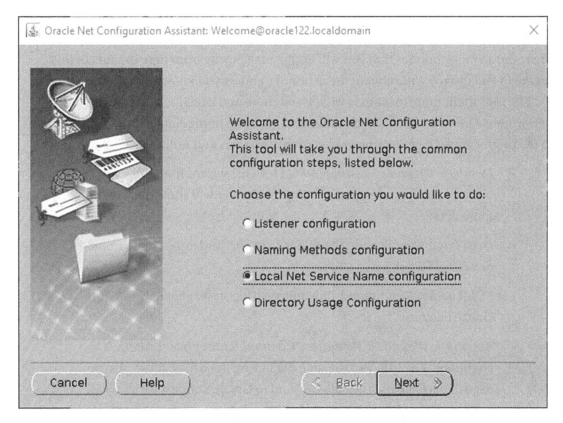

Figure 11-15. *NETCA initial screen*

On the next screen, we can add, reconfigure, delete, rename, or test a TNS alias. The wizard walks you through the rest.

As stated, most Oracle database administrators edit the configuration files by hand. On occasion, they will run into issues where the syntax is not working correctly. Using the NETCA is a great way to make sure the syntax gets formulated properly.

Other Tools and Utilities

This chapter has touched on a few of the tools and utilities that you may use as an Oracle database administrator. Most of your time will be spent with SQL*Plus and/or SQL Developer. Many database administrators use Enterprise Manager throughout the day as well. This chapter could not spend a lot of time discussing these tools in more detail due to space constraints. After all, Enterprise Manager deserves a book of its own. Like anything with Oracle, you will have to explore and learn more on your own.

The tools and utilities do not stop with what we have seen so far in this chapter. There are so many utilities that you will find yourself using from time to time. In this section, I will discuss a number of these utilities and let you know what they are used for. The important thing to learn is what is out there and what job each tool is good at performing. Once you know which tool to use, you can immediately focus your attention in the proper area. The following is a list of various tools and utilities:

- *Database Upgrade Assistant (DBUA):* A GUI wizard that walks you through the upgrade process. A future chapter will show this tool in more detail.

- *Data Pump*: A collection of utilities to export and import data from one Oracle database to another.

- *SQL*Loader*: A command-line utility to import text file data into an Oracle database.

- *Automatic Diagnostic Repository Command Interpreter (adrci)*: A command-line utility to manage diagnostic trace files. It can also be used to package up trace files to send to Oracle Support for analysis.

- *Database Verify (dbv)*: A command-line utility to check the database's data file for corruption.

- *Character Set Scanner (csscan)*: A comand-line utility to scan the database before changing its character set. This utility will help spot issues resulting from a character set conversion.

- *Listener Control (lsnrctl)*: A command-line utility to manage the Listener. We have seen a number of examples throughout this book already.

- *Oracle Error (oerr)*: A command-line utility to display the error messages for a specific error code. For example, in a Terminal window, type "oerr ora 100" to get text help for the ORA-00100 error message.

- *Oracle Password Utility (orapwd)*: A command-line utility to manage Oracle's password file, which is used for external authentication to SYSDBA and SYSOPER accounts.

- *Orion*: A command-line utility to benchmark disk performance.

- *Relink*: A command-line utility to recompile the Oracle software.

- *Recovery Manager (RMAN)*: A command-line utility to back up and restore the Oracle database. RMAN was discussed in Chapter 7.

- *tkprof*: A command-line utility that can reformat some trace files into more human-readable output.

- *TNS Ping (tnsping)*: A command-line utility to determine that the TNS alias will reach a valid Listener. This utility was discussed in Chapter 9.

- *sqlcl*: A command-line utility that is a replacement for SQL*Plus. SQL*Plus has not seen major changes in many years. The sqlcl utility is provided by the same team at Oracle that creates SQL Developer. It is billed as "SQL Developer meets SQL*Plus." This is the one Oracle product on the list that is not installed by default.

- *Swingbench*: A free utility available at www.dominicgiles.com that lets you performance test your Oracle database. This is not an Oracle product and is not installed by default.

- *HammerDB*: An open source utility that lets you performance test Oracle and other database platforms. This is not an Oracle product and is not installed by default.

Most of the tools and utilities in this list are supplied by Oracle Corporation and are present when you install the Oracle database software. There are plenty of third-party tools at your disposal as well. Some of those typically require extra fees. You and your company will have to evaluate those products to see if they are worth the extra cost.

Moving On

This chapter spent some time discussing some of the tools at the Oracle DBA's disposal. As you work with these tools, you will learn more about them and how to use them to do your work.

In the next chapter, we will move on to Oracle diagnostic files. It is important that the database administrator know how to leverage the diagnostics and trace files to learn more about what is going wrong with the Oracle database.

CHAPTER 12

Diagnostics

In previous chapters, we set up a database and started using it. In this chapter, we will leverage diagnostic and trace files to learn more about the issues that may be plaguing our Oracle database. If the Oracle instance fails to start or it crashes, the diagnostic files are a great place to start digging into the problem.

Diagnostic Destination

Today's Oracle database engine combines its diagnostic and trace files into a singular location called the Diagnostic Destination. Prior to Oracle Database 11g, the files were scattered over multiple locations, making it harder to find what you were looking for. By default, the Diagnostic Destination is a sub-directory in the Oracle Base location. If you are unsure where this is, you can use a simple SQL*Plus command, show parameter, to find out, as shown in Listing 12-1. The show parameter command can be used to see the value of any initialization parameter.

Listing 12-1. Diagnostics Destination

```
SQL> show parameter diagnostic_dest

NAME                 TYPE        VALUE
-------------------- ----------- ----------------
diagnostic_dest      string      /u01/app/oracle
```

The output above corresponds to the Oracle Base location. The diagnostics files are in a subdirectory named diag. Within /u01/app/oracle/diag (or similar location on your system), there are a number of other subdirectories, one for each component that might create diagnostic and trace files. For example, the database engine will write its trace files in the rdbms subdirectory. The Oracle Listener will write its trace files in the tnslsnr subdirectory. Listing 12-2 shows the multiple subdirectories of /u01/app/oracle/diag on our testbed.

© Brian Peasland 2019
B. Peasland, *Oracle DBA Mentor*, https://doi.org/10.1007/978-1-4842-4321-3_12

Listing 12-2. Diag Dest Contents

```
[oracle@dbamentor ~]$ cd /u01/app/oracle/diag
[oracle@dbamentor diag]$ ls -l
total 0
drwxrwxr-x. 2 oracle oinstall  6 Sep 29  2017 afdboot
drwxrwxr-x. 2 oracle oinstall  6 Sep 29  2017 apx
drwxrwxr-x. 2 oracle oinstall  6 Sep 29  2017 asm
drwxrwxr-x. 2 oracle oinstall  6 Sep 29  2017 asmtool
drwxrwxr-x. 2 oracle oinstall  6 Sep 29  2017 bdsql
drwxrwxr-x. 3 oracle oinstall 24 Jul 10 00:14 clients
drwxrwxr-x. 2 oracle oinstall  6 Sep 29  2017 crs
drwxrwxr-x. 2 oracle oinstall  6 Sep 29  2017 diagtool
drwxrwxr-x. 2 oracle oinstall  6 Sep 29  2017 dps
drwxrwxr-x. 2 oracle oinstall  6 Sep 29  2017 em
drwxrwxr-x. 2 oracle oinstall  6 Sep 29  2017 gsm
drwxrwxr-x. 2 oracle oinstall  6 Sep 29  2017 ios
drwxrwxr-x. 2 oracle oinstall  6 Sep 29  2017 lsnrctl
drwxrwxr-x. 2 oracle oinstall  6 Sep 29  2017 netcman
drwxrwxr-x. 2 oracle oinstall  6 Sep 29  2017 ofm
drwxrwxr-x. 2 oracle oinstall  6 Sep 29  2017 plsql
drwxrwxr-x. 2 oracle oinstall  6 Sep 29  2017 plsqlapp
drwxrwxr-x. 3 oracle oinstall 17 Sep 29  2017 rdbms
drwxrwxr-x. 4 oracle oinstall 38 Jul 30 10:30 tnslsnr
```

As you work with Oracle during your career, you will find yourself visiting many of these subdirectories, and others will never need your attention. If you use Oracle's Automated Storage Manager (ASM), then you may need to look into the asm subdirectory on occasion. If you never use ASM, then you will never need this component's trace files and the directory will likely be empty. Other common ones you may visit are

- *crs*: If you have installed Oracle's Grid Infrastructure (GI), any GI trace files will be written here. In the old days, GI used to be known by the name Cluster Ready Services (CRS), hence the directory name.

- *em*: If you have Enterprise Manager (EM) installed and running on this system, you can find its files here.

- *rdbms*: As stated earlier, this directory is where an Oracle database engine writes its diagnostic trace files.

- *tnslsnr*: The Oracle Listener will write its files here.

The other subdirectories of /u01/app/oracle/diag are rarely used.

Because a server can support multiple Oracle databases, each Oracle instance will write trace files into a directory path similar to /u01/app/oracle/diag/rdbms/*db_name*/*instance_name*.

For our testbed, the Oracle instance name is the same as the database name. The only time the instance differs from the database name is when running Oracle Real Application Clusters (RAC). Since our database does not use RAC, the directory path to our database's diagnostic and trace files is /u01/app/oracle/diag/rdbms/orcl/orcl.

The Oracle Listener will write its diagnostic and trace files into a path similar to /u01/app/oracle/diag/tnslsnr/*hostname*/listener.

We will see more of these files as we progress through this chapter.

Alert Log

There is a special file that you will rapidly become familiar with as you administer Oracle databases, and that is the Alert Log. It is likely that you have already had some exposure to this file, even early in your career. On our testbed, the Alert Log is stored in /u01/app/oracle/diag/rdbms/orcl/orcl/trace. The instructions in Chapter 6 created a database named "orcl". If you used a different name, then the directory path will differ slightly.

The Alert Log is always named with the convention of alert_*instance*.log, using the instance name. As said before, unless you are running Oracle RAC, the instance name is the same as the database name. Oracle also creates an XML-based Alert Log in /u01/app/oracle/diag/rdbms/orcl/orcl/alert where each entry in the log file is wrapped in XML markup tags. I find the XML version of the log file hard to read, but this file is very useful for tools that parse the log file. If you work with Oracle support, they may ask you to send the XML-based Alert Log so they can parse it with their tools. Otherwise, I never look at the XML-based Alert Log.

Listing 12-3 shows the text-based Alert Log in our testbed.

Listing 12-3. Alert Log Location

```
[oracle@dbamentor ~]$ cd /u01/app/oracle/diag/rdbms/orcl/orcl/trace/
[oracle@dbamentor trace]$ ls -l alert*
-rw-r-----. 1 oracle oinstall 466338 Jul 30 14:09 alert_orcl.log
```

The Alert Log should be one of the first places the Oracle DBA looks to troubleshoot problems with the Oracle database. Oracle will not write information here for errors or issues with each and every session. Doing so would be too resource intensive. Rather, the Alert Log is for issues affecting the Oracle database and its instance, as a whole. We will see Oracle instance startup and shutdown messages in the Alert Log.

When an Oracle instance starts up, it writes a great deal of informational messages into the Alert Log. In Listing 12-4, we can see some of the information in the Alert Log. Much of the information has also been removed for brevity. See if you can spot the following from what is included:

- Date and time the instance was started

- Number of cores on the database server

- Oracle database version

- Oracle home directory

- Database server name and its OS version

- Location of the parameter file (spfile)

- Non-default parameters in use

- Date and time the instance was open for business

Listing 12-4. Alert Log Instance Startup

```
2018-07-30T15:21:00.796201-05:00
Starting ORACLE instance (normal) (OS id: 23853)
2018-07-30T15:21:00.801613-05:00
*********************************************************************
LICENSE_MAX_SESSION = 0
LICENSE_SESSIONS_WARNING = 0
Initial number of CPU is 1
Number of processor cores in the system is 1
```

Number of processor sockets in the system is 1

Using LOG_ARCHIVE_DEST_1 parameter default value as /u01/app/oracle/
product/12.2.0.1/dbs/arch

Autotune of undo retention is turned on.

IMODE=BR

ILAT =51

LICENSE_MAX_USERS = 0

SYS auditing is enabled

NOTE: remote asm mode is local (mode 0x1; from cluster type)

NOTE: Using default ASM root directory ASM

NOTE: Cluster configuration type = NONE [2]

Oracle Database 12c Enterprise Edition Release 12.2.0.1.0 - 64bit
Production.

ORACLE_HOME: /u01/app/oracle/product/12.2.0.1

System name: Linux

Node name: dbamentor.localdomain

Release: 4.1.12-103.6.1.el7uek.x86_64

Version: #2 SMP Wed Sep 20 12:15:11 PDT 2017

Machine: x86_64

Using parameter settings in server-side spfile /u01/app/oracle/
product/12.2.0.1/dbs/spfileorc

l.ora

System parameters with non-default values:

```
  processes               = 300
  nls_language            = "AMERICAN"
  nls_territory           = "AMERICA"
  sga_target              = 4G
  control_files           = "/u01/app/oracle/oradata/orcl/control01.ctl"
  control_files           = "/u01/app/oracle/oradata/orcl/control02.ctl"
  db_block_size           = 8192
  compatible              = "12.2.0"
  undo_tablespace         = "UNDOTBS1"
  remote_login_passwordfile= "EXCLUSIVE"
  dispatchers             = "(PROTOCOL=TCP) (SERVICE=orclXDB)"
  audit_file_dest         = "/u01/app/oracle/admin/orcl/adump"
```

```
    audit_trail                = "DB"
    db_name                    = "orcl"
    open_cursors               = 300
    pga_aggregate_target       = 773M
    diagnostic_dest            = "/u01/app/oracle"
ALTER DATABASE    MOUNT
2018-07-30T15:21:04.148241-05:00
Using default pga_aggregate_limit of 2048 MB
2018-07-30T15:21:05.924180-05:00
Network throttle feature is disabled as mount time
2018-07-30T15:21:05.930822-05:00
Successful mount of redo thread 1, with mount id 1510662109
2018-07-30T15:21:05.931015-05:00
Database mounted in Exclusive Mode
Lost write protection disabled
Using STANDBY_ARCHIVE_DEST parameter default value as /u01/app/oracle/
product/12.2.0.1/dbs/ar
ch
Completed: ALTER DATABASE    MOUNT
2018-07-30T15:21:05.987184-05:00
ALTER DATABASE OPEN
2018-07-30T15:21:05.990548-05:00
```

In the next example, shown in Listing 12-5, I have simulated the loss of a control file. When the instance is started, an error is raised.

Listing 12-5. Failed Startup

```
SQL> startup
ORACLE instance started.

Total System Global Area 4294967296 bytes
Fixed Size                   8628936 bytes
Variable Size              939525432 bytes
Database Buffers          3338665984 bytes
Redo Buffers                 8146944 bytes
ORA-00205: error in identifying control file, check alert log for more info
```

As the error message says, we should check the Alert Log. Toward the end of the Alert Log, we can see errors similar to Listing 12-6.

Listing 12-6. Alert Log Missing Control File

```
2018-07-30T15:33:25.549374-05:00
Errors in file /u01/app/oracle/diag/rdbms/orcl/orcl/trace/orcl_m000_25234.trc:
ORA-00202: control file: '/u01/app/oracle/oradata/orcl/control02.ctl'
ORA-27037: unable to obtain file status
Linux-x86_64 Error: 2: No such file or directory
```

The error messages are telling us exactly which file is missing, control02.ctl, and that there is no such file or directory. Fixing this problem is easy. Control files are multiplexed, meaning any other control file is an exact duplicate. If we have control01.ctl, we can simply copy it as our missing file and restart the instance. Listing 12-7 shows how easy it was to resolve the issue.

Listing 12-7. Fixing Our Control File

```
SQL> !ls -l
total 7867508
-rw-r-----. 1 oracle oinstall 5368717312 Jul 30 15:28 apps_ts01.dbf
-rw-r-----. 1 oracle oinstall   10600448 Jul 30 15:28 control01.ctl
-rw-r-----. 1 oracle oinstall  209715712 Jul 30 15:21 redo01.log
-rw-r-----. 1 oracle oinstall  209715712 Jul 30 15:21 redo02.log
-rw-r-----. 1 oracle oinstall  209715712 Jul 30 15:28 redo03.log
-rw-r-----. 1 oracle oinstall  807411712 Jul 30 15:28 sysaux01.dbf
-rw-r-----. 1 oracle oinstall  734011392 Jul 30 15:28 system01.dbf
-rw-r-----. 1 oracle oinstall   20979712 Jul 30 00:51 temp01.dbf
-rw-r-----. 1 oracle oinstall  492838912 Jul 30 15:28 undotbs01.dbf
-rw-r-----. 1 oracle oinstall    5251072 Jul 30 15:28 users01.dbf

SQL> !cp control01.ctl control02.ctl

SQL> shutdown abort
ORACLE instance shut down.
SQL> startup
ORACLE instance started.
```

```
Total System Global Area 4294967296 bytes
Fixed Size                  8628936 bytes
Variable Size             939525432 bytes
Database Buffers         3338665984 bytes
Redo Buffers                8146944 bytes
Database mounted.
Database opened.
```

The directory is obviously missing that control file, so I simply copied it from the other control file. I then terminated the instance that was partially up and running and started it back up with success.

The Alert Log also contains useful information when the instance is shut down, although not the same volume of information. See if you can spot the following in the excerpt of the log seen in Listing 12-8:

- Date and time the shutdown was started

- Date and time the shutdown was completed

Listing 12-8. Alert Log Instance Shutdown

```
2018-07-30T15:28:43.622558-05:00
Shutting down instance (immediate) (OS id: 24764)
2018-07-30T15:28:45.143579-05:00
Stopping background process SMCO
2018-07-30T15:28:46.160809-05:00
Shutting down instance: further logons disabled
2018-07-30T15:28:46.168713-05:00
Stopping background process CJQ0
License high water mark = 1
2018-07-30T15:28:48.203074-05:00
Dispatchers and shared servers shutdown
ALTER DATABASE CLOSE NORMAL
Stopping Emon pool
Stopping Emon pool
2018-07-30T15:28:48.260284-05:00
Shutting down archive processes
2018-07-30T15:28:49.260600-05:00
```

```
Archiving is disabled
2018-07-30T15:28:49.262589-05:00
Thread 1 closed at log sequence 42
Successful close of redo thread 1
2018-07-30T15:28:49.320837-05:00
Completed: ALTER DATABASE CLOSE NORMAL
ALTER DATABASE DISMOUNT
Shutting down archive processes
Archiving is disabled
Completed: ALTER DATABASE DISMOUNT
2018-07-30T15:28:50.329124-05:00
ARCH: Archival disabled due to shutdown: 1089
Shutting down archive processes
Archiving is disabled
2018-07-30T15:28:59.607117-05:00
Instance shutdown complete (OS id: 24764)
```

If the instance ever crashes, the best place to find out why is in the Alert Log. The first thing the DBA should do is to start the instance and get it up and running as quickly as possible to restore access to the data. The second thing the DBA should do is figure out why the instance crashed. In the Alert Log entries shown in Listing 12-9, we can see that the instance was critical. A background process named SMON died unexpectedly. Since SMON must be up and running, another process, PMON, detected the condition and terminated the Oracle instance.

Listing 12-9. Alert Log Instance Crash

```
2018-07-30T15:40:21.276295-05:00
Instance Critical Process (pid: 22, ospid: 26021, SMON) died unexpectedly
PMON (ospid: 25978): terminating the instance due to error 474
2018-07-30T15:40:21.323557-05:00
System state dump requested by (instance=1, osid=25978 (PMON)),
summary=[abnormal instance termination].
System State dumped to trace file /u01/app/oracle/diag/rdbms/orcl/orcl/
trace/orcl_diag_25999_20180730154021.trc
2018-07-30T15:40:21.790622-05:00
```

```
Dumping diagnostic data in directory=[cdmp_20180730154021], requested by
(instance=1, osid=25978 (PMON)), summary=[abnormal instance termination].
2018-07-30T15:40:22.882068-05:00
Instance terminated by PMON, pid = 25978
```

We know what happened. A required background process died. We still do not know why SMON died. Later in this chapter, we will see the trace files generated by the various background processes.

On some occasions, it is helpful to be able to write a custom message to the Alert Log. Since the instance is writing to the file, you do not want to open it in a text editor to add text. It is possible to use OS commands to append to the file, similar to the following:

```
cat "text to alert log" >> alert_orcl.log
```

By doing so, you run the risk of trying to write to the file at the same time as the instance is writing to the file. A better way would be to run a command in the instance to write the message. The example in Listing 12-10 uses the DBMS_SYSTEM package to write an entry to the Alert Log. The relevant portion of the Alert Log is then shown.

Listing 12-10. Writing to the Alert Log

```
SQL> exec dbms_system.ksdwrt(2,'Shutting down for db maintenance - BP');

PL/SQL procedure successfully completed.

SQL> !tail -2 alert_orcl.log
2018-07-30T15:47:18.866067-05:00
Shutting down for db maintenance - BP
```

In the example above, I wrote a custom message indicating that I am taking down the instance for database maintenance. I included my initials at the end of the message so that some other database administrator on the team would know who performed the action.

I have grown accustomed to using OS utilities to see the contents of the Alert Log no different than viewing any text file. In Oracle 11g, a new fixed view was introduced that let you query the contents of the Alert Log with any SQL statement. In Listing 12-11, we can see how to find any occurrences of the ALTER command in the Alert Log.

Listing 12-11. Querying the Alert Log

```
SQL> select originating_timestamp,message_text
  2  from x$dbgalertext
  3  where upper(message_text) like '%ALTER%'
  4  order by originating_timestamp;

ORIGINATING_TIMESTAMP              MESSAGE_TEXT
--------------------------------   ------------------------------------------
29-SEP-17 10.51.16.369 AM -05:00   ALTER DATABASE DEFAULT TEMPORARY
                                   TABLESPACE TEMP
29-SEP-17 11.04.28.706 AM -05:00   ALTER DATABASE CLOSE NORMAL
29-SEP-17 11.04.30.011 AM -05:00   Completed: ALTER DATABASE CLOSE NORMAL
29-SEP-17 11.04.30.012 AM -05:00   ALTER DATABASE DISMOUNT
29-SEP-17 11.04.30.018 AM -05:00   Completed: ALTER DATABASE DISMOUNT
29-SEP-17 11.04.46.162 AM -05:00   ALTER DATABASE MOUNT
29-SEP-17 11.04.50.247 AM -05:00   Completed: ALTER DATABASE MOUNT
29-SEP-17 11.04.50.264 AM -05:00   ALTER DATABASE OPEN
29-SEP-17 11.04.50.950 AM -05:00   Completed: ALTER DATABASE OPEN
```

Now that we can leverage the power of SQL, we can perform filtering very easily. For example, if we know when an issue occurred, we can search for any message that occurred in that timeframe.

Listener Log

Another useful trace file is the Listener Log. If the Listener is experiencing any problems, it will write entries to its log file. Listing 12-12 shows the location of the Listener Log. There should only be one file in this directory, the Listener Log.

Listing 12-12. Listener Log Location

```
[oracle@dbamentor ~]$ cd /u01/app/oracle/diag/tnslsnr/dbamentor/listener/
trace/
[oracle@dbamentor trace]$ ls -l
total 12
-rw-r-----. 1 oracle oinstall 11514 Jul 30 16:02 listener.log
```

Looking at the Listener Log, it is a little more difficult to see where it starts. We have to look for the line that says "Started with pid." After that message is info on the host, port, and network protocol the Listener is working with. In the last line, we can see that the instance has registered the service "orcl" with the Listener. Listing 12-13 shows the portion of the Listener Log where it was started and the service registered with the Listener.

Listing 12-13. Listener Startup

```
[oracle@dbamentor trace]$ cat listener.log
2018-07-30T16:15:52.354897-05:00
Log messages written to /u01/app/oracle/diag/tnslsnr/dbamentor/listener/
alert/log.xml
Trace information written to /u01/app/oracle/diag/tnslsnr/dbamentor/
listener/trace/ora_29203_140321849041280.trc

Started with pid=29203
Listening on: (DESCRIPTION=(ADDRESS=(PROTOCOL=tcp)(HOST=localhost)
(PORT=1521)))
30-JUL-2018 16:16:46 * (ADDRESS=(PROTOCOL=tcp)(HOST=::1)(PORT=33928)) *
service_register * orcl * 12542
```

When the Listener is shut down, the log file will contain a small bit of information indicating such, as shown in Listing 12-14.

Listing 12-14. Listener Shutdown

```
2018-07-30T16:19:38.049565-05:00
No longer listening on: (DESCRIPTION=(ADDRESS=(PROTOCOL=tcp)
(HOST=localhost)(PORT=1521)))
```

Unfortunately, the Listener's log file doesn't say explicitly that someone started or stopped the Listener. In Listing 12-14, all we see is that the Listener is no longer listening on that host and port.

Typically we would not use the Listener Log to monitor startup and shutdown of the Listener. The previous examples were used to illustrate how to find information in the Listener's log file. If you want true monitoring of the Listener, use a product like Enterprise Manager.

Background Process Trace Files

The Oracle database engine is composed of multiple processes running in the background. Each has a different job to do for Oracle to be operational. You may have already dealt with some of these processes like PMON, SMON, and CKPT. Chapter 21 will provide more information on these processes if you want to know more.

Each of these processes can write to their own trace file. The background process trace files are located in the same directory as the Alert Log. The files are typically named *instance_process_pid*.trc, which is the instance name, followed by the process name, followed by the operating system's process identifier. For example, I have a trace file named orcl_pmon_25978.trc. This file is for my orcl instance's PMON process when it was running with OS pid 25978.

Many times, you will find these files when no problem exists. The simple act of the process starting up will generate one of these trace files. Normally, the contents are just informational. It is when you are having a problem with a specific background process that you will want to examine its trace file. Remember earlier in this chapter the Alert Log showed the instance terminated because SMON had died. PMON detected the condition and terminated the instance. The PMON trace file shows this event, as we can see in Listing 12-15.

Listing 12-15. PMON Trace File

```
[oracle@dbamentor trace]$ cat orcl_pmon_25978.trc
Trace file /u01/app/oracle/diag/rdbms/orcl/orcl/trace/orcl_pmon_25978.trc
Oracle Database 12c Enterprise Edition Release 12.2.0.1.0 - 64bit
Production
Build label:    RDBMS_12.2.0.1.0_LINUX.X64_170125
ORACLE_HOME:    /u01/app/oracle/product/12.2.0.1
System name: Linux
Node name:    dbamentor.localdomain
Release:      4.1.12-103.6.1.el7uek.x86_64
Version:      #2 SMP Wed Sep 20 12:15:11 PDT 2017
Machine:      x86_64
Instance name: orcl
Redo thread mounted by this instance: 1
Oracle process number: 2
Unix process pid: 25978, image: oracle@dbamentor.localdomain (PMON)
```

```
*** 2018-07-30T15:40:21.285277-05:00
*** SESSION ID:(2.57305) 2018-07-30T15:40:21.285291-05:00
*** CLIENT ID:() 2018-07-30T15:40:21.285294-05:00
*** SERVICE NAME:(SYS$BACKGROUND) 2018-07-30T15:40:21.285297-05:00
*** MODULE NAME:() 2018-07-30T15:40:21.285300-05:00
*** ACTION NAME:() 2018-07-30T15:40:21.285302-05:00
*** CLIENT DRIVER:() 2018-07-30T15:40:21.285304-05:00

Instance Critical Process (pid: 22, ospid: 26021, SMON) died unexpectedly
Background process SMON found dead
...
*** 2018-07-30T15:40:21.301322-05:00
PMON (ospid: 25978): terminating the instance due to error 474
ksuitm: waiting up to [5] seconds before killing DIAG(25999)
```

The first part of the trace file is just informational and was generated when the process started. At the end of Listing 12-15, we can see that PMON knows that SMON died unexpectedly. After a long stack trace that mostly looks like gibberish, omitted for brevity, we can see that PMON terminated the instance.

User Trace Files

Any end user's database session can create a trace file as well. A session's trace file is very useful because it may contain a record of each and every SQL statement issued to the database for the duration of the trace. Sometimes an end user will report a problem and neither the end user nor the database administrator knows what SQL statement is causing problems. The DBA can start a trace in the user's session and try to figure out what the user is executing against the database.

By default, sessions do not generate a trace file. The simplest way to start a trace is to modify the session's SQL_TRACE parameter and set it to a value of TRUE, shown in Listing 12-16.

Listing 12-16. Starting SQL Trace

```
SQL> alter session set sql_trace=true;

Session altered.

SQL> select 'this is my trace',sysdate from dual;

'THISISMYTRACE'   SYSDATE
---------------- ---------
this is my trace 31-JUL-18

SQL> alter session set sql_trace=false;

Session altered.

SQL> select spid as os_pid from v$process
  2  where addr in (select paddr from v$session
  3                 where sid=sys_context('USERENV','SID'));

OS_PID
------------------------
5765
```

In the preceding example, the user started SQL Trace, issued a SQL statement to the database, then ended the trace. At the end, the user used V$SESSION and V$PROCESS to learn the session's OS process identifier. All user trace filenames have the format *instance*_ora_*pid*.trc, where the ora is constant. Since we know the instance is named ORCL and we now know the OS pid, we know to look for a file named orcl_ora_5765.trc in our RDBMS trace directory, which also contains the Alert Log.

If we open the trace file with a text editor, we can see some introductory information, and if we scroll down, we can find the SQL statement that was issued to the database. The trace file generated in Listing 12-16 is shown in Listing 12-17.

Listing 12-17. Raw Trace File Contents

```
=====================
PARSING IN CURSOR #139855599918944 len=43 dep=0 uid=0 oct=3 lid=0
tim=8201176343
6 hv=2979390255 ad='70aa7700' sqlid='az5q2d6stbstg'
select 'this is my trace',sysdate from dual
```

```
END OF STMT
PARSE
#139855599918944:c=0,e=567,p=0,cr=0,cu=0,mis=1,r=0,dep=0,og=1,plh=13887349
53,tim=82011763436
EXEC #139855599918944:c=520,e=2029,p=0,cr=0,cu=0,mis=0,r=0,dep=0,og=1,
plh=1388734953,tim=82011765502
FETCH #139855599918944:c=0,e=7,p=0,cr=0,cu=0,mis=0,r=1,dep=0,og=1,
plh=1388734953,tim=82011765583
STAT #139855599918944 id=1 cnt=1 pid=0 pos=1 obj=0 op='FAST DUAL
(cr=0 pr=0 pw=0 str=1 time=2 us cost=2 size=0 card=1)'
FETCH #139855599918944:c=0,e=1,p=0,cr=0,cu=0,mis=0,r=0,dep=0,og=0,
plh=1388734953,tim=82011766311

*** 2018-07-31T09:16:25.618519-05:00
CLOSE #139855599918944:c=0,e=7,dep=0,type=0,tim=82020618587
=====================
```

The output is a bit of a nightmare to read, but we can clearly make out the SQL statement. If we look at the lines below the SQL statement, we can see the Parse phase, the Execution phase, and the Fetch phase. SQL statements are typically parsed to ensure that they are syntactically correct and that that user has permissions on the statement's objects. The statement is then executed. All SQL statements undergo these three phases. If the SQL statement returns rows, the results are the fetched and returned to the user.

A trained Oracle DBA might be able to make sense of what follows. For example, the c= value tells us how much time that phase spent processing on the CPU. The e= value tells us how much elapsed time was spent on that phase.

Thankfully, we do not have to read this raw trace file. Introduced in Chapter 11, Oracle provides a nice utility called tkprof that will format the trace file into something more human readable. We can call the tkprof utility by passing it two parameters, the trace file and the output file. Listing 12-18 shows how to use the tkprof utility for our raw trace file.

Listing 12-18. tkprof Execution

```
[oracle@dbamentor trace]$ tkprof orcl_ora_5765.trc tkprof.out

TKPROF: Release 12.2.0.1.0 - Development on Tue Jul 31 09:40:13 2018

Copyright (c) 1982, 2017, Oracle and/or its affiliates. All rights reserved.
```

In the example above, the output will be placed in a file named tkprof.out. If we look at the file's contents, we can see the information presented in a form that is much easier to read, as shown in Listing 12-19.

Listing 12-19. tkprof Output

```
SQL ID: az5q2d6stbstg Plan Hash: 1388734953

select 'this is my trace',sysdate
from
 dual
```

call	count	cpu	elapsed	disk	query	current	rows
Parse	1	0.00	0.00	0	0	0	0
Execute	1	0.00	0.00	0	0	0	0
Fetch	2	0.00	0.00	0	0	0	1
total	4	0.00	0.00	0	0	0	1

From the output above, we can easily see the three phases of the SQL statement.

The tkprof utility has many options to help format the trace file to suit your specific needs. Just type "tkprof" with no additional parameters and the utility will display some helpful information. One of my favorite ways to use tkprof is to sort the SQL statements in order of the elapsed run time so that the longest-running SQL statement is last in the output. If a user is experiencing slowness, it is often the longest-running SQL statement causing them the most pain.

It is very common for the end user to be unable to issue the ALTER SESSION command to start the SQL Trace. End users typically access the database through some application that does not let them enter any SQL statement they want. Oracle includes the ability for the DBA to start a trace in that user's session. The DBA just needs to determine the session's identifier and serial number. In the example in Listing 12-20, the DBA has queried V$SESSION to learn those values. Once known, the DBA calls the DBMS_MONITOR package to start a trace in that session. After a period of time, the DBA ends the trace.

Listing 12-20. SQL Trace in Another Session

```
SQL> select sid,serial# from v$session
  2  where username='PEASLAND';

       SID    SERIAL#
---------- ----------
        61      21753

SQL> exec dbms_monitor.session_trace_enable(session_id=>61,serial_num=>21753);

PL/SQL procedure successfully completed.

SQL> exec dbms_monitor.session_trace_disable(session_id=>61,serial_num=>21753);

PL/SQL procedure successfully completed.
```

The resulting trace file is no different than if the user issued the ALTER SESSION command on their own.

This section has introduced SQL Trace and the tkprof utility. The ability to trace a user's actions and the SQL statements they execute is a valuable tool for the database administrator. Most of the time, a SQL Trace is used when trying to resolve performance problems. Performance tuning is a large topic and is not going to be discussed in this book. If you want to learn more about performance tuning, the Oracle documentation is a great place to start, as we will discuss in the next chapter.

SQL Trace files are also useful when trying to determine which SQL statement is resulting in an error when you do not have access to the application code. For example, the application is telling the user that an ORA-00942 error has been reached. The database administrator can start a trace in their session and then search the resulting trace file for 942 to see which SQL statement is getting this error.

ADRCI

It used to be, prior to Oracle 11*g*, that the database administrator needed to manage all the trace files. Oracle does not remove the files automatically, so the DBA needed a regularly scheduled job to remove files older than a specific period of time. The other problem with these trace files was that if you needed to enlist the help of Oracle Support to resolve an issue, they often requested a trace file or two and the DBA had a challenging time identifying the files that Support needed. The DBA then sent all trace files to Oracle Support. Oracle now includes the Automatic Diagnostic Repository Command Interpreter (adrci), which is a command-line utility to manage these trace files.

Let's start by seeing how adrci can help package up the trace files Oracle Support may need to resolve an issue. In Listing 12-21, we start by asking adrci to give us a list of problems it has tracked in our Oracle database.

Listing 12-21. adrci Problems

```
adrci> show problem

ADR Home = /u01/app/oracle/diag/rdbms/orcl/orcl:
*********************************************************************
PROBLEM_ID    PROBLEM_KEY    LAST_INCIDENT    LASTINC_TIME
------------  -----------    -------------    ---------------------------------
3             ORA 445        222031           2016-12-10 04:30:31.338000 -06:00
```

Only one problem is logged here. Let's create a package to send to Oracle Support, shown in Listing 12-22.

Listing 12-22. adrci Creating Package

```
adrci> set home diag/rdbms/mspstg/mspstg
adrci> ips create package problem 3 correlate all
Created package 1 based on problem id 3, correlation level all
adrci> ips generate  package 1 in "/home/oracle"
Generated package 1 in file /home/oracle/IPSPKG_20180731101513_COM_1.zip,
mode complete
```

The adrci utility has created a zip file for us to upload to Oracle Support. Do not worry if all of the adrci commands sound confusing. Oracle Support will provide all the instructions you will need should they want you to send them trace files this way.

Prior to adrci, the database administrator had to take matters into their own hands in managing the trace files. Leave them on the server for too long and the storage will fill up. On Unix/Linux systems, database administrators often used commands in crontab to schedule the removal of trace files older than a certain age. The problem was that the DBA needed to remove trace files from multiple subdirectories. If a new version of Oracle was released, the routine to purge old files needed to be updated.

The adrci can remove trace files and handle any changes a future version might throw at you. The command to remove the trace files is very simple, as shown in Listing 12-23.

Listing 12-23. ADRCI Purge Trace Files

```
adrci> purge -age 10080 -type trace
```

The command above will remove any files older than 10,080 minutes, or 7 days. All the DBA needs to do is put this in a script and schedule it on the database server.

Moving On

This chapter has shown us where the various diagnostic and trace files reside on the database server. We have seen a few examples of how to use the Alert Log and other trace files to help with problem resolution. This chapter also has shown us how to start a SQL Trace in order for the DBA to get information on the SQL statements the end user issues to the database. Trace files can be difficult to read, but they are necessary to decipher to obtain diagnostic data to help resolve issues. At the very least, they will be sent to Oracle support for an analyst to read.

The next chapter will focus on a subject that too many Oracle professionals seem to despise, the Oracle documentation. Do not skip the next chapter as it contains important information that you will need to grow your Oracle DBA career. The reason many people do not like the documentation is because it is so voluminous that it becomes difficult to find what you are looking for. The next chapter will sort this out for you and help you learn to find what you need to know.

CHAPTER 13

Oracle Documentation

In the first eight chapters, we discussed some introductory material and set up our testbed. In Chapters 9–12 we then turned to the topic of using our Oracle database, where we spent time connecting to Oracle, running test cases, and examining various tools we will use in our administration duties.

This chapter shifts focus to learning more about Oracle. My primary reason for writing this book was to teach you how to become a self-sufficient DBA. Technology books are a great resource and I have a large number of them on my bookshelf, but most technology books are self-contained guides that teach you what is written but do not help you expand upon that knowledge going forward. As I've said before, what makes this book different is that it will teach you to learn on your own. This chapter and the three that follow are at the heart of what you need to focus on as you read this book.

If you work with other database systems, you can still leverage the techniques in these four chapters to help grow your career there as well. We will be covering the Oracle product documentation in this chapter, the data dictionary in the next chapter, Oracle's support site in Chapter 15, and using social media in Chapter 16. If you are working with another database platform, such as SQL Server or DB2, then you can reference its documentation set, data dictionary, support sites, and related social media sites. The ideas hold as you move from platform to platform. I've even used these same focus areas to learn about non-database systems as well. You have probably been using some of them thus far in your career.

In the end, no one can teach you everything you will possibly need to know for your DBA career. You will have to spend time learning more. Undoubtedly, you will rely on multiple sources of information to help you learn more so that you can do your job. All of the great database administrators I know are very adept at leveraging each of the avenues of information presented here and in Chapters 14 through 16. This is not an accident.

The primary source of information for the many Oracle experts out there in the world is the Oracle documentation, as we discuss in this chapter. During my career, I've seen too many Oracle professionals that avoid the Oracle documentation set at

© Brian Peasland 2019
B. Peasland, *Oracle DBA Mentor*, https://doi.org/10.1007/978-1-4842-4321-3_13

all costs. The documentation is their resource of last resort. Readers of this book will know that the documentation should be one of your first stops when you need more information. When I ask people why they do not look up the information in the Oracle documentation, they may give me examples of errors in the books. Fair enough. Any book can have errors. As I dig deeper, I almost always conclude the person doesn't like the documentation because it is hard to use. In this chapter, you will find out how easy and beneficial the documentation is.

RTFM

You may have seen the acronym before. The polite version is Read The Fine Manual. There is a more offensive version of the acronym that you'll likely hear in the field, which does not need to be repeated here. If you ever ask anyone a question and they reply with "RTFM," they are telling you the answer is in the documentation. No matter if the responder to your question has a polite or rude intent, the direction you need to pursue is to look in the documentation.

As any parent can tell you, one of their jobs is to help teach their children how to be polite members of society. We are continually reminding our kids to say "please" and "thank you." The other day my son asked me, "Can you help me please?" and I told him I would. The next words he said were "come here." I always tell my kids that if they want someone's help, they should burden them as little as possible. I tell them "If you want my help, you come to me." For some reason I always think of this when I hear an RTFM question. You want my help in finding your Oracle answer, but you're not willing to do a little work to look it up yourself? Oracle professionals that answer questions do it willingly of their own time. They do not like to be bothered with simple questions you could answer yourself. We are not here to do your job for you. If you ever ask a question that is a candidate for an RTFM response, make sure you preemptively point out that you already looked in the Oracle documentation and are having difficulty finding the answer, if it is there.

Every Oracle guru I have ever met has spent countless hours poring over Oracle's documentation set. I have long been of the opinion that part of the reason they are so good at this job is because of the time spent with the documentation. It's not the only reason they are experts in their field, but I can definitely say that I have never met an Oracle expert or guru that has not read the documentation. If you want to grow your Oracle DBA career, then reading the Oracle documentation is important. If you read the Oracle documentation guides I discuss in this book and take some time to learn what is in them, you can easily find yourself as one of the top database administrators. All of the top DBAs have read the documentation over and over again, and they will tell you to do the same. Probably the most important guide for the DBA is the Oracle Database Concepts Guide, which we will discuss in this chapter. If you really want to be one of the best Oracle DBAs around, you will know the information in the Oracle Database Concepts Guide very well.

If you want to raise yourself to guru status, you need to study the documentation with a fine-toothed comb. Pour over every detail. Take the examples given in the documentation and use them to form test cases and play around with the concept. I'm always amazed when I read a blog post by some guru-level DBA who has taken a small section of the Oracle documentation that I have completely glossed over and has examined every minute detail.

I hope I've convinced you that you need to use the Oracle documentation to improve your skill set and advance your career. So far in this book, I have referred you to the *Database Installation Guides* (Chapter 5); the *Database Backup and Recovery User's Guide* and *Database Backup and Recovery Reference* (Chapter 7); and the *Database 2 Day + Security Guide* and *Database Security Guide* (Chapter 8). I have left it to you to pursue those guides in the documentation set for reading on your own. The decision to leave it up to you, the reader, is a purposeful one. **You must get used to the idea of reading the documentation.**

Tip   Read the Oracle documentation. It is a must for advancing your skillset.

I have worked with some products where the documentation was a 20- or 40-page PDF file. It was easy to read it from start to finish. Unfortunately for us, the Oracle documentation set is very, very lengthy. When you go to `https://docs.oracle.com`, you will find 15 different categories, starting with Solutions all the way to Industries. Right away, you may not be sure where to go with so many different categories. You can see the first eight of these categories in Figure 13-1.

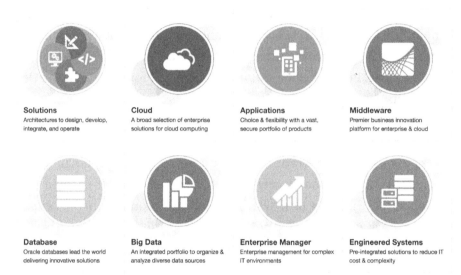

Figure 13-1. *Oracle documentation categories (partial view)*

We have already navigated to the Oracle database documentation in previous chapters. However, we will go through the steps here for thoroughness. For our purposes, we will always be clicking the Database category. Once you click that category, there are five subcategories, ranging from Oracle Database to Other Databases. For this book, we will always click Oracle Database, the bottom-left button in Figure 13-2.

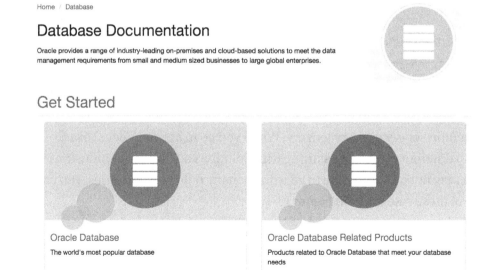

Figure 13-2. *Database documentation subcategories (partial view)*

What may not be obvious when you land on the next page is that the Oracle Database category contains 147 different documentation books for the Oracle 18c version. This is why people do not like to read the Oracle documentation. If there are 147 different books to read just for the Oracle database, how many other books exist on `https://docs.oracle.com` in other categories? There are so many different documentation books out there that it is very difficult to know which one to read. You might be thinking, "Just getting to the Oracle Database documentation set was not an easy task and now you want me to pick through 147 different books?" Don't worry, as this chapter will help you sort it out. The more you work with the documentation set, the better you'll be able to leverage it to your advantage.

Tip   Do not let the volume of Oracle documentation overwhelm you.

The people at Oracle who write the documentation have done a good job with their website in their effort to organize the documentation set so that you can more easily find what you are looking for. It is no easy task to make navigating to the book you need more efficient. As I've worked with this documentation set over my career, I have noticed that it grows with every release of Oracle and navigation becomes more complex. There are many DBAs out there that hate the way Oracle has decided to lay out the documentation set, but it is what we have to work with.

After clicking the Oracle Database button shown in Figure 13-2, we can see the major topics in Figure 13-3.

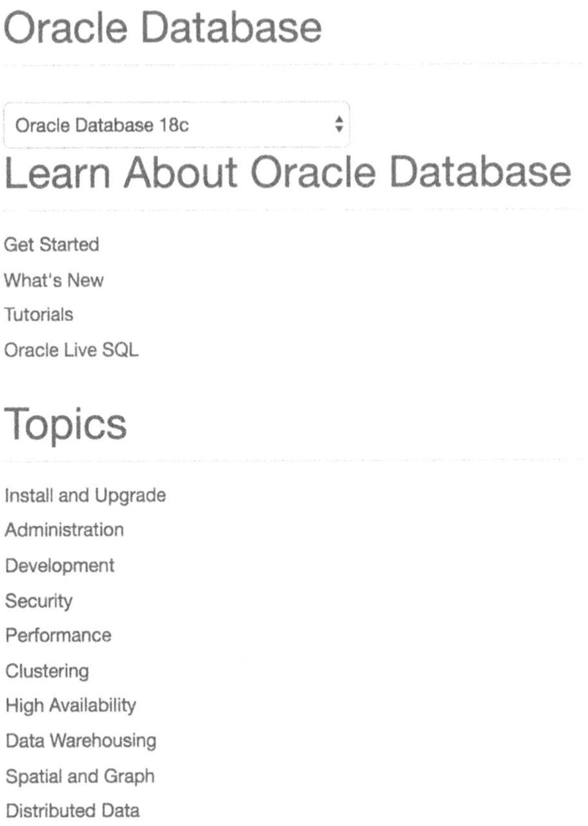

Oracle Database

Oracle Database 18c   ⇕

Learn About Oracle Database

Get Started
What's New
Tutorials
Oracle Live SQL

Topics

Install and Upgrade
Administration
Development
Security
Performance
Clustering
High Availability
Data Warehousing
Spatial and Graph
Distributed Data

Figure 13-3. *Oracle Database documentation navigation*

The first thing to notice is the drop-down menu near the top. Each new version is different from its predecessors, and some of the information in the documentation changes from version to version. New features are introduced and documented. Older features may change and the changes are documented. At the time of writing, the drop-down menu contains versions 11.2, 12.1, 12.2, and 18c. After this chapter was written, the Oracle 19c documentation has now become available. The last item in the drop-down menu is Earlier Releases, which provides access to documentation for releases going all the way back to Oracle 7.3.4. Whenever you are reading the Oracle documentation, make sure to select the proper version you are working with to get to the most accurate information possible. Whenever you are reading a page of the documentation, the navigation breadcrumbs at the top of the page will tell you which version you are browsing.

Whenever I read the documentation, I'm always trying to learn something. However, the most important thing I try to learn is what piece of information is located in which spot in the documentation. With so much documentation to read, it is impossible to remember everything. Thankfully, you do not have to memorize it all. You can always go back and find what you read at a later date. For example, when reading the *Database Installation Guide for Linux*, I do not need to memorize that an Oracle database requires 4GB of swap if the server has 4GB of RAM. Instead, I just need to memorize that the swap space information is in the *Installation Guide*. Later on, when I am installing Oracle, I can easily refer back to the *Installation Guide* now that I know where to go. With 147 books to read on Oracle Database, you will most likely not be able to memorize it all.

Tip   The most important thing is to learn what is where in the documentation.

This is the biggest piece of advice I can give you. Learn what is where in the documentation set. Once you know that, the volume of information is much less overwhelming and you will start using the documentation more. Like anything, the more you use it, the better you become at it. Use the Oracle documentation as much as you can and you will find it an invaluable tool. I must visit the documentation so much, when I want to start typing docs.oracle.com in the address bar of my browser window, the browser automatically suggests this site after typing "do".

As you read, you may be tempted to take notes. I find taking notes to be beneficial. Any time I write down something I learn, it helps me remember the concept. Often, my notes become blog posts to share what I learned. Blogging will be discussed in Chapter 16.

Before moving on to discussing the documentation in more detail, I want to add one final item. Read the documentation with each new version. As I stated earlier, things can and will change from one Oracle version to the next. When a new version is released, the first thing I read is the latest *Database New Features Guide*, which gives me a high-level overview of the new goodies found in the new version. After that, I read a few of the core books that we will discuss in this chapter. Doing so solidifies existing knowledge after I have read the information again and also surprises me with a few new tidbits here and there related to the new version. I've even learned things that were relevant to an older version but were never explained in that older version's documentation.

Do not be afraid of the documentation. Start using it more and more and you will expand your knowledge of the Oracle database more than you ever thought possible. I feel very strongly about this. Do not think of the documentation as something you can get to later. Make it a primary resource for your Oracle knowledge.

Installing and Upgrading

In the Oracle Database category for the Oracle 18c version, there is a link to a section named Install and Upgrade. It is under the Topics heading, as shown in Figure 13-4.

Topics

Install and Upgrade

Figure 13-4. *Install and Upgrade link*

Clicking that link brings us to a section with several books related to installing and upgrading Oracle databases, part of which is shown in Figure 13-5.

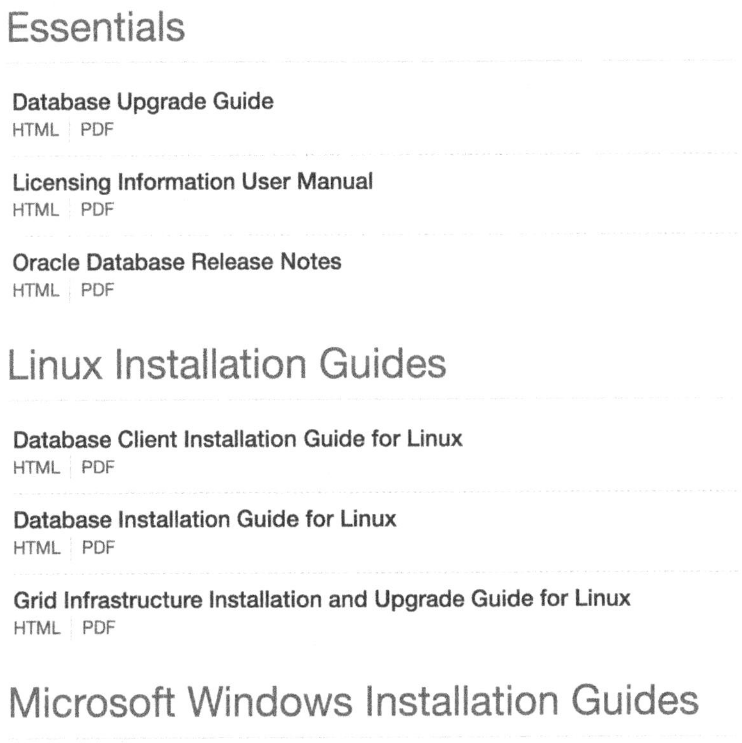

Essentials

Database Upgrade Guide
HTML   PDF

Licensing Information User Manual
HTML   PDF

Oracle Database Release Notes
HTML   PDF

Linux Installation Guides

Database Client Installation Guide for Linux
HTML   PDF

Database Installation Guide for Linux
HTML   PDF

Grid Infrastructure Installation and Upgrade Guide for Linux
HTML   PDF

Microsoft Windows Installation Guides

Figure 13-5. *18c Installation Guides (partial view)*

We will talk about the *Database Upgrade Guide* in Chapter 18. The *Licensing Information User Manual* is a must-read for all Oracle database administrators. This book explains how Oracle is licensed and is important so that you do not get your organization into a situation where they are using Oracle improperly and exposing themselves to extra fees or worse. If you are ever audited by Oracle for your license usage, you will be thankful you read this manual and complied with the information therein.

What follows next on the page are sections for installing Oracle on different platforms. We explored the *Installation Guide for Linux* in Chapter 5. Hopefully you have at a minimum, scanned this documentation to see the information presented there. If you are asked at a later date to install Oracle on Windows, Solaris, or AIX, you already know which documentation you have to read to achieve a successful installation.

Administration

Because this book is focused on Oracle database administration, the main area of the documentation to read is related to the topic of administration. As shown in Figure 13-6, the link for books in the Administration category is below the Install and Upgrade link under Topics.

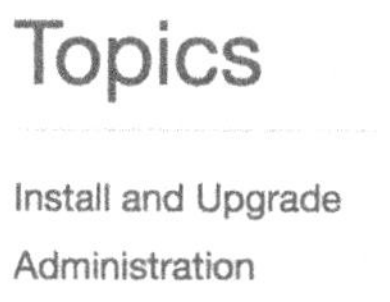

Topics

Install and Upgrade
Administration

Figure 13-6. *Administration topic*

Once you click the Administration link, you will be presented several books to read, a partial list of which is shown in Figure 13-7.

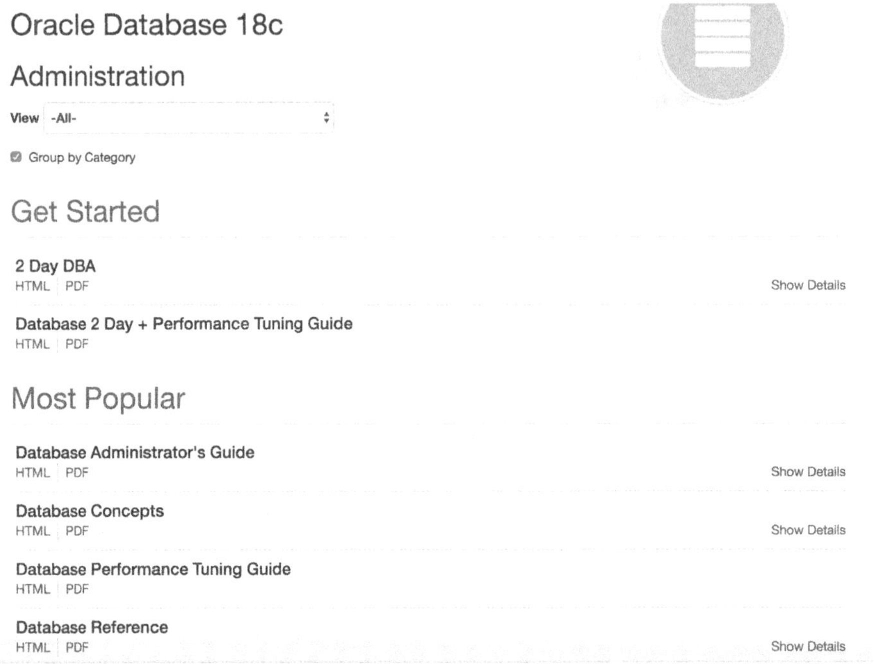

Oracle Database 18c

Administration

View -All-   ‡

☑ Group by Category

Get Started

2 Day DBA
HTML   PDF   Show Details

Database 2 Day + Performance Tuning Guide
HTML   PDF

Most Popular

Database Administrator's Guide
HTML   PDF   Show Details

Database Concepts
HTML   PDF   Show Details

Database Performance Tuning Guide
HTML   PDF

Database Reference
HTML   PDF   Show Details

Figure 13-7. *18c Administration books (partial view)*

Figure 13-7 shows the documentation for the Oracle 18c version. If you want the documentation for a different version, go back to the previous page and select your version from the drop-down menu. We will discuss the books you see listed here in more detail next. Try to become familiar with this section of the documentation because you will be spending a lot of time here over the course of your DBA career.

2 Day Guides

Oracle Corporation must have recognized how daunting the documentation set can be for its customers. Oracle launched a few books in its "2 Day" series. We can see two of these books listed in Figure 13-7. Oracle also provides a *Database 2 Day Developer's Guide* and a *Database 2 Day + Java Developer's Guide* as well. These books are a great way to obtain introductory material on the topic at hand and get your feet wet. These books are not meant to be the only books you read on the subject. After reading the 2 Day guides, delve further into the subject with the rest of the documentation set.

The *2 Day DBA* book listed in Figure 13-7 includes a chapter on how to install and create an Oracle database, a chapter on how to administer the database with various tools, and chapters on how to configure the network, manage storage, provide database security, and perform back and recovery. There is a chapter devoted to performance tuning as well. This 2 Day guide starts to sound a lot like this book and others on the market. We've covered the same areas topically in this book as well. Use the *2 Day DBA* book as another resource in your library.

The *Database 2 Day + Performance Tuning Guide* gets you started down the road of the very large but exciting topic of performance tuning for the Oracle database. This is one of my favorite subjects, and even though I have been performance tuning Oracle databases for 20 years, I still learn something every day. The 2 Day + Performance Tuning Guide just scratches the surface but it is a great place to start.

Make sure to spend some time with the 2 Day guides. After reading them, you will have questions and want to seek answers. Those are often found in the other books we will discuss in this chapter.

Concepts Guide

If you only had time to read one or two Oracle books, I would tell you that there are two books in the documentation set that every Oracle DBA must read. The first is the Concepts Guide and the second is the *Database Administrator's Guide,* discussed in the next section. The Concepts Guide is a must-read. This book is so important to your DBA career, you should read it multiple times, cover to cover.

Tip   Read the Concepts Guide! It is too important to miss!

The Concepts Guide goes over many of the theories and models that make the Oracle database engine work. Ever wondered how Oracle processes database transactions? It's in there. Ever wondered how Oracle stores data? It's in there. Need to know more about indexes? It's in there.

As you read the Concepts Guide, you may find yourself moving to other books to get more information on that subject, which is an acceptable way to consume this information. I would recommend reading the Concepts Guide from cover to cover just to get an idea of what's in there. Then go back and read a chapter with the goal of trying to learn more about that topic. If needed, then branch out to other sources of information. Come back and read the next chapter and repeat.

The Concepts Guide contains six major parts:

> Part I, "Oracle Relational Data Structures," covers tables, indexes, and other schema objects and how to ensure data integrity.
>
> Part II, "Oracle Data Access," covers SQL and PL/SQL.
>
> Part III, "Oracle Transaction Management" covers how transactions work and how to ensure data consistency.
>
> Part IV, "Oracle Database Storage Structures," covers physical files on disk and logical storage implementation.
>
> Part V, "Oracle Instance Architecture," covers how Oracle uses processes and memory to make the engine work.
>
> Part VI, "Oracle Database Administration and Application Development," covers how to administer and develop for an Oracle database.

Remember that earlier in this chapter I mentioned the important thing is to learn what is where in the documentation set. The Concepts Guide breaks the rule. This is one book you will want to learn from front to back. It may take multiple passes through the book before everything makes sense and you may need to hop around to other sources. Reading the Concepts Guide is not a race, so take your time with it. After decades of working with Oracle, I'm still reading the book.

Administrator's Guide

The *Administrator's Guide* is the second book that is vitally important to read. Whereas the Concepts Guide presents the ideas of how things should work, the *Administrator's Guide* shows you how to do it. These books go hand in hand. I often find myself bouncing between the two.

Tip   Read the *Administrator's Guide*! It is too important to miss!

Again, this book is so important to read, you will not want to focus on just remembering what is in there. You will want to spend time to digest the information presented in the book and learn as much as you can.

The *Administrator's Guide* contains six major parts:

> Part I, "Basic Database Administration," covers how to create and manage an Oracle database, including startup/shutdown and many of the things we discussed earlier in this book.

> Part II, "Oracle Database Structure and Storage," covers how to manage control files, data files, temp files, redo logs, and undo.

> Part III, "Schema Objects," covers how to manage tables, indexes, views, and more.

> Part IV, "Database Resource Management and Task Scheduling," covers how to leverage the Resource Manager to ensure important users do not get overrun by less important ones and how to schedule database jobs.

> Part V, "Distributed Database Management," covers how to perform transactions spanning multiple databases. If you do not have distributed databases, you can skim this section.

> Part VI, "Managing Read-Only Materialized Views," covers how to use Materialized Views that have the potential to improve application performance. You may be fine with skimming this section as well.

The first four parts of the book are vital to your success as an Oracle DBA. Skim through the last two parts. You may never need the information in those sections, but if you do, you will know where to look.

Performance Tuning Guide

Getting optimal performance out of any database engine will become a focus sooner or later in your database administration career. The database is at the heart of what users will interact with. Users want access to the data and they want it to be fast. Every DBA will get a call that performance is terrible, and it is up to the DBA to diagnose the root cause of the issue and figure out how to return performance back to acceptable levels.

So much can and has been written about the topic of performance tuning. Early in my career, Oracle did not document performance tuning very well, but the *Database Performance Tuning Guide* is now a must-read for all Oracle DBAs. Performance tuning is a large topic and takes a lot of work to be good at it. Start with this guide and then look to other sources.

The *Performance Tuning Guide* has four parts:

> Part I, "Database Performance Fundamentals," covers the foundation to begin your performance tuning efforts.

> Part II, "Diagnosing and Tuning Database Performance, covers how to measure existing performance and gather information about performance problems.

> Part III, "Tuning Database Memory," covers how to size your Oracle instance for optimal performance.

> Part IV, "Managing System Resources," covers how to optimize your system configuration for optimal performance.

If you are a junior-level DBA, then start by skimming this guide to get a feel for what it contains. As you progress over your career and grow your skillset, you will most likely be tasked with more performance tuning cases and you will delve into this book more and more.

Error Messages

Oracle Database Error Messages is not really a book that you read in the traditional sense. Rather, the book is a reference that contains a list of all the documented Oracle error messages you may encounter. What you want to look for here is how to navigate the book for the time you run across some error message you do not understand. For example, if you see the ORA-00020 error, you can find it in the book and see the description (or similar) shown in Figure 13-8.

ORA-00020: maximum number of processes (*string*) exceeded

Cause: All process state objects are in use.

Action: Increase the value of the PROCESSES initialization parameter.

Figure 13-8. Sample error message

All of the error messages in the book will have a Cause section and an Action section. Many times, the error message alone may not be meaningful enough, in which case the Cause and Action sections typically can help you sort out the issue and help you resolve the problem. Sadly, some Cause and Action sections are blank.

Backup and Recovery

In Chapter 7, we discussed the topic of backup and recovery. In that chapter, I pointed you to the *Backup and Recovery User's Guide*. Hopefully you have had time to at least skim through it. Because we covered that book in some depth already, we will not spend any more time discussing it in this chapter.

Chapter 7 also mentioned another book to examine, the *Database Backup and Recovery Reference*. Any time you see the term *Reference* in the book's title, it means the contents of that book detail each and every option for that topic. For example, although the *Backup and Recovery User's Guide* shows you how to use Recovery Manager (RMAN) for backing up and recovering your database, including examples on using the BACKUP and RECOVER and RESTORE commands, there is so much more to those commands than what is shown in that guide. Each of those commands has many options, and the guide only shows the most commonly used options to those commands. The *Backup and Recovery Reference*, on the other hand, shows details on each of the command options. If you want to know every little detail of these commands, look in the reference. Not only does it tell you everything you need to know about each command, it also includes syntax diagrams so that you can properly formulate the command. Many times, I have put command options in the wrong order or defined a command incorrectly. If I go to this reference, I can see exactly how to formulate my command and avoid errors. Take some time to peruse this reference so that you know what it contains.

SQL Language Reference

The only way to interact with an Oracle database is to send it SQL commands. Every SQL command is documented in detail in the *Oracle Database SQL Language Reference*. For example, see if you can find the CREATE ROLE command in this book. (Hint: The SQL Statements are presented alphabetically in Chapters 10 through 19.) The first thing you will see is the Purpose section, describing the purpose of the command. The Prerequisites section describes what you need before you can successfully issue the command. In this example, you need the CREATE ROLE system privilege. The Syntax section diagram shows how to correctly formulate the statement. The Semantics section then discusses, in depth, each of the options for this command. Lastly, the Examples section provides a few examples of various options to illustrate how the command works.

In addition to the various SQL commands documented in this reference, the book also discusses the default data types and functions supplied by Oracle. Also discussed are operators and expressions you could use in a SQL statement.

Take time to peruse this document. You might be surprised to see how much information is in there about everyday SQL statements you issue to an Oracle database on a regular basis.

PL/SQL Packages and Types Reference

The *Oracle Database PL/SQL Packages and Types Reference* often goes under the radar, which is why I mention it here. As you progress through your Oracle DBA career, you will use more and more of the PL/SQL packages Oracle provides for us. You may have already used a few of them by now. The ones Oracle supplies start with "DBMS_" in their name. You may have been exposed to DBMS_SCHEDULER or DBMS_OUTPUT to name a few. This reference provides all of the details on every package Oracle gives to us out of the box.

This reference gives us an overview of what each package is used for, a list of data types and constants exposed to us through the API, and any usage notes. It is the usage notes that help us when we have permissions issues. You may have permissions to execute the PL/SQL package, but you may also need other permissions. For example, if you try to use the DBMS_STATS package to GATHER_TABLE_STATS and run into a permissions error, this reference tells you that you need to either own the table or have the ANALYZE ANY system privilege.

Take some time to peruse this reference. Obviously, you cannot memorize the entire contents of this book. The next time you use an Oracle-supplied PL/SQL package, take a few moments to look up that package in this book and learn more about it. If you are having problems when trying to use a supplied PL/SQL package, look it up in this reference and see if you can solve the issue.

Bookshelf

When we access a version's documentation set, Oracle is nice enough to give us different categories, like the one that we have been looking at in this chapter, Administration. Sometimes, it is hard to find a book we are looking for because we cannot determine the correct category. If we are on the main landing page of the Oracle Database documentation, below the list of Topics is a section called Access Our Bookshelf, shown in Figure 13-9.

Access Our Bookshelf

Browse
Download

Figure 13-9. *Browse bookshelf link*

If you have selected one of the topics, the same link is on the left side, below the list of topics. In Figure 13-10, you can see I have selected the Administration topic and below that is the link for Books.

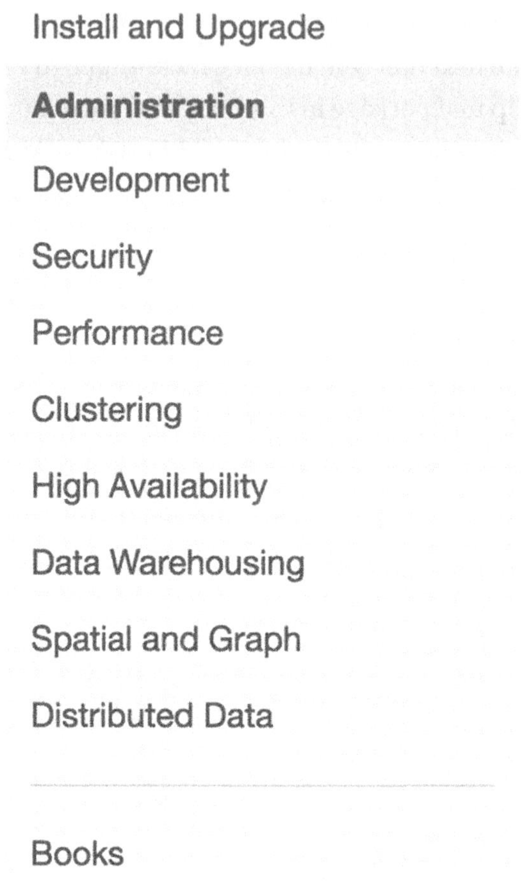

Install and Upgrade

Administration

Development

Security

Performance

Clustering

High Availability

Data Warehousing

Spatial and Graph

Distributed Data

Books

Figure 13-10. *Books link*

No matter how you get there, you will be taken to a complete list of books for that Oracle database version. Figure 13-11 shows a sampling of these books (the page goes on much longer than shown).

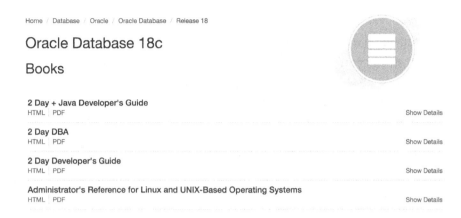

Figure 13-11. *Oracle Database 18c books*

If you scroll through the list of books, you can see they are presented in alphabetical order. If you cannot find the book you are looking for, come to this listing of all the books and do a simple text search in your browser for a keyword. Most browsers use Ctrl-F to bring up a text search window. If I'm looking for a book on JSON or Multitenant, I can easily find it by searching for those words.

It is a good idea to read the book titles so that you know what is out there. You don't have to read the books. At most, just skim through them. Again, the whole point of this chapter is to learn how to navigate the documentation set and learn what is where so that you can more easily find what you are looking for in the future. If you see a book title that looks interesting, click the Show Details link to get a sentence or two describing the book's contents.

Other Books

I want to end this chapter by discussing, at a very high level, a few of the other Oracle documentation books that may be important to you as you advance through your Oracle career. Take some time to examine these books so that you know what they contain. You will most likely end up reading most of the books in this list at some point in the future.

> *Automatic Storage Management User's Guide*: If you use ASM for your Oracle databases, you will need to consult this guide to understand how to work with your files in the storage.

Database New Features Guide: As mentioned earlier in this chapter, when a new version is released, this is the first thing I read. It shows you the new features for that version. If you are just starting out, everything is new. At some point in the future, you will upgrade to a higher version, and this book lets you know what to look forward to.

Database Security Guide: Everyone needs to secure their database. This book, introduced in Chapter 8, provides lots of great details on the topic.

Database Utilities: Learn how to use Data Pump to export and import data. Learn how to use SQL*Loader and external tables to move data from a text file into the database and back again.

Multitenant Administrator's Guide: Oracle has stated that Multitenant is the future direction of Oracle. At that point, all Oracle databases will have at least a single tenant. This guide can be used to learn how to manage the Multitenant feature, even if you have only one tenant.

Net Services Administrator's Guide: This book shows you how to configure the Oracle network.

SQL Tuning Guide: This book is for performance tuning, but focuses on how to write well-performing SQL statements.

This list is not exhaustive. You may certainly need to read other books. Many of the books pertain to features you may be required to use, like Oracle Text or Real Application Clusters. If you do not use those features, you can skip those books. Cloud technologies are starting to demand more of our attention, and Oracle has documentation on its cloud database services (click the Cloud button at `https://docs.oracle.com`).

Moving On

To the uninitiated, reading the Oracle documentation is not something you want to do. Early in your career, it can even be a bit scary due to its overwhelming size. Hopefully, having read this chapter, you no longer feel intimidated by its volume. You should have an understanding of the key books that are vital to your career. You are becoming familiar with the information, format, and structure presented in these books. You should be excited because you have now been exposed to a treasure trove of knowledge. Just reading these books will improve your skill set, guaranteed. Digging into the books, playing with the concepts discussed, and working through the features in your testbed will grow your knowledge of Oracle more than anything else.

Every Oracle DBA I have ever met that is any good at their job has spent a large amount of time not only reading the documentation, but also learning how to leverage it to the best of their ability. Remember that it is not important to memorize everything you read. Rather, learn what is where so that you can look it up again in the future. Like anything, the more you do it, the easier it becomes, so start using the Oracle documentation today.

The two exceptions to the rule of learning what is where are the *Concepts Guide* and *Administrator's Guide*. I am of the opinion that these two guides are required reading. After you are done reading this book, I strongly encourage that you read these two guides. They are that important.

In the next chapter, we will learn more about the data dictionary. We will discover how we can ask the Oracle database questions about itself. After all, no book on the market will be able to tell you with 100% certainty where the DBA put the data files on disk or which user owns a table named RPT30_180101. For those types of questions, we need to ask the data dictionary.

CHAPTER 14

Data Dictionary

In the previous chapter, we discussed the Oracle documentation set. Hopefully you have had a chance to explore the documentation so that it is becoming more familiar to you, and thus much more useful to you as well. In this chapter, we turn to a different type of documentation, the data dictionary. We will also examine some of the various dynamic performance views at our disposal.

The documentation we will see in this chapter is in every one of your Oracle databases. It can tell you more about your database than any book can. Every database engine, Oracle, SQL Server, Postgres, etc., has some sort of data dictionary.

Everything in this chapter is documented in the *Oracle Database Reference* for your specific version. The *Oracle Database Reference* was not mentioned in the previous chapter about the Oracle documentation set because we would be mentioning it here. If you ever have a question about any of the views you see here, feel free to explore more in the *Database Reference*. Take a moment to skim through this book to see how it is laid out.

Data Dictionary

Every database engine worth using has some form of a data dictionary. Sometimes it will be referred to as a *catalog, system catalog,* or a *data repository*. When Edgar Codd pioneered the rules for relational databases, one of those rules dictated a relational catalog be created. How each database engine implements the data dictionary will vary, but they all have it in some form or another.

So what is a data dictionary? The most common answer is that the data dictionary is metadata about the data itself. Basically, the data dictionary contains the information you may need to read to know more about what is in your database.

No matter how the data dictionary is implemented, you interact with it the same way you would interact with any other database table. You query it. In Oracle, you query the data dictionary through SQL statements. Some database engines give you

243

B. Peasland, *Oracle DBA Mentor*, https://doi.org/10.1007/978-1-4842-4321-3_14

stored procedures to execute. The manner in which you get information out of the data dictionary is the same means you can use for the rest of your application data.

The curious thing is that the data dictionary is also updated the same way you update data in your application tables. When you create a table, Oracle performs an INSERT statement into a data dictionary table that contains a list of all tables in the database. Oracle inserts other rows into another table that contains a list of all columns of all tables in the database. Oracle interacts with the data dictionary in the same manner you would interact with your tables.

You should never directly modify the data in the data dictionary tables yourself. Doing so may cause data dictionary corruption and leave your database in an inoperable state. Let the database engine update the data dictionary for you. You should only ever query the data dictionary.

Base Tables

The data dictionary is composed of a number of base tables. There are over a thousand base tables in today's Oracle versions. All the base tables are owned by the SYS user. It is common to hear that SYS is the data dictionary or that SYS owns the data dictionary. Without the data dictionary, the database is not operable, so it must be protected at all times. That being said, it is fun to explore these base tables and see what they contain. I should also mention that we almost never query the base tables directly. Rather, we use the data dictionary views that Oracle has supplied for us. As we will see in this section, the information in the base tables can be cryptic and may be difficult or impossible to decipher. Oracle does not publish much information about the base tables. However, it is fun to start exploring Oracle database internals and seeing how the database works under the covers.

Let's look at one of these base tables. The SYS.TAB$ table contains a list of all tables in the database. It is common to see the dollar sign in the base table names. In Listing 14-1, we can see a description of the SYS.TAB$ table.

Listing 14-1. SYS.TAB$ Base Table

```
SQL> desc sys.tab$
 Name                            Null?        Type
 ------------------------------- -----------  ---------------
 OBJ#                            NOT NULL     NUMBER
 DATAOBJ#                                     NUMBER
 TS#                             NOT NULL     NUMBER
 FILE#                           NOT NULL     NUMBER
 BLOCK#                          NOT NULL     NUMBER
 BOBJ#                                        NUMBER
 TAB#                                         NUMBER
 COLS                            NOT NULL     NUMBER
 CLUCOLS                                      NUMBER
 PCTFREE$                        NOT NULL     NUMBER
 PCTUSED$                        NOT NULL     NUMBER
 INITRANS                        NOT NULL     NUMBER
 MAXTRANS                        NOT NULL     NUMBER
 FLAGS                           NOT NULL     NUMBER
 AUDIT$                          NOT NULL     VARCHAR2(38)
 ROWCNT                                       NUMBER
 BLKCNT                                       NUMBER
 EMPCNT                                       NUMBER
 AVGSPC                                       NUMBER
 CHNCNT                                       NUMBER
 AVGRLN                                       NUMBER
 AVGSPC_FLB                                   NUMBER
 FLBCNT                                       NUMBER
 ANALYZETIME                                  DATE
 SAMPLESIZE                                   NUMBER
 DEGREE                                       NUMBER
 INSTANCES                                    NUMBER
 INTCOLS                         NOT NULL     NUMBER
 KERNELCOLS                      NOT NULL     NUMBER
 PROPERTY                        NOT NULL     NUMBER
 TRIGFLAG                                     NUMBER
```

245

SPARE1	NUMBER
SPARE2	NUMBER
SPARE3	NUMBER
SPARE4	VARCHAR2(1000)
SPARE5	VARCHAR2(1000)
SPARE6	DATE

Some of the column names in this base table make sense if you have spent any time creating Oracle tables. We can see PCTFREE$, INITRANS, and DEGREE, all of which are options you can specify at table creation time. One thing that is absent is the table's owner and name. To know that piece of information, we have to look at the base table describing all database objects, SYS.OBJ$. We can see a description of SYS.OBJ$ in Listing 14-2.

Listing 14-2. SYS.OBJ$ Base Table

```
SQL> desc sys.obj$
 Name                  Null?      Type
 -------------------   ---------  ---------------------------
 OBJ#                  NOT NULL   NUMBER
 DATAOBJ#                         NUMBER
 OWNER#                NOT NULL   NUMBER
 NAME                  NOT NULL   VARCHAR2(128)
 NAMESPACE             NOT NULL   NUMBER
 SUBNAME                          VARCHAR2(128)
 TYPE#                 NOT NULL   NUMBER
 CTIME                 NOT NULL   DATE
 MTIME                 NOT NULL   DATE
 STIME                 NOT NULL   DATE
 STATUS                NOT NULL   NUMBER
 REMOTEOWNER                      VARCHAR2(128)
 LINKNAME                         VARCHAR2(128)
 FLAGS                            NUMBER
 OID$                             RAW(16)
 SPARE1                           NUMBER
 SPARE2                           NUMBER
 SPARE3                           NUMBER
```

SPARE4	VARCHAR2(1000)
SPARE5	VARCHAR2(1000)
SPARE6	DATE
SIGNATURE	RAW(16)
SPARE7	NUMBER
SPARE8	NUMBER
SPARE9	NUMBER

Right away, it should be obvious that we need at least two tables to learn about any table in the database, SYS.TAB$ and SYS.OBJ$. Notice that in SYS.OBJ$, we do have the object's NAME but none of those columns tell us the owner. Instead, we would have to use the OWNER# column to join to the USER# column of the SYS.USER$ table and we have now introduced a third base table to the mix.

The base tables can also contain columns that do not make much sense to us. In SYS. TAB$, we have columns named FLAGS, PROPERTY, TRIGFLAG, and multiple SPARE columns. If you have ever wanted to know more about the columns of the base tables, all it takes is a little detective work in the $ORACLE_HOME/rdbms/admin directory. As we will see in a bit, we would typically use the DBA_TABLES view, not the SYS.TAB$ table. So let's go to the directory and see which script creates the DBA_TABLES view. Listing 14-3 shows how to find the scripts that create the DBA_TABLES view.

Listing 14-3. Finding DBA_TABLES Creation

```
[oracle@dbamentor ~]$ cd $ORACLE_HOME/rdbms/admin
[oracle@dbamentor admin]$ grep -i dba_tables *|grep -i create|grep -i view
catspace.sql:create or replace view DBA_TABLESPACES
catspace.sql:execute CDBView.create_cdbview(false,'SYS','DBA_
TABLESPACES','CDB_TABLESPACES');
catspace.sql:create or replace view DBA_TABLESPACE_GROUPS
catspace.sql:execute CDBView.create_cdbview(false,'SYS','DBA_TABLESPACE_
GROUPS','CDB_TABLESPACE_GROUPS');
catspace.sql:create or replace view DBA_TABLESPACE_USAGE_METRICS
catspace.sql:execute CDBView.create_cdbview(false,'SYS','DBA_TABLESPACE_
USAGE_METRICS','CDB_TABLESPACE_USAGE_METRICS');
cdcore.sql:create or replace view DBA_TABLES
cdcore.sql:execute CDBView.create_cdbview(false,'SYS','DBA_TABLES','CDB_
TABLES');
```

```
depssvrm.sql:  CREATE OR REPLACE VIEW DBA_TABLESPACE_THRESHOLDS
depssvrm.sql:execute CDBView.create_cdbview(false,'SYS','DBA_TABLESPACE_
THRESHOLDS','CDB_TABLESPACE_THRESHOLDS');
e1002000.sql:create or replace view dba_tablespaces as select null nn from
dual;
```

In Listing 14-3, I used grep to give me a list of all files that contain the string DBA_TABLES. I then filtered for only those that had CREATE and VIEW in that same line. Some of the lines returned are for other database objects, but we can see that the file cdcore.sql creates the view DBA_TABLES. Open the file in a text editor and look for the line that creates this view. Do not make any changes to this file! In this file, we can see how Oracle uses nine different SYS-owned tables to create this view, plus some cryptic X$ tables, which I will get to in a bit.

Hopefully after looking at how DBA_TABLES was created, and all of those different joins, we can understand why we do not use the data dictionary base tables directly. The views, as we will explore in this chapter, make things much easier for us. Another reason to use the views instead of the base tables is that Oracle may make changes to columns and the data in the base tables with a new Oracle version. When they do that, they update the view to handle the changes. If you query the base tables directly, you may have to rewrite your SQL statements. If you query the view, things should work the same in the new version.

So what about those X$ tables like X$KSPPCV and X$KSPPI that are part of the DBA_TABLES view? Those X$ tables are a mechanism for Oracle to be able to look into the contents of its own memory. This way, Oracle can query to see what is in its own memory by a simple SQL statement. The DBA_TABLES view gets some information from various data dictionary tables and the rest of the information from what is stored in Oracle's memory.

For most of your job, these base tables and X$ memory tables are not important to your database administration job. You will be able to have a long career without spending too much time on them. I only mention them because it is inevitable that as you progress through your Oracle profession, you may be more interested in how things work behind the scenes. Curiosity is great here. For the most part, we will interact with the data dictionary with the information presented in the rest of this chapter, but you should continue to develop a healthy curiosity about how Oracle works behind the scenes.

Static Dictionary Views

Oracle classifies a number of their data dictionary views as *static*. This definition is used because the data in those views stays static unless a transaction occurs in the database to make a change. For example, if you query DBA_TABLES over and over again, it will return the exact same information. If someone creates a new table, that transaction will cause the data returned by DBA_TABLES to change. Querying DBA_TABLES after the change will result in the same data being returned until someone drops or creates another table.

DBA_, ALL_, USER_, and CDB_

Most of the static data dictionary views start with DBA_, ALL_, or USER_. What follows is often seen in all three. We have talked about DBA_TABLES, but there is also an ALL_TABLES and a USER_TABLES view. All three of these views let us query the data dictionary for information about tables. The difference is the scope of information we can see from these views as illustrated in the following list:

> USER_: These views are for what we own.

> ALL_: These views are for what we own and we have privileges to access.

> DBA_: These views are for the entire database.

> CDB_: These views are for Oracle Multitenant. The CDB_ view shows the same information as its corresponding DBA_ view, but for all pluggable databases.

From the above list, we can correctly surmise that USER_TABLES shows us the tables we own. ALL_TABLES shows us the tables we own and have privileges to access. DBA_TABLES shows us all tables in the entire database. In Listing 14-4, we can see that each of the views shows us how many tables we can see in those categories.

Listing 14-4. Table Counts

```
SQL> select count(*) From dba_tables;

  COUNT(*)
----------
     23048
```

```
SQL> select count(*) from all_tables;

  COUNT(*)
----------
     23048

SQL> select count(*) from user_tables;

  COUNT(*)
----------
     1
```

The user that issued the SQL statements above owns just one table. They have access to 23,048 tables and there are 23,048 tables in the entire database. The reason ALL_TABLES and DBA_TABLES show us the same number of tables is because the user issuing the queries in Listing 14-4 is a DBA user. They have access to all tables in the database. Consider the user in Listing 14-5 that is not a DBA user.

Listing 14-5. Table Counts Non-DBA User

```
SQL> select count(*) From dba_tables;
select count(*) From dba_tables
                      *
ERROR at line 1:
ORA-00942: table or view does not exist

SQL> select count(*) from all_tables;

  COUNT(*)
----------
      4360

SQL> select count(*) from user_tables;

  COUNT(*)
----------
     5
```

In the code above, the user owns 5 tables and has access to 4,360 tables. The query to DBA_TABLES returns an error because this user does not have privileges to access that view.

It should be noted that the USER_ views do not contain a column named OWNER. It is understood that the output of these views is owned by the user querying the view. The ALL_ and DBA_ tables typically have an OWNER column, where it applies.

Being a DBA, I am constantly querying the DBA_ views. Non-DBA users rarely query the DBA_ views. I never query the ALL_ views because as a DBA, they often return the same information as the corresponding DBA_ views.

Since this book is geared toward database administrators, the code will use the DBA_ views. If you look up the DBA_ view in the *Database Reference*, it will most likely direct you to the corresponding ALL_ view instead. This is not a problem because DBA_ and ALL_ views show you the same thing, just different scopes. All that differs is which rows are returned, depending on the user querying the view.

DICT

There are lots of DBA_ views to query. So many that it can be difficult finding the one that you need. Each new version brings with it more static data dictionary views. In Listing 14-6, we can see a count of the total number of DBA_ views in an Oracle 12.1.0.2 database.

Listing 14-6. Oracle 12.1.0.2 DBA View Count

```
SQL> select count(*) From dba_objects where object_name like 'DBA_%' and
object_type="VIEW";

  COUNT(*)
----------
      1905
```

In Oracle 12.2.0.1, there are 2,022 DBA_ views. So how can we find the view that can get us the information we need? Thankfully, Oracle creates a data dictionary view that gives us a description of data dictionary views, called DICT, which is short for Dictionary. When I am having a hard time remembering which view contains the information I seek, I will query DICT to see what it provides. DICT has two columns, the table name and a comment. The word "table" is erroneous because it most likely refers to a view, not a real table.

I often use wildcards in my searches since I may not know the real name. For example, if I want to know which views start with DBA and contain the word INDEX, I would issue a query similar to Listing 14-7.

Listing 14-7.   Index Views

```
SQL> select * from dict where upper(table_name) like 'DBA%INDEX%';

TABLE_NAME                 COMMENTS
------------------------   ----------------------------------------------
DBA_INDEXES                Description for all indexes in the database
DBA_INDEXTYPES             All indextypes
DBA_INDEXTYPE_ARRAYTYPES   All array types specified by the indextype
DBA_INDEXTYPE_COMMENTS     Comments for user-defined indextypes
DBA_INDEXTYPE_OPERATORS    All indextype operators
DBA_PART_INDEXES
DBA_XML_INDEXES            Description of all XML indexes in the database

7 rows selected.
```

Hopefully, one of the seven rows contains the dictionary view I am interested in. I may also query the COMMENTS column. In the example in Listing 14-8, querying the TABLE_NAME column did not give me a list of views that describe materialized views, but querying the COMMENTS column did.

Listing 14-8.   Materialized Views

```
SQL> select * from dict where upper(table_name) like '%MATERIALIZED%';

no rows selected

SQL> select * from dict where upper(comments) like '%MATERIALIZED%';

TABLE_NAME  '             COMMENTS
---------------------   --------------------------------------------------
DBA_BASE_TABLE_MVIEWS   All materialized views with log(s) in the database
DBA_MVIEWS              All materialized views in the database
```

I can see that DBA_MVIEWS contains information on the materialized views in the database. I can also see why it was not found when I queried the table name. The output above was trimmed for brevity as it returned 42 rows in my database.

Querying DICT is a great way to figure out what data dictionary views are at your disposal. The other way is to read the *Database Reference*.

Common DBA Views

In this section, I will go over a number of the common data dictionary views that you might use, along with a brief description. Undoubtedly, you will use more than what is in this list.

DBA_BLOCKERS: Shows which session is blocking who.

DBA_CONSTRAINTS: Shows the constraints applied to all of the tables in the database.

DBA_DATA_FILES: Shows the files that make up the database.

DBA_DEPENDENCIES: Shows objects dependent on other objects in the database.

DBA_FREE_SPACE: Shows how much free space is in each tablespace.

DBA_IND_COLUMNS: Shows the column of each index in the database.

DBA_INDEXES: Shows all of the indexes in the database.

DBA_OBJECTS: Shows all of the objects in the database.

DBA_ROLES: Shows all of the roles in the database.

DBA_ROLE_PRIVS: Shows roles granted to others in the database.

DBA_SCHEDULER_JOBS: Shows all scheduled jobs in the database.

DBA_SEGMENTS: Shows all objects that are segments, i.e., tables and indexes.

DBA_SEQUENCES: Shows all sequence objects in the database.

DBA_SOURCE: Shows the source code that makes up views, procedures, packages, triggers, etc.

DBA_SYS_PRIVS: Shows all system privileges assigned to others

DBA_SYNONYMS: Shows all synonyms in the database.

DBA_TAB_COLUMNS: Shows all columns for all tables in the database.

DBA_TAB_COMMENTS: Shows comments on all tables in the database.

DBA_TAB_PRIVS: Shows privileges on all tables assigned to others.

DBA_TABLES: Shows all tables in the database.

DBA_TABLESPACES: Shows all tablespaces in the database.

DBA_TEMP_FILES: Shows all temporary files for temp tablespaces in the database.

DBA_TRIGGERS: Shows all triggers on all tables in the database.

DBA_USERS: Shows all users in the database.

DBA_VIEWS: Shows all views in the database.

You have probably been querying a number of the views in this list in your career. If there are some that are unfamiliar to you, take some time to see what information they contain.

Useful Views

There are a number of useful static data dictionary views that do not start with DBA_, ALL_, USER_, or CDB_ that you will want to be familiar with.

DATABASE_PROPERTIES: Shows permanent database properties such as the timezone and language.

DICT: Shows all of the data dictionary views.

RECYCLE BIN: Shows tables that are in the recycle bin and may be able to be restored from an accidental drop.

SESSION_PRIVS: Shows the privileges available to your session.

SESSION_ROLES: Shows the roles enabled for your session.

Dynamic Performance Views

With the static data dictionary views, a transaction of some sort is needed to change the output. With the dynamic performance views, no such transaction is needed. Consider the example in Listing 14-9 showing how many sessions are connected to the Oracle instance.

Listing 14-9. Session Count

```
SQL> select count(*) from v$session;

  COUNT(*)
----------
    36

SQL> select count(*) from v$session;

  COUNT(*)
----------
    37
```

The first time the query was issued, 36 sessions were connected to the Oracle instance. The second time, 37 sessions were connected. Because this is a controlled environment, I know that none of the user sessions generated any transactions, yet the value changed. This is why this category of views is called *dynamic*. The values can and will change over time, even without any user transactions in the database.

There is one other big difference between the static and the dynamic performance views and that deals with instance shutdown. If there are 1,498 tables in the database and you shut it down, then on startup, there better be 1,498 tables. With the dynamic performance views, when the instance is shut down, all of the information is lost. Any of the counters returned by these views starts over from the beginning when the instance starts back up.

Most of the dynamic performance views start with V$. In the example in Listing 14-9, we can see a query of V$SESSION. The V$ views are normally used by database administrators to get an idea of what is going on in their database. If you are looking for a specific V$ view, you can query DICT or look in the *Database Reference*.

Common V$ Views

The following list shows many of the commonly used V$ views. As with the DBA_ views, there are many others at your disposal that you may use from time to time.

> V$ACCESS: Shows which session has a lock on an object in the library cache.

> V$CACHE: Shows the contents of the buffer cache.

> V$CONTROLFILE: Shows the status of the control files.

> V$DATABASE: Displays information about the database that is recorded in the control files.

> V$FILESTAT: Shows I/O statistics on the database's files.

> V$INSTANCE: Shows information about the currently running instance.

> V$LOG: Shows information about the online redo logs.

> V$LOGFILE: Shows the online redo log members.

> V$MYSTAT: Shows statistics about your current session.

> V$PARAMETER: Shows the parameter sessions for your current session.

> V$SESSION: Shows the currently connected sessions to the instance.

> V$SESSION_EVENT: Shows what events each session has been waiting on since the session started.

> V$SESSION_WAIT: Shows details about what each session is currently waiting on.

> V$SGAINFO: Shows how each component of the SGA is sized.

> V$SPPARAMETER: Shows the parameter values as stored in the SPFILE.

> V$SQL: Shows details about the SQL statements stored in the shared pool.

> V$VERSION: Shows the Oracle version.

Of course, there are many more V$ views you can and will use over the course of your career. You may have already used some of what you see in the list above. If there are some that are unfamiliar to you, take some to query each and investigate further.

GV$ Views

It is time to throw in an extension to the V$ views discussed in the prior section. In our testbed, when we start Oracle, there is one instance for the database. An extra-cost option for the Oracle database is Real Application Clusters (RAC), which lets you start multiple instances over multiple servers for that same database. Oracle RAC is used for high availability and high scalability.

The V$ views show you the current instance only. If you are using Oracle RAC, then there are other instances in the configuration. The GV$ views are beneficial in Oracle RAC because they let you query the information for all instances of the database. I've always thought of these as Global V$ views. If you query V$SESSION in Oracle RAC, it shows you the sessions connected to the same instance you are connected to. If you query GV$SESSION, it shows you all sessions over all instances.

If you are not using Oracle RAC, the GV$ views still work, but they only have one instance's information, the only one running. The GV$ views also contain an additional column, INST_ID, to denote which instance the row of information is coming from. In a non-RAC, single-instance environment, the INST_ID column is always 1.

Useful Examples

This chapter has discussed the Oracle data dictionary, both the static views and the dynamic performance views. The data dictionary is where you can learn so much about your database. In this section, I will provide some useful examples. You can use many of the scripts in this section and even tailor them for your specific needs. Please follow this section to learn examples on how to leverage the data dictionary.

Every Oracle DBA has at one point or another during their career inherited a database someone else set up. The DBA in this situation often needs to find out some introductory information about the database to learn more about it. When encountering an existing database for the first time, I often run a series of queries against the data dictionary in order to become more familiar with the system. One of the first things I do is to make sure I know the instance name, hostname, and the database's version, shown in Listing 14-10.

Listing 14-10. V$INSTANCE Query

```
SQL> select instance_name,host_name,version,startup_time
  2  from v$instance;
```

INSTANCE_NAME	HOST_NAME	VERSION	STARTUP_T
orcl	dbamentor.localdomain	12.2.0.1.0	20-AUG-18

Next, I determine the tablespaces that make up the database using a query similar to Listing 14-11.

Listing 14-11. Database's Tablespaces

```
SQL> select tablespace_name from dba_tablespaces
  2  order by tablespace_name;
```

```
TABLESPACE_NAME
------------------------------
APPS_TS
SYSAUX
SYSTEM
TEMP
UNDOTBS1
USERS
```

I am naturally curious about where the tablespaces' data files reside on disk storage. In addition to the data files, I also want to know where the temp files, control files, and online redo logs are located. All of this information is stored in different data dictionary views, but I can perform a UNION operation to put it all together, as shown in Listing 14-12.

Listing 14-12. Databases Files

```
SQL> select 'DATA' as type,file_name,bytes from dba_data_files
  2  union all
  3  select 'TEMP',file_name,bytes from dba_temp_files
  4  union all
  5  select 'REDO',lf.member,l.bytes
```

```
 6  from v$logfile lf join v$log l on lf.group#=l.group#
 7  union all
 8  select 'CTL',value,NULL from v$parameter2 where name='control_files';
```

```
TYPE FILE_NAME                                              BYTES
---- ------------------------------------------------- ----------
DATA /u01/app/oracle/oradata/orcl/system01.dbf          734003200
DATA /u01/app/oracle/oradata/orcl/sysaux01.dbf         1184890880
DATA /u01/app/oracle/oradata/orcl/undotbs01.dbf         492830720
DATA /u01/app/oracle/oradata/orcl/users01.dbf             5242880
DATA /u01/app/oracle/oradata/orcl/apps_ts01.dbf        5368709120
TEMP /u01/app/oracle/oradata/orcl/temp01.dbf             20971520
REDO /u01/app/oracle/oradata/orcl/redo01.log            209715200
REDO /u01/app/oracle/oradata/orcl/redo02.log            209715200
REDO /u01/app/oracle/oradata/orcl/redo03.log            209715200
CTL  /u01/app/oracle/oradata/orcl/control01.ctl
CTL  /u01/app/oracle/oradata/orcl/control02.ctl
```

I now have a better idea of what the storage configuration looks like for this database. I want to make sure the tablespaces are not running low on space, so I can issue a query similar to Listing 14-13.

Listing 14-13. Tablespace Free Space

```
SQL> select f.tablespace_name, to_char(f.bytes,'99,999,999,999,999') as
bytes_alloc,
  2  nvl(to_char(se.bytes,'99,999,999,999,999'),LPAD('Empty',19)) as
     bytes_used,
  3  to_char(nvl(trunc((se.bytes/f.bytes)*100,2),0),'990.00') as pct_used
  4  from
  5  ( select df.tablespace_name, sum(bytes) as bytes
  6    from dba_data_files df group by df.tablespace_name) f,
  7  ( select s.tablespace_name, sum(bytes) as bytes
  8    from dba_segments s group by s.tablespace_name ) se
  9  where f.tablespace_name=se.tablespace_name (+)
 10  order by f.tablespace_name;
```

TABLESPACE_NAME	BYTES_ALLOC	BYTES_USED	PCT_USE
APPS_TS	5,368,709,120	Empty	0.00
SYSAUX	1,184,890,880	1,122,566,144	94.74
SYSTEM	734,003,200	730,726,400	99.55
UNDOTBS1	492,830,720	13,959,168	2.83
USERS	5,242,880	Empty	0.00

I can see that two tablespaces are empty and the SYSTEM and SYSAUX tablespaces are more than 90% full.

Next, I often want to learn about the users in the database. Oracle includes a number of users created to support internal database operations. I typically only care about the non-Oracle-maintained users, as shown in Listing 14-14.

Listing 14-14. Non-Oracle Users

```
SQL> select username,account_status from dba_users
  2  where oracle_maintained='N' order by username;

USERNAME                       ACCOUNT_STATUS
------------------------------ --------------------------------
PEASLAND                       OPEN
TEST_USER                      OPEN
HR                             OPEN
```

When discussing user accounts, security should be at the forefront of everyone's mind. Next, I'll query the data dictionary to determine the security profile in use, shown in Listing 14-15.

Listing 14-15. User's Profile

```
SQL> select username,profile from dba_users
  2  where oracle_maintained='N' order by username;

USERNAME                       PROFILE
------------------------------ ------------------------------
PEASLAND                       DEFAULT
TEST_USER                      DEFAULT
```

I see the profile named DEFAULT is in use by the users. To learn more about this profile, I can query the data dictionary again as shown in Listing 14-16.

Listing 14-16. Default Profile Settings

```
SQL> select resource_name,limit from dba_profiles
  2  where profile='DEFAULT';

RESOURCE_NAME                   LIMIT
------------------------------- -------------------------------
COMPOSITE_LIMIT                 UNLIMITED
SESSIONS_PER_USER               UNLIMITED
CPU_PER_SESSION                 UNLIMITED
CPU_PER_CALL                    UNLIMITED
LOGICAL_READS_PER_SESSION       UNLIMITED
LOGICAL_READS_PER_CALL          UNLIMITED
IDLE_TIME                       UNLIMITED
CONNECT_TIME                    UNLIMITED
PRIVATE_SGA                     UNLIMITED
FAILED_LOGIN_ATTEMPTS           5
PASSWORD_LIFE_TIME              90
PASSWORD_REUSE_TIME             730
PASSWORD_REUSE_MAX              8
PASSWORD_VERIFY_FUNCTION        ORA12C_VERIFY_FUNCTION
PASSWORD_LOCK_TIME              .0069
PASSWORD_GRACE_TIME             7
INACTIVE_ACCOUNT_TIME           365
```

If any of the above profile settings are out of line for my security expectations, I can work toward closing the gap.

It is useful to learn which users in the database are granted the powerful DBA role. Listing 14-17 shows a simple query to determine the users with the DBA role.

Listing 14-17. DBA Users

```
SQL> select grantee from dba_role_privs
  2  where granted_role='DBA';

GRANTEE
-------------------------------
PEASLAND
SYSTEM
SYS
```

I always expect to see the SYSTEM and SYS users with this role. Any other users should be part of the DBA team.

Next, I often try to learn more about the database's initialization parameters in use. I only care about those parameters that are set to something other than the default value for the parameter, so my query in Listing 14-18 will give me the non-default values.

Listing 14-18. Non-Default Parameters

```
SQL> select name,value from v$parameter
  2  where isdefault='FALSE'
  3  order by name;

NAME                            VALUE
-----------------------------   ----------------------------------------
audit_file_dest                 /u01/app/oracle/admin/orcl/adump
audit_trail                     DB
compatible                      12.2.0
control_files                   /u01/app/oracle/oradata/orcl/control01.c
                                tl, /u01/app/oracle/oradata/orcl/control
                                02.ctl

db_block_size                   8192
db_name                         orcl
diagnostic_dest                 /u01/app/oracle
dispatchers                     (PROTOCOL=TCP) (SERVICE=orclXDB)
nls_language                    AMERICAN
nls_territory                   AMERICA
```

```
open_cursors                    300
pga_aggregate_target            810549248
processes                       300
remote_login_passwordfile       EXCLUSIVE
sga_target                      4294967296
undo_tablespace                 UNDOTBS1
```

Next, I determine the scheduled jobs in the database. I do not care about Oracle's jobs for its internal operations, so I ignore those jobs owned by SYS and ORACLE_OCM, as shown in Listing 14-19.

Listing 14-19. Scheduled Jobs

```
SQL> select owner,job_name,repeat_interval
  2  from DBA_scheduler_jobs
  3  where owner<>'SYS' and owner<>'ORACLE_OCM'
  4  order by 1,2;

OWNER     JOB_NAME          REPEAT_INTERVAL
--------- ----------------- -------------------------------------------
HR        EMP_ROLLUP_JOB    freq=daily;byhour=01;byminute=01;bysecond=01
```

In just a few queries, and a quick trip through the data dictionary, I have learned quite a bit about this database I inherited. As with anything in life, when we learn the answer to a question, it will likely bring about new questions. All we need to do is find the appropriate data dictionary view and learn more about this specific database.

No author can write a book containing specific information about your database. The best I can do is show you how to leverage the data dictionary. You now have the power to learn more about your specific database you are managing.

Moving On

The data dictionary is the database's internal documentation. As an Oracle DBA, you will find yourself constantly querying the data dictionary to learn answers to many of the questions you will have. The Oracle documentation tells you how Oracle databases work in general. The data dictionary tells you about your database, specifically.

In the next chapter, we will discuss My Oracle Support. This valuable resource lets you learn more about the Oracle database than what is written in the documentation. It helps you discover if an issue is related to a bug and if there is a known workaround or a patch. If the Oracle documentation and the data dictionary cannot answer your question, My Oracle Support is often the next destination.

PART IV

Maintaining the Oracle Database

CHAPTER 15

My Oracle Support

After you finish reading this book, you will likely have additional questions and want to learn more. In the prior two chapters, we started a journey into the depths of the Oracle documentation. As you've discovered, the Oracle documentation is a great resource for learning more about Oracle. The documentation set is very large, and the biggest obstacle is figuring out which book contains the information you seek, which is why we spent two chapters exploring how to navigate the documentation.

In the previous chapter, we discussed the Oracle data dictionary. All good database engines are self-documenting in the form of the data dictionary or database catalog. The biggest obstacle to using the data dictionary is figuring out which view contains the information you seek.

If you have a problem and the Oracle documentation and data dictionary do not contain the answers you seek, the next place to look is in normally with My Oracle Support.

Logging Into My Oracle Support

My Oracle Support, often abbreviated MOS, is Oracle Corporation's support portal. MOS users can search the knowledge base, obtain patches, and file a request for assistance. MOS handles all of Oracle's products. MOS provides much more functionality as well, as we will see in this chapter.

To access My Oracle Support, point a web browser to `http://support.oracle.com` and sign in with your Oracle Single Sign-On (SSO) account, as shown in Figure 15-1. Recall that you used your Oracle SSO account to download software from the Oracle Technology Network in Chapters 3 and 5. If you do not have an Oracle SSO account, you can create one for free. Figure 15-1 shows the button to sign into MOS. If you do not have an Oracle SSO account, click the New User link. When creating an account, I typically

© Brian Peasland 2019
B. Peasland, *Oracle DBA Mentor*, https://doi.org/10.1007/978-1-4842-4321-3_15

use my corporate e-mail address for the user ID. All Oracle SSO accounts use an e-mail address for the user ID. If you ever fill out a service request for a support issue, Oracle Support will send you notifications to that e-mail address.

Sign In

Language [English ♦]

[Sign In...]

Forgot User ID / Password?

New user? Register here

Use of My Oracle Support is subject to the My Oracle Support Terms of Use and the Oracle Privacy Policy

Figure 15-1. *My Oracle Support Sign In screen*

After you have signed in, you will be directed to the MOS Dashboard tab. To the right of the dashboard tab is a number of other tabs to navigate to the different areas of MOS, as you can see in Figure 15-2.

ORACLE MY ORACLE SUPPORT   PowerView is Off

Dashboard | Knowledge | Service Requests | Patches & Updates | Community | Certifications | Systems | Collector | Advanced Customer Services | Settings

Figure 15-2. *MOS navigation tabs*

CSI

While access to MOS is free, you will not be able to do much there unless your company has an Oracle Support contract in good standing. When a support contract is first purchased for the company's Oracle products, Oracle provides a Customer Service Identification (CSI) number. You can continue to use the CSI so long as the maintenance contract is renewed on an annual basis. It is possible that you will have multiple CSI numbers if your company has bought Oracle products at different times.

The first MOS account to enter in a valid CSI number becomes the CSI administrator. If someone else is already the CSI administrator for your company, when you enter the CSI into your MOS account, the administrator will have to approve your use of the CSI number.

If your company already has its CSI numbers entered into MOS, ask the rest of your database administration team which CSI values you should use. Then sign in to My Oracle Support and click the Settings tab. As shown on the left side of Figure 15-3, click the My Account link.

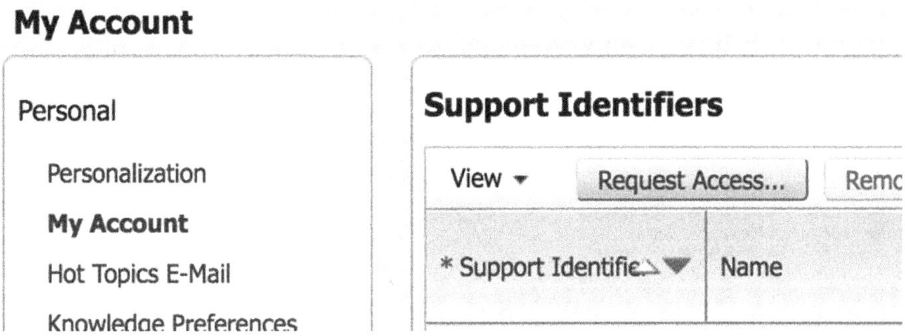

Figure 15-3. *Support Identifiers*

In the section for Support Identifiers, you should see the CSI numbers associated with your MOS account. Click the Request Access button. You will be taken to the screen shown in Figure 15-4 to add the CSI to your account.

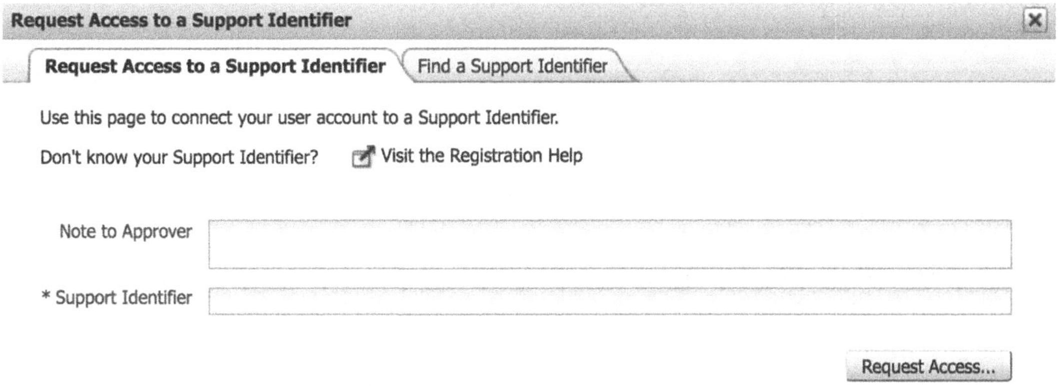

Figure 15-4. *Adding new CSI*

Enter in the value of the CSI you need access to. This will automatically send an e-mail to the CSI administrator in your organization.

The CSI admin will need to go to the same Settings tab in MOS and click the Pending User Requests link to approve your access. Once approved, you will be able to use this CSI value for your needs.

Dashboard

When you first sign on to My Oracle Support, you will land on the Dashboard tab, as shown in Figure 15-5. If you ever want to get back to the Dashboard, simply click its tab at the top of the page.

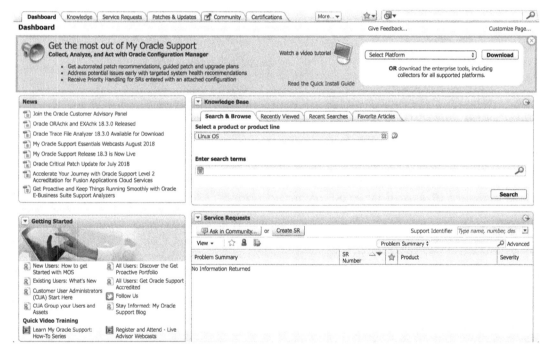

***Figure 15-5.** MOS Dashboard*

The Dashboard tab is a great place to start. It contains sections for the latest news, for a quick search of the knowledge base, for a summary of your outstanding service requests, and for getting started.

Most people live with the default settings of the Dashboard, but you can tailor it to suit your needs if you choose. In the top-right corner of the page, click the Customize Page link. From there, you can remove some of the Dashboard panels if you do not want to see them. You can click the Add Content button to add panels for a Bug Tracker, a Patch Search, and more.

Tutorial Videos

In the dashboard's Getting Started section there is a link titled "Learn My Oracle Support: How-To Series." I highly recommend that you click that link and spend some time watching some videos on how to use MOS. These videos will augment what you read in this chapter. If you click that link, you will see a page similar to Figure 15-6. Click any of the buttons under Play Video to learn more.

ORACLE SUPPORT - VIDEO TRAINING SERIES

The My Oracle Support How-To Video Training Series is a valuable resource that provides just-in-time training, whenever and wherever you need it.

Cloud and on-premise customers alike can access step-by-step instructional videos covering key topics related to My Oracle Support. The feature-based videos are arranged by experience level, role, and task. New users learn how to search for answers in the knowledge base, ask questions using My Oracle Support Community, and more. Advanced users can learn to improve their search capability with PowerViews and improve how they manage content with tips on Favorites and Hot Topics. Cloud Users, Customer User Administrators (CUAs), and anyone that creates and manages Service Requests, will find training videos targeted to their roles.

New to MOS?	Adv. MOS User	Create SRs	CUA Tasks	Cloud Users			
Week	Topic Area	Video Description			Video Length MM:SS	Play Video	Learn More
1	Get Familiar about SI and Terminology	**My Oracle Support Getting Started** — Learn what to do with your Support Identifier. This video steps through the Oracle Account creation process, using your business email address as your username. How to Sign In and associate Support Identifiers to your account. How to request Management Attention should your account not be authorized with a 3 working day period.			07:49		
1	Get Familiar with the Portal	**My Oracle Support Overview** — This video is a basic introduction to the core areas most users make use of. Additional detailed videos deep dive into specific areas with more detailed step by step guides.			06:05		
		Configure your Dashboard — Get familiar with your Dashboard. Remove features you don't need and add features you may need.			05:30		
1	Explore how to use the Knowledge Base	**Understanding the My Oracle Support Knowledge Tab** — Discover the basics of knowledge settings, global search, how results are displayed and the knowledge tab layout. Download the KM ICON Lists			10:01		

Figure 15-6. *MOS training videos*

Figure 15-6 shows the New to MOS tab, which provides videos for those new to My Oracle Support. There are a number of short videos describing much of the functionality. Feel free to click the other tabs to discover what videos await.

Knowledge Base

The knowledge base is where I spend most of my time when I am accessing My Oracle Support. If you have a problem and neither the Oracle documentation nor the data dictionary can help you solve it, the MOS knowledge base is often the next place to look.

Searching the knowledge base is pretty easy. It is very similar to performing a search of the Web with Google or another search engine. Simply enter in your search text and click the magnifying glass icon to begin the search. You can enter your search text into the box in the Knowledge Base section of the Dashboard or you can click the Knowledge tab. At the top of each page is a search box similar to Figure 15-7.

Figure 15-7. *MOS search box*

I typically use the search box at the top of the page because I know it's always there no matter where I am in MOS. The drop-down menu on the left of the search box shows a history of your recent search terms.

As with doing any web search, the more specific you are in your terminology, the better your chances of obtaining a relevant hit (result). If you search for "Oracle" only, you are going to get lots of hits and many of them will not help you with your problem. It is often helpful to copy and paste your exact error message into the search box.

Figure 15-8 shows the results of one search conducted with an error message. The search text is still in the box.

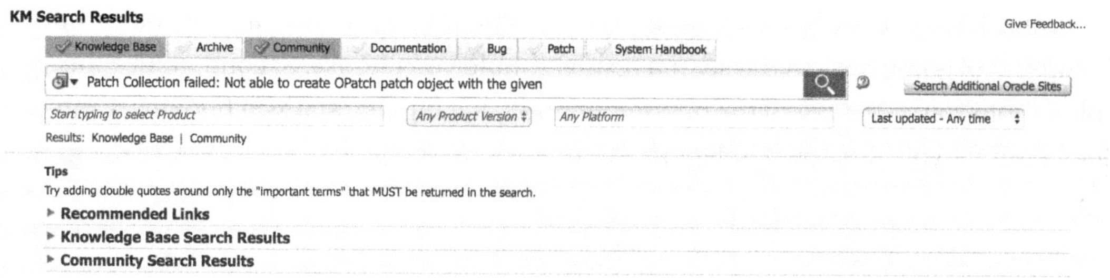

Figure 15-8. *Knowledge base search results*

MOS will break down the search hits into various sections. In the example in Figure 15-8, the sections are Recommended Links, Knowledge Base Search Results, and Community Search Results. Click the blue triangle to expand each section. At the top of Figure 15-8, you will see a green check mark next to Knowledge Base and Community. You can click that green check mark to turn those off and remove hits from those areas in your results. Click the check mark again to show the hits in the results.

If I click the blue triangle next to Knowledge Base Search Results in Figure 15-8 and then click the first hit, I am taken to the My Oracle Support Note shown in Figure 15-9. Every document in MOS is called a Note, and they all have an ID number. In the example in Figure 15-9, I am viewing MOS Note 1475147.1. In the older days of Oracle Support, Notes were referred to by their document ID, or Doc ID for short. You may still see people reference Doc IDs instead of Notes. Even the article in Figure 15-9 says "Doc ID". Today's Oracle DBA will use Doc ID and Note interchangeably.

Figure 15-9. *MOS document*

It is a violation of your support agreement to disclose the contents of the MOS Notes outside of My Oracle Support. You will notice in Figure 15-9 that I am only including the title and not the actual contents of the document. Also note the words "Oracle Confidential" at the top of the page.

There are two things to point out once you display a document from your search results. First, on the left side is a list of the documents found matching your search criteria. You can use this to easily get to the next document of interest rather than having to bounce back and forth from search results to document and over again. You do have the option of going back to the search results should you choose. Second, notice the hollow gold star to the left of the document title. Clicking that star will bookmark the document for you, as shown in Figure 15-10.

Figure 15-10. *MOS bookmark*

You can see the gold star next to the document title is now filled in, meaning it has been bookmarked. So where do you access your bookmarks? Look to the left of the search box at the top of the screen. You should see a gold star drop-down menu. Click that gold star and then select Documents to see what you have bookmarked. As you collect more and more bookmarks, you may want to organize them by topic. In that same drop-down menu, you can select Manage Favorites to create folders for better organization.

As I stated earlier, the knowledge base is where I spend a lot of my time when I am using MOS. If I cannot solve a problem, typically others have had the same issue and Oracle Support has documented it for your consumption. This saves everyone a great deal of time. Oracle Support does not have to spend time working with you one on one if you can read the MOS Note and solve the issue yourself, and you do not have to wait for Oracle Support to get around to helping you. If you remember from Chapter 13, covering the Oracle documentation, I indicated that when you are asking for help, it is better to show that you have done some work in advance. Just like we should not be asking RTFM questions, we should not be asking simple questions that can be found with an easy MOS search. Do your own legwork and save everyone, including yourself, some time.

Like any type of searching, the more you search MOS, the better you will get. The more specific you are, the better your results will be. Do not search for "ORA-700"; instead, search for "ORA-700 [kesqsMakeSql-invstat:elpsTime]" if that is what your error message states. The text in those brackets is pretty unique and will narrow down the results rather quickly.

Service Requests

Suppose that you have an issue that you cannot solve. Nothing in the Oracle documentation helps. You've been searching MOS Notes for an hour and none of them really solves your issue or answers your questions. The next step is often to perform a Google search. If that proves unsuccessful, where do you turn? Often, the option of last resort is to file a service request (SR) with Oracle Support. In MOS, click the Service Requests tab. Your screen should look like Figure 15-11.

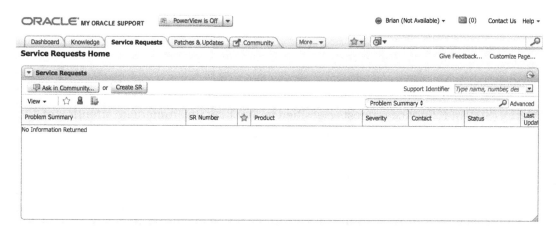

Figure 15-11.   *MOS Service Requests tab*

In the Service Requests tab, you can see a list of your open SRs. You can also click the Create SR button. When you create a new service request, you will be asked for a bunch of information that will help get the request assigned to the correct support analyst. Perhaps most important is identifying the severity of your request, as shown in Figure 15-12.

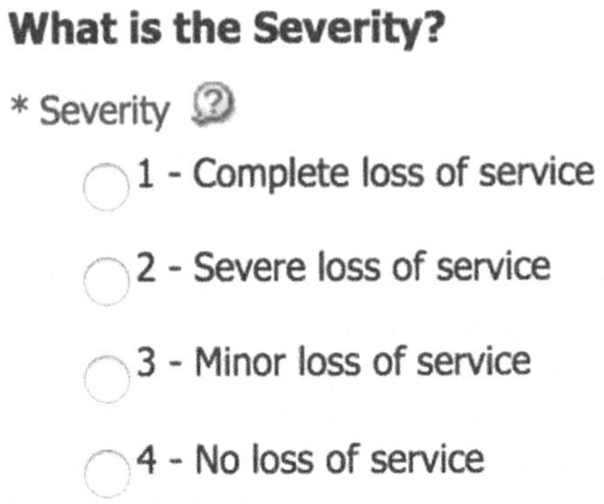

What is the Severity?

* Severity ⑦

⚬ 1 - Complete loss of service

⚬ 2 - Severe loss of service

⚬ 3 - Minor loss of service

⚬ 4 - No loss of service

Figure 15-12. *SR severity options*

If this is a production system and you have a complete loss of service, choose a Severity (Sev) of 1. Service requests classified as Sev 1 get the immediate attention of Oracle Support. If you have a Sev 1 request, expect to be available when Oracle responds to you. Very few of your service requests will be in the Sev 1 or Sev 2 category. Most of your issues will have a lower severity rating.

After selecting the severity, you will need to describe the problem. If you have exact error messages, include them, as it will help in the initial diagnosis. In Figure 15-13, I am entering in a service request for a specific ORA-600 error in production.

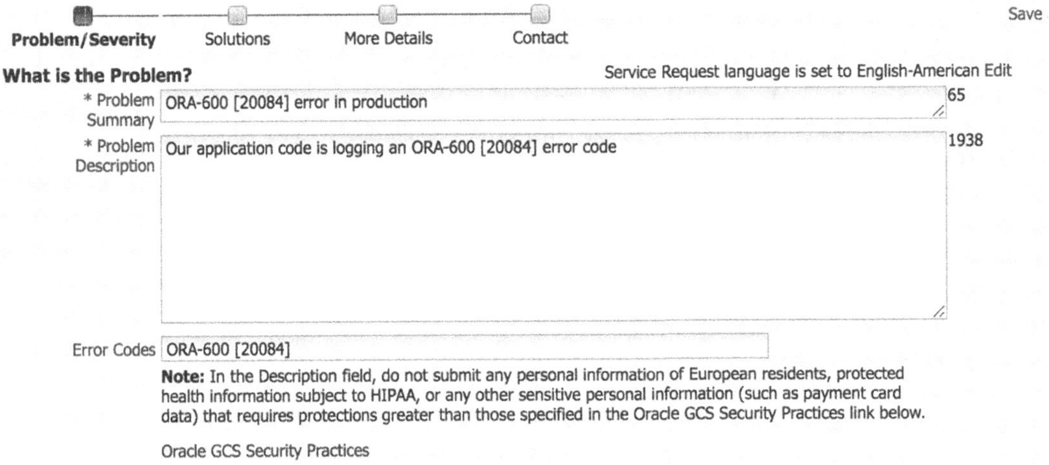

				Save
Problem/Severity	Solutions	More Details	Contact	

What is the Problem?   Service Request language is set to English-American Edit

* Problem Summary	ORA-600 [20084] error in production	65
* Problem Description	Our application code is logging an ORA-600 [20084] error code	1938

Error Codes ORA-600 [20084]

Note: In the Description field, do not submit any personal information of European residents, protected health information subject to HIPAA, or any other sensitive personal information (such as payment card data) that requires protections greater than those specified in the Oracle GCS Security Practices link below.

Oracle GCS Security Practices

Figure 15-13. *SR problem summary*

Next, you need to include some details about where the problem lies. In the Product box, start typing the product name. A pop-up menu will show you which products match what you are typing. In Figure 15-14, I typed "database" and was able to choose the Oracle Database Enterprise Edition product.

Where is the Problem?   Autofill this section using: **SR Profile** or **Existing SR**

| Configuration | **Software** |

* Product Oracle Database - Enterprise Edition

* Product Version 12.1.0.2

* Product Languages English

* Operating System/Version Linux x86-64 - Oracle Linux 7

* Problem Type Internal Errors and Core Dump (ORA-600, ORA-700, ORA...)
Internal Errors and Core Dump (ORA-600, ORA-700, ORA-7445, ORA-4030, ORA-4031, ORA-3137) > ORA-600 / ORA-7445 / ORA-700 / Core Dump

ⓘ **The following questions are designed to improve problem definition. Your answers can help decrease the time to resolve this Service Request.**

* Support Identifier *Type name, number, description, or org., or selec...*

Figure 15-14. SR problem area

After you choose the product, you can then select a specific version of the product in the Product Version field. Always include the version number, as some issues could be version-specific. In Figure 15-14, I chose version 12.1.0.2. I then chose Oracle Linux 7 from the Operating System/Version drop-down list.

The hardest part about filling out this section is selecting the correct type of problem from the Problem Type drop-down menu. The problem type is one of the criteria in determining which Oracle analyst will receive your problem. If you choose incorrectly, expect the service request to take longer, as the analyst that receives the issue will need to determine where to route the request. Read through all problem types before selecting. Lastly, enter in your CSI number in the Support Identifier field. If you put the cursor in that box, a pop-up menu will show you all of the CSI numbers you have access to.

When you are ready, click the Next button. In the old days, that was all there was to submitting a service request. With Oracle Support today, you have more work to do. For better or worse, you will have to provide more information up front. MOS will also be looking at the information you have provided to determine if there is a known resolution to the problem. In my case, I am filling out an SR for an ORA-600 error, so MOS asks me a question, as shown in Figure 15-15.

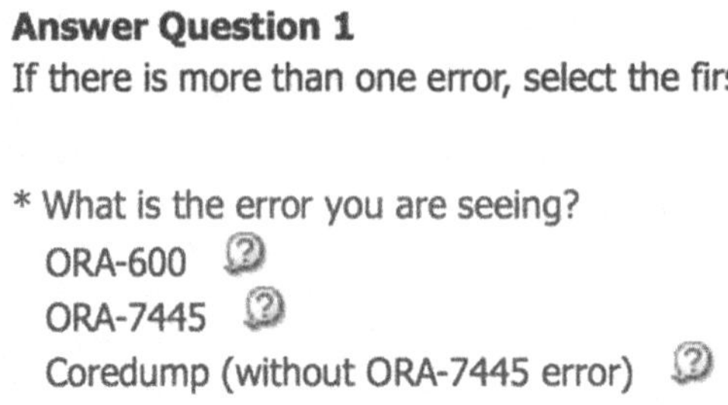

Answer Question 1
If there is more than one error, select the first in the group.

* What is the error you are seeing?
ORA-600
ORA-7445
Coredump (without ORA-7445 error)

Figure 15-15. *SR Question 1*

I am experiencing an ORA-600 error, so I will click the first link. If you have a different issue, it is most likely that you will see a completely different question. Based on the answer I provided, MOS gives me a Note that it thinks will help me, as shown in Figure 15-16.

☆   **ORA-600 Troubleshooting Tool (Doc ID 2024861.1)**

Modified: **Aug 4, 2018**   Type: **DIAGNOSTIC TOOLS**

In this Document

Main Content

ORA-600 Troubleshooting Tool

References

Figure 15-16. *SR suggested Note*

Sometimes, the suggested Note solves my problem. Sometimes it does not. This is the big reason why you are asked to do more work when filing a service request. Like I said, in the old days you would fill out a problem statement and your SR would be created. Today, MOS wants to save you and the support analysts as much time as possible. After asking you a few more problems, you may well solve your problem right out of the gate. In Figure 15-17, we can see that we can let MOS know if the recommendations solved our issue or if we want to go to the next step.

Save as Draft   Solved Issue   Back   Next   Cancel

Figure 15-17. *SR navigation buttons*

If my problem is not yet resolved, I click the Next button. The next screen lets me provide more details that can help the analyst narrow down the root cause of my problem. Figure 15-18 shows MOS asking for more details for my service request.

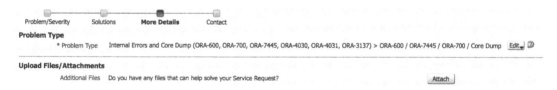

Figure 15-18. *SR More Details request*

In this case, MOS is asking me to upload any files that may help. If the database has created any trace files, now is the time to upload them to MOS. Other details you may be asked to provide will depend on the nature of the problem.

When you click the Next button, you will be on the Contact screen. Fill in your name, phone number, e-mail address, and preferred contact method. Normally these are auto-populated from your profile information. Then click the Submit button and your SR is now in the system.

When an support analyst is working on your problem, they will usually ask for additional information. You will be notified via your preferred contact method when they update the SR. Modify the SR with the requested information and help the analyst help you.

It typically takes some back and forth where the analyst looks at what you provided, determines it isn't enough information, and updates the SR asking you for more pieces to the puzzle. They may ask you to try a few things to work around the issue or fix it. Hopefully, this will enable you to resolve your problem to your satisfaction.

Patches and Updates

One of the main tabs in MOS is Patches & Updates. This section is where you can download any needed patches. Normally, you would only download a patch when working with a support analyst via a service request. When the analyst wants you to apply a patch, they will often include a direct link to the patch in the SR. If you know the patch number, you can type it into the patch search field, as shown in Figure 15-19.

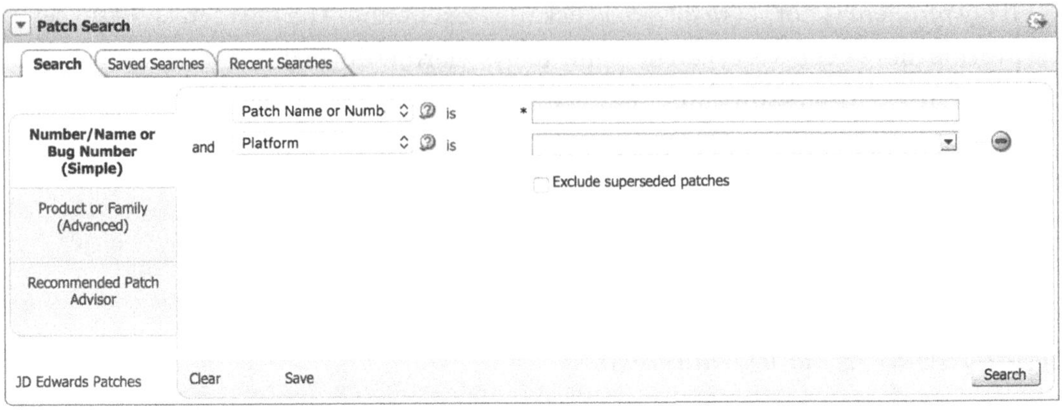

Figure 15-19. MOS patch search

While not required, it is often helpful to specify the platform as well. Click the Search button in the lower-right corner of the screen and you will be taken to links to download the patch. We will discuss patching Oracle databases in Chapter 17.

Certifications

I often see people ask questions like "Is Oracle 18c supported on Windows 2012?" The person wants to know if a specific Oracle version is certified for a specific operating system. You can answer a question like that via the Certifications tab, which has a section showing some quick links, as you can see in Figure 15-20.

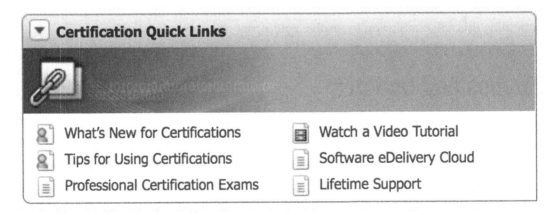

Figure 15-20. MOS Certification Quick Links

It is a good idea to spend some time watching the tutorial video. But we will move on to an example of how to use the search feature in this tab of MOS. In the Certification Search section, place the mouse cursor in the Product box and start typing "database"; a pop-up menu will let you pick any product that matches what you have typed. After selecting the Oracle Database product, as shown in Figure 15-21, click in the Release box. You can select any of the product versions shown. In our example, we will select the 18.0 version. For now, leave the Platform box set to the default value of Any. Click the Search button.

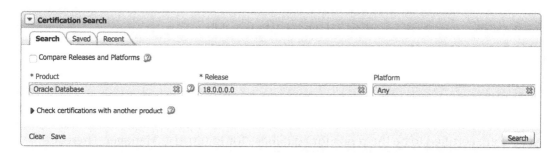

Figure 15-21. *MOS Certification Search section*

At the time of writing, Oracle 18c is only certified for Linux and Solaris platforms. More specifically, MOS showed me that 18c is certified for SLES12, RHEL 6 and 7, and Oracle Linux 6 and 7 for the Linux platforms. At this time, Windows operating systems do not appear on the list. So, to answer the original question, Oracle 18c is not supported on Windows 2012. By the time you read this book, I expect Oracle 18c to be certified for some Windows OS versions, so your results should vary.

For another example, let's do a certification search for the product "Enterprise Manager Base Platform – OMS" and the version 13.3 for any platform. The results in Figure 15-22 show a section of the operating systems certified to run this version of Enterprise Manager 13.3 Cloud Control. If we expand the Databases section of the results, we get a bit more information.

▽ **Databases (10 Items)**

IBM DB2 (Managed Target)	1 Release (9
Microsoft SQL Server (Managed Target)	5 Releases (
Microsoft SQL Server AlwaysOn (Managed Target)	3 Releases (
Microsoft SQL Server Failover Cluster (Managed Target)	3 Releases (
Oracle Audit Vault (Managed Target)	2 Releases (
Oracle Audit Vault and Database Firewall (Managed Target)	14 Releases
Oracle Database (Managed Target)	13 Releases
Oracle Database (Repository)	3 Releases (
Oracle Exadata Storage Server (Managed Target)	37 Releases
Oracle TimesTen In-Memory Database (Managed Target)	1 Release (1

Figure 15-22. *MOS EM certification results*

The two lines I wanted to point out in Figure 15-22 are the Oracle Database (Managed Target) and Oracle Database (Repository) lines. You can see that only three releases are certified to be the repository database for Enterprise Manager. There are 13 different releases that are certified to be managed targets that EM can monitor and control. I specifically cropped out the version numbers on the right so as to not divulge any privileged information accessible only to those with a valid CSI number. The point of this example is that the Certifications tab shows more than just the OS the product can run on. If you were to search on the Oracle Client product, the results would show you which Oracle database versions Client is supported to connect to.

Relative Time

By default, My Oracle Support shows what is called "relative time." Instead of giving me a specific date, MOS will show me something like "2 days ago." Have a look at the dates in Figure 15-23 from a number of service requests in MOS.

Last Updated
10+ months ago
11+ months ago
1+ year ago
1+ year ago
1+ year ago
1+ year ago
2+ years ago
2+ years ago
2+ years ago
2+ years ago
3+ years ago

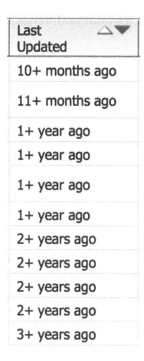

Figure 15-23. *MOS relative time*

It is a matter of personal preference, but to me something like "1+ year ago" is not descriptive enough. Was that 12 months ago? Or does + indicate it could be 18 or even 23 months ago? My preference is to show the exact date. In the View menu, you can uncheck Show Relative Time and you will then see the dates as shown in Figure 15-24.

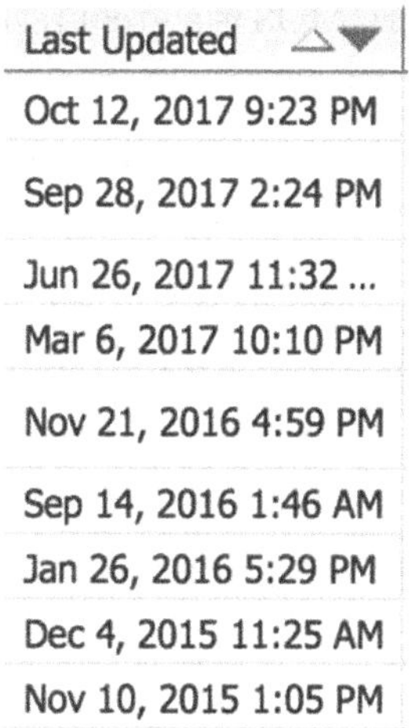

Last Updated
Oct 12, 2017 9:23 PM
Sep 28, 2017 2:24 PM
Jun 26, 2017 11:32 ...
Mar 6, 2017 10:10 PM
Nov 21, 2016 4:59 PM
Sep 14, 2016 1:46 AM
Jan 26, 2016 5:29 PM
Dec 4, 2015 11:25 AM
Nov 10, 2015 1:05 PM

Figure 15-24. *MOS regular time*

To me, that looks better. However, your preference may differ, which is why MOS gives us the option.

If you have relative time turned on in the Service Requests tab, that setting will carry over when you view the details of an SR. In Figure 15-25, the dates on each entry of the service request's history show relative time of ten months or more.

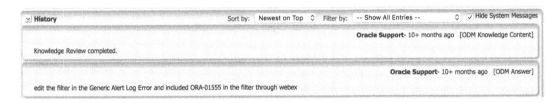

Figure 15-25. *MOS regular time in SR*

If you want to see the exact date, you have to go back to the Service Requests tab and turn off relative time, then enter the SR again.

As stated, relative time is turned on by default. I mentioned it in this book because it is not obvious how to control the behavior should you have a different preference.

Moving On

This chapter continues the focus on how to learn things on your own. Remember that no single source, not even this book, can teach you everything you need to know to advance your DBA career. You will have to consult the Oracle documentation, the data dictionary, and maybe even My Oracle Support. MOS is a great resource for those that have a valid Oracle Support contract.

In the next chapter, we will continue with the notion of learning how to learn. The next chapter discusses social media and its role in today's Oracle DBA career. Social media is a great way to stay on top of the fast-moving Oracle ecosystem. It is also a great way to find answers when even My Oracle Support fails you.

CHAPTER 16

Social Media

In Chapter 13, we discussed how to leverage the Oracle documentation to answer many of the questions we might have as well as learn more about how the Oracle database engine works. In the next chapter, we discovered the data dictionary and explored how it could answer questions about what is contained in our specific Oracle database. Chapter 15 discussed My Oracle Support, another resource for obtaining answers to questions you might have throughout your Oracle DBA career. In this chapter, we examine the role of social media to assist today's database administrator. Social media is not specific to Oracle DBAs. If you work on another platform, you may find the information in this chapter beneficial as well.

When I first drafted the outline for this book, I had this chapter right before the one on My Oracle Support. I've heard many people say they use social media outlets first and use My Oracle Support only as a method of last resort. The reason for this viewpoint is that My Oracle Support has a bad reputation when it comes to responding to service requests. Many times, service requests take a very long time and it seems to appear that a resolution to the problem is nowhere in sight. Personally, I have had bad experiences with MOS and have had to rely on social media for my answers.

At the time I wrote this book, I flipped the order of the social media and My Oracle Support chapters. There are two reasons for this change from the initial draft. One, aside from service requests, MOS has a great knowledge base and is the only place you should obtain patches and updates. Second, social media often contains misinformation. Even though MOS has its issues, it is an authoritative source and the information in MOS is very reliable. Over time, you will learn when to leverage MOS and when to turn to social media.

© Brian Peasland 2019
B. Peasland, *Oracle DBA Mentor*, https://doi.org/10.1007/978-1-4842-4321-3_16

Social Media Definition

What is social media? Social media comprises all the computer technologies that foster the creation and sharing of information, ideas, and careers. When people think of social media, they often think of platforms like Facebook, LinkedIn, and Twitter. These platforms connect people to each other based on their common interests. Facebook was initially designed to connect family and friends with each other, but businesses use it to connect to their customers. LinkedIn was created to connect job seekers with potential employers, but people are using it more often to share ideas and discuss non-career items. Twitter was created to be able to send short messages to people who might want to hear what you say, but today it has evolved into a platform for obtaining newsworthy information as it is happening.

Social media platforms evolve over time, and so do our careers. While the creators of a social media platform might have designed their system with a specific intent in mind, it is the users that make it work for their needs. The creators respond by giving the users a better experience to meet their needs, and the platform evolves.

When I first started in the Information Technology field, the Internet was largely a research project. The best way to get any information was to read all the manuals a vendor supplied to you. When I first started with Oracle databases, Oracle Corporation would send customers a box filled with hard copy manuals included with the CD to install the Oracle software. Over time, Oracle started providing the manuals in soft copy form and customers could install the documentation set on their computers. Like many vendors, Oracle stopped shipping hard copy books of their documentation.

Technology changes the way we work, and most documentation is now accessed through the Internet. Software vendors set up support portals, which are just a specific form of social media. Not only can you access documentation from the vendor, but the support portals let you ask questions, read best practices, and so much more. Although limited to those with a current support contract, My Oracle Support can be thought of as a form of social media, but a very important one for the Oracle DBA. Because of its importance, I devoted an entire chapter to it in this book, Chapter 15.

Because things evolve, so will the definition for the term *social media*. In this chapter, we will explore more than just traditional social media platforms. This chapter will extend the term social media to cover search engines, blogs, forums, and networking with conferences and user groups. While some of these are not true social media outlets, they are still important for the success of your career.

Search Engines

I spend a large amount of my time looking for answers with search engines. What are the hours of the hardware store near my house? How old is Lionel Messi? How long do I boil eggs? Just type the question into your favorite search engine and you learn the answers. People put an astounding amount of information on the Internet, and search engines are the gateway to finding what you need.

In my professional life, the only thing that changes are the questions. What is the meaning of Oracle error PRVG-2027? What do I do when the .patch_storage directory gets too large? When was Oracle 7 released? How do I create a multitenant database?

Typically, when people think of a search engine, they mean Google. Other search engines exist, but Google reigns supreme. You can use Yahoo, Bing, or others should use desire. They all lead to the same Internet. Google is the most often used because it is thought to provide the most relevant hits for your searches, but Google is not perfect. You may want to use other search engines if Google is not finding what you seek. Some search engines are better for a specific geography. For example, in China, you might use Baidu.

No matter what search engine you use, the search results may be more relevant to you the more specific you are in your search terms. If you search for "Oracle" you probably will not get any hits helping you solve a problem with a foreign key constraint. If you search for "oracle foreign key" you will get plenty of hits related to showing you how to create foreign keys, but if you are searching for a solution to disable foreign keys, you will miss the mark. Instead, search for "oracle disable all foreign key constraints on a table" and your search will be more successful. The more specific you are in your search terms, the quicker you will find what you are looking for.

One trick I typically use is to include the database platform in the search terms. If I search for "disable all foreign key constraints on a table," Google responds with information on the SQL Server platform as its first two results. Adding the word "Oracle" to the search terms narrows down the results more quickly to my platform. There are times you will want to include your Oracle version. The term "oracle 12.2" will ensure that results from the old Oracle 10.1 version do not appear. Including the platform and its version is one trick to help obtain the most relevant results of your search.

Many times, you will need to include multiple lines from your issue in your search terms. I once ran into the problem shown in Listing 16-1 while trying to patch an Oracle database.

Listing 16-1. Example Problem

```
Queryable inventory could not determine the current opatch status.

Execute 'select dbms_sqlpatch.verify_queryable_inventory from dual'

and/or check the invocation log

/u01/app/oracle/cfgtoollogs/sqlpatch/sqlpatch_25889_2016_11_09_22_26_12/
    sqlpatch_invocation.log

for the complete error.
```

I wasn't sure how to resolve this problem. I tried to determine what message in the output above would be a good search term. The first line looks generic, so that probably wouldn't work. The second link contains something specific, dbms_sqlpatch.verify_queryable_inventory, so I used that as my search team. Unfortunately, the results were not related to my problem. When I looked in the log file mentioned in the output above, I could see the additional information shown in Listing 16-2.

Listing 16-2. Example Problem Log File

```
verify_queryable_inventory returned ORA-20008: Timed out, Job
Load_opatch_inventory_1execution time is
more than 120Secs

Queryable inventory could not determine the current opatch status.
```

I now have something even more specific. My search term is now "dbms_sqlpatch. verify_queryable_inventory ORA-20008 Timed Out". By making the search term very specific, I can hone in on the most relevant results as quickly as possible.

For many readers, this advice may seem like common sense. However, I have found that people who do not find relevant information in a web search are often using terms that are too generic. It is helpful if you include any error codes in your search, for example. If the hits are still too broad, then include the error code and the error message, as some errors can have multiple messages. If your issue has multiple error codes, include them all in your search terms. All of these are a tips I have learned over the years when trying to research problems on the Web.

Blogs

A blog is a website where you can post any content you desire, normally to share information or start a discussion. The author of the blog writes an article and posts it to the website. The articles are typically arranged in reverse order of the date they were posted, with the most recent article at the top.

As you will see later in this section, I strongly recommend that all readers start a blog for their database career. Over the course of your career, expect your blog to change nature and scope as your career grows. Eventually, you will find your niche and provide meaningful content for the worldwide community to enjoy.

The two most commonly used blog sites are Blogger (`www.blogger.com`) and WordPress (`www.wordpress.com`). Each of these sites includes an editor that lets you quickly and easily create content. You can choose from many predefined themes to give your blog a look and feel that suits your style. Both platforms allow for free blogs to be hosted on their systems. Many Internet service providers also provide the capability to host your own blog on other systems.

Many people start a blog for multiple reasons. Blogs were not in existence during my first few years. After a while, web searches kept leading me to other blogs that people had started. Over time, I learned that blogs all start with sharing something the author has to say. When I write a blog post as a DBA, it is typically for one of three categories:

- Whenever I have a tricky problem that I resolved, I will write a blog entry detailing the specifics of the issue and what I did to resolve it.

- Whenever I learn something new, I will write a blog article showing the new concept in action. I try to include any tips I learned along the way that are not written or obvious in the documentation.

- Something is on my mind and I want to share with it people.

You will find that most database-related blog posts fall into these main categories. There are always exceptions to the rule, of course, and you can make your blog unique. One of the great things about blogging is that the author defines the content. You may have a different idea for a blog than what I have enumerated above.

I encourage all readers to start their own blog. In addition to the altruistic endeavor of sharing information with the database community at large, there are self-serving reasons for blogging as well. If you read my blog and learn something from it, that is excellent! However, I also blog for myself.

One reason I blog is because the act of writing down my own thoughts enhances my own understanding. Whenever I must write something and explain it to someone else, I learn more about the subject than if I had not written anything at all. There is something magical that happens inside the human brain where the simple act of relating content to someone makes you understand it better yourself. For many people, writing also helps them remember the topic easier as well.

The second reason I blog is because my blog is a piece of my documentation. The Oracle documentation cannot explain everything. It covers a lot but there are things missing in the documentation as well. For example, when Oracle 12c introduced IDENTITY columns, very similar to a feature long available in SQL Server, there were a few things I learned about this new feature. I wrote a blog entry about the subject over five years ago. Over time, I could not remember the exact details of what I had learned, so I referred to my blog post to remind myself of the specifics. It was not vitally important that I retain every piece of information in that blog post; rather, I just had to remember that I had written it and I could easily refer to it. A quick Google search of "`www.peasland.net` identity" was all that I needed to do and I could quickly find my blog's entries for this information.

As I stated earlier in this section, I will often write a blog entry whenever I have solved a tricky problem. Throughout my career, I have run into problems that were not solved through My Oracle Support or by a Google search. Once I solve a problem, I know that others have yet to see the solution, and my solution becomes an immediate candidate for a blog entry. I post the details and the solution to my blog. I have been rewarded many times over the years with wonderful comments on how much time I saved someone by resolving their issue, all because of my blog post.

Now here's a secret most bloggers will not tell you. My blog helps me most of all! I cannot tell you the number of times I have written up a difficult problem on my blog. Years later, I run into the issue again. By now, I have forgotten that I already solved the problem. My mind is totally blank on the issue. It's like this is the first time I have ever seen the problem in my life. I do a quick search on My Oracle Support and do not see any resolutions to my problem. I head to Google and search for my specific issue and, sure enough, right there near the top of the search results is a blog entry I wrote a long time ago. I click the link to my own blog and the post describes in exact detail the problem I am experiencing today, and it even gives me a nice resolution. Yet I do not remember even writing the blog entry. So much for the idea that writing helps with memory retention.

> **Tip**   Start a blog today. Your career will only grow as a result.

While writing to share and help others is certainly a noble endeavor, it will help your career as well. Most bloggers are reluctant to admit there is a bit of self-serving activity in their blogging, but it is there. In addition to the previously mentioned benefits of blogging, you may also see career growth. I have personally been approached by web magazines and asked to write content for them, in part because they read articles on my blog. I know of some database administrators that monetize their blog and get paid for posting ads. If you are an independent consultant, blogging will be essential so that your customers can gauge your level of expertise.

Start your own blog today. You can use Blogger or WordPress, as I mentioned, for free. At first, you may struggle to find what you want to write about. The more you write, the more you will find your own voice and, I promise, the more your Oracle career will grow. Blogging does not have to be terribly time consuming. You can write a post as seldom or as often as you like. I often go in spurts and will post a couple times a month and then be dormant for a period. Some bloggers are more regular and try to post at least once a week.

There are many great blogs to follow out there. The following is a list of candidates for you to consider. I follow all of these bloggers and learn a great deal from them.

- Brian Peasland (`www.peasland.net`): My blog, of course!

- Connor McDonald (`https://connor-mcdonald.com`): Oracle employee who is one of the driving forces behind the popular Ask TOM site.

- Jonathan Lewis (`https://jonathanlewis.wordpress.com`): The world's foremost expert on how the Oracle Optimizer works.

- Tim Hall (`https://oracle-base.com/blog`): Tim Hall does a great job showcasing most everything you want to know about how to use Oracle.

- Jeff Smith (`www.thatjeffsmith.com`): Oracle product manager for the SQL Developer tool. This blog always has great tips on how to get the most out of the product.

- Mike Dietrich (`https://mikedietrichde.com`): Oracle product manager for patches and upgrades.

Please do not feel offended if your blog did not make the list. The blogs above are a few that I follow on a regular basis and recommend as a great start for you. As you advance through your career and build networks in your database community, you will learn of other useful blogs that you may want to follow.

Almost all blogs include the ability to sign up for an RSS feed. RSS lets you be informed of updates to the blog. You need a news reader that can handle the RSS feeds. I use a product called NewsBlur, which requires a small annual subscription. There are other news readers out there and some are even free. I visit the news reader in the morning to see what new blog posts have been created for me to read, rather than visiting each blog individually only to find out many of them do not have any new content that day.

Twitter

Twitter is a social media platform for sending messages to several people, called followers. You can follow anyone with a Twitter account and anyone can follow you. When you send a message, called a tweet, everyone who follows you will see it in their Twitter feed. Likewise, your twitter feed will show the tweets of those you follow.

It wasn't that long ago that tweets were limited to 140 characters, which meant the messages needed to be brief. If someone wanted to post a longer message, they sent it as an image or video. Due to its shorter message length, Twitter is often best suited for getting the news to your audience of followers.

What constitutes news may vary from person to person. Some Oracle professionals think that their choice of morning coffee is news. Others think it is important to tell me how many miles they ran over the lunch break. Personally, I do not find that as news, and even though they may be a top-notch Oracle professional, I tend not to follow those types of individuals on Twitter. Similarly, you will not see me tweet about my non-professional life, but as they say, to each his own. You may find that learning more about a person's non-Oracle day as a fantastic way to bond and connect with that individual. You can make Twitter what you want it to be and do not need to share my views on the subject.

The Twitter accounts I follow often fall into two categories, individuals and companies. While not an exhaustive list, here are some of the individuals I follow:

- Mike Dietrich (@MikeDietrichDE): Oracle product manager of upgrades and patches

- Christian Antognini (@ChrisAntognini): Oracle performance specialist

- Franck Pachot (@FranckPachot): Oracle DBA

- Markus Michalewicz (@OracleRACPM): Oracle product manager for Real Application Clusters

- Tim Hall (@oraclebase): The same Tim Hall whose blog I follow

- Jeff Smith (@thatjeffsmith): Oracle product manager for SQL Developer

- Jonathan Lewis (@JLOracle): Oracle Optimizer expert

And here are some of the companies I follow on Twitter:

- Orachrome (@orachrome): Twitter feed for the makers of the awesome Lighty product for Oracle performance tuning

- Oracle DB Support (@OracleDBSupport): Twitter feed for Oracle Support

- Oracle SQL Developer (@OracleSQLDev): Twitter feed for the Oracle SQL Developer product

- Oracle VirtualBox (@virtualbox): Twitter feed for the Oracle VirtualBox product

There are many more that I follow as well. The list is just a sampling. I am currently following 88 different Twitter accounts. I know of people who follow a lot more than I do. Once you start following a few accounts, Twitter will recommend others to follow. Feel free to follow me on Twitter at @BPeaslandDBA if you like.

Twitter is not a great resource to seek help, although I have seen people try to use it for problem resolution. The platform does not easily allow for a back and forth discussion with significant detail. Thankfully, we have much better platforms for resolving problems.

Ask TOM

Almost every Oracle professional has used Oracle's Ask TOM website at one time or another. Many years ago, Oracle Corporation employed a consultant by the name of Tom Kyte. In addition to being sent to client sites to resolve Oracle issues for customers, Tom Kyte set up a website where you could ask him questions, and Ask TOM was born. You can visit this site at `https://asktom.oracle.com`. The web page has evolved over time and now looks like Figure 16-1.

Figure 16-1. *Ask TOM home page*

On the home page, you can immediately start searching for answers to questions. Do not let the title fool you. This site is for database administrators as well as Oracle Developers. Always perform a search first, before asking any questions of your own. Chances are good that someone else has asked the question in the past.

Even though the Ask TOM site has changed over the years, all of the old answers are still available. The site provides a rich history of questions and answers in amazing detail with lots of examples. Bookmark this website in your browser and use it often, especially when you are stuck with a problem in Oracle.

In 2016, Tom Kyte retired from Oracle Corporation. Oracle did not want the Ask TOM resource to fade away, as it has become too valuable to the Oracle worldwide community. Upon Tom Kyte's retirement, Oracle turned to other employees, namely Connor McDonald and Chris Saxon, to keep the site going. Soon after, they expanded it to include many employees, each with their own expertise. Ask TOM no longer refers to a specific individual, but is now rebranded as Ask TOM or Ask The Oracle Masters. Oracle

Corporation still uses the same name, but changed the branding to reflect a team of experts rather than a specific individual.

If you are trying to obtain an answer to your Oracle-related question, and a search of the Ask TOM archives does not provide anything relevant, you can post your own question. Simply click the Questions tab and fill out the required information.

Discussion Forums

Discussion forums are a great way to interact with Oracle professionals from around the globe. These forums are where you can ask questions and discuss the issue back and forth until a resolution is obtained. Today's discussion forums are typically accessed with a web browser. There are many discussion forums out there, but only a few see a good amount of traffic to make them worthwhile in my opinion.

Oracle-L (`www.freelists.org/list/oracle-l`) has been around a very long time. This one is really a discussion list. Visit the URL above to subscribe to the list and you will receive each and every update by e-mail. If you choose to subscribe to Oracle-L, make sure you set up an e-mail rule and route the e-mails to a folder instead of clogging up your Inbox. The way you respond to threads of discussion is to respond to the e-mail you receive. Oracle-L was designed before discussion forums became web based. While the interaction with the discussion group is a bit archaic by today's standards, this discussion list deserves mention simply because of the talent level of the individuals that still respond to questions there.

The Oracle Groundbreakers forum (`https://community.oracle.com/community/technology_network_community`) used to be known as the Oracle Technology Network (OTN) Community before they changed the name. Oracle Groundbreakers is a free to use discussion forum. All you need is an Oracle Single Sign-On account to obtain access. You may have created this account when you downloaded Oracle software earlier in this book to create our testbed.

The My Oracle Support Community (MOSC) (`https://community.oracle.com/community/support/`) is another web-based discussion forum. This site is integrated with Oracle Developer Community. If you access both of them, you use the same site essentially. This makes it easy because you do not have to bounce from one site to another. When you subscribe to discussion spaces in either site, the new content appears in one Inbox.

If there are two sites and they are integrated, why have two sites at all? Oracle Groundbreakers is for everyone, open to the public. MOSC is for Oracle customers who have a paid Oracle Support contract, hence its name. You can even enter MOSC from within My Oracle Support by clicking the Community tab. When you create a service request in MOS, you do have the option of starting a discussion in MOSC instead by clicking the button to ask a question in the Community, as you can see in Figure 16-2.

Figure 16-2. *MOS Ask in Community button*

The main differentiator between the two sites is that Oracle Support employees will often participate and provide answers in MOSC. Thankfully, you do not have to choose between the two sites because they are integrated and work nicely together.

No matter which discussion forum you use, there are a few rules to follow. Failure to adhere to these rules will result in the numerous forum trolls who like to flame new victims. It is unfortunate, but there are too many people in any discussion forum that are rude and condescending. The best way around their poor attitudes is to participate under some well-known guidelines:

- The subject line should contain a brief description of the problem, not state the entire problem.

- Post your Oracle version. Your version is not "12c" but rather something like 12.1.0.2 or 12.2. Too many answers are version-specific. Knowing your version gets you the correct answer to your question. Failure to include your version will get terse responses like "Which version?" or flames from the forum trolls.

- Do not post RTFM questions. Thanks to Chapter 13 of this book, you now know how to use the Oracle documentation. If you can Read The Fine Manual, you can answer these questions yourself. Do not waste the valuable time of volunteers by posting questions that you could have looked up yourself.

- Do not post questions you could easily search for. Earlier in this chapter, we discussed how to use search engines to find answers. If you can easily find the answer by a simple web search, it should not be posted to discussion forums. People will often reply "LMGTFY," which is short for Let Me Google That For You. Their reply will then be followed by a link to `http://lmgtfy.com` showing Google search results.

- If possible, post sample code showing your work and also include what is not working. For example, if you are working on a SQL statement, post code to create a sample table and populate it with sample data. Then post the SQL statement that does not work and do your best to explain how it should work. With all of this information, the responder can create the table in their database and try the same SQL statement to figure out how to resolve the issue.

- Post entire error messages. If you say you are receiving an ORA-00942 error and provide nothing else, you are not likely to obtain a good answer. Post the SQL statement that received the error and then copy and paste the entire error stack into your initial post.

- Never ask for immediate help or say that your request is urgent. The people who answer questions are not paid for their work. They are volunteers and they have their own jobs to do. They will answer your questions when they have time. If you want an immediate resolution, file a service request with My Oracle Support.

As you interact with these discussion forums, start participating as a respondent to questions. All too often, I see people who only ask questions and never share their knowledge. The discussion forums are better when we have more people looking at the problem. In the beginning stages of your career, you may not have the skill set needed to answer a lot of different questions, which is to be expected. Try to answer a few questions anyway. As I stated in the section discussing blogging, something magical happens when you try to explain something in written form: you actually learn more yourself. The same thing holds true in discussion forums. The more questions you answer, the better you will understand how Oracle works. In the beginning, try to answer one question a day. Make it an easy question if you can find one. Then start working your way up.

Another reason for answering questions and becoming a major participant in the discussion forums is that you will learn the Oracle documentation very well. I can typically look up anything I need in the Oracle documentation with a few clicks of the mouse because I know exactly where to look. It wasn't until I started answering questions that I became better at knowing how to use the documentation. When I answer a question, I try to include a link to the relevant portion of the documentation if I can. That way, the reader can find more information. It does take extra time to find that link, but I save time from typing lots of extra information that the reader can see in the documentation. The documentation also serves as a way of proving what I am saying is true in case there is a doubt.

The last reason I answer questions on the discussion forums is because I learn so much every day. People will post some of the oddest problems that I would have never seen in my regular job. Additionally, someone will respond to a question with something I did not know before. No matter how much I know about the Oracle product, I will never know everything. Everyone can teach me something. Just reading different discussion threads often teaches me a great deal. On many occasions during my career I have come across a problem that I had been exposed to at a previous time in some discussion forum. I already have an introduction to this problem. All I need to do is find the forum thread that discussed the problem and I easily have a solution.

If you do answer questions in discussion forums, prepare to be wrong. It takes a while to learn how to answer questions properly. Too many people will jump on you for being wrong, sometimes very rudely. Ignore the negativity and figure out where you went wrong and how you can respond better the next time. Do not let the negativity deter you from answering future questions. Like anything, the more you do it, the better you will be at it. Answering questions is the same.

YouTube

More and more, I see Oracle professionals posting videos on YouTube. I started with sharing information via blogging and discussion forums, in written form. For me, trying to share Oracle concepts in video form was a foreign concept. I have put out a few videos in a YouTube channel, but it's just not for me. It's not something I do well. Thankfully, there are some Oracle professionals that do it very well and have posted great videos on YouTube. You may enjoy creating some videos of your own to share your knowledge.

Most of the Oracle-related content on YouTube are how-to videos. Because the video is prerecorded, it is difficult for the platform to serve the same role as a discussion forum. For examples, search for "Oracle SQL Developer" on YouTube and you will find many videos showing how to use specific features of the product.

When you find a person that publishes content to your liking, subscribe to their YouTube channel. This way you will be notified when they publish something new.

Conferences and User Groups

Oracle professionals live and work all over the world. We interact with each other in all of the social media platforms discussed in this chapter, but nothing compares to face-to-face communication. This is where conferences and user groups come into play.

Conferences draw a lot of people to them. In 2014, Oracle's annual OpenWorld conference hosted over 60,000 attendees. That's a lot of people all talking about Oracle! OpenWorld is a great place to hear the latest and greatest news about Oracle. You get a chance to talk with Oracle employees in a one-on-one setting in the demo grounds. Oracle employees are willing to walk you through a demonstration of a particular product and you can ask questions along the way. You can attend many of the conference's sessions and learn from presenters who are experts in the field. You can also meet up with the people you interact with in social media. When you interact with a person in a discussion thread in some forum, your conversation often sticks to the thread's subject. When you meet them in person, your conversation may go off in other directions, tangential to the initial topic. This is a great way to foster discussion of things you may never talk about in your normal settings. If you cannot attend a conference in person, see if they offer the ability to attend virtually through live streaming of keynote addresses and breakout sessions.

The Independent Oracle Users Group (IOUG) hosts an annual conference as well, called COLLABORATE. You will find a lot of the same vendors and database experts at IOUG's COLLABORATE as you will at OpenWorld. The big difference between the conferences is that OpenWorld's content is defined by Oracle Corporation whereas IOUG's content is defined by the IOUG members.

Many regions have their own, independent user groups focusing on Oracle. To find a user group close to you, search in Google. For example, if you live in Dallas, search for "Dallas Oracle User Group" and you will see a link for the DOUG. Many large cities have their own user group. Joining one of these groups is a great way to network with people in your region. You do not have to travel very far to participate in their events. Most regional user groups have one- or two-day mini-conferences you can attend. These conferences are usually attended by individuals local to that area. Some regional user groups host larger conferences, like the Denver area's Rocky Mountain Oracle User Group's (RMOUG) Training Days conference, which draws attendees from all over the nation. User group conferences are not limited to the United States. Many areas all over the world have Oracle user groups and conferences.

Take some time to find an Oracle user group in your area. Become a member and start interacting with your Oracle peers. Not only will you learn more about Oracle, you will create a network of valuable resources that you can lean on during your career. This network can help you resolve issues or even find a job.

As your career progresses, you should be answering questions on discussion forums and writing blog posts, if you have been following the advice in this chapter. Over time, your Oracle knowledge will grow and you will be ready to share more of what you have learned. The next step is presenting at an Oracle conference. Conferences are always looking for presenters. They want to provide a ton of information to their attendees. Simply put, they need people to provide that information. Prior to the conference, the organizers will ask for people to submit *abstracts*. These are short descriptions of a presentation that you may be interested in providing at the conference. Typically, an abstract is one paragraph in length and explains what you want to discuss and how it is of value to the attendees. Always be on the lookout for the calls for abstracts to conferences. When you are ready to present at a conference, start filling out the calls for abstracts to see if you are chosen. Start by presenting at your local user group conferences and work your way up from there. Presenting at a conference gives you the same benefits as writing blogs or answering your questions. If you are going to explain something to someone, you will learn it better that if you had not. Another great benefit is that many of the organizers will give you free attendance to the rest of the conference just for presenting. The larger conferences provide free gifts to their presenters. You will also start to be recognized by others in your community for your skill.

Moving On

We have spent the last few chapters discussing how you can learn more about Oracle and even resolve issues. It starts by reading the Oracle documentation. The documentation provides a plethora of information. The hardest part of using the Oracle documentation is trying to find the information you seek, due to its sheer size. The more you use the Oracle documentation, the easier it will be to navigate.

We then discussed the Oracle data dictionary. The data dictionary helps you learn details about your specific database. The data dictionary is documentation of the database's contents.

If the documentation or data dictionary cannot help you, the next place to look is often My Oracle Support. You can search its extensive knowledge base for answers. You can file a service request and obtain help from a support analyst.

If you have exhausted all of these sources and are not able to resolve your issue, then the next place to turn is to social media. There are many social media outlets at your disposal, as we have covered in this chapter.

In the next chapter, we shift gears to maintaining our Oracle database. After we have installed Oracle and created our database, we need to learn how to apply patches and keep it up to date. The following chapter will discuss how to upgrade your Oracle database to a new version.

CHAPTER 17

Patching

In the previous four chapters, we discussed the different avenues for you to learn and grow your Oracle DBA career. The Oracle documentation is a must read. Eventually, you will have to interact with Oracle Support. Hopefully you are starting to use social media to expand your interactions with Oracle professionals around the world.

This chapter shifts the focus toward maintaining your Oracle database. Recall that earlier in the book we built a virtual machine and created our first Oracle database to serve as a testbed. Subsequent chapters helped harden the installation by discussing recovery and backups and database security. Now it's time to keep that database working for the lifetime of the system.

Patching Overview

Oracle patches are inevitable if you are doing a proper job. Sadly, I have met a number of Oracle database administrators that have never patched an Oracle database, even ones that have been around for years. You should be applying patches, regularly.

Oracle patches are often applied for one of two reasons:

- *To fix a known issue*: These patches should only be applied under the direction of Oracle Support.

- *To keep your database software up to date*: Notably, to plug security holes. These patches should be applied as they are released.

Patches are only available from My Oracle Support. You will need a paid Oracle Support contract to be able to download patches. If you come across a patch from a third party, do not download and install it. For starters, the patch is not official, and you may run into support and legal issues down the road. Additionally, you have no guarantees that the third party has not introduced some sort of malware into the patch.

© Brian Peasland 2019
B. Peasland, *Oracle DBA Mentor*, https://doi.org/10.1007/978-1-4842-4321-3_17

Tip   Only download patches from MOS. You will need a valid support contract.

Every patch you will ever download from MOS will contain a Readme file, either in text or HTML form. Always read the Readme file. While that may sound like obvious advice, I constantly see questions on Oracle discussion forums asking how to apply a certain patch. The Readme file is there for a reason. It contains step-by-step instructions on how to apply the patch. The Readme file also contains known issues with the patch and known installation issues as well. If you have to roll back the patch, instructions are in the Readme file. Even if you are familiar with applying patches, read the Readme file every time. Just when you think you know the process, Oracle will change something and the old way of installing the patch will not work correctly.

Tip   Always read the patch's Readme file.

Whenever you apply a patch, never, ever apply it in production first. Always apply the patch through your development lifecycle infrastructure. If you have them, apply the patch in development databases first. Then apply in test databases. Finally, apply in production. Take a break between patching each of these stages. If you can, wait at least one week between the time you apply in dev to the time you apply in test. Then wait another week before you apply to production. This means it will take about two weeks to run through the chain of databases. You want this intentional delay so that any issues caused by the patch are found before the patch is in production. By the time the patch is in production, you should be confident in your ability to apply it and that it will not break any application or database functionality.

Many times, I will apply the patch to a testbed before installing it in my development databases. My testbed does not have the same schema objects as dev, test, and prod but it does let me practice the patch installation on a system that no one else is using. While we often treat development and test as non-production platforms, I am fond of saying that "development is production for someone." If your development database is down, application developers may not be able to work. We take more risks with development and test than we do in production, but we can also minimize risk by working in a testbed prior to development.

Oracle Versions

The Oracle database we installed for our testbed in Chapter 5 is the Oracle 12.2.0.1 version. It is possible that you have older and newer versions in your enterprise today. New versions are released and we migrate our database forward, a process known as upgrading that we will cover in the next chapter. Oracle Corporation will also refer to these versions are *releases*. You can use the terms release and version interchangeably.

Unless we are talking with other database administrators, Oracle Support analysts, or others that want to know the exact technical details, we often say "Oracle 12c." This notation is not a proper version. The letter *c* is a marketing label.

I started my database administration career working with the Oracle 7.1 version. Back then, there were no marketing labels on the versions. I upgraded my first Oracle database to Oracle 7.2 and then to the Oracle 8.0 version. Right about the time Oracle 8.1 was set to be released, the Internet had exploded. Some people referred to this as the "dot-com era." Many web-enabled applications were already running with an Oracle database backend, but Oracle Corporation wanted to say they had a database ready for the Internet. The first Oracle 8.1 version was marketed as Oracle8*i* Database, where the *i* stood for Internet. The IT industry was just wrapping up tagging everything with an *e* for electronic, such as e-mail, e-documents, etc. Now every IT vendor on the planet wanted to be known as an Internet company and we started seeing the letter *i* popping up everywhere. Still today, we have the iPhone, iPad, and iTunes from Apple.

Oracle Corporation, always wanting to distance themselves from the competition, started changing the marketing label every so often. After Oracle8*i*, we were treated to Oracle9*i* Database. As we were getting ready for the next major Oracle database version to be released, we Oracle professionals that were not Oracle employees started referring to the next version as 10*i*, but we were mistaken. When Oracle 10 was released, it had the marketing label Oracle Database 10*g*, where the letter *g* stood for *grid* computing. Oracle 10*g* was the version where Oracle Corporation really started pushing Oracle's Real Application Clusters (RAC) and other Grid Infrastructure technologies. This marketing label stuck with us through the Oracle 11*g* version as well. As you can imagine, before the launch of the first Oracle 12 database, we non-Oracle employees started referring to it as Oracle 12*g*, only to be wrong once again. By the time Oracle 12 was released, *cloud* computing was the favorite topic of IT vendors around the world. So, Oracle gave us Oracle Database 12*c* instead.

None of these letters really tells us the Oracle version. Oracle8*i* was really Oracle versions 8.1.5, 8.1.6, and 8.1.7. Oracle9*i* ran through a number of versions, from 9.0.1 up to 9.2.0.7. Oracle 12*c* has provided Oracle 12.1.0.1, 12.1.0.2, 12.2.0.1, and 12.2.0.2. As you can see, each marketing label has a number of different versions associated with it.

If you are talking with Oracle professionals, the exact version may make a difference in your conversation. You should not refer to Oracle 12*c*, but the full version. Each version, however small of a difference in the version number, changes features and functionality, which can make a big difference in your discussion. If you are talking with non-Oracle people, using the marketing label is normally sufficient.

Tip   Know your audience when referring to specific Oracle versions.

Then there were the patchsets. When Oracle 8.1.7 was released, its version number was 8.1.7.0. After a period of time, Oracle Corporation released a patchset fixing a number of bugs. The database administrator installed the 8.1.7.1 patchset over the top of the existing 8.1.7.0 Oracle home directory. When the 8.1.7.2 patchset was released, the DBA installed this on top of the same home directory. Oracle also released the 8.1.7.3 and 8.1.7.4 patchsets, the latter being the end of the line for the 8.1.7 version. Back in those days, when you moved from 8.1.6 to 8.1.7, it was a database *upgrade*, and patchsets changed the fourth number in the version.

Of course, things change over time. Beginning with Oracle 11.2, Oracle stopped releasing patchsets as we used to think of them. What looked like a patchset was now a full version. Oracle changed the fourth digit in the version number to signify an upgrade rather than a patchset. The Oracle 11.2.0.2 version was not installed on top of 11.2.0.1, but rather into a new Oracle home directory. If you look back a few paragraphs to where Oracle 12*c* was discussed, you will see the versions in the list all have four places in the digits because we started to think about those Oracle versions differently than in the past.

It used to be common wisdom that no one ever trusted a critical production IT system to the first version. When Oracle 8.0 was released, that was thought of as the first Oracle 8 version, so people shied away from it. They waited for the first or second patchset. Better yet, the cautious DBA waited for the first patchset after the first change from the dot-zero release, meaning the first patchset after 8.1 was released. The idea was that the first version was buggy and letting someone else sort out these problems was wiser. Our systems are too critical to be exposed to bugs. We will wait for a good, stable release before we move forward with our Oracle versions.

After the initial release of Oracle 11g, we started seeing Oracle Corporation make major changes before the next major version. Oracle 11.1 was available and Oracle 11.2

introduced the SCAN Listeners and other new features to Grid Infrastructure. After Oracle 12.1.0.1 was released, the 12.1.0.2 version introduced to Oracle's new In-Memory database features. What used to be a patchset version change was now introducing big changes. The point is that if you are fearful of changes causing problems and you want a stable release, each new release is going to bring changes yet you have to keep moving forward.

In discussion forums, I see questions asked all the time about what version of Oracle is a stable release. The answer is any supported version you are using today. At the time of writing, the fully supported versions are Oracle 11.2.0.4, 12.1.0.2, and 18. (I'll get to the fact that the Oracle 18 version has no number after it shortly.) The Oracle database is a mature product that is over 30 years old. Many companies use Oracle for their database needs and quite simply cannot have transactions fail or systems that are down for an extended period of time, and they trust today's Oracle versions. This is not to say that Oracle versions are free from defects. There are always bugs in the software and there always will be.

Why did Oracle Corporation start introducing new functionality in their product before the next major release? The answer is because they wanted to be quicker to market to ward off their competitors who were releasing new features at a faster rate. The entire IT world has shifted for more rapid deployments of new features in software. This shift has brought about agile development methodologies, added DevOps personnel in the organization, and contributed to the rise of cloud computing that facilitates a faster pace of change. Oracle Corporation is not alone in adopting this faster pace.

If you have paid attention, there is no Oracle 13, 14, 15, 16, or 17 version. We jumped from Oracle 12c to Oracle 18c. Oracle 12.1 was introduced in 2013. Oracle 12.2 was released in 2016 for Oracle's cloud customers and in 2017 for on-premises deployments. Because of Oracle Corporation's desire to release more regularly, they changed the numbering scheme to match the calendar year of release. Oracle 18 is denoted as such because it was released in 2018. When Oracle released it's new version in 2019, it was named Oracle 19. Depending on the patch you apply to your Oracle 18c database, the version number may be 18.1, 18.2, and so on.

If you're not totally confused by all of these version numbers so far, Oracle's quarterly patches, which we will discuss in this chapter, change the version number to denote the patch that was applied. If you applied the July 2018 patches to an Oracle 12.1.0.2 database, the version is technically 12.1.0.2.180717 to denote that the patch from July 17, 2018 has been applied.

These version numbers are enough to start making one's head dizzy. I mentioned the history of these version numbers so that you can have a better understanding of why the number scheme has changed over the years and what the digits mean. Oracle Corporation changed the patches and how it affects the versions, once again, for the Oracle 18c release, as we will see later in this chapter.

OPatch

Oracle now uses a Java-based utility to apply patches to its database software. That utility is named OPatch, which is obviously short for Oracle Patch. Because this utility is Java based, it is the same utility no matter which platform you run Oracle on, a feature that makes it easier for the Oracle DBA. If we are in charge of Oracle on different platforms, such as Linux and Windows, we do not have to patch differently. It is usually the same process on both systems.

Most patches will tell you a minimum OPatch version that must be used to apply the patch. You may have to patch the patch software first. To see the current OPatch version, use the example in Listing 17-1.

Listing 17-1. OPatch Version

```
[oracle@dbamentor ~]$ $ORACLE_HOME/OPatch/opatch version
OPatch Version: 12.2.0.1.6

OPatch succeeded.
```

When you install the Oracle database software, it will automatically include OPatch in the $ORACLE_HOME/OPatch directory. Normally, the installed OPatch version is already out of date and there is a newer version you should be using. In Listing 17-1, we can see the OPatch version is 12.2.0.1.6, which is the version that was installed when we installed the Oracle 12.2 software on our testbed.

To obtain the latest version, we need to sign on to My Oracle Support and then click the Patches & Updates tab. OPatch is downloaded via patch 6880880, and you can enter that patch number in the appropriate search box. Then click the Search button. You will need to select the OPatch version and platform you seek. Figure 17-1 shows that I have selected the Linux x86-64 platform and the 12.2 release to match my testbed.

Patch 6880880

| Simple Search | Advanced Search | Quick Links | Saved Searches |

Description   **OPatch 12.2.0.1.14 for DB 12.2 releases (JUL 2018)**
Product   **Oracle Global Lifecycle Management OPatch**
Select a Release   OPatch 12.2.0.1.0
Platform or Language ⓘ Linux x86-64
Last Updated   **11-JUL-2018**
Size   **94M (99183505 bytes)**
Entitlement Class ⓘ   **Software**
Classification ⓘ   **General**

| Download | View Readme | View Digest |

Figure 17-1. *OPatch download*

Download the OPatch update to your testbed. You should view the Readme file for instructions as well. The Readme file will tell you to unzip the download file in the $ORACLE_HOME directory. It is always a good idea to back up your old OPatch version first. I have placed the downloaded zip file in the $HOME directory. I will now install OPatch into $ORACLE_HOME. First, the OPatch directory is moved to a backup location. The zip file is copied to $ORACLE_HOME and then unzipped. I then check the new OPatch version to make sure it is higher than 12.2.0.1.6 that was installed by default. These steps are shown in Listing 17-2.

Listing 17-2. Updating OPatch

```
[oracle@dbamentor ~]$ cd $ORACLE_HOME
[oracle@dbamentor 12.2.0.1]$ mv OPatch OPatch.old
[oracle@dbamentor 12.2.0.1]$ cp $HOME/p6880880_122010_Linux-x86-64.zip .
[oracle@dbamentor 12.2.0.1]$ unzip p6880880_122010_Linux-x86-64.zip
[oracle@dbamentor 12.2.0.1]$ $ORACLE_HOME/OPatch/opatch version
OPatch Version: 12.2.0.1.14

OPatch succeeded.
```

We have successfully updated OPatch as we are now ready to apply some patches.

Tip   OPatch is always updated by downloading patch 6880880.

Quarterly Patches

Every quarter, Oracle Corporation releases a new bundle of patches. The patches are released in January, April, July, and October every year, usually released on the Tuesday closest to the 17th of the month.

Oracle will only provide patches for fully supported versions. In the next chapter, we will discuss how to upgrade your database to a newer version. The quarterly patches are just one reason you will want to keep your database version up to date.

When Oracle Corporation first started releasing quarterly patches, the patches only contained fixes to plug security holes in the software. The patch became known as the quarter's Cumulative Patch Update (CPU). The patches are cumulative as the name states, meaning a patch released for a quarter contains all the fixes for that quarter plus fixes for the previous quarters as well. If you install Oracle 12.2.0.1 as we did in our testbed, you do not have to find each and every CPU released for that version. Just apply the latest and greatest CPU and you are all caught up.

Keeping up with the quarterly CPU is one of the ways you can help secure your organization's database infrastructure. Many organizations have a policy that the security patches must be applied. Sadly, too many companies do not have any such policy and the database goes unpatched and, as a result, has gaping security holes all over it. If your organization does not have any such policy, work with management to get one implemented, if for nothing else other than the databases.

If you want to be notified when the security patches are released, sign on to `http://otn.oracle.com` with your Oracle Single Sign-On account. Then mouse over the Account button and click the Account link. Next, click Subscriptions. Expand the section named "Oracle security notifications" and check the box next to Security Alerts. Click the Save button.

When the quarterly patches contained only security fixes, downloading and installing was easy because you only had one choice. Over time, things became much more difficult. Oracle Corporation decided to create a new quarterly patch type called the Patch Set Update (PSU). The PSU contained the same security fixes as well as other bug fixes they deem to be safe for everyone's environment. When the PSU was created, the CPU was renamed to be the Security Patch Update (SPU). I think they could have done a better job with the acronyms because PSU and SPU are too similar. Oracle started referring to the collection of SPU and PSU as the CPU. Today, if you ever hear of the CPU, it is meant to refer to a collection of quarterly patches. Oracle also changed the name to Critical Patch Updates, but they are still cumulative.

Up until Oracle 11.2, you had your choice of SPU or PSU to apply each quarter. Many database administrators around the world would apply only the SPU because it introduced the least amount of change in their Oracle environments. However, Oracle Corporation's official recommendation was to apply the PSU, but the choice was up to the DBA. When Oracle 12.1 was released, the SPU was no longer supplied for that version. Oracle releases just the PSU for the 12.1 version. Oracle Corporation took away that choice for 12*c*. To make matters even more confusing, it was recommended for DBAs who ran Oracle on Windows to apply the Bundle Patch (BP) instead of the PSU. The BP contains everything in the PSU plus even more bug fixes.

Oracle 12.2 changed the quarterly patches. Oracle 12.2 introduced the Release Update (RU) and the Release Update Revision (RUR) patches. A Release Update contains security fixes and bug fixes just like a PSU does. The RU also contains fixes to the Oracle Optimizer, which is responsible for determining an efficient method to execute all SQL statements sent to the database.

At some point, Oracle 18 was released. The following quarter, Oracle released the 18 RU, which changes the Oracle version to 18.1. The second RU changes the Oracle version to 18.2, and so on. If you apply the RU to an Oracle 18 database, you will have the most fixes you possibly can. Please note that applying the RU to an Oracle 18 database changes the version to make it look as if an Oracle upgrade has taken place, but this is not the case. The RU is a patch, not an upgrade. Making the issue even more confusing is that applying the RU to an Oracle 12.2 database does not change the version to 12.3 or higher.

Some people do not like making so many changes to the Oracle Optimizer. One bad change can make the Optimizer choose inefficient execution plans, and application performance will suffer. Oracle provides us with the RUR, which contains the same security and bug fixes as the RU but does not have the Optimizer fixes in it, which means the RUR keeps the Optimizer at the same level of functionality. The first quarter after Oracle 18 was released, only the RU was available. The second quarter, the DBA had a choice to apply the next RU or apply the RUR. However, the Optimizer changes are frozen for only six months, so the RUR only buys you a little time. Oracle Corporation is recommending you apply the RU every quarter. Their position is that the RUR is only for special circumstances.

All of that can be confusing, especially with all of the acronyms. To make matters easier, the following are the recommendations for each Oracle version for your quarterly patches. Unless you have a specific reason, follow Oracle's recommendation to determine which quarterly patch to apply.

- Versions prior to 11.2.0.4: Upgrade to a more recent version

- Oracle 11.2.0.4: Apply the PSU

- Oracle 12.1: Apply the PSU (or BP if on Windows)

- Oracle 12.2: Apply the RU

- Oracle 18 and 19: Apply the RU

For some reason that I have never been able to figure out, getting these quarterly patches is not as easy as you might think. Oracle publishes a link for us, but you need to click a few more times before you can actually download the patch. We will walk through how to find the quarterly patch. Point a web browser to `http://otn.oracle.com` and look for the box titled Essential Links, partially shown in Figure 17-2.

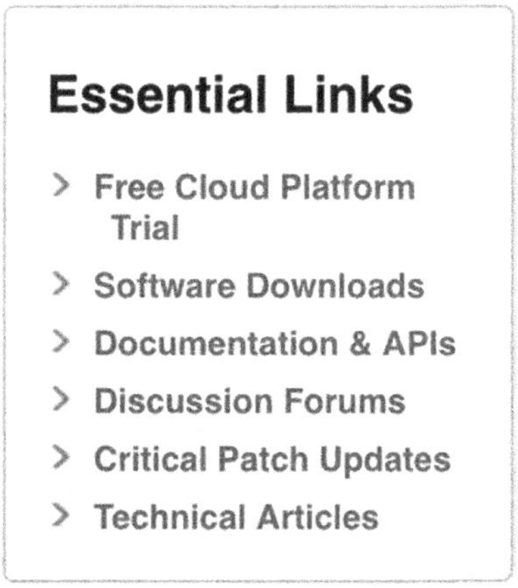

Essential Links

> Free Cloud Platform Trial
> Software Downloads
> Documentation & APIs
> Discussion Forums
> Critical Patch Updates
> Technical Articles

Figure 17-2. *OTN Essential Links*

In that list, you can see the link for Critical Patch Updates. Click that link. Note that you can find a similar link on the Dashboard of My Oracle Support. Either link takes you to the Critical Path Updates, Security Alerts and Bulletins page. Scroll down just a bit until you see the section titled Critical Patch Updates, shown in Figure 17-3.

Critical Patch Updates

Critical Patch Updates are collections of security fixes for Oracle products. They are available to customers with valid support contracts. They are released on the Tuesday closest to the 17th day of January, April, July and October. The next four dates are:

- 16 October 2018
- 15 January 2019
- 16 April 2019
- 16 July 2019

A pre-release announcement will be published on the Thursday preceding each Critical Patch Update release.

The Critical Patch Updates released since 2014 are listed in the following table. Critical Patch Updates released before 2014 are available here.

Critical Patch Update	Latest Version/Date
Critical Patch Update - July 2018	Rev 6, 4 September 2018
Critical Patch Update - April 2018	Rev 3, 23 May 2018
Critical Patch Update - January 2018	Rev 8, 20 March 2018
Critical Patch Update - October 2017	Rev 10, 15 February 2018
Critical Patch Update - July 2017	Rev 6, 20 March 2018
Critical Patch Update - April 2017	Rev 5, 20 June 2017
Critical Patch Update - January 2017	Rev 5, 18 May 2017
Critical Patch Update - October 2016	Rev 4, 21 November 2016
Critical Patch Update - July 2016	Rev 2, 18 October 2016
Critical Patch Update - April 2016	Rev 3, 20 December 2016
Critical Patch Update - January 2016	Rev 2, 12 February 2016
Critical Patch Update - October 2015	Rev 6, 27 October 2015
Critical Patch Update - July 2015	Rev 4, 30 July 2015
Critical Patch Update - April 2015	Rev 3, 28 April 2015
Critical Patch Update - January 2015	Rev 2, 10 March 2015
Critical Patch Update - October 2014	Rev 5, 21 November 2014
Critical Patch Update - July 2014	Rev 2, 24 July 2014
Critical Patch Update - April 2014	Rev 2, 28 April 2014
Critical Patch Update - January 2014	Rev 1, 14 January 2014

Figure 17-3. *CPU links*

The first part of this section tells you the next four CPU release dates so that you are informed in advance. The table that follows contains a link to each quarter's patches. You can download every CPU for the past few years, but there is rarely a reason to download anything but the most recent CPU, which is at the top of the table. Click the most recent CPU link.

The next page is the Critical Patch Update Advisory for that quarter. The table that follows the description contains patches for each and every Oracle product they provide. The list is quite extensive and in alphabetical order. You need to scroll down to find Oracle Database Server, as shown in Figure 17-4.

Oracle Communications User Data Repository, versions 10.x, 12.x	Oracle Communications User Data Repository
Oracle Database Server, versions 11.2.0.4, 12.1.0.2, 12.2.0.1, 18.1, 18.2	Database
Oracle E-Business Suite, versions 12.1.1, 12.1.2, 12.1.3, 12.2.3, 12.2.4, 12.2.5, 12.2.6, 12.2.7	E-Business Suite

Figure 17-4. *Oracle Database Server link*

Do not click the link on the left with the different versions in it. Instead, click the link on the right side of that table that says just Database. You will then be asked to provide credentials to connect to MOS if you have not authenticated recently. Everything up to this point is in the public domain, but the next page is a MOS Note, which means you need a paid support contract.

The MOS Note for the quarterly patch provides relevant information you will want to read. One section details what is new for that quarter. In the section of new information, Oracle provides what they call Post Release Patches. When the CPU is first released, it is only available for a handful of platforms. Other platforms are released a short period of time later. This section will tell you when those platforms are scheduled to release that quarter's patch.

Section 3 of this MOS Note gives details on the patch. I am only interested in patches for Oracle Database at this time. Section 3.1.4, shown in Figure 17-5, lists links to patches for each currently supported version.

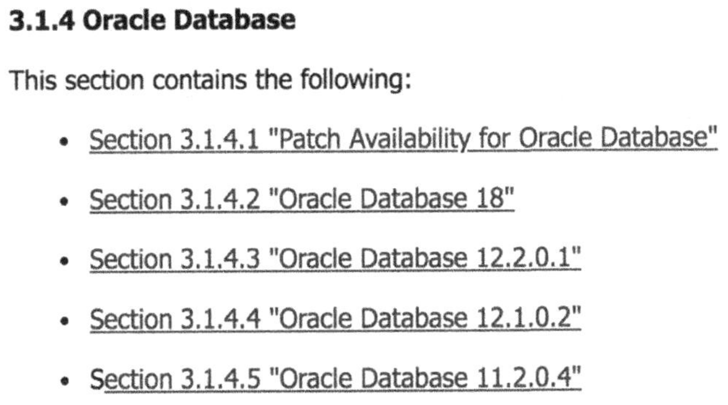

3.1.4 Oracle Database

This section contains the following:

- Section 3.1.4.1 "Patch Availability for Oracle Database"

- Section 3.1.4.2 "Oracle Database 18"

- Section 3.1.4.3 "Oracle Database 12.2.0.1"

- Section 3.1.4.4 "Oracle Database 12.1.0.2"

- Section 3.1.4.5 "Oracle Database 11.2.0.4"

Figure 17-5.   *Oracle Database version list*

Our testbed contains the 12.2.0.1 version, so click that link to be taken to Section 3.1.4.3. If you have a different Oracle version, you can click appropriately. Notice that the version list is pretty short. Only supported versions are shown. Any version not on the list is unsupported and will not receive the quarterly patches. You must upgrade to one of the versions on the list.

After clicking the database version, the browser will show a table listing the patches for that version. After all of that clicking, we are now at a place where we can see the patch numbers to download. If you want to include the Oracle Java Virtual Machine (OJVM) patches, they are in the first box in the table. The second box is shown in Figure 17-6 and it does not contain the OJVM patches.

Patch Availability for Oracle Database 12.2.0.1

Product Home	Patch	Advisory Number
Oracle Database Server home	Combo OJVM Update 12.2.0.1.180717 and Database Update 12.2.0.1.180717 Patch 28317292 for UNIX, or Combo OJVM Update 12.2.0.1.180717 and GI Update 12.2.0.1.180717 Patch 28317269, or Quarterly Full Stack download for Exadata (Jul2018) 12.2.0.1 Patch 28183343 for Linux x86-64 and Solaris x86-64, or Quarterly Full Stack download for SuperCluster (Jul2018) 12.2.0.1 Patch 28183354 for Solaris SPARC 64-Bit	CVE-2017-15095, CVE-2018-2939, CVE-2018-3004, CVE-2018-3110
Oracle Database Server home	Database Jul 2018 Update 12.2.0.1.180717 Patch 28163133 for UNIX, or Database Jan 2018 Revision 12.2.0.1.180717 Patch 27872031, or Database Apr 2018 Revision 12.2.0.1.180717 Patch 27848049, or GI Update 12.2.0.1.180717 Patch 28183653, or	CVE-2017-15095, CVE-2018-2939

Figure 17-6. *Oracle CPU patch links*

Our testbed is on Linux, which is in the UNIX category. Click the Patch 28163133 link in the table shown in Figure 17-6 (this patch is the first one listed in the second row of the table).

The next page contains a link for each of the UNIX platforms. Scroll down to the line for the Linux x86-64 platform and click the link to the left. We can see in Figure 17-7 that this is just one of many patches on the page. Also notice that because this is an Oracle 12.2 database, we are downloading a Release Update (RU) type of patch.

28183133	DATABASE JUL 2018 RELEASE UPDATE 12.2.0.1.180717 (Patch)	12.2.0.1.0	Systems (32-bit) (American English)
28163133	DATABASE JUL 2018 RELEASE UPDATE 12.2.0.1.180717 (Patch)	12.2.0.1.0	Linux x86 (American English)
28183653	GI JUL 2018 RELEASE UPDATE 12.2.0.1.180717 (System Patch)	12.2.0.1.0	IBM AIX on POWER Systems (64-bit)

Figure 17-7. *Patch download for Linux*

If you click the wrong hyperlink, you will have problems installing the patches on your system. Make sure you selected the proper one. On the next screen, shown in Figure 17-8, make sure the platform is correct. Even though you may have clicked the correct hyperlink for your platform, there are times MOS gets it wrong here, so double-check the platform.

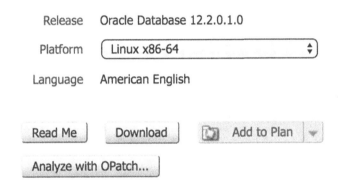

Figure 17-8. *PSU Platform Selection*

You can view the patch's Readme file by clicking the Read Me button. The Readme file will also be in the download. Click the Download button and the screen in Figure 17-9 will appear.

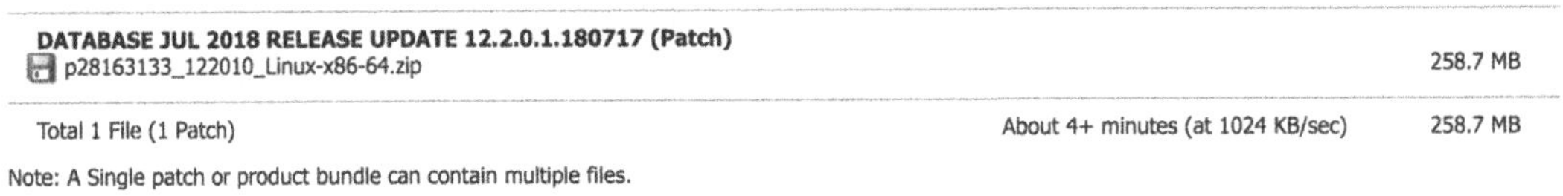

DATABASE JUL 2018 RELEASE UPDATE 12.2.0.1.180717 (Patch)		
p28163133_122010_Linux-x86-64.zip		258.7 MB
Total 1 File (1 Patch)	About 4+ minutes (at 1024 KB/sec)	258.7 MB

Note: A Single patch or product bundle can contain multiple files.

Figure 17-9. *Download link*

We are finally here! I wish it was easier, but after all of that clicking, we can now actually download the patch. Click the link to begin the download. After the download is complete, unzip the patch in its own, empty directory.

Installing the PSU

Most any patch you will ever apply is a two-step process. First, the Oracle software is updated. Then the internal database is updated. Some patches may only have one of the steps, but most have two. Applying the PSU is always a two-step process. OPatch is used for the first step, and another utility, datapatch, is used for the second step. Do not worry about updating the datapatch utility. It is part of OPatch and was updated when you updated OPatch.

Now that the PSU has been downloaded and unzipped, let's define our environment variables. The PATH environment variable will have both the $ORACLE_HOME/bin and $ORACLE_HOME/OPatch directories.

After unzipping the patch file in an empty directory, there are three files, a subdirectory named with the patch number, the zip file, and a file named PatchSearch. xml, as you can see in Listing 17-3. Environment variables are also declared in this code sample.

Listing 17-3. Ready for Patching

```
[oracle@dbamentor PSU]$ ls
28163133  p28163133_122010_LINUX-x86-64.zip  PatchSearch.xml
 [oracle@dbamentor PSU]$ export ORACLE_HOME=/u01/app/oracle/product/12.2.0.1
[oracle@dbamentor PSU]$ export PATH=$ORACLE_HOME/OPatch:$ORACLE_HOME/bin:$PATH
[oracle@dbamentor PSU]$ export ORACLE_SID=orcl
```

Patch filenames are usually of the form **p***number_version***_platform.zip**. In Listing 17-3, the patch file is in bold text and we can see this is patch number 28163133 for the 12.2.0.1 database on Linux x86-64 platforms. The next quarter's PSU will have a completely different patch number.

To apply the patch, we must first stop all Oracle software running out of this home directory. We also change to the directory created from the unzip operation. In Listing 17-4, we shut down Oracle software on our testbed.

Listing 17-4. Shutting Down Oracle

```
[oracle@dbamentor PSU]$ sqlplus /nolog

SQL*Plus: Release 12.2.0.1.0 Production on Sat Sep 8 19:32:03 2018

Copyright (c) 1982, 2016, Oracle.  All rights reserved.

SQL> connect / as sysdba
Connected.
SQL> shutdown immediate
Database closed.
Database dismounted.
ORACLE instance shut down.
SQL> exit
Disconnected from Oracle Database 12c Enterprise Edition Release
12.2.0.1.0 - 64bit Production
[oracle@dbamentor PSU]$ cd 28163133/
```

Next, we run the opatch apply command to install the patch. Please note that while I am showing you the steps to apply the patch, this is no substitute for reading the patch's Readme file for complete instructions.

When OPatch starts, it always shows information such as the OPatch version, the Oracle Home directory, and the location of the log file generated for this execution of OPatch. OPatch will run some prerequisite checks to ensure a smooth installation of the patch. If any of the prerequisite checks fail, OPatch will end execution here. The database administrator will need to resolve the issue and then run opatch again. In Listing 17-5, we tell opatch to apply the patch in our current directory.

Listing 17-5. opatch apply Prerequisite Checks

```
[oracle@dbamentor 28163133]$ opatch apply
Oracle Interim Patch Installer version 12.2.0.1.14
Copyright (c) 2018, Oracle Corporation.  All rights reserved.

Oracle Home       : /u01/app/oracle/product/12.2.0.1
Central Inventory : /u01/app/oraInventory
   from           : /u01/app/oracle/product/12.2.0.1/oraInst.loc
```

```
OPatch version      : 12.2.0.1.14
OUI version         : 12.2.0.1.4
Log file location : /u01/app/oracle/product/12.2.0.1/cfgtoollogs/opatch/
opatch2018-09-11_22-54-18PM_1.log

Verifying environment and performing prerequisite checks...
OPatch continues with these patches:   28163133

Do you want to proceed? [y|n]
```

Once everything checks out, the opatch utility asks if it is okay to proceed with the patch installation. You will want to make sure all Oracle software running out of this home is down and then respond with y. The opatch utility will ask you to confirm that everything is down, as shown in Listing 17-6.

Listing 17-6. OPatch Confirmation

```
Do you want to proceed? [y|n]
y
User Responded with: Y
All checks passed.

Please shutdown Oracle instances running out of this ORACLE_HOME on the
local system.
(Oracle Home = '/u01/app/oracle/product/12.2.0.1')

Is the local system ready for patching? [y|n]
```

Once you respond with y, the opatch utility will begin to do its work. The first thing it does is make a backup of any files it will be modified in ORACLE_HOME. This way, should you need to roll back the patch, the opatch utility will simply restore those files from the backups.

The opatch utility may inform you that there are patches for optional components that are not present in the current ORACLE_HOME directory. This message is informational and the opatch utility will skip that portion of the patch. After that, we can see the opatch utility applying the patches to various components that are installed in that home. I trimmed the output in Listing 17-7 for brevity, as we do not need to see each and every component that the opatch utility updated.

Listing 17-7. OPatch Installing the Patch

```
Is the local system ready for patching? [y|n]
y
User Responded with: Y
Backing up files...
Applying interim patch '28163133' to OH '/u01/app/oracle/product/12.2.0.1'
ApplySession: Optional component(s) [ oracle.oid.client, 12.2.0.1.0 ] ,
[ oracle.has.crs, 12.2.0.1.0 ] , [ oracle.ons.daemon, 12.2.0.1.0 ] , [
oracle.network.cman, 12.2.0.1.0 ]  not present in the Oracle Home or a
higher version is found.

Patching component oracle.assistants.server, 12.2.0.1.0...

Patching component oracle.rdbms.rman, 12.2.0.1.0...

Patching component oracle.rdbms.rsf.ic, 12.2.0.1.0...

Patching component oracle.rdbms, 12.2.0.1.0..

Patching component oracle.sdo, 12.2.0.1.0...
Patch 28163133 successfully applied.
Log file location: /u01/app/oracle/product/12.2.0.1/cfgtoollogs/opatch/
opatch2018-09-11_22-54-18PM_1.log

OPatch succeeded.
```

There are two messages we want to see after the opatch utility is done. The first message is "Patch *xxxxx* successfully applied." The second message is "OPatch succeeded." If we do not see those messages, then something went wrong and we will need to look into the log file for clues to help resolve the issue.

Once the opatch utility has done its work, the first phase of updating the software is complete. It is time to start up the Listener and the database and then run the datapatch utility to complete the second phase. The Listener and the database instance are started in Listing 17-8.

Listing 17-8. Starting Oracle After Patching

```
[oracle@dbamentor 28163133]$ lsnrctl start

LSNRCTL for Linux: Version 12.2.0.1.0 - Production on 11-SEP-2018 23:06:22

Copyright (c) 1991, 2016, Oracle.  All rights reserved.

Starting /u01/app/oracle/product/12.2.0.1/bin/tnslsnr: please wait...

TNSLSNR for Linux: Version 12.2.0.1.0 - Production
Log messages written to /u01/app/oracle/diag/tnslsnr/dbamentor/listener/
alert/log.xml
Listening on: (DESCRIPTION=(ADDRESS=(PROTOCOL=tcp)(HOST=dbamentor)(PORT=1521)))

Connecting to (ADDRESS=(PROTOCOL=tcp)(HOST=)(PORT=1521))
STATUS of the LISTENER
------------------------
Alias                     LISTENER
Version                   TNSLSNR for Linux: Version 12.2.0.1.0 - Production
Start Date                11-SEP-2018 23:06:22
Uptime                    0 days 0 hr. 0 min. 0 sec
Trace Level               off
Security                  ON: Local OS Authentication
SNMP                      OFF
Listener Log File         /u01/app/oracle/diag/tnslsnr/dbamentor/listener/
                          alert/log.xml
Listening Endpoints Summary...
  (DESCRIPTION=(ADDRESS=(PROTOCOL=tcp)(HOST=dbamentor)(PORT=1521)))
The listener supports no services
The command completed successfully
[oracle@dbamentor 28163133]$ sqlplus /nolog

SQL*Plus: Release 12.2.0.1.0 Production on Tue Sep 11 23:06:25 2018

Copyright (c) 1982, 2016, Oracle.  All rights reserved.
```

```
SQL> connect / as sysdba
Connected to an idle instance.
SQL> startup
ORACLE instance started.

Total System Global Area 1660944384 bytes
Fixed Size                  8621376 bytes
Variable Size             989856448 bytes
Database Buffers          654311424 bytes
Redo Buffers                8155136 bytes
Database mounted.
Database opened.
SQL> exit
Disconnected from Oracle Database 12c Enterprise Edition Release
12.2.0.1.0 - 64bit Production
```

Next, we'll run the datapatch utility. The only command-line option is to tell datapatch to use verbose mode in its output, as we can see in Listing 17-9.

Listing 17-9. Datapatch Utility

```
[oracle@dbamentor 28163133]$ datapatch -verbose
SQL Patching tool version 12.2.0.1.0 Production on Tue Sep 11 23:08:42 2018
Copyright (c) 2012, 2018, Oracle.  All rights reserved.

Log file for this invocation: /u01/app/oracle/cfgtoollogs/sqlpatch/
sqlpatch_9674_2018_09_11_23_08_42/sqlpatch_invocation.log

Connecting to database...OK
Bootstrapping registry and package to current versions...done
Determining current state...done

Current state of SQL patches:
Bundle series DBRU:
  ID 180717 in the binary registry and not installed in the SQL registry
```

```
Adding patches to installation queue and performing prereq checks...
Installation queue:
  Nothing to roll back
  The following patches will be applied:
    28163133 (DATABASE JUL 2018 RELEASE UPDATE 12.2.0.1.180717)

Installing patches...
Patch installation complete.  Total patches installed: 1

Validating logfiles...
Patch 28163133 apply: SUCCESS
  logfile: /u01/app/oracle/cfgtoollogs/sqlpatch/28163133/22313390/28163133_
  apply_ORCL_2018Sep11_23_08_53.log (no errors)
SQL Patching tool complete on Tue Sep 11 23:09:54 2018
```

Datapatch will connect to the database and apply the current patch. We want to see the message "Patch *xxxxx* apply:SUCCESS" near the end of the output.

Any time we apply patches and update the internal part of the database, we run the risk of making some data dictionary objects become invalid. We can run the utlrp.sql supplied script, shown in Listing 17-10, to recompile any invalid objects.

Listing 17-10. Running utlrp.sql

```
[oracle@dbamentor 28163133]$ sqlplus /nolog

SQL*Plus: Release 12.2.0.1.0 Production on Tue Sep 11 23:12:06 2018

Copyright (c) 1982, 2016, Oracle.  All rights reserved.

SQL> connect / as sysdba
Connected.
SQL> @?/rdbms/admin/utlrp.sql

PL/SQL procedure successfully completed.
```

I omitted output in the middle of the script invocation and the end of execution in Listing 17-10 for brevity.

Congratulations! The patch has now been applied without any issues. The only thing that remains is to verify that the database thinks it is patched. We do this by querying a DBA view, as shown in Listing 17-11.

Listing 17-11. Querying DBA_REGISTRY_SQLPATCH

```
SQL> select description,status from dba_registry_sqlpatch;

DESCRIPTION                                        STATUS
-------------------------------------------------- ----------
DATABASE JUL 2018 RELEASE UPDATE 12.2.0.1.180717   SUCCESS
```

We can see from the DBA_REGISTRY_SQLPATCH view that the RU was successfully applied to this database. There have been occurrences where the opatch utility noted everything was successful, as did datapatch, yet this view was not populated correctly. If you use Oracle Enterprise Manager (EM) to monitor your database, EM will query this view to determine if the most recent patch was applied. Querying this view yourself at the end of the patch is a great way to ensure that EM will get the proper information.

Moving On

Patching your Oracle database is necessary to fix bugs in the database's operation and to close security holes and help keep the data safe. You should be applying the quarterly CPU patches for your database regularly. Never put an Oracle database into production status unless it has the latest and greatest CPU applied for your version.

As was stated in this chapter, the quarterly CPU patches are released for fully supported versions of Oracle. At some point, no matter who you are, your current version will go out of date and Oracle Corporation will stop releasing patches for it. Every database administrator will have to upgrade their database to a newer version at some point in their career. The next chapter discusses various upgrade techniques.

CHAPTER 18

Upgrades

After a database is created for the first time, the database administrator will maintain it by applying regular quarterly patches, as we saw in the previous chapter. The DBA may also have to apply, under the direction of Oracle Support, other patches to fix bugs. After some period of time has passed, maybe months or even years, the database administrator will need to upgrade the database to a newer version. This chapter will discuss the different upgrade paths and provide some best practices.

Reasons to Upgrade

I have met a number of database administrators that are afraid to upgrade their Oracle databases to a newer version. The most common reason for refusing to upgrade is the mantra, "If it ain't broke, don't fix it." Everything is working fine with their current configuration and the system is critical, so they choose to just leave it be. Their mindset is that upgrading any database always incurs a certain amount of risk, and the issues that could arise after an upgrade make upgrading not worth it. The inverse is true—the benefit far outweighs the risk. There are many reasons why you should upgrade your Oracle database, even if everything is working great today. This section will detail a number of reasons to upgrade your Oracle database, in no particular order.

As we saw in Chapter 17, security patches released on a quarterly basis are available only for fully supported versions. At the time of writing, the patches are available only for the 11.2.0.4, 12.1.0.2, 12.2.0.1, and 18 versions. If your Oracle database is not on this list, you have security holes that will never be plugged. While the database and its application may be running just fine, a hacker will love to exploit your approach. Always be on a supported version to obtain the security patches and make your database environment as secure as it can be.

© Brian Peasland 2019
B. Peasland, *Oracle DBA Mentor*, https://doi.org/10.1007/978-1-4842-4321-3_18

Oracle Support may also request that you upgrade to a supported version if you file a service request. If you are running on an unsupported version, the support analyst's favorite response is to upgrade and check to see if the problem still exists. Bugs are fixed all the time, and why should the analyst waste any time tracking down your issue if it is a known bug that has already been fixed? The analyst is hoping that the database upgrade will resolve the problem and they can close the ticket with minimal effort on their part.

Your company has likely paid for an Oracle Support contract. Upgrades are part of this contract. If you do not upgrade your databases, you are overpaying for support. You already paid for the newer database version, so enjoy it. That being said, there is one reason to refuse to upgrade your Oracle database. If you do not have a paid support contract, then upgrading to a newer version may land you in legal trouble with Oracle Corporation. If your support contract ends, you cannot upgrade to a version that was released after that contract expired. If you do not have a support contract, do not upgrade. If you do not have a support contract, this database must not be very important to the company.

Your new database version has many new features. When you upgrade, many new features are available to you. While it may take a good amount of effort to complete an Oracle upgrade, these new features are often great time savers. Some new features reduce the workload on database administrators. Others may shorten application development time. New features can let you move your database architecture in a different direction that benefits the organization's needs.

It is crazy the number of times I see people on discussion forums ask how to install a very old Oracle version on a new operating system. Oracle versions are certified for different OS platforms, and Oracle Corporation is not going to make the effort to ensure that the very old Oracle 8.0.5 version will work on Windows Server 2016, a much newer operating system. System administrators have no problems replacing hardware on a regular basis after the server has passed its warranty period. When hardware is replaced, admins often use the hardware replacement as a time to upgrade the operating system as well. If your company is replacing older hardware, as it should, the DBA should be upgrading Oracle as well, as they should.

As we will see later in this chapter, you can perform direct upgrades to a newer Oracle version from a limited subset of older versions. For example, you cannot directly upgrade an Oracle 7.3.4 database to Oracle 12.2.0.1 no matter how hard you try. You will have to upgrade to an intermediary version. If your database is very old, you may need multiple upgrades. The more upgrades you must complete before you reach your final version, the harder it may be to track down any upgrade issues. Was it the first, second, or third upgrade that caused your problem? If you are keeping current on your Oracle versions, the upgrades are less painful.

In addition to support from Oracle, and to maintain a certified combination with your operating system, the database administrator also needs to be mindful of the support from application vendors. Third-party applications are certified for specific database versions. If you want to upgrade an application, you may need to upgrade the database to keep pace. Sadly, too many application vendors lag behind the most current Oracle versions. I frequently hear database administrators complain they cannot upgrade their database because the application vendor has yet to support it, even if the Oracle version was released years ago! If your application vendor is very behind the current Oracle versions, you might want to reconsider your future business with that vendor.

In Chapter 16, we discussed how to interact with Oracle professionals from around the world through social media. Many of these people are very willing to help you resolve your Oracle problems and teach you more about the Oracle database. While many have worked with Oracle for a very long time, please do not expect them to remember the exact details of the very old versions. I have worked with Oracle since the 7.1 version, but I remember very little about it other than what still holds true in today's versions. I barely remember the intimate details that are specific to the Oracle 9.2 version. I will answer questions on discussion forums, but I am not going to be as helpful as you might want if your version is old. I have become adept at looking things up in the Oracle documentation, but I am not going to dig up an old documentation set, just to answer one question. I am more likely to respond, as politely as I can, to upgrade to a newer version. Oracle professionals that help you are doing so voluntarily. Very few of them are paid to provide you that service, so help them help you by keeping your version up to date.

Hopefully this section has helped convince you to upgrade your databases. You do not need to upgrade the moment a new version has been released, and it is perfectly acceptable to skip a version once in a while. For example, I have many production databases that are running Oracle 12.1.0.2 but will upgrade to Oracle 18.3, skipping the 12.2.0.1 version. It is my best practice to skip at most one version. I will not go from the 12.1.0.2 version to 19c, even if it is possible. The risks of skipping two versions, 12.2 and 18, are too great.

Upgrade and New Features Guides

Whenever a new Oracle version is released, there are two books that are a must read, cover to cover. Chapter 13 discussed the Oracle documentation set. By now, you know how to access it, so I will skip those details in this chapter.

The *Database Upgrade Guide* contains information on how to upgrade to the new version. This book contains instructions on how to upgrade your database. You must read this so that you reduce your chances of error during the upgrade process. This chapter will cover material you will find in that book, but you must still read it anyway. If you have performed many database upgrades and a new version comes out, read the new version's *Upgrade Guide*. Oracle changes the upgrade process all the time. Most of the upgrade process is the same, but they will throw in a few different changes here and there. The *Upgrade Guide* contains the details you need to know for a successful upgrade.

Tip   Read the *Upgrade Guide*!

After you have upgraded your database, make sure to read the *Database New Features Guide* for that version. Every new version has new features to explore. Some of those features may be of little value to you and your organization. Other new features will be a welcome change in your enterprise.

In addition to introducing new features for that version, the *New Features Guide* also contains a list of deprecated and obsolete features. A *deprecated* feature is one that is still available and still fully supported. It is a myth that deprecated features are not supported. Any feature still available in the Oracle database is supported so long as that version is supported. When a feature is deprecated, Oracle Corporation is telling us the feature will be going away in the future. Oracle never tells us when the feature will become unavailable. The LONG and LONG RAW datatypes have been deprecated for as long as I can remember, but they are still around. Sometimes, a feature is deprecated in one major release and gone in the next release. When a feature is deprecated, it is the database administrator's responsibility to figure out if that impacts the organization and to determine how to remediate it. Many times, a deprecated feature is replaced by a new feature and the DBA just needs to move to the replacement feature.

An *obsolete* feature is one that is no longer available. If the DBA is doing a proper job, this should not be a surprise because the feature was previously deprecated and the DBA has moved that functionality to something else. For example, the DBA has worked with the application development team to move from LONG and LONG RAW columns to CLOB and BLOB respectively. Once LONG and LONG RAW are obsolete, the DBA has no worries.

Things do slip through the cracks on occasion and a feature becomes obsolete before we have had a chance to take action. If we upgrade the database to the new version, we may have problems. The DBA should read the *New Features Guide* in the earlier planning stages of their upgrade activity and determine if any of the obsolete features are going to be a problem.

Upgrade Methodology

There are different upgrade methods available to you, as will be discussed in the next section. No matter which method you choose to upgrade an Oracle database, there are certain steps that you should always take to give yourself the best chance of success. Upgrading a production database does involve a certain amount of risk and mistakes can be perilous. Follow these steps and you will significantly reduce that risk:

1. Read the *Installation Guide* for the new version. You have likely read the guide for your current version. The new version may have new installation requirements.

2. Read the *Upgrade Guide* for the new version. Learn as much as you can about what it takes to upgrade successfully.

3. Create a testbed similar to what we have done in this book. Install your current version and create a database. Install the new database version and upgrade your database to this target version. You may learn a few things about upgrading to this version. Document any lessons learned.

4. Pick an upgrade method that you will be using to upgrade your production database. Each upgrade method has its own pros and cons. Once you determine the upgrade method that will work best for your specific situation, use that method to upgrade as you advance through development and test environments. If you do not have development or test environments, do whatever you need to get them for your organization. A change should not be pushed to production unless the change has been properly vetted in non-production environments.

5. Install the new version on a development database that is as close to production as possible. As you install the new version, document the process, step by step.

6. Upgrade the database using the method chosen in step 4. Document the process step by step. Make note of the length of downtime needed for the upgrade, as this will be used for planning the maintenance window for the production upgrade.

7. Test the application against the upgraded database. If your company has them, leverage automated testing tools to ensure nothing has broken and performance is still at acceptable levels. If something is broken, determine how to fix the problem. If performance is unacceptable, determine how to resolve the issue. In either case, determine how to mitigate the problem as you move forward. This testing period should last at least two weeks and could be longer depending on how active end users are in the development database. The more activity in the database, the quicker issues will be seen. If the database is barely used, it may take longer to spot problems.

8. If possible, have at least one development database that is not yet upgraded. If you run into an issue with a database that is upgraded, you can try the same process on the older version to see if the problem exists there. If the problem does exist in the older version, the upgrade did not cause the issue.

9. After everyone in the IT team is comfortable with the first development upgrade, plan to upgrade any remaining development databases, except for one as noted in the step above. Use the instructions in steps 5 and 6 as your guide. Upgrading other development environments is a chance to fine-tune the documentation you created.

10. Install and upgrade the test database using your documentation. Ideally, everything should go as planned according to your instructions. If something is different with the installation and upgrade processes, update your documentation accordingly.

11. Wait at least two weeks with the test database at the new version. During this time, you should be looking for any new issues due to the upgrade. By the end of this cycle, you should have tested the application in both development and test and have confidence that the upgrade will not cause any application issues in production. You should also have confidence in the upgrade process itself.

12. Arrange for a downtime window for the production upgrade. All relevant members of the IT team should be involved in the plan. Everyone should know what is happening and when the upgrade will take place.

13. Prior to the downtime window, install the new Oracle version on the database server. The software installation does not require any downtime and can be done in advance. Use the documentation created in step 5 as your play-by-play instructions and the installation should go smoothly.

14. It is now time to upgrade the production database. Take a good backup of the database right before the upgrade begins. Should something fail in the upgrade process, it may leave the database in a state where it is no longer operational. You will want to have this backup on hand in case you need to get to a state just prior to upgrade.

15. Upgrade the production database. Use the documentation created in step 6 as your play-by-play instructions. This will give you confidence that the upgrade will go smoothly. It will also reduce the chances of human error and lead to a shorter downtime window because you will know the next step no matter where you are in the process. If desired, print out the documentation and cross off each step as you complete it.

16. Take a good backup of the database right after the upgrade ends. The database upgrade is not a trivial task. Should you have a failure of the server or the disk, you now have a copy of the upgraded database to restore just in case. Do not skip steps 14 and 16 as, one day, they may very well save you from a catastrophe.

17. Continue to monitor the application functionally and performance for a few weeks after the upgrade is complete. Very few testing efforts in development and test environments will cover everything the application and its end users perform against production.

Oracle documents the installation and upgrade in two different books that you can read in steps 1 and 2 above. However, those books are written for generic environments. Your environment is specific to your organization. Do not skip writing your own step-by-step documentation because this is your playbook as to how you accomplish the installation and upgrade, specifically for you. More than once, this simple task of documentation has saved myself from many upgrade mistakes.

Do not skip the backups both before and after the upgrades. You may never need them and they may seem like unnecessary steps. However, it only takes one bad upgrade to be thankful you did the extra work.

Upgrade Methods

There are three different upgrade methods you could use. All will get your database to the new version. As you can imagine, there are three different methods because they do things a bit differently and they each have their own strengths and weaknesses, as we will see in this section. The three methods are to use the Database Upgrade Assistant (DBUA), perform a manual upgrade, and use some form of export/import to move the database.

One special note needs to be mentioned before we explore these methods in detail. No matter which method you choose, Oracle Corporation recommends that you apply the latest and greatest Patch Set Update (PSU) or Revision Update (RU) to your database before you begin the upgrade process. On rare occasions, a bug in the old version has caused problems when trying to upgrade to a new version. The bug was not necessarily causing problems with the database running on the old version, but reared its ugly head only when upgrading. If your database version is up to date, you reduce the chances of running into such upgrade problems.

Database Upgrade Assistant

The Database Upgrade Assistant (DBUA) is a Java-based, graphical wizard-style utility that will walk you through the upgrade process. Answer a few questions, click the Next button a number of times, and watch the DBUA do the work for you. Because the DBUA is written in Java, it is the same utility no matter which OS platform your Oracle database is running on. The DBUA also has a silent mode where you can automate the process and run it in command-line mode.

My recommendation is to use the DBUA as much as possible for your database upgrades. This method of upgrading the database often has the shortest downtime window. The downtime window is not determined by the database size. The DBUA significantly reduces the chances of human error because it automates much of the process for you. The DBUA even runs prerequisite checks and, if it finds issues, stops before attempting the upgrade.

The shorter downtime window and the reduced risk are the two benefits of using the DBUA. One downside to this utility is that the upgrade cannot be used to simultaneously move the database to a different server. Another downside is that the DBUA also requires that the database to be upgraded be one of a few different versions. This is called a *direct upgrade*. In this chapter, we will be upgrading the database in our testbed to the Oracle 18.3 version. A direct upgrade to 18.3 is only possible if the source database is version 11.2.0.3, 11.2.0.4, 12.1.0.1, 12.1.0.2, or 12.2.0.1. If your database is a different version, you cannot use the DBUA to upgrade to the 18.3 version.

The *Database Upgrade Guide* always lists the versions that can have a direct upgrade. If you are running a different version, then you have two options. Perform an upgrade to one of the versions supporting a direct upgrade, or use export/import tools. The export/import upgrade path will be discussed shortly.

As an example, if the database is version 10.2.0.5, you can upgrade to 11.2.0.4 and then upgrade to 18.3. This scenario would require two upgrades to be performed. If this situation applies to you, I highly recommend you perform one upgrade and then wait awhile, making sure there are no issues. After you are confident things are running fine on the 11.2.0.4 version, upgrade to 18c. Do not attempt to upgrade from 10.2.0.5 to 11.2.0.4 then to 18.3 all in the same downtime window.

Manual Upgrade

You always have the option of performing a manual upgrade. Before the DBUA existed, this method was the most preferred. The manual upgrade has two of the same characteristics as using the DBUA. One, you can only perform a manual upgrade for versions that support a direct upgrade. The DBUA is actually performing the same steps as a manual upgrade, it is just automating the process for you. Two, the downtime window is similar, but in actuality will take a little bit longer because the database administrator will need to perform some of the steps the DBUA is much quicker in doing. The manual upgrade's biggest downside is that the steps are performed manually by the DBA and the chances of human error increase greatly. Because of the increased risk, the DBUA is recommended over the manual upgrade almost every time.

When a manual upgrade is performed, the database administrator must prepare the new Oracle home directory for the database. The database is then shut down cleanly. The DBA changes their environment to use the new software version. The database is started in MIGRATE mode and scripts are run to upgrade the database. Once complete, the DBA restarts the database with the new version.

If the DBUA is a better option, why perform a manual upgrade? The only reason to do so is that the database administrator can intervene midway during the upgrade process. The DBUA will do what it was programmed to do. There may be certain situations where you want to perform the upgrade steps and introduce a step in the middle of the process. Such situations would be very, very rare. As such, the manual upgrade is not likely to be performed in today's Oracle environments.

Export/Import

The last upgrade path is to use export and import utilities. There are many different type of utilities you could use. When people talk about export/import upgrade paths, they often mean to use Oracle's Data Pump utilities, impdp and expdp. You could export the data to text files and import with SQL*Loader, as another example. Data replication tools, like Oracle GoldenGate, can also be used to move the data to a newer Oracle version. You could also use third-party utilities that have similar functionality.

With the export/import upgrade path, you create a database running the new version. You export the data from the old database and import into the new database. Technically, this is not a database upgrade because the new database is not changing versions at all.

There are two main reasons to use the export/import upgrade path. One, you want to perform the upgrade in one step and your current Oracle version does not support a direct upgrade. Using export/import, you can go from Oracle 7.1 to 18.3 in one step, as an example. Two, you can move to a different database server at the same time. You will export the data on one server and move the dump file(s) to the new server and import there. If you use Data Pump, you can transfer the data from one database to the other over the network.

There are two big problems with this approach. One, the length of time is dependent on the database size. The larger the database, the longer it will take to export and the longer it will take to import, pure and simple. If your database is very large, the amount of time to complete this upgrade method may be unacceptable. Two, there is a certain amount of risk making sure you move everything. If you export to text files, you will be missing indexes, constraints, stored procedures, views, and so many more schema objects. You will have to move those separately. If you use Data Pump, the dump file can contain all of the schema objects, reducing this risk. Data Pump was introduced in Oracle 10*g*. If you are upgrading from an older version, you can alternatively use the legacy export and import utilities, exp and imp.

Which to Choose?

For the most part, database administrators use the DBUA to perform their upgrades. Choose this upgrade method so long as you can perform a direct upgrade. Use the export/import method if you are moving to a different server or your version is very old and you want to avoid multiple upgrades. The manual upgrade is almost never done today.

Installing 18c

Before we can upgrade our testbed database, we need to install a newer version of the database software on our virtual machine. In Chapter 5 we walked through installing the Oracle 12.2.0.1 software on our testbed. It is now time to upgrade that database we created in Chapter 6. Using the information in Chapter 5, download the newer version from the Oracle Technology Network at `https://otn.oracle.com` by clicking Software Downloads in the Essential Links section and then clicking the Database 18c Enterprise/Standard Editions link. For brevity's sake, I will not repeat the subsequent instructions from Chapter 5 here. The only thing that changes is the version being downloaded. After you download the software to the virtual machine, unzip the file in its own directory. One change with the 18c version is that you unzip that file into the Oracle home directory you want. The downloaded zip file is an image of the home directory. This is a minor change from previous versions.

First, create the home directory, as shown in Listing 18-1.

Listing 18-1. Creating 18c Home Directory

```
[oracle@dbamentor ~]$ cd /u01/app/oracle/product
[oracle@dbamentor product]$ mkdir 18.3
[oracle@dbamentor product]$ cd 18.3
[oracle@dbamentor 18.3]$ pwd
/u01/app/oracle/product/18.3
```

Then place the download file in this directory and unzip it.

Once the download file is unzipped, launch the runInstaller utility. In this section, I will show screenshots from things that have changed compared to the 12.2 version we installed in Chapter 5. Right away, we can see from Figure 18-1 that the initial screen is a bit different.

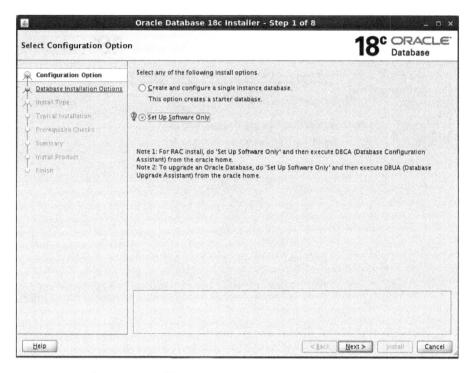

Figure 18-1. *Oracle 18c Installer Step 1*

The option to set up the software only is chosen because we already have a database on this system. Note 2 in Figure 18-1 confirms this is the proper choice for our testbed. Click Next. On the next screen, Step 2, choose the option to perform a single-instance installation and then click Next. On the next screen, Enterprise Edition is selected. Click Next.

On the screen for Step 4, we need to ensure the Oracle base directory is correct. In previous versions, the OUI would ask us for the Oracle home directory. In 18c, the OUI assumes the product is being installed where it was unzipped. We can see from Figure 18-2 that the software location is correct for our home. We are not given the option to change the software location. Click Next.

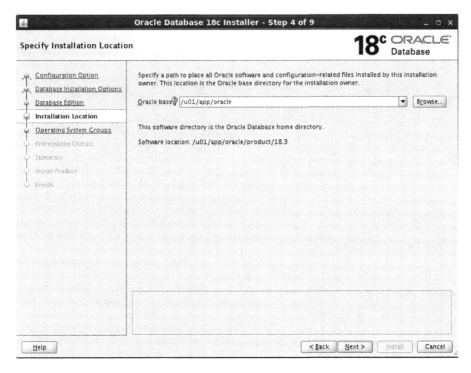

Figure 18-2. *Oracle 18c Installer Oracle home*

The next screen asks for the operating system groups; the defaults are acceptable, so click Next. In Step 6, the Oracle Universal Installer (OUI) performs its prerequisite checks. Figure 18-3 shows we have one failed check on the testbed system.

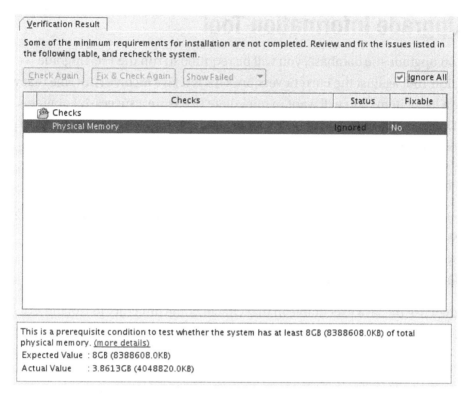

Figure 18-3. *Oracle 18c prerequisite checks*

The OUI has discovered that the database server does not have enough physical memory. This was not an issue when we installed the Oracle 12.2 version. Every Oracle version is a bit different in its requirements, and this version has raised the amount of memory we need. Since this is a virtual machine, we can easily shut it down, increase the memory, and start it back up again. Make sure your host workstation or laptop has enough memory to devote to the virtual machine. Being that this is a testbed, we can choose the other option to ignore the findings and continue, hence the Ignore All box is checked in Figure 18-3. After confirming we intended to ignore the issue, we can then click the Install button.

The installation will proceed and the OUI will ask to run a script as root. When running this script, you will be asked to confirm if it is okay to overwrite the oraenv and coraenv files. We were not asked this question when the 12.2 version was installed because these files did not exist yet. We will overwrite them with newer versions just in case 18c has changed the file contents. The new version is now installed and ready for the database upgrade.

Pre-Upgrade Information Tool

Before you upgrade the database, you will be required to run the Pre-Upgrade Information Tool against the current version. This is a Java archive (JAR) file that will generate a list of items you will want to remediate to ensure a successful upgrade. To run the Pre-Upgrade Information Tool, we set our session's environment variables to point to the current database, as shown in Listing 18-2.

Listing 18-2. Pre-Upgrade Setting Environment Variables

```
[oracle@dbamentor ~]$ export ORACLE_HOME=/u01/app/oracle/product/12.2.0.1
[oracle@dbamentor ~]$ export ORACLE_BASE=/u01/app/oracle
[oracle@dbamentor ~]$ export ORACLE_SID=orcl
[oracle@dbamentor ~]$ export PATH=$ORACLE_HOME/bin:$PATH
```

We then use the Java executable in that Oracle home directory to run the JAR file. Listing 18-3 shows a sample run of the Pre-Upgrade utility.

Listing 18-3. Running Pre-Upgrade Information Tool

```
 [oracle@dbamentor ~]$ $ORACLE_HOME/jdk/bin/java -jar /u01/app/oracle/
product/18.3/rdbms/admin/preupgrade.jar
==================
PREUPGRADE SUMMARY
==================
  /u01/app/oracle/cfgtoollogs/orcl/preupgrade/preupgrade.log
  /u01/app/oracle/cfgtoollogs/orcl/preupgrade/preupgrade_fixups.sql
  /u01/app/oracle/cfgtoollogs/orcl/preupgrade/postupgrade_fixups.sql

Execute fixup scripts as indicated below:

Before upgrade log into the database and execute the preupgrade fixups
@/u01/app/oracle/cfgtoollogs/orcl/preupgrade/preupgrade_fixups.sql

After the upgrade:

Log into the database and execute the postupgrade fixups
@/u01/app/oracle/cfgtoollogs/orcl/preupgrade/postupgrade_fixups.sql

Preupgrade complete: 2018-09-14T14:21:32
```

The Pre-Upgrade Information Tool has created three files for us. A log file, and two fixup scripts, one pre- and one post-upgrade. The first stop is to read the contents of the preupgrade.log file. The initial part of the log file, shown in Listing 18-4, gives some basic information such as the version of the current database and the version we are upgrading to.

Listing 18-4. Pre-Upgrade Log File Introductory Information

```
Report generated by Oracle Database Pre-Upgrade Information Tool Version
18.0.0.0.0 on 2018-09-14T14:21:32

Upgrade-To version: 18.0.0.0.0

========================================
Status of the database prior to upgrade
========================================
      Database Name:  ORCL
     Container Name:  ORCL
       Container ID:  0
            Version:  12.2.0.1.0
         Compatible:  12.2.0
          Blocksize:  8192
           Platform:  Linux x86 64-bit
      Timezone File:  26
  Database log mode:  ARCHIVELOG
           Readonly:  FALSE
            Edition:  EE

Oracle Component                        Upgrade Action    Current Status
----------------                        --------------    --------------
Oracle Server                           [to be upgraded]  VALID
JServer JAVA Virtual Machine            [to be upgraded]  VALID
Oracle XDK for Java                     [to be upgraded]  VALID
Oracle Workspace Manager                [to be upgraded]  VALID
Oracle XML Database                     [to be upgraded]  VALID
Oracle Java Packages                    [to be upgraded]  VALID
```

The next section of the log file, displayed in Listing 18-5, shows us actions we will need to complete.

Listing 18-5. Log File Actions

```
==============
BEFORE UPGRADE
==============

  REQUIRED ACTIONS
  ================
  None

  RECOMMENDED ACTIONS
  ===================
  1.  (AUTOFIXUP) Gather stale data dictionary statistics prior to database
      upgrade in off-peak time using:

         EXECUTE DBMS_STATS.GATHER_DICTIONARY_STATS;

      Dictionary statistics do not exist or are stale (not up-to-date).

      Dictionary statistics help the Oracle optimizer find efficient SQL
      execution plans and are essential for proper upgrade timing. Oracle
      recommends gathering dictionary statistics in the last 24 hours before
      database upgrade.

      For information on managing optimizer statistics, refer to the 12.2.0.1
      Oracle Database SQL Tuning Guide.
```

The tool has not found any required actions we need to complete. It does recommend one action at this time, which is to upgrade stale data dictionary statistics. Always try to follow any recommended actions to ensure a smoother upgrade. The log file gave us the exact command to execute, as we can see in Listing 18-6.

Listing 18-6. Updating Dictionary Stats

```
SQL> EXECUTE DBMS_STATS.GATHER_DICTIONARY_STATS;

PL/SQL procedure successfully completed.
```

The Pre-Upgrade Information Tool continues to provide us some valuable information. In our case, this utility is informing us that two tablespaces will automatically extend during the upgrade. It also informs us that the archive log destination will need about 3GB of space so we need to ensure the space is available. Both of these can be seen in Listing 18-7.

Listing 18-7. Pre-Upgrade Information Section

```
INFORMATION ONLY
================
2.  To help you keep track of your tablespace allocations, the following
    AUTOEXTEND tablespaces are expected to successfully EXTEND during the
    upgrade process.

                                        Min Size
    Tablespace                    Size  For Upgrade
    ----------                    ----------  -----------
    SYSTEM                        720 MB      1140 MB
    TEMP                          20 MB       150 MB

Minimum tablespace sizes for upgrade are estimates.

3.  Ensure there is additional disk space in LOG_ARCHIVE_DEST_1 for at least
    3139 MB of archived logs.  Check alert log during the upgrade that there
    is no write error to the destination due to lack of disk space.

Archiving cannot proceed if the archive log destination is full during
upgrade.

Archive Log Destination:
 Parameter    :  LOG_ARCHIVE_DEST_1
 Destination  :  /u01/app/oracle/oradata/arch/

The database has archiving enabled.  The upgrade process will need free
disk space in the archive log destination(s) to generate archived logs
to.
```

The log file then concludes the pre-upgrade section with information on a script we can run before the upgrade to remediate any issues. Listing 18-8 contains the pre-upgrade script for the testbed.

Listing 18-8. Pre-Upgrade Fixup Script

```
ORACLE GENERATED FIXUP SCRIPT
==============================
All of the issues in database ORCL
which are identified above as BEFORE UPGRADE "(AUTOFIXUP)" can be resolved
by executing the following

  SQL>@/u01/app/oracle/cfgtoollogs/orcl/preupgrade/preupgrade_fixups.sql
```

The pre-upgrade utility cannot generate the commands to fix everything that might need attention prior to the upgrade. If there was something the fixup script could not handle, the utility would have informed us of this fact. Just to be safe, we run the pre-upgrade fixup script in our database, as shown in Listing 18-9.

Listing 18-9. Pre-Upgrade Fixup Script Execution

```
SQL> @preupgrade_fixups.sql
Executing Oracle PRE-Upgrade Fixup Script

Auto-Generated by:      Oracle Preupgrade Script
                        Version: 18.0.0.0.0 Build: 1
Generated on:           2018-09-14 14:21:30

For Source Database:    ORCL
Source Database Version: 12.2.0.1.0
For Upgrade to Version: 18.0.0.0.0

Preup                           Preupgrade
Action                          Issue Is
Number  Preupgrade Check Name   Remedied    Further DBA Action
------  ---------------------   ----------  ----------------------------
    1.  dictionary_stats        YES         None.
    2.  tablespaces_info        NO          Informational only.
                                            Further action is optional.
    3.  min_archive_dest_size   NO          Informational only.
                                            Further action is optional.
```

The fixup scripts have been run and resolved what they can. However, there are still issues originally identified by the preupgrade that have not been remedied and are still present in the database. Depending on the severity of the specific issue, and the nature of the issue itself, that could mean that your database is not ready for upgrade. To resolve the outstanding issues, start by reviewing the preupgrade_fixups.sql and searching it for the name of the failed CHECK NAME or Preupgrade Action Number listed above. There you will find the original corresponding diagnostic message from the preupgrade which explains in more detail what still needs to be done.

PL/SQL procedure successfully completed.

Back in the log file, the post-upgrade section is all that remains. Listing 18-10 shows the continuation of the Pre-Upgrade Information Tool's log file.

Listing 18-10. After Upgrade Information

```
=============
AFTER UPGRADE
=============

  REQUIRED ACTIONS
  ================
  None

  RECOMMENDED ACTIONS
  ===================
  4.  Upgrade the database time zone file using the DBMS_DST package.

      The database is using time zone file version 26 and the target 18.0.0.0.0
      release ships with time zone file version 31.

      Oracle recommends upgrading to the desired (latest) version of the time
      zone file. For more information, refer to "Upgrading the Time Zone File
      and Timestamp with Time Zone Data" in the 18.0.0.0.0 Oracle Database
      Globalization Support Guide.
```

5. (AUTOFIXUP) Gather dictionary statistics after the upgrade using the command:

   EXECUTE DBMS_STATS.GATHER_DICTIONARY_STATS;

   Oracle recommends gathering dictionary statistics after upgrade.

   Dictionary statistics provide essential information to the Oracle optimizer to help it find efficient SQL execution plans. After a database upgrade, statistics need to be re-gathered as there can now be tables that have significantly changed during the upgrade or new tables that do not have statistics gathered yet.

6. Gather statistics on fixed objects after the upgrade and when there is a representative workload on the system using the command:

   EXECUTE DBMS_STATS.GATHER_FIXED_OBJECTS_STATS;

   This recommendation is given for all preupgrade runs.

   Fixed object statistics provide essential information to the Oracle optimizer to help it find efficient SQL execution plans. Those statistics are specific to the Oracle Database release that generates them, and can be stale upon database upgrade.

   For information on managing optimizer statistics, refer to the 12.2.0.1 Oracle Database SQL Tuning Guide.

```
ORACLE GENERATED FIXUP SCRIPT
==============================
All of the issues in database ORCL
which are identified above as AFTER UPGRADE "(AUTOFIXUP)" can be resolved by
executing the following

  SQL>@/u01/app/oracle/cfgtoollogs/orcl/preupgrade/postupgrade_fixups.sql
```

The output in the log file tells us there are no required actions. It is recommended to upgrade the timezone information and gather dictionary and fixed object statistics. The Pre-Upgrade Information Tool has generated a post-upgrade fixup script that we can execute to perform these recommended actions.

We are now ready to begin our database upgrade. The new Oracle software has been installed and the Pre-Upgrade utility was executed. Any actions recommended by the utility were performed in advance of the upgrade.

Upgrading the Database

For this upgrade, we will use the Database Upgrade Assistant. Most Oracle upgrades use this utility because it results in the shortest downtime window and has the least amount of risk by automating the upgrade process.

First, we need to set our session's environment variables to point to the new software home, but retain the same Oracle SID. Then, we need to launch the DBUA utility. Listing 18-11 shows how we set the environment variables for our Linux testbed and start the DBUA.

Listing 18-11. Setting Environment to Upgrade

```
[oracle@dbamentor ~]$ export ORACLE_HOME=/u01/app/oracle/product/18.3
[oracle@dbamentor ~]$ export ORACLE_SID=orcl
[oracle@dbamentor ~]$ export PATH=$ORACLE_HOME/bin:$PATH
[oracle@dbamentor ~]$ dbua
```

On the initial screen, shown in Figure 18-4, the DBUA asks which database to upgrade. If there are multiple databases on the server, the DBA will need to choose from the list. Our testbed only has one database. If we were running this utility from another server, we would have to supply SYSDBA credentials. Typically, you run this utility from the database server itself, so the SYSDBA username and password can be left blank.

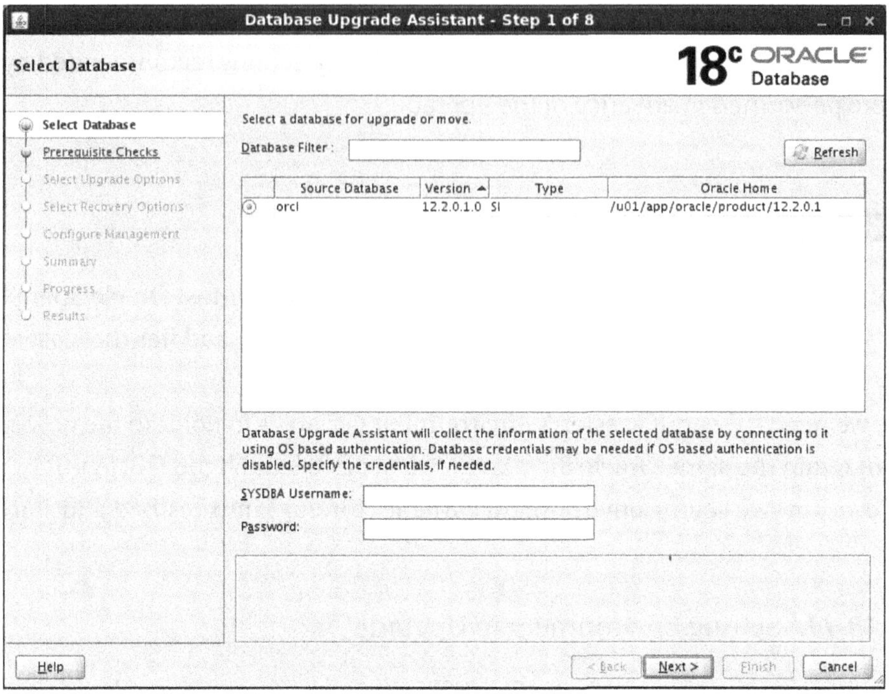

Figure 18-4. *DBUA upgrade target selection*

After you click the Next button, the DBUA will then take a few minutes to gather information about the database to be upgraded. After the DBUA has completed that task, it will perform some prerequisite checks. Figure 18-5 shows the results of those checks.

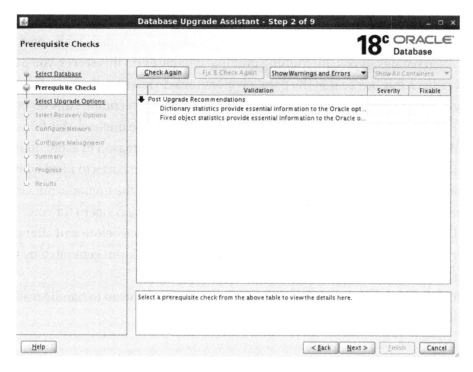

Figure 18-5.   *DBUA Prerequisite Checks screen*

If we did a good job remediating any findings from the Pre-Upgrade Information Tool, the prerequisite checks should pass without any additional findings. In Figure 18-5, the only information is some post-upgrade recommendations that we already know and will handle at the end.

After clicking Next, we are asked to provide some upgrade options, as shown in Figure 18-6.

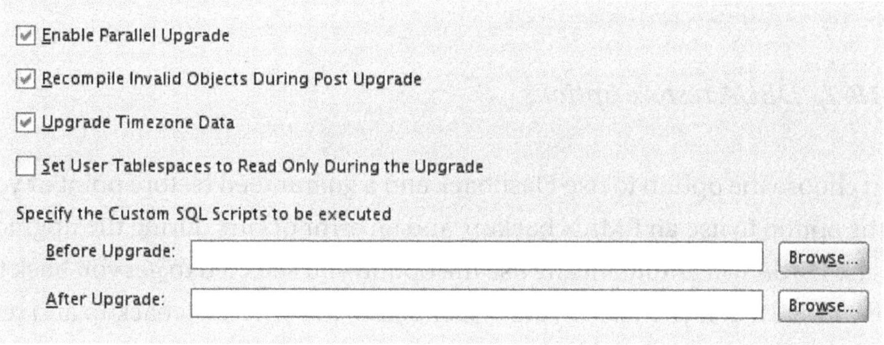

Figure 18-6.   *DBUA upgrade options*

The first three options in Figure 18-6 were selected by default and we normally leave those options as they are. The first one lets the upgrade process run faster by performing many tasks in parallel. If you are running multiple databases on this server, you may want to uncheck this box so that the parallel operations do not negatively impact other database performance. The second option will run a script to recompile any objects that became invalid during the upgrade. There is no good reason to uncheck this box. The third option upgrades the timezone data. Again, there is little reason to avoid doing so.

The fourth option instructs the DBUA to change user tablespaces to Read Only. This option is used to facilitate fast fallback during a failure in the upgrade, but Oracle recommends that you use a guaranteed restore point if that is a concern for you.

The last part of DBUA Step 3 lets you execute custom scripts before and after the upgrade. You could point the After Upgrade part to that fixup script generated by the Pre-Upgrade Installation Tool if you desire.

In Step 4, shown in Figure 18-7, the DBUA asks us how we want to handle restoring the database should a failure occur in the upgrade process.

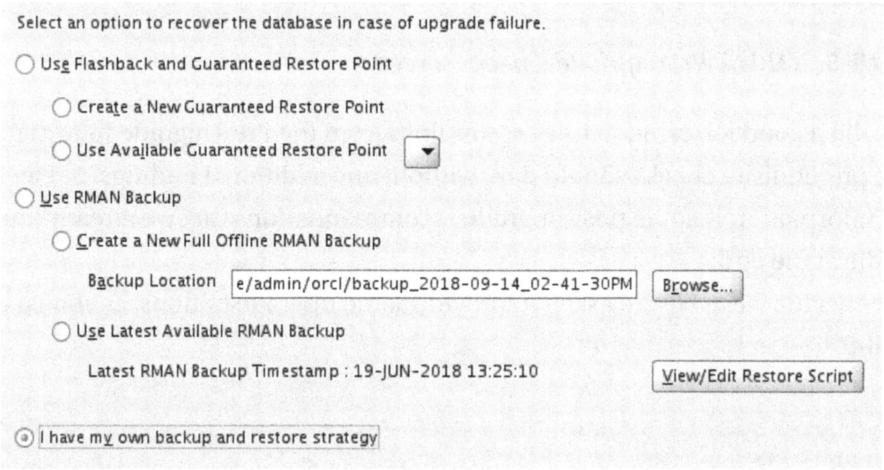

Figure 18-7. DBUA restore options

If you choose the option to use Flashback and a guaranteed restore point or you choose the option to use an RMAN backup, and an error occurs during the upgrade process, the DBUA will automatically use the option you selected to get you back to the place you started. If you choose the last option to use your own backup and restore strategy, the DBUA will not be able to recover for you. You will have to perform the recovery on your own.

As stated earlier, Oracle's recommendation is to use a guaranteed restore point. This is the fastest way to get you back to the pre-upgrade state, but you must have a Flashback Recovery Area already defined. Another great option is an RMAN backup.

Remember that I said you need to perform a backup before you begin the upgrade process? Step 4 of the DBUA is where you define that strategy. If you choose the last option, your backup should take place right before you start the DBUA.

Since this is a testbed, I am going to choose to use my own backup and restore strategy and click Next to move on to the next screen of the DBUA, as shown in Figure 18-8. Step 5 of the DBUA asks us to create a new Listener.

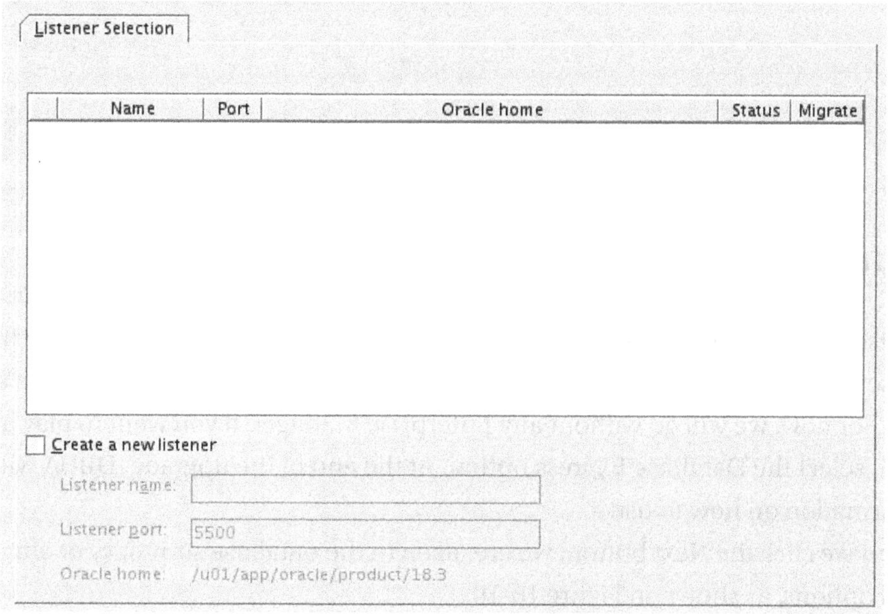

Figure 18-8. *DBUA Listener Selection*

The DBUA does not see the current Listener because it is running out of an old Oracle home directory. It does give us the option to create a new Listener, but we do not want two running on the server. After the upgrade is complete, I will show you how easy it is to move the Listener to the new home. Accept the defaults on this step and click the Next button.

In Step 6, the DBUA asks us to define management options, meaning do we want to manage this database with Oracle Enterprise Manager (EM) Database Express or EM Cloud Control. By default, EM Database Express is chosen. I have deselected that option in Figure 18-9.

Specify the management options for the database.

☐ Configure Enterprise Manager (EM) database express

    EM database express port: 5500

    ☐ Configure EM database express port as global port

☐ Register with Enterprise Manager (EM) cloud control

    OMS host:

    OMS port:

    EM admin username:

    EM admin password:

    DBSNMP user password:

    ASMSNMP user password:

Figure 18-9. *DBUA management options*

If I use Cloud Control, I can easily add this database at a later date. I can use the Database Configuration Assistant (DBCA) to add Database Express in the future, should I desire. For now, we will go without any Enterprise Manager. If you want to play around with EM, select the Database Express option. At the end of the upgrade, DBUA will give you information on how to use it.

When we click the Next button, we are taken to the database summary of our selected options, as shown in Figure 18-10.

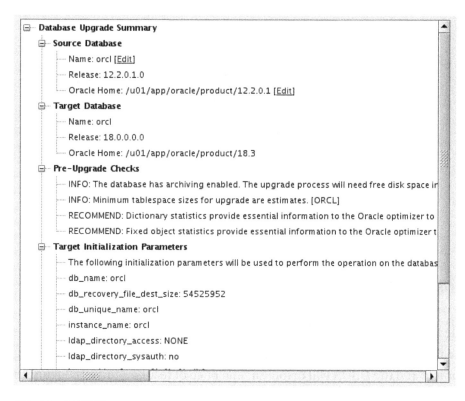

Figure 18-10. DBUA summary

This screen is our last chance to verify everything is correct before proceeding. Up until now, the DBUA has not made any changes nor attempted to upgrade the database. When you click the Finish button, the upgrade will start. It is at this time that the database will be unavailable. You can get to this point in advance of your downtime window and save yourself some time when the upgrade is scheduled to begin.

It is now time to let the DBUA do all of the hard work for us. Click the Finish button and sit back and watch it work. We can see an example of the Progress screen in Figure 18-11.

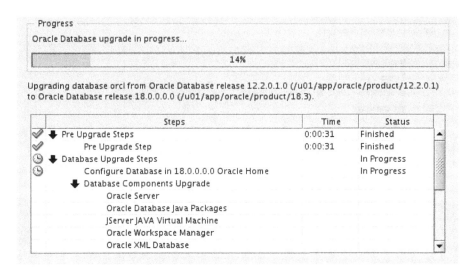

Figure 18-11. *DBUA Progress screen*

While the DBUA is upgrading the database, it will continue to display the Progress screen so that you can keep track of where it is. After some period of time, the upgrade will complete and the DBUA will display a final page of results similar to Figure 18-12.

Upgrade Results

Database upgrade has been completed successfully, and the database is ready to use.

	Source Database	Target Database
Name:	orcl	orcl
Release:	12.2.0.1.0	18.0.0.0.0
Oracle Home:	/u01/app/oracle/product/12.2.0.1	/u01/app/oracle/product/18.3

Figure 18-12. *DBUA Upgrade Results page*

The upgrade results show the database was upgraded from 12.2 to 18c. If you scroll down the results a bit, the Upgrade Details section will show how long each step took to complete, illustrated in Figure 18-13.

Upgrade Details

A detailed summary of the upgrade of the Database components is available at
"/u01/app/oracle/cfgtoollogs/dbua/upgrade2018-09-14_02-41-30PM/orcl/upg_summary.log".

The following summary lists the steps performed during the upgrade process. Log files for all the steps, as
well as this summary, are available at

"/u01/app/oracle/cfgtoollogs/dbua/upgrade2018-09-14_02-41-30PM/orcl".

Step Name	Log File Name	Status	Time
Pre Upgrade	PreUpgrade.log	Successful	0:00:31
Configure Database in 18.0.0.0.0 Oracle Home	Migrate_Sid.log	Successful	0:01:00
Database Components Upgrade	Oracle_Server.log	Successful	0:18:29
Recompile Invalid Objects	Utlprp.log	Successful	0:03:26
Timezone Upgrade	UpgradeTimezone.log	Successful	0:02:31
Post Upgrade	PostUpgrade.log	Successful	0:01:15
Generate Summary	generateSummary.log	Successful	0:00:00
Total Upgrade Time			0:27:12

Figure 18-13. *Upgrade Details section*

It might be interesting to note that we upgraded to the 18.3 version, but the Upgrade Details in Figure 18-13 show the 18.0 version instead. We can see that for this testbed, the total upgrade time was about 27 minutes. I typically plan for one hour of downtime even for very large databases. Hopefully you will have a good time estimate from when you upgraded the development and test databases. When you are satisfied with the results, click the Close button to end the DBUA session.

Post Upgrade

After the upgrade is complete, there are a few extra tasks to take care of. We already know that we need to run the post-upgrade fixup script the Pre-Upgrade Installation Tool generated for us. We will need to change our environment to the new Oracle home directory and then execute the script. In Listing 18-12, we set our environment to the new software home and run the post-upgrade fixup script.

Listing 18-12. Post-Upgrade Fixup Script

```
[oracle@dbamentor ~]$ export ORACLE_HOME=/u01/app/oracle/product/18.3
[oracle@dbamentor ~]$ export ORACLE_SID=orcl
[oracle@dbamentor ~]$ export PATH=$ORACLE_HOME/bin:$PATH
[oracle@dbamentor ~]$ sqlplus /nolog
```

```
SQL*Plus: Release 18.0.0.0.0 - Production on Fri Sep 14 16:31:20 2018
Version 18.3.0.0.0

Copyright (c) 1982, 2018, Oracle.  All rights reserved.

SQL> connect / as sysdba
Connected.
SQL> @/u01/app/oracle/cfgtoollogs/orcl/preupgrade/postupgrade_fixups.sql
Executing Oracle POST-Upgrade Fixup Script

Auto-Generated by:        Oracle Preupgrade Script
                          Version: 18.0.0.0.0 Build: 1
Generated on:             2018-09-14 14:21:32

For Source Database:      ORCL
Source Database Version: 12.2.0.1.0
For Upgrade to Version:   18.0.0.0.0
```

Some of the script output has been removed for brevity.

One of the checks I always perform is to make sure the DBUA has updated the oratab file to point to the new home directory for this database. The DBUA has never skipped this step, but I still check it anyway, maybe out of habit. Listing 18-13 shows my oratab file has been updated.

Listing 18-13. Oratab Update

```
[oracle@dbamentor ~]$ cat /etc/oratab
#

# This file is used by ORACLE utilities.  It is created by root.sh
# and updated by either Database Configuration Assistant while creating
# a database or ASM Configuration Assistant while creating ASM instance.

# A colon, ':', is used as the field terminator.  A new line terminates
# the entry.  Lines beginning with a pound sign, '#', are comments.
#
# Entries are of the form:
#   $ORACLE_SID:$ORACLE_HOME:<N|Y>:
#
```

```
# The first and second fields are the system identifier and home
# directory of the database respectively.  The third field indicates
# to the dbstart utility that the database should , "Y", or should not,
# "N", be brought up at system boot time.
#
# Multiple entries with the same $ORACLE_SID are not allowed.
#
#
orcl:/u01/app/oracle/product/18.3:Y
```

The oratab file does point to the new Oracle home directory.

If you remember from earlier in this chapter, the DBUA asked how we wanted to handle the Oracle Listener. We did instruct the DBUA to do nothing with the Listener. It is always a good idea to have the Listener running as the same version as your highest database version. If you are running an Oracle 12.2 database as well as an Oracle 18 database on the same server, use the Oracle 18 Listener.

To move over to the new Listener, simply shut down the old one, copy any configuration files to the new home, and start up the Listener with the new version. The steps are shown in Listing 18-14.

Listing 18-14. Listener Upgrade

```
[oracle@dbamentor ~]$ export ORACLE_HOME=/u01/app/oracle/product/12.2.0.1
[oracle@dbamentor ~]$ $ORACLE_HOME/bin/lsnrctl stop

LSNRCTL for Linux: Version 12.2.0.1.0 - Production on 14-SEP-2018 16:35:57

Copyright (c) 1991, 2016, Oracle.  All rights reserved.

Connecting to (ADDRESS=(PROTOCOL=tcp)(HOST=)(PORT=1521))
The command completed successfully
[oracle@dbamentor ~]$ cp /u01/app/oracle/product/12.2.0.1/network/admin/*.
ora /u01/app/oracle/product/18.3/network/admin/.
cp: cannot stat `/u01/app/oracle/product/12.2.0.1/network/admin/*.ora': No
such file or directory
[oracle@dbamentor ~]$ export ORACLE_HOME=/u01/app/oracle/product/18.3
[oracle@dbamentor ~]$ $ORACLE_HOME/bin/lsnrctl start
```

```
LSNRCTL for Linux: Version 18.0.0.0.0 - Production on 14-SEP-2018 16:36:55

Copyright (c) 1991, 2018, Oracle.  All rights reserved.

Starting /u01/app/oracle/product/18.3/bin/tnslsnr: please wait...

TNSLSNR for Linux: Version 18.0.0.0.0 - Production
Log messages written to /u01/app/oracle/diag/tnslsnr/dbamentor/listener/
alert/log.xml
Listening on: (DESCRIPTION=(ADDRESS=(PROTOCOL=tcp)(HOST=dbamentor)(PORT=1521)))

Connecting to (ADDRESS=(PROTOCOL=tcp)(HOST=)(PORT=1521))
STATUS of the LISTENER
------------------------
Alias                     LISTENER
Version                   TNSLSNR for Linux: Version 18.0.0.0.0 -
                          Production
Start Date                14-SEP-2018 16:36:55
Uptime                    0 days 0 hr. 0 min. 56 sec
Trace Level               off
Security                  ON: Local OS Authentication
SNMP                      OFF
Listener Log File         /u01/app/oracle/diag/tnslsnr/dbamentor/listener/
                          alert/log.xml
Listening Endpoints Summary...
  (DESCRIPTION=(ADDRESS=(PROTOCOL=tcp)(HOST=dbamentor)(PORT=1521)))
Services Summary...
Service "orcl" has 1 instance(s).
  Instance "orcl", status READY, has 1 handler(s) for this service...
Service "orclXDB" has 1 instance(s).
  Instance "orcl", status READY, has 1 handler(s) for this service...
The command completed successfully
```

The copy command looks for any *.ora files in the old home's network/admin subdirectory. It did not find any in Listing 18-14, so the copy command gave us an error. The Listener is not required to have any configuration files. The default configuration, without any config files, is usually sufficient. While the Listener is being changed to the new home, incoming connections will not be possible, so you may need a small downtime window for this move.

Next, I check the database to see what version it thinks it is, as shown in Listing 18-15.

Listing 18-15. Version Check

```
SQL> select banner_full from v$version;

BANNER_FULL
--------------------------------------------------------------------------
Oracle Database 18c Enterprise Edition Release 18.0.0.0.0 - Production
Version 18.3.0.0.0

SQL> select version from v$instance;

VERSION
-----------------
18.0.0.0.0
SQL> select comp_name,version,status from dba_registry;

COMP_NAME                              VERSION     STATUS
-------------------------------------- ----------  ----------
Oracle Database Catalog Views          18.0.0.0.0  VALID
Oracle Database Packages and Types     18.0.0.0.0  VALID
JServer JAVA Virtual Machine           18.0.0.0.0  VALID
Oracle XDK                             18.0.0.0.0  VALID
Oracle Database Java Packages          18.0.0.0.0  VALID
Oracle Real Application Clusters       18.0.0.0.0  OPTION OFF
Oracle XML Database                    18.0.0.0.0  VALID
Oracle Workspace Manager               18.0.0.0.0  VALID
```

All of the version information checks out. Oracle is saying this is an 18.0 database, but if you look at the first query, we can see the banner shows the version is 18.3 as we expected. Furthermore, all of the components in the DBA_REGISTRY view show as valid or the option is off.

The final check is to look for invalid objects. We had the DBUA recompile any invalid objects, but we want to double-check the recompile got everything, shown in Listing 18-16.

Listing 18-16. Invalid Object Check

```
SQL> select count(*) from dba_objects where status='INVALID';

  COUNT(*)
----------
     0
```

If the query above returns a non-zero count, we need to investigate further and determine what objects are invalid and why they remain that way. If the objects are part of an application schema, it is most likely they are invalid due to some reason other than the database upgrade. If there are invalid objects in Oracle-supplied schemas, you will want to work with Oracle Support to fix them.

At this point we are satisfied the upgrade was a success. There is only one more task remaining and that is to take a good backup of the database. We do not want to have to repeat this process again after all of our hard work.

Downgrading

Most people never consider downgrading an Oracle database. I once created a poll on a discussion forum asking how many people had ever practiced an Oracle downgrade. Out of 675 respondents, only 14 had practiced an Oracle downgrade, a figure that totally baffles me to this day. I wish more Oracle database administrators would practice a downgrade at least once in a while.

Downgrades are an avenue of last resort. If you have performed adequate testing of the application on the new Oracle version, and if you have tested the upgrade process, you will never need to downgrade. While I have practiced a downgrade, I have never needed to downgrade a production database, although I came very close once. I only consider a downgrade if I cannot fix problems in the database after the upgrade is complete. For example, when upgrading to 12.1.0.2, I ran into many Optimizer issues leading to poorly performing queries. As I came close to pulling the trigger on a database downgrade, I learned others had the same problem and Oracle had some hidden initialization parameters that would fix my problem.

You should have taken backups both before and after the upgrade, which means you have the capability of going back in time to either point. Now consider what happens if you discover a problem after the upgrade is complete, after you have opened the database for business to the application users. Those application users have generated transactions in the database since the upgrade completed. You cannot use the backup taken after the upgrade because that backup is for the new version. If you want to use the backup taken prior to the upgrade, you can certainly revert to the old version, but you will not be able to roll forward any transactions after the upgrade. If you want to use that pre-upgrade backup, you will experience data loss, pure and simple.

In an ideal world, the morning after a database upgrade, I come into the office and no one says anything. End users never know the database is now a shiny new version. No one complains and there are no reported issues. Sometimes things happen and it is the database administrator's job to fix the database because the upgrade broke something. Some problems are easy to fix and others can be difficult. Solve the problems as quickly as you can because you really do not want to revert to the old version. In rare circumstances, you may need to make the decision that the upgrade was not a good thing to do and you need to go back to the old version. You have two choices to make. Restore from the pre-upgrade backup and lose all transactions since that time, or perform a downgrade. To me, data loss is a bad option and the downgrade is the better choice, which is why I am surprised when so many database administrators do not give downgrades any thought. This is so important, I'll say it again to emphasize the point. Downgrades may be your only option to revert to an older database version without any data loss.

The Oracle *Upgrade Guide* for the new version always devotes one chapter to downgrading Oracle. If you have to perform a downgrade, you will want to read that chapter very thoroughly. It will contain step-by-step instructions on how to perform a downgrade. The steps depend on the various options you may be using and have installed, so this chapter will not repeat the process. At a high level, the downgrade steps are to shut down the database, start in DOWNGRADE mode with the old version software, and then run the catdwgrd.sql script.

The DBUA does not perform downgrades. Downgrades are a manual process. It is my recommendation that you practice an Oracle downgrade on a testbed at different points in your career. Our testbed makes a perfect place to practice. Simply shut down the virtual machine and take a snapshot of the server and its storage. Start it all up and follow the steps in the *Upgrade Guide* to downgrade to the old version. When the database has been downgraded, you can either revert to the snapshot and be instantaneously on the new version, or you can practice the upgrade all over again, which is not a bad idea.

Moving On

This chapter has discussed how to upgrade Oracle databases to a new version. We walked through the upgrade process on our testbed and now have an Oracle 18c database up and running to play around with. We discussed the importance of database upgrades and reading the Oracle documentation. We even touched on database downgrades.

In the next chapter, we will focus more on maintaining an Oracle database. We will look at capacity planning so that we can ensure the database will be able to handle the load for the future. What you built may work for today, but be too small for tomorrow.

CHAPTER 19

Capacity Planning

In the last two chapters, we have kept our Oracle databases moving forward by applying patches and performing upgrades, both vital tasks for the database administrator. Sometimes, applying patches is a reactive task to fix a problem. Most of the time, applying patches is a proactive endeavor. Upgrading your database is a way to keep current, maintain support, and enjoy new features that keep the database moving forward to support the infrastructure.

In this chapter, we will discuss capacity planning for the Oracle database. By itself, capacity planning does not impact your current environment. Rather, capacity planning is an activity that you perform today to help you make better decisions for the future.

The Complexity

If you talk to experts in the capacity planning field, they will be more than happy to let you know how complex and important their work is to ensure a successful operational environment for today and for the future. While I am not trying to dismiss or demean their efforts, I take a more simplistic approach to capacity planning, as I will outline in this chapter. My approach has served me well over the course of my DBA career. After reading this chapter, you may find you need more and want to be more detailed in your capacity planning efforts. If this chapter falls short of what you need for capacity planning going forward, then by all means learn more about the subject on your own and after you read this chapter to become more in-depth on the subject than I usually am. For many of you, the information in this chapter will provide much of what you need and you can probably sustain your database administrator career with it.

When I first started in this business, resources for a computer system were in very limited supply. Software developers squeezed every single byte of memory. It was a common task to refactor one's code into more efficient, smaller bodies of work that did the same thing so as to use less memory. Back then, disk space was very limited and

© Brian Peasland 2019
B. Peasland, *Oracle DBA Mentor*, https://doi.org/10.1007/978-1-4842-4321-3_19

DBAs only stored the information they needed and nothing more. If you asked for more memory or more disk space, you needed to know exactly how much more. Organizations did not buy more than was necessary.

I remember when I first started as an Oracle DBA that I had discovered an Excel spreadsheet where you plugged in a few values, and the document would tell you exactly how big an index was going to be. You put in the index's column datatype and precision, added the expected number of rows, and the spreadsheet factored that information, along with all of the Oracle overhead needed for an index, and one of the cells magically gave you a figure in kilobytes. To be honest, this spreadsheet was actually very good for the Oracle versions of that day. I remember using it to get an estimate for the index size, then creating the index in real life and the estimate was proven to be very good, time after time.

After using this spreadsheet over and over again for a project, I came to the realization that there were many problems with this approach. For starters, this approach was very time consuming. The DBA had to fill in values in the spreadsheet, get the estimate, and then repeat for each and every index. I found it much easier to fill a table with sample data, create an index, and then ask Oracle how much space it required. If the sample data was approximately 10% of the expected data volume, I could then simply multiply the index's size by a factor of ten and receive a good estimate. Not only would I have an estimate of the index's size, but also of the table's size. This meant I could ditch the spreadsheet helping me size tables as well.

Another problem with the spreadsheet approach is that while it seemed very precise and offered up an exact number, the inputs to the spreadsheet were sometimes estimates themselves. If the inputs are not exact, then no matter how good the tool is, the output will not be exact either. So, let's save all of the detailed analysis for something better. Instead, let's get to an answer as easily as possible. After all, it's just an estimate.

Lastly, while you may have done some fine work in your initial estimates, it has been my experience that shortly after the estimates are defined, they are wrong. For example, I once worked on a system that would be receiving data points from a satellite. My job was to create and design a database that would be able to handle the data received from the object orbiting our planet. The creators of the satellite knew precisely how much data was captured every minute of every day. My estimate of the expected data volume was spot on. I loaded some sample data and was able to determine exactly how much disk space I would need month to month. When we started populating the database with data in a production setting, the estimates I generated were in agreement with our real-world system. Then requirements changed. Things worked so well there was talk of adding another system's data to this same database. Well, that should be easy enough. Simply multiply the expected growth by a factor of two. However, this new system would have additional data the original satellite lacked. There went my exact estimate right out the window. The point is that no matter how accurate your initial estimate is, requirements and data usage patterns can change. Very few of us work on a database system that receives a steady stream of data with the same regularity that can be counted on to be able to accurately make determinations of the total data volume over time.

Over the course of my career, I have learned that it is often better to become less precise in our estimates of expected system usage. Instead of getting down into the nitty-gritty details, I often take a completely opposite approach, and that is to look at system usage from a higher level.

Capacity Planning

Before we can proceed, we need to define *capacity planning*. The name may be obvious, but I have found it can mean different things to different people. Before we can learn more in this chapter, the term needs to be defined so that we are all on the same page, no pun intended.

All computer systems have a set of resources that perform work. For the most part, the only resources I look at are CPU usage, memory usage, and disk usage. The latter can be broken down into the amount of disk being used, and by corollary the amount of free disk space, and the time spent servicing requests. There are certainly other resources in a computer system, but CPU, memory, and disk are the big three.

As requests are made of the system, the resources get used. Once the request is complete, the resource becomes available to service the next request. Unfortunately, there is a finite supply of the resources on the system. Ask too much of any one resource, and performance will suffer. If my request is using all of the CPU resources, your request will have to wait and you will rightfully complain that the system is slow. Not only are resources limited, they need to be shared by multiple people and processes all at the same time. Your job as a database administrator is to ensure there are sufficient resources for the end users so that they do not notice any performance issues. In other words, you need to ensure there is sufficient *capacity* for the workload.

Part of the database administrator's job is to determine how many resources are needed for the initial launch of the system. To put it a different way, the DBA needs to *plan* the resource utilization. After the initial launch, the DBA needs to forecast the resource utilization for the future. It is very common to see the demands placed on the resources grow over time. The DBA needs to *plan* for future growth so that resources can be made available before they are needed.

Capacity planning is the activity of making sure adequate resources are available today and for the future to meet expected demand. This activity is a proactive approach. If you ever find yourself performing capacity planning in a reactive mode, it is too late and you may lose customers.

To me, the hardest part of capacity planning is not in forecasting for the future but rather in setting up the system for its initial launch for an unknown product. Forecasting for the future is looking at where you are today and multiplying by a best-estimate factor and seeing where the trendline on a graph leads you. It's an easy task. If the product is known, then you can look at what the product has required from previous deployments. If this product is from a third party, the vendor will typically supply resource recommendations to ensure their product performs properly.

Setting up an unknown system for the first time is harder because we know so little about the resource utilization. Someone in management may say things like "We expect 100,000 users in the first month and 1 million users by six months." Those figures are something, but they do not tell us how much CPU or memory the users will require. In short, it's an unknown system and its resource requirements are unknown as well. For unknown systems, the best course of action is for the DBA to take is to learn all of the known requirements that have been defined. Then try to see what other systems they have worked on in the past that may mimic these details and use those as a guide. If no other such systems exist, the DBA can only make an initial guess. In either case, the DBA needs to let others on the team know that the initial estimates do not have enough background information to have a high degree of confidence.

I've seen people ask questions over the years that want to know something like "How much memory do I need to support one million users?" I hate to break it to them, but there is no magic formula or table that can answer that question. One million application users in my system can have totally different resource requirements than one million users in another system.

Because this is an unknown system, it will need to be developed and tested prior to being place into a production status. During development, the DBA should be looking at resource utilization to determine if the initial guess is still on track or needs to be redefined. Once the system goes to testing, the DBA should get to see the system under load. Automated testing tools help by simulating a large number of simultaneous users without involving real people. You can use Swingbench or HammerDB to simulate a testload, but keep in mind that those may not be representative of your application. I have used JMeter to exercise a web-based application in the past simulating multiple users.

If possible, have a number of real users exercise the application. I have been known, from time to time, to enlist the help of the entire IT staff to exercise the application all at the same time, even if it is only for 10 or 15 minutes. Doing so gives me a much better idea of how resources are utilized in a real-world setting before the real world gets its hands on it.

Enterprise Manager

If you do not already have it installed in your infrastructure, I strongly encourage you to get Oracle Enterprise Manager (EM) up and running. You will be happy you took the time to install, configure, and start using EM. Entire books have been written about EM, so we will not cover the details here. If you do not have EM in your environment, this chapter will show you some of the information at your fingertips, which may convince you to add it to your DBA infrastructure in the near future.

Enterprise Manager is constantly looking at your system and capturing information about its configuration as well as its resource utilization and performance of both the database and the operating system. As we will see in this chapter, you can certainly create your own routines to capture resource utilization, but as the saying goes, why reinvent the wheel? Let's look at examples of the information EM is gathering for us, out of the box with no additional customization. In EM Cloud Control, you can go to Targets ➤ Hosts and then click a specific server of interest. Scroll down the summary screen a bit and you can see some charts showing the CPU and memory utilization of that server, as shown in Figure 19-1.

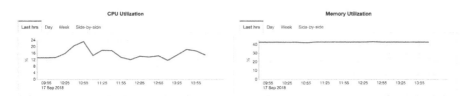

Figure 19-1. *EM utilization summaries*

The two charts show us the CPU and memory utilization of this server. When we initially land on this page, the charts default to the last four hours of activity. Four hours is not sufficient for capacity planning. Instead, this view is used to help spot immediate performance problems. If you want to see the information over a longer period of time, you can click the Day tab or Week tab. Figure 19-2 shows the same server looking at the past week.

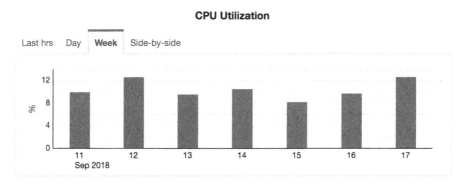

Figure 19-2. *EM CPU utilization in the past week*

One of the more interesting charts is the side-by-side view, as shown in Figure 19-3.

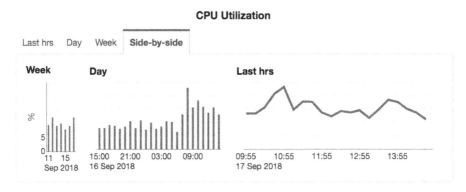

Figure 19-3. *EM CPU utilization side-by-side view*

The chart in Figure 19-3 shows us all three charts side by side, as the name suggests. Unfortunately for this chapter, the data here only goes back seven days. One week is hardly enough historical data to help spot trends in resource utilization. The point is that Enterprise Manager is capturing this information for us. We just need to harness it. For accurate capacity planning, we need as many data points as possible. A week's or even a month's worth of data may not be sufficient. I recommend at least a year's worth of metrics, however, I tend to keep mine around for the life of the system.

While in EM still looking at that same host, select Host ➤ Monitoring ➤ CPU Details. This takes us deeper into EM's metrics for that resource on that server, as shown in Figure 19-4.

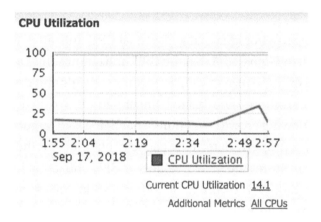

Figure 19-4. *EM CPU utilization details*

In the chart in Figure 19-4, we can see the CPU utilization over the past hour. Click the CPU Utilization hyperlink in the chart's legend to be taken to the next screen, shown in Figure 19-5. By default, the view shows the last 24 hours, but here the View Data drop-down menu near the top was changed to 31 days.

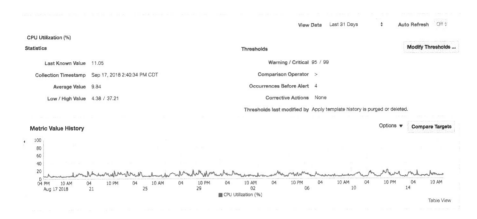

Figure 19-5. EM CPU utilization in the last 31 days

Now we are getting a better idea of the historical CPU utilization for this server. We can see from the chart in Figure 19-5 that the CPU utilization shows a relatively steady state of consumption over the past month. Sure, there are ups and downs within each day, but overall the chart shows a horizontal, linear pattern. We do not see any spikes, and the chart is not showing growth over time. That being said, arguably, 31 days' worth of data is not enough to properly determine capacity planning for the future.

Enterprise Manager stores the metric values for CPU utilization in its repository. I used the query in Listing 19-1 to obtain the CPU utilization of a server from the Enterprise Manager repository.

Listing 19-1. EM CPU Utilization Repository Query

```
select rollup_timestamp,trunc(average,2) as host_avg,
          trunc(maximum,2) as host_max
from sysman.mgmt$metric_daily
where metric_column='cpuUtil'
    and target_name='myhost.acme.com' and metric_label='Load'
order by rollup_timestamp;
```

If you run the query above in your EM repository database, you can see how much data is in there. Typically, it will be 90 days' worth or less. Note that this is your EM repository database, not the database on that server.

It is a simple operation to pull out the data values with that query and store them in an Excel spreadsheet. By offloading to Excel, you can keep the data points around much longer than EM will in its repository. You can also create charts with this information. Figure 19-6 shows a simple chart I created from that same query storing the data values over time.

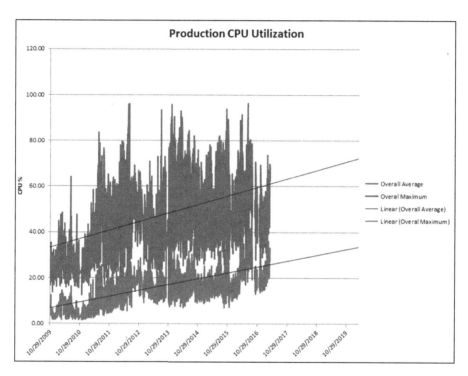

Figure 19-6. *CPU trendline*

In the chart in Figure 19-6, I added a linear trendline forecasting the resource utilization over the next three years. To do so, I just right-clicked the line graph, chose Add Trendline, and modified the trendline's properties to forecast forward 1,095 days, about three years.

This was not that difficult. Enterprise Manager is already capturing this data for me. All I did was store it in Excel and create a quick and easy chart. I now have a good idea of what my needs will be in the future. The chart used seven years' worth of data, which means I also have a high degree of confidence in my forecast.

Remember in Chapter 17 we discussed knowing your audience? Charts like the one shown in Figure 19-6 are easy for most people to understand. The blue line is the average

CPU consumption per day. The red line is the maximum CPU consumption per day. The trendlines show our forecast. You do not need to be an Oracle expert to get the idea. IT managers and other members of the IT team can instantly benefit from this easy analysis.

Similarly, we can obtain the memory usage of a monitored server from the EM repository with the query in Listing 19-2.

Listing 19-2. EM Memory Utilization Repository Query

```
select rollup_timestamp,trunc(average,2) as host_avg,
          trunc(maximum,2) as host_max
from sysman.mgmt$metric_daily
where metric_column='usedLogicalMemoryPct'
    and target_name='myhost.acme.com'
order by rollup_timestamp;
```

Again, we copy the data points from the query above to an Excel spreadsheet and graph over time. The chart in Figure 19-7 shows memory usage from a different production system.

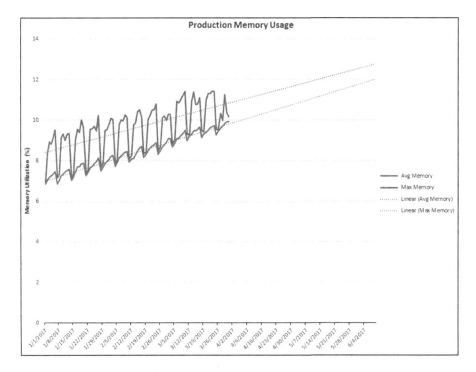

Figure 19-7. *Memory trendline*

In the chart in Figure 19-7, we can still see linear growth, but trending upward. Like the CPU chart, this chart shows the average daily utilization as well as the maximum daily utilization. When planning for capacity, we need to be able to handle the maximum values. We need to be able to handle the spikes in demand for that resource.

Such a simple graph generated in Excel goes a long way toward forecasting and explaining your resource needs. If the chart showed I would hit some resource limit in the forecasted future, it would be easy to justify spending the additional money to provide more of that resource.

Similar to the CPU and memory queries from the Enterprise Manager repository, we can also get a look at the disk utilization as measured in Input/Output Operations per Second (IOPS). The query in Listing 19-3 can be used to obtain those values for a monitored server in the EM repository.

Listing 19-3. EM Disk Utilization Repository Query

```
select rollup_timestamp,trunc(average,2) as host_avg,
          trunc(maximum,2) as host_max
from sysman.mgmt$metric_daily
where metric_column='totiosmade'
    and target_name='myhost.acme.com'
order by rollup_timestamp;
```

Again, the output from the query above is easily written to an Excel spreadsheet and charted over time to display a graph similar to Figure 19-8.

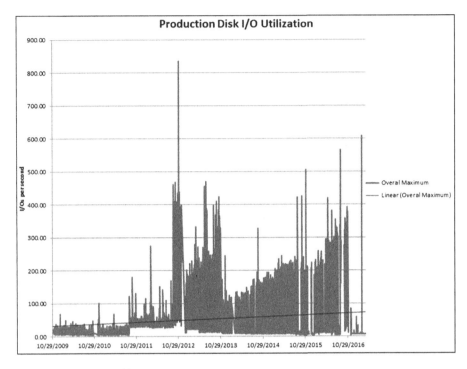

Figure 19-8. *Disk trendline*

The chart in Figure 19-8 shows the maximum IOPS seen during any given day from a real production system. There is a trendline generated by Excel, but we can see most of the data points are above the trendline, and in many cases, well above that trendline. The chart is a good example of being able to handle many different spikes in resource utilization. This system has generated over 400 IOPS on multiple occasions. No matter what the trendline shows, the disk subsystem needs to be able to handle all of those spikes in the graph.

The CPU, memory, and disk utilization charts shown so far obtained the data from the Enterprise Manager repository. EM holds many more metrics if one cares to look at them. I tend to focus on the big three as previously stated, but there are occasions to look at other metrics as well. When the server target has been selected, choose Host ➤ Monitoring ➤ All Metrics to see the breadth of data you can use. Figure 19-9 shows only a few of the categories to choose from. Each item in that list can be expanded to view the metrics in that category.

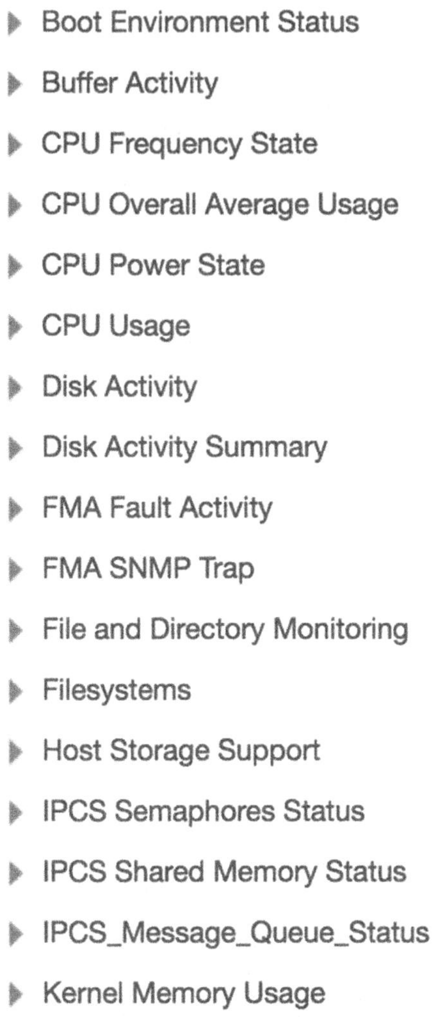

▶ Boot Environment Status

▶ Buffer Activity

▶ CPU Frequency State

▶ CPU Overall Average Usage

▶ CPU Power State

▶ CPU Usage

▶ Disk Activity

▶ Disk Activity Summary

▶ FMA Fault Activity

▶ FMA SNMP Trap

▶ File and Directory Monitoring

▶ Filesystems

▶ Host Storage Support

▶ IPCS Semaphores Status

▶ IPCS Shared Memory Status

▶ IPCS_Message_Queue_Status

▶ Kernel Memory Usage

Figure 19-9. *EM metrics categories*

As stated earlier, EM will keep the metrics for a period of time, but typically not long enough to support capacity planning decision making. For that, you will have to pull the data out of the EM repository and store it elsewhere. The queries shown in this chapter can give you a start on figuring out where the data is stored in that repository. If you do not have access to Enterprise Manager, stand up an EM environment today. EM is already included in your Oracle license, so it costs you nothing extra. You may use third-party tools as well, but you may need to pay extra for them.

Data Dictionary

In Chapter 14, we explored the data dictionary and its role in the Oracle database. There are many metrics that every Oracle database keeps track of and lets you view in the data dictionary. One of the key metrics you may want to use for capacity planning is the overall database size. The data dictionary will only tell you the current size of the database. If you want to keep this information to chart over time, as you normally would expect for capacity planning, then you have to store the data in a table. In Listing 19-4, we create a table to hold the total allocated space and the total space used by segments in the database. The INSERT statement that follows can be used to populate the table with the current date's values. Simply schedule the INSERT statement to run monthly in an Oracle job.

Listing 19-4. Tracking DB Size

```
CREATE TABLE db_size (
   date_collected  DATE,
   gb_allocated    NUMBER,
   gb_used   NUMBER);

INSERT INTO db_size
SELECT sysdate, df.gb_alloc, ds.gb_used
FROM (SELECT round(sum(bytes)/1024/1024/1024,2) AS gb_alloc
              FROM dba_data_files) df
JOIN (SELECT round(sum(bytes)/1024/1024/1024,2) AS gb_used
          FROM dba_segments) ds;
```

If we track the growth over time, we can generate a graph similar to Figure 19-10, again in Excel with a trendline added.

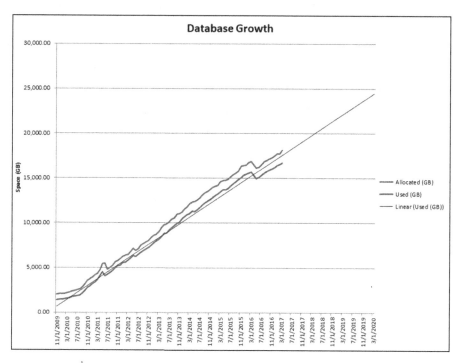

Figure 19-10. *DB growth trendline*

In the chart in Figure 19-10, we can see that the growth of this database over time is very linear, which makes it easy to generate an accurate forecast. One of the things we need to know is when the capacity will reach its limit. In the charts shown for CPU and memory, the utilization rate is expressed as a percentage of the total available. For example, in Figure 19-6, the CPU utilization was over 60% and even approached 100% on occasion. But none of the days shown in the chart reached the 100% mark, so we still have resources to spare. In the chart in Figure 19-10, the values are expressed in total gigabytes. We need to know how much disk space is available to the database. If we know the disks can hold 20TB of data, then we will run out of disk space when the trendline crosses the 20,000GB line. If the disk can hold 25TB of data, we have more time. Because the trend was consistent, we can accurately forecast the date we will run out of disk space. This lets us buy more disk for our servers well in advance of hitting the threshold.

So far in this chapter, we have seen easy charts to cover the big three areas, CPU, memory, and disk, and we broke down the disk area into IOPS and database size. These four charts are ones that I generate on a monthly basis for my production database systems and are what I find to be the most useful in capacity planning.

The Oracle data dictionary has more metrics than you will ever know what to do with. If the charts in this chapter are not sufficient for your capacity planning needs, you should be able to obtain the metrics from the data dictionary with a query. Then create a table and populate it with data. Make sure the table has a column to show when that metric was collected. This column will become the crucial one to sort on so as to display the metric values in a proper time sequence.

If you want to look at different metrics in the data dictionary, start by querying V$SYSSTAT. One thing to note about this and most of the other V$ views is that the statistics are incremented over the lifetime of the instance. The statistics will get reset back to zero when the instance is started anew.

The Tough Questions

Let's assume you have the metrics shown so far in this chapter for CPU, memory, and disk. Your manager comes to you and asks if your database can support doubling the number of concurrent users. The question sounds very specific, but it really isn't that simple. In order to know the answer, you need to determine if the new users will be doing the same exact activity as the current users or if they will be doing something new in the database. If they are doing something new, what exactly will they be doing? If you can define what they will be doing, can you turn that into an analysis of how that will impact the big three resources? Taking this simple, specific question and turning it into a capacity planning activity can be extremely difficult. The problem is that there are too many variables and too many unknowns. It becomes a bit like making a long-range weather forecast, and we have all seen how many times those forecasts miss the mark.

The easiest way to answer questions like these is to extrapolate from our graphs, and then make a big caveat. For example, if we look at the memory utilization in Figure 19-7, we can see the utilization is well under 20%, so we can easily handle doubling the demands on server memory. If we look at the CPU utilization in Figure 19-6, we can easily determine the CPU cannot handle twice the requests from the extra users.

So the answer to the question would be that memory can handle the additional users, but CPU resource cannot. If we need to double the number of concurrent users, then we need to increase CPU resources in advance.

You can show similar charts to your manager and explain your findings. You must then provide a big caveat to the answer, which is "all things being equal." If these extra users are just like the current ones, then here is how it shapes the resource utilization. But if those users are different, they can impart new demands these charts cannot account for with any certainty.

For the most part, if we can translate the tough question into a factor we can apply to our charts, we can provide a capacity planning answer. The translation can be as simple as increasing the demands on the database by some quantity will multiply the chart values by that same factor. Doubling the users means to double the chart values. Quadrupling the data volume means multiplying the database growth chart by four. Keep the capacity planning simple. You cannot account for every detail and every variable, and you will make capacity planning a full-time job if you attempt to do so. Database administrators have other duties to perform in addition to capacity planning.

These charts can also be used to predict when you will run out of resources. For example, the memory utilization in Figure 19-7 is under 20%. We know that 100% is five times 20%, so our factor is five. We can predict that we can support five times as many concurrent users with this memory configuration. If we are using 30% of our total disk capacity, then we can predict when we will run out of disk if we double the data growth.

By now you may be saying to yourself that I am making this overly simplistic, and you would be right. You may be thinking I am glossing over a great many details, and you would be right again. What some people do not want to admit is that all of the details, the minutiae as to how to plan the capacity of your system, do not matter for the most part. I use summary details at a high level and it works for me every time. There is no database administrator that can take a requirement like multiplying the number of concurrent users by a factor of ten and turn that into a detailed analysis that says something like the number of logical read requests will grow by a factor of X in response and in turn the number of physical read requests will grow by a factor of Y. The 10× increase in concurrent users may increase the logical read requests by the same factor of 10× and yield a zero-net change in the number of physical read requests, or the physical reads may double, or triple. No one can say with any accuracy how every metric will change as a result because there are too many unknowns and too many variables, as I have said before.

Instead of spending a ton of your valuable time trying to get the most accurate answer as possible, answer the tough questions with simple factors applied to your current metrics and get on to other important work. By the time your organization procures new hardware, it will have new specifications that you did not account for anyway, throwing any of your previous calculations off the mark. Every hardware purchase means the new equipment is bigger, stronger, and faster than the old machines.

The cloud can make capacity planning both easier and tougher at the same time. Capacity planning in the cloud can be tougher if the cloud provider does not let you obtain metrics on your resource utilization. If they do let you see the resource utilization, it may be in a form that does not let you store the metric values over an extended period. Work with your cloud provider to understand how you can best obtain high-level resource metrics for your capacity planning needs. Where the cloud can make capacity planning easier is not so much in the planning but in the implementation of your plans. Need twice the CPU resources? I'm sure your cloud provider will just add more CPUs to your environment. Need more memory? That's an easy fix. It has become so easy to add resources that many IT administrators just quit planning all together. What could be easier than just stopping the activity of capacity planning? Instead of trying to determine how much we will need in the future, we'll have our cloud provider flip a switch and give us more resources. The cloud providers often allude to this in their sales pitch. I do not like this approach because those additional resources cost your organiation extra money. Every organization I have worked for has budgets and needs to plan their expenditures. While the CPU, memory, and disk resource increase is easy, paying for it may not be so simple.

Moving On

This chapter introduced capacity planning. At a high level, we need to capture CPU, memory, and disk utilization metrics and graph them over time. Once we have the data points, we can easily add trendlines to obtain a good idea of where resource utilization is headed for the future. Keep it simple. There are too many variables and unknowns to account for. You can use your time more wisely by keeping your capacity planning efforts at a very high level.

In the next chapter, I will provide overviews of the Oracle database architecture. The chapter is not meant to make you an expert in each of those areas, but rather to give you exposure to how the Oracle database works.

PART V

Appendixes

CHAPTER 20

Oracle Architecture

In this chapter, we will discuss the Oracle database architecture. We discuss the memory structures, processes, and files that comprise an Oracle database. Knowing how Oracle works is important because otherwise it's just a black box sitting on the shelf.

Consider an automobile and its engine. For many people, a vehicle is a black box. They start it up and drive. Then one day, the engine will not start. If you have no knowledge of how to fix a car's engine, what do you do? You take it to an expert in the field, an automobile mechanic. They know how to fix the black box that takes you back and forth to work every day. Some readers of this book may know a great deal about car engines and have no problems repairing them, no matter what is broken. Other readers are in the middle and may know a bit about the combustion engine, just enough to fix minor issues, but not enough to fix major problems.

As an Oracle database administrator, your organization is relying on you to fix this black box they use to store their valuable data. Just like a mechanic needs to have an in-depth knowledge of how engine components all come together to make the vehicle go, the DBA needs to understand how the Oracle components work in conjunction with each other. Your organization employed you to be the database mechanic.

If you are reading this book, then you probably do not fall in the category of the expert who knows exactly how Oracle works, but you are not one who treats Oracle as a black box either. You are most likely somewhere in the middle. If so, then this chapter is for you. After all, you are most likely reading this book because you want to make the journey from entry-level DBA or higher all the way up to an expert in the field.

In Chapter 13, I recommended that you read the *Oracle Database Concepts* guide. That book in the Oracle documentation provides a wealth of information on how the Oracle database engine works. Please read that guide. In this chapter I will be discussing the same topic from my viewpoint. I will also be touching on the areas I think are vital to understanding the Oracle architecture. This chapter is no substitute for reading the *Database Concepts* guide. While you're in the Oracle documentation, read the *Database Administrator's Guide* as well, as I recommended in Chapter 13.

© Brian Peasland 2019
B. Peasland, *Oracle DBA Mentor*, https://doi.org/10.1007/978-1-4842-4321-3_20

As you work with the Oracle database over the course of your career, you will learn more and more about this architecture. When I first started as an Oracle DBA, it was trying to understand how Oracle worked that was the biggest puzzle to solve, and the most fun too. Even though I have been working with Oracle for more than 20 years, I am still learning new details about the Oracle architecture. Not only am I getting deeper and deeper into Oracle internals, but Oracle changes the architecture a bit here and there with each new release.

Database vs. Instance

In the Oracle architecture, there is a big distinction between the Oracle database and the Oracle instance. These are not the same thing. As a database administrator, you need to understand the two, what they mean, and how they interact.

An Oracle *database* is the collection of files on disk. These files include the tablespace's data files, the control files, and the online redo logs. The database is what survives when Oracle is not up and running. The Oracle software is down, but the files are there. The database is still on disk, but no one can access it. To see the database, we can issue a query as shown in Listing 20-1.

Listing 20-1. Database Files

```
SQL> select file_name as database_files
  2  from dba_data_files
  3  union
  4  select value from v$parameter2
  5  where name='control_files'
  6  union
  7  select member from v$logfile
  8  union
  9  select file_name from dba_temp_files;
```

```
DATABASE_FILES
--------------------------------------------------
/u01/app/oracle/oradata/hr_test/DB10.DB
/u01/app/oracle/oradata/hr_test/DB11.DB
/u01/app/oracle/oradata/hr_test/control01.ctl
/u01/app/oracle/oradata/hr_test/control02.ctl
/u01/app/oracle/oradata/hr_test/redo01.log
/u01/app/oracle/oradata/hr_test/redo02.log
/u01/app/oracle/oradata/hr_test/redo03.log
/u01/app/oracle/oradata/hr_test/sysaux01.dbf
/u01/app/oracle/oradata/hr_test/system01.dbf
/u01/app/oracle/oradata/hr_test/temp01.dbf
/u01/app/oracle/oradata/hr_test/undotbs01.dbf
/u01/app/oracle/oradata/hr_test/users01.dbf
```

The SQL statement above queries for the data files, control files, online redo logs, and temp files. This collection of files is the Oracle *database*. You may recall we issued a similar query in Chapter 7 when we discussed backup and recovery.

You will hear people say things like "I cannot connect to the database." Technically speaking, you can never connect to an Oracle database. The software application is normally running on a different machine, maybe even a web server, accessed by a browser. The application does not have direct access to the files, so it cannot connect to the database. This is where the DBA needs to know their audience. To the end user, Oracle is just a black box and they will use the term "database." When the DBA talks to end users, they should use the same terminology to facilitate the conversation, even though the DBA knows the term is not factually correct.

Users and applications connect to an Oracle *instance*, not the database. The instance is the collection of processes and allocated memory that is a result of starting the Oracle software. User sessions spawn processes on the database server which interact with allocated memory as well as the database's files, as we will see in this chapter.

When the DBA starts Oracle, they are starting the instance. When the DBA shuts down the instance, the database is still there on disk. The *instance* is the collection of processes and memory. The *database* is the files on disk. When talking with other Oracle professionals you will want to use the correct terminology. When talking with others, feel free to use the term "database."

File Types

For the Oracle database, there are eight different file types, each of which is detailed here:

- *Data files*: Each tablespace is composed of one or more data files on disk. A data file can belong to only one tablespace, but a tablespace can have multiple data files.

- *Temp files*: Any temporary tablespaces are composed of one or more special files called temp files. Oracle makes the distinction between data files that contain data to survive an instance shutdown, and temp files that are cleared out when an instance is started up. With this difference known between the two file types, Oracle RMAN can back them up differently. RMAN does not have to waste time backing up the contents of a temp file because the data won't be there when the instance starts up again. Temp files are used when a SQL statement performs a sort or join operation that is too big for its memory space. The work is broken into pieces and temporarily stored in the TEMP tablespace.

- *Online redo logs*: When a transaction occurs, Oracle needs to be able to replay, or redo, that transaction to aid in any recovery efforts. The redo information is written to the online redo logs (ORLs). The ORLs are created in groups. You should have a minimum of three and usually no more than five ORL groups. When redo information is written, it all goes to one ORL group. When that group is filled, Oracle will perform a *log switch* where redo is written to the next ORL group. Once the last ORL group is filled, the next log switch will go back to the first ORL group, overwriting what was there. Ideally, the ORL groups should be large enough so that there are only three or four log switches during a peak hour of transactional activity in the instance. The ORLs are vital to database operations. As such, the ORL groups should be *multiplexed*, which means Oracle maintains a mirror copy of the file. The two copies should not be on the same disk.

- *Archived redo logs*: As stated above, the ORL groups will eventually be overwritten. If the DBA needs to save the redo records for longer periods of time, the database must be configured in archivelog mode. When a log switch occurs, Oracle will copy the previous ORL to an archivelog destination. In Chapter 7, we turned on archivelog mode for our testbed database.

- *Undo tablespace files*: The undo tablespace has its own data files. Technically, Oracle considers the files for the Undo tablespace to be just like regular data files. However, the data in the undo tablespace will not survive instance shutdown, which makes the undo tablespace's data files more similar to temp files. I classify these files differently than regular files if for no other reason than to know they are different than regular data files.

- *Control files*: The control file is the master pointer for the database. When an Oracle instance starts, the instance has no clue where the database's files are located. But the instance does know the location of the control files from the required CONTROL_FILES initialization parameter. The instance reads the data file locations from the control files. The control files also contain any other information Oracle may need before the instance is started. The control files also contain information about RMAN backups and the database's name and unique identifier. You should create production databases with three control files, all on different disk units.

- *Parameter file*: When an Oracle instance starts, it first needs to find the control files. The instance also needs to know how much memory to allocate and several other settings that are controlled by the various parameters influencing Oracle. These parameters are stored in the parameter file. Technically, the parameter file is not part of the "database" but it is an important file to be aware of.

- *Password file*: This optional file is used whenever someone attempts to connect to the instance from a different machine than the database server and they are attempting a SYSDBA or SYSOPER connection. Again, this file is not part of the database, but you will want to understand its role.

Memory Structures

When an Oracle instance is started, it allocates memory on the database server. The memory used by Oracle falls under two distinct categories, the Program Global Area (PGA) and the System Global Area (SGA). Both are sized differently. The PGA usage is dynamic, responding to changes in user demands. The SGA is usually of a fixed size, although the DBA can change the SGA's size on the fly if the database is configured correctly.

PGA

The Program Global Area is the simplest to understand. A user's session makes a connection to the Oracle instance. The session will need memory to store that session's data and control information. What will take up the most space in the PGA is when a user performs an operation that needs temporary sorting space. Any time the session issues a query that includes ORDER BY, GROUP BY, and even a join over two or more tables, Oracle needs space to store the intermediary results. Oracle uses the session's PGA.

The name Program *Global* Area is a bit misleading. Each session will allocate its own PGA. Sessions are forbidden from seeing another session's PGA contents. The memory in the PGA is not shared so the term "global" may not seem appropriate. As each session allocates PGA memory, the total PGA for the instance will grow. As sessions disconnect from the instance, the total instance PGA will fall. The example in Listing 20-2 shows how to calculate the total allocated instance PGA for an Oracle instance. I repeated the query a few more times to show how the total PGA allocation rises and falls.

Listing 20-2. Total PGA Allocation

```
SQL> select to_char(sysdate,'HH24:MI:SS') as sample_time,
  2  trunc(sum(pga_alloc_mem)/1024/1024,2) as pga_mb
  3  from v$process;

SAMPLE_T     PGA_MB
-------- ----------
13:29:44    3571.84

SQL> /
```

```
SAMPLE_T    PGA_MB
--------  ----------
13:33:31    3606.75

SQL> /

SAMPLE_T    PGA_MB
--------  ----------
13:36:52    3526.39
```

For this system, seeing 3.5GB of total PGA usage is normal. Every system will be different because the PGA usage is determined by the end users and their activity with the Oracle instance.

There are two initialization parameters that control the PGA memory usage. These parameters can be defined by the database administrator. The two initialization parameters are shown in Listing 20-3.

Listing 20-3. PGA Initialization Parameters

```
SQL> show parameter pga

NAME                                 TYPE        VALUE
------------------------------------ ----------- --------------------------
pga_aggregate_limit                  big integer 20G
pga_aggregate_target                 big integer 10G
```

The PGA_AGGREGATE_TARGET parameter defines the total amount of memory the PGA can allocate. Unfortunately, this is a soft limit. As the parameter's name implies, this is a target value, but targets are often missed. If your sessions demand more PGA, they can easily exceed the target setting. Oracle 12.1 introduced the PGA_AGGREGATE_LIMIT parameter to define a hard limit to PGA consumption. Oracle will not allow the total instance PGA to exceed the defined limit. If the limit is reached, Oracle will first abort any calls for sessions that have the most untunable memory allocated to them. If this action does not reduce the PGA allocation below the limit, Oracle will then kill some of those sessions.

It is never good for a session to be killed, yet we cannot let sessions just allocate as much memory as they would like. We need a way of determining an optimal setting for the PGA_AGGREGATE_TARGET parameter. Oracle includes the V$PGA_TARGET_ ADVICE view that helps us understand the impact of raising or lowering this parameter value, which is shown in the code of Listing 20-4.

Listing 20-4. PGA Target Advice

```
SQL> select pga_target_factor,estd_extra_bytes_rw,estd_overalloc_count
  2  from v$pga_target_advice;
```

PGA_TARGET_FACTOR	ESTD_EXTRA_BYTES_RW	ESTD_OVERALLOC_COUNT
.125	2.0558E+11	3195
.25	1.0327E+10	141
.5	1360508928	0
.75	1360508928	0
1	1360508928	0
1.2	0	0
1.4	0	0
1.6	0	0
1.8	0	0
2	0	0
3	0	0
4	0	0
6	0	0
8	0	0

The line where the PGA_TARGET_FACTOR column equals 1 is our current setting. The rest of that factor column shows what occurs if we increase or decrease the PGA by the value in that row. For example, the last row shows the effect of increasing the PGA by a factor of 8. The first row shows the effect of decreasing the PGA by a factor of 0.125 (one-eighth). The second and third columns show how much extra work is needed by the database if the PGA changes by that factor. We want to size the PGA such that the values in the second and third column are 0. We can see in the row where the factor equals 1 that we have a nonzero value, so we should consider increasing the PGA. The next row has all zeros for the second and third columns, so this view is telling us to increase the PGA by a factor of 1.2. Increasing the PGA by a larger factor will not bring any benefit.

SGA

The System Global Area (SGA) is memory that is shared, globally, for all sessions in the Oracle instance. This memory structure is divided into many different components, all with a different job to perform. In this section, we will discuss various components of the SGA.

Buffer Cache

The Buffer Cache stores copies of blocks from the data files into memory for fast, efficient retrieval. If the database engine had to read data from disk every time it needed it, performance would be miserable. Reading the data from memory is much faster. When the instance is started, the Buffer Cache is initially empty. As SQL statements are issued to the database, the statements will attempt to read or modify data in the database. Before the data can be modified or returned to the user, the data file's block is read into the Buffer Cache. The idea is that if your session wanted to access the data, another session might want similar access in the near future. If we cache the data in memory, we can save the expensive operation to read the data from disk for any subsequent requests.

When talking to non-Oracle professionals, I simply refer to this structure as the "database's cache." Many people are familiar with the concept of a cache, so using a simple term helps us communicate more effectively. I lump other cache structures in the SGA, which we will discuss soon, in with this term as well. When talking with Oracle database administrators, I will be very specific regarding which cache component in the SGA I am referring to.

Unless the database is relatively small, the server may lack sufficient memory to cache the entire database's contents. The Buffer Cache needs to manage its contents so that the most requested data stays in memory. Oracle uses a modified "least recently used" algorithm to determine the data to purge from the cache should it be needed for another request.

On certain occasions, especially for those where the Oracle engine thinks the data will only be requested once, the Buffer Cache may be skipped. The data is read from disk and passed directly to the user's session, which Oracle calls a *direct path read*. A direct path read can avoid the time it takes to find and possibly clear out a portion of the Buffer Cache before reading the data from disk. However, if the data is accessed again, it will have to be read from disk again.

The Buffer Cache is so named because each block of space in the cache is called a *buffer*. The buffer size is equal to the database's DB_BLOCK_SIZE initialization parameter. If your database's block size is 8K in size, then each buffer in the cache is a contiguous 8K chunk of memory. The Buffer Cache is the collection of these chunks or buffers.

As stated earlier, when the instance starts up, the Buffer Cache is empty. Each buffer in the cache has a state of *unused*. A session then issues a SELECT statement to read data from a table. The blocks are read from disk and placed into buffers in the cache. At this point, the data has not yet been modified so the buffer has a state of *clean*. If a session changes the data in the buffer, the state changes to *dirty*. When the transaction commits the change, the buffer stays in the cache marked as dirty.

It is important to note that the act of committing the transaction does not cause Oracle to write the contents of the dirty buffer to disk. The dirty buffers are written to the data files only when Oracle performs a checkpoint. The following events will trigger a checkpoint:

- A redo log is switched to the next group.

- The LOG_CHECKPOINT_INTERVAL has been reached.

- The LOG_CHECKPOINT_TIMEOUT value has passed.

- Someone issues the ALTER SYSTEM CHECKPOINT command.

Another important item to note is that dirty buffers can be written to disk even if the transaction that modified the buffer has yet to commit. This can happen when there is space pressure for the Buffer Cache.

Shared Pool

Another important SGA component is the Shared Pool. The Shared Pool is a collection of memory structures all lumped in this category. We could think of the subcomponents separately, but for whatever reason, Oracle decided to group them into the Shared Pool. These subcomponents, also called sub-pools, are defined next.

Library Cache

The Library Cache is where Oracle keeps all the SQL statements it has processed. When a user issues a SQL statement to the instance, there is a lot of work that goes on well before Oracle starts returning data. The statement must be parsed to ensure that it is syntactically correct. Next, the Oracle Optimizer must determine an efficient execution plan to return the data as quickly as possible. If another user issues the same SQL statement, it would be nice if they could benefit from the prior work. Oracle stores all this information in the Library Cache. When a user submits a SQL statement, Oracle first checks the Library Cache to see if that statement is there. If it is in the cache, all the preprocessing can be skipped.

Data Dictionary Cache

The Buffer Cache stores data from application tables. Remember that the data dictionary is stored in tables as well, owned by the SYS user. The data dictionary tables are essential to the database operations and, as such, they get their own cache, a subcomponent of the Shared Pool. Instead of holding blocks, or buffers, in the cache, the data dictionary Cache holds rows of data. As such, you will sometimes see this referred to as the *row cache* in older Oracle literature.

Result Cache

If a SQL statement returns a consistent result, the DBA can leverage the Result Cache to store that result rather than having to recompute the result every time the SQL statement is executed. The next time a user issues the same SQL statement, Oracle will look in the Library Cache and see the best way to execute it is to just get the results from the Result Cache. The Result Cache can greatly improve the performance of these SQL statements. This functionality works best with SQL statements whose underlying data does not change frequently and where the result set is not very large. Very few SQL statements will benefit from the Result Cache, but for those that do, Oracle needs memory and the Result Cache is the place.

Redo Log Buffer

The Redo Log Buffer, also called the Log Buffer, is another component of the SGA. When a transaction makes changes to data, Oracle must store the information to be able to replay, or redo, that transaction. The redo records will be written to the online redo logs, but writing redo records directly to disk would take too much time. Transactions write redo to memory instead, to the Redo Log Buffer.

The Redo Log Buffer is a circular memory structure. If enough data is written to the buffer, eventually older contents will be overwritten. Oracle will need to write the redo records to the online redo logs prior to the buffer filling up.

Large Pool

The Large Pool is space set aside for memory needs that are larger than other Shared Pool needs. Typically, the Large Pool is used as buffer space for parallel SQL statements and RMAN slave processes.

Java Pool

The Java Pool is where Oracle stores Java code that is executed within the database's Java Virtual Machine (JVM).

Fixed SGA

The SGA needs a certain amount of space for internal housekeeping activities. This space is fixed in size and cannot be changed, hence its name Fixed SGA. However, a new Oracle version may require a larger Fixed SGA.

Sizing SGA Components

It used to be that the Oracle database administrator specified different initialization parameters to specify the size of the SGA components, including the Shared Pool, the Buffer Cache, etc. Today's Oracle DBA uses the SGA_TARGET initialization parameter to define the total SGA size and lets the Oracle instance determine the best size of the individual components so long as they all fit within the parameter's setting. By using this parameter, there are two benefits. First, sizing the SGA is easier because only one parameter must be accurately set. Second, the Oracle instance can adjust the individual components in response to changing workloads. If more space is needed for the Buffer Cache, it can be taken from the Shared Pool if there is plenty available there.

Similar to determining a proper size for the PGA, Oracle includes the V$SGA_TARGET_ADVICE view. In Listing 20-5, the row where the size factor equals 1 is our current SGA setting.

Listing 20-5. SGA Target Advice

```
SQL>  select sga_size_factor,estd_db_time,estd_physical_reads
  2  from v$sga_target_advice;
SGA_SIZE_FACTOR ESTD_DB_TIME ESTD_PHYSICAL_READS
--------------- ------------ -------------------
            .25        53470             4175955
             .5       686730            42630654
            .75        77000            29370744
              1        60692             4175955
           1.25        59958             3005852
            1.5        59703             3005852
           1.75        59581             3005852
              2        59521             3005852
```

In the output above, our current SGA has an estimated DB time value of 60,692 and an estimated number of physical reads of 4,175,955. If we increase the SGA by 25% (factor=1.25), the estimated DB time drops a little, as does the estimated physical reads. Notice that if we increase the SGA by a factor of 50%, the estimated physical reads do not change. This view is showing us that doubling the SGA size would not give us that much better performance than increasing by a more modest amount of 25%.

Oracle includes another parameter, MEMORY_TARGET, that is used to size both the SGA and the PGA. This singular parameter makes it even easier for database administrators to size the memory structures to support the Oracle instance. However, you cannot use MEMORY_TARGET if your database server has implemented Huge Pages for shared memory allocation. If you are running Oracle on Linux, then you will most likely want to use Huge Pages, which means you need to determine proper values for the SGA_TARGET and PGA_AGGREGATE_TARGET initialization parameters.

Background Processes

Allocating all that memory is fine, but no work will get accomplished with simple memory allocation. Something needs to move data in and out of memory. In Unix and Linux environments, Oracle makes heavy use of different processes, or small programs, running on the server. Each process has its own job to do. Together, the processes work together to make the Oracle instance function. On Windows servers, the work is done by different threads in the same process.

When you start an Oracle instance, memory is allocated and several processes automatically start. These are called *background processes* because they work in the background managing the instance. This differs from processes that are specific to user sessions.

Some background processes are *mandatory*. If a mandatory process dies, the instance will terminate. After all, an instance cannot survive if a process it requires is absent. Other processes are *optional* and are started depending on the configuration of the instance. Recall that in Chapter 7 we set up archivelog mode for our testbed. When configured this way, the Oracle instance will start a process to copy the contents of an ORL to the archivelog destination. That's the process's only job. Because archivelog mode is not required, the process to support it is not required either. If an optional process abnormally terminates, the instance will stay up and running. Typically, one of the mandatory processes will detect the optional process is down and attempt to restart it.

Each new Oracle version can bring with it new processes, some mandatory and some optional. Consult the *Database Concepts* guide for your specific version to understand the different processes the instance may spawn. Sometimes new processes are created to support new functionality. Other times, Oracle Corporation creates new processes to split out work done by a process that has become overburdened. For example, as long as I can remember, every Oracle version has had a PMON process. PMON still exists, but Oracle 12c now has taken part of PMON's duties and pushed them into the CLMN and CL*nn* processes, as we will see in the next section.

Mandatory Processes

This section describes the mandatory processes for an Oracle 12.2 instance.

- *Process Monitor (PMON)*: This process is responsible for monitoring and cleaning up after other processes. PMON will clean up the Buffer Cache. Once a user's session ends, PMON will release any resources that session held, including any transaction locks. PMON includes a few helper processes in Oracle 12c, CLMN and CL*nn*.

    - *Cleanup Main Process (CLMN)*: When PMON knows a user's process needs cleanup work, it delegates the job to CLMN. CLMN is then responsible for seeing that the work is completed. Because the cleanup work can be a job all on its own and leaves little time for oversight, CLMN delegates the real work to the next process.

    - *Cleanup Helper Processes (CL*nn*)*: These are the processes that do the real cleanup work. CLMN is the supervisor and CL*nn* does the actual work. The *nn* is a placeholder for a two-digit number. You might see CL01 and CL02 processes if multiple processes are running.

- *Process Manager (PMAN)*: This process monitors and controls dispatcher and shared server processes, job queue processes, and any background processes that can be restarted.

- *System Monitor (SMON)*: This process performs cleanup of the system. PMON and its helpers take care of process cleanup. SMON takes care of the rest. When an instance is started, SMON will perform recovery of any uncommitted transactions. SMON will also clean up any temporary segments.

- *Listener Registration (LREG)*: This process tells the Listener the instance is up and running and ready for connection requests. It periodically updates the Listener with the number of current connections to the instance. Prior to 12*c*, this process's work was performed by SMON.

- *Database Writer (DBWn)*: This process, also known as DBWR, is responsible for writing dirty blocks in the Buffer Cache back to the database files. While there is typically one process (DBW0), a heavy workload may dictate multiple processes.

- *Log Writer (LGWR)*: This process is responsible for writing the contents of the Redo Log Buffer to the online redo logs.

- *Checkpoint (CKPT)*: This process starts the checkpoint activity. When a checkpoint occurs, it prompts DBWR to take action. CKPT will update the control files and update every datafile header with the most recent System Change Number (SCN).

- *Manageability Monitor (MMON)*: This process updates and manages the Automatic Workload Repository (AWR).

  - *Manageability Monitory Lite (MMNL)*: This process reads statistics from the Active Session History buffer and writes the data to disk, all part of the AWR.

- *Recoverer Process (RECO)*: This process cleans up failures in any distributed transactions. A distributed transaction is one that involves more than one Oracle database.

Optional Background Processes

Not all processes are mandatory. This section details the optional background processes.

- *Archiver Processes (ARCn)*: These processes copy the contents of the online redo logs to the archivelog destination. This process is only started when the database is in archivelog mode.

- *Job Queue Processes (CJQ0 and Jnnn)*: These processes execute jobs in the Oracle Scheduler. CJQ0 is the master job coordinator process. Each running job will execute in a different slave process, J*nnn*.

- *Parallel Query Slaves (Pnnn)*: These processes are responsible for doing work to support parallel SQL statements. The user's session is the master process and pieces out the work to the parallel query slaves.

- *Data Guard Monitor (DMON)*: This process is started when the Data Guard Broker is implemented to support standby databases.

- *Managed Recovery Process (MRP)*: This process runs on a standby database to replay transactions.

- *Queue Monitor Process (QMNn)*: This process manages Oracle Streams and Advanced Queueing.

- *Lock Monitor (LMON)*: This process helps manage locks for Real Application Clusters (RAC) databases.

As you can imagine looking at the list above, if you are not using archivelog mode, parallel query, standby databases, or RAC, you will not see these processes on your system.

There are many, many other optional background processes as well. The list above shows the most common.

User Processes

The last category of processes to discuss are those for user sessions. After this section, we will attempt to put it all together—processes, files, and memory structures—and build an architecture diagram.

Users always connect to an Oracle instance by using some application. That application may be as simple as SQL*Plus or some command-line tool, but they are still applications. The application runs in its own process on a computer. Normally in today's computer environments, the applications run on a machine other than the database server.

When the application requests a connection to the instance, Oracle will create a *server process* on the database server. Depending on the configuration, that process make be earmarked solely for the user, in which case it is called a *dedicated server process*, or the process may be used by multiple application connections, in which case it is called a *shared server process*. Oracle Corporation created the capability to share the server process in response to the explosion of the Internet age. Databases needed to be able to support many more users than prior to the birth of web-based applications. Oracle Corporation decided to give us the ability to have shared server processes. About the same time, those who made the web servers we use gave us wonderful things like connection pooling. It is much more common to use connection pooling in the application tier than it is to use shared server processes. Every Oracle database I have administered has used dedicated server processes. I recommend avoiding shared server processes if possible due to the extra management it requires from the DBA. Just know that the capability is there should the need warrant its implementation. For the rest of this chapter, we will refer to the term *server process* to mean either the dedicated type or the shared type, depending on the database configuration.

No application connects directly to the instance. When the application does request a connection, Oracle ensures a server process is available. The application communicates only to the server process. The server process talks to the instance on behalf of the application. You can think of the server process as the middleman. The Listener accepts the incoming connection request and facilitates the connection between the application and the server process. After that, the Listener is no longer involved in whatever occurs between the two. It is a myth that the application always goes through the Listener.

Putting It Together

We have discussed the various files that make up the database as well as the memory structures and processes that make up the instance. Now it's time to make some sense of it all and see how these components work together. We'll start where we left off and view the interaction between the application, the Listener, and the server process, as shown in Figure 20-1.

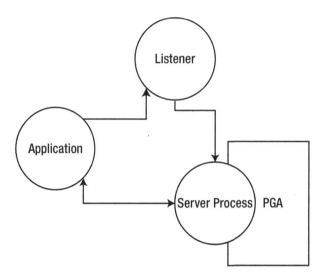

Figure 20-1. *Application connection*

As stated in the previous section, the application contacts the Listener, which brokers the connection request and gets the application process talking to the server process. The server process allocates the PGA for its use.

At some point, the application is going to make a request by issuing a SQL statement. We will assume that the data blocks needed to satisfy this request are not currently in the Buffer Cache. The blocks need to be read into the Buffer Cache. What may surprise some is that it is the server process for the user's session that reads from the data file, as shown in Figure 20-2.

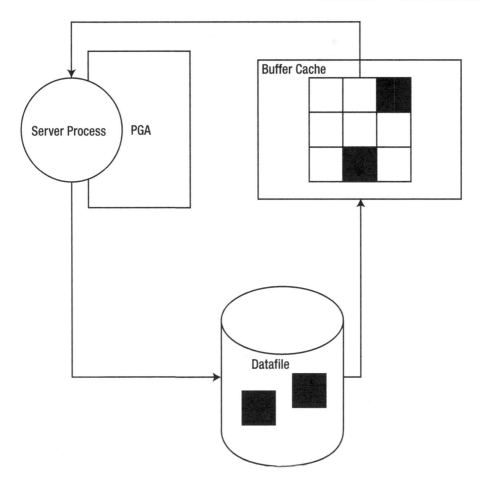

Figure 20-2. *Reading block into Buffer Cache*

Once the block is in the Buffer Cache, the server process can access the data. If the block was already in the Buffer Cache, the read from the data file is not necessary. If the SQL operation results in a direct path read, the arrow from the data file goes back to the server process and the Buffer Cache is not used.

The user's session then modifies the contents of a data block in the cache through a transaction. The block is now marked as dirty. Information is written to the Redo Log Buffer to be able to replay the transaction if necessary. Eventually, LGWR writes the redo information to the online redo logs and DBW*n* writes the dirty block to the data files, but not necessarily at the same time. Figure 20-3 shows the interactions with the Buffer Cache, Redo Log Buffer, and the background processes.

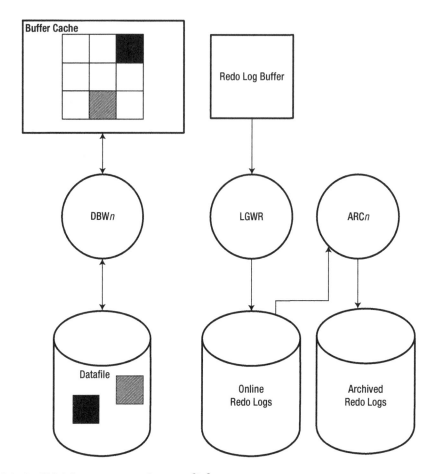

Figure 20-3. *Writing transaction to disk*

If archivelog mode is turned on, the Archiver Process will copy the online redo logs to the archivelog destination.

Interactive Quick Reference

Rather than rely on my diagrams of the Oracle architecture, you could look in the *Database Concepts* guide for some nice visualizations. In addition, Oracle Corporation has provided an interactive web page that lets you explore the Oracle architecture. You can find this web page at the following URL:

```
www.oracle.com/webfolder/technetwork/tutorials/obe/db/12c/r1/poster/OUTPUT_
poster/poster.html
```

Once on that web page, click the Database Architecture tab. This will bring you to a complex diagram, reproduced in Figure 20-4, showing every piece of the architecture.

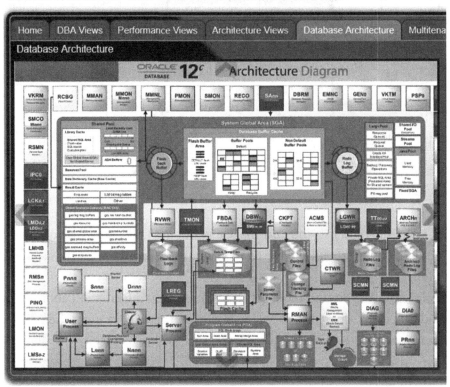

Figure 20-4. *Interactive Quick Reference Database Architecture tab*

We can see all of the processes and memory structures and follow the flow of activity through this architecture. There is so much more than was written in this chapter. Processes and memory structures not discussed here are not as significant as the ones mentioned, but they may be important to you as you explore more about how Oracle works.

To interact with the diagram, double-click it. You will be zoomed into the image and you can use your mouse to move it to an area of interest. If you want to learn more about an item in the diagram, click it. In Figure 20-5, I clicked the Checkpoint Process.

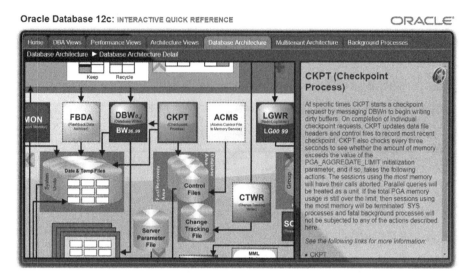

Figure 20-5. *Interactive Quick Reference CKPT details*

The pane on the right lists the information about the CKPT process I clicked. At the bottom of these details are links to the Oracle documentation that discusses the item in greater detail.

If you click the Background Processes tab, you can get information about all of the background processes. There are so many processes, this site arranges them by various categories. In Figure 20-6, I clicked the General category.

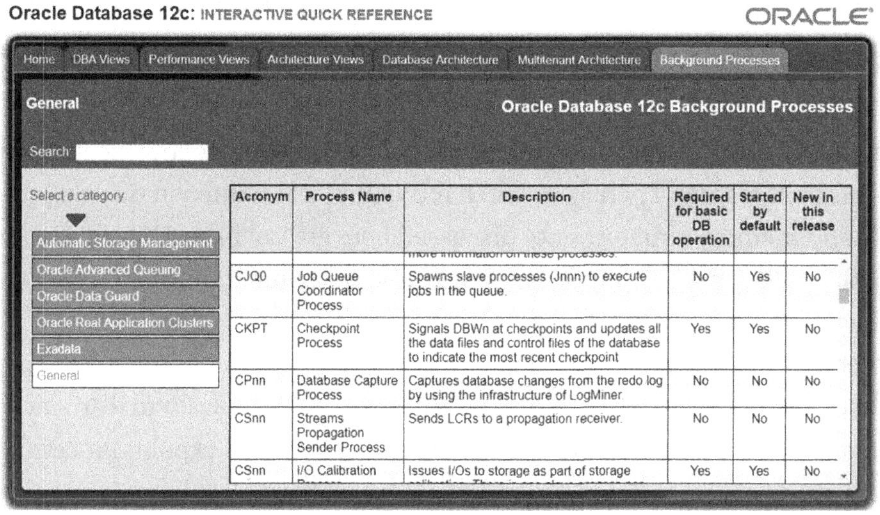

Figure 20-6. *Interactive Quick Reference Background Processes tab*

Recall that in Chapter 14 we discussed the data dictionary. This interactive tool also provides documentation on the data dictionary views. Click the DBA Views, Performance Views, or Architecture Views tab. In Figure 20-7, the Storage category is selected on the DBA Views tab. We can see how views are related to each other by following the lines in the diagram. The search box can be used to more easily find a view if you know part of its name.

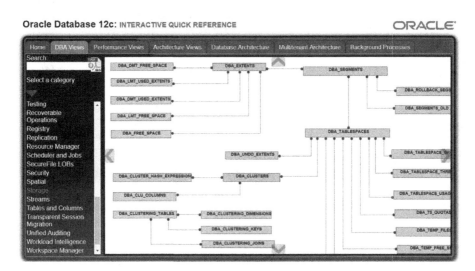

Figure 20-7. *Interactive Quick Reference DBA Views tab*

Clicking a view will bring up its description. If we click the DBA_TABLESPACES view, we can see all of its columns, similar to Figure 20-8.

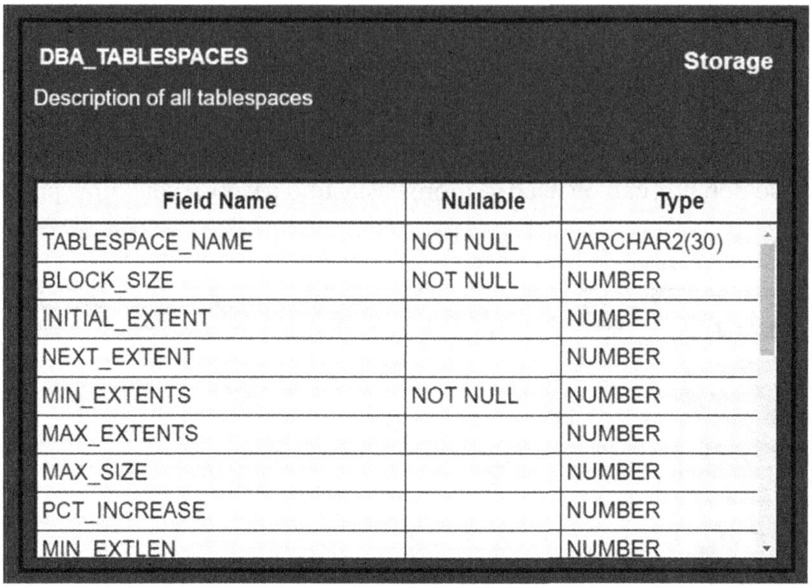

DBA_TABLESPACES   Storage
Description of all tablespaces

Field Name	Nullable	Type
TABLESPACE_NAME	NOT NULL	VARCHAR2(30)
BLOCK_SIZE	NOT NULL	NUMBER
INITIAL_EXTENT		NUMBER
NEXT_EXTENT		NUMBER
MIN_EXTENTS	NOT NULL	NUMBER
MAX_EXTENTS		NUMBER
MAX_SIZE		NUMBER
PCT_INCREASE		NUMBER
MIN_EXTLEN		NUMBER

Figure 20-8. *Interactive Quick Reference DBA_TABLESPACES description*

Give the Interactive Quick Reference a tour and see if it can help you in your career. Oracle does not publish a similar product for the Oracle 18c version, most likely because 18c was originally to be named 12.2.0.2 before Oracle Corporation decided to change its version numbering scheme.

An Oracle 11*g* Interactive Quick Reference guide is published at the following URL:

```
www.oracle.com/webfolder/technetwork/tutorials/obe/db/11g/Poster/11g_
interactive.html
```

The 11*g* version of this tool does require Adobe Flash in your browser.

Instance Startup

When an Oracle instance is started, the instance goes through three stages: NOMOUNT, MOUNT, and OPEN, in that order. In Listing 20-6, we have connected to an idle instance, meaning it is not yet running. The instance is then started in NOMOUNT mode, then advanced to MOUNT, and finally to OPEN.

Listing 20-6. Moving Instance Through Startup Stages

```
SQL> connect / as sysdba
Connected to an idle instance.
SQL> startup nomount
ORACLE instance started.

Total System Global Area 2147483648 bytes
Fixed Size                   2926472 bytes
Variable Size              687868024 bytes
Database Buffers          1442840576 bytes
Redo Buffers                13848576 bytes
SQL> alter database mount;

Database altered.

SQL> alter database open;

Database altered.
```

The database administrator can start the instance and have it proceed to any of the three stages. In the example above, the DBA started the instance in NOMOUNT mode. But the DBA could have specified STARTUP MOUNT or STARTUP OPEN to proceed to those stages. If no stage is specified on the STARTUP command, the default action is to proceed to the OPEN stage.

When an instance is started in NOMOUNT mode, the only file accessed on disk is the parameter file. The instance starts, memory is allocated, and background processes necessary to support the instance are spawned. When the instance moves to MOUNT mode, the control file is accessed for the first time. When the instance is moved to OPEN mode, the rest of the database's files are accessed. If needed, SMON will perform recovery to roll back any uncommitted transactions from when the instance was terminated. Once complete, the database is then open for business and connections are allowed to the instance.

You would use NOMOUNT mode when you need to perform work on the control files. Remember that the control files are not yet accessed in this stage. If you need to manually re-create the control files, you need to be in NOMOUNT mode.

The MOUNT mode is used when you need access to the control files but not to the rest of the data files. You would use this stage if you wanted to move or rename data files. MOUNT mode is also used when configuring the archivelog mode for the database or performing full database recovery.

Most of the time, you will use the OPEN stage. After all, we want the instance open and ready for business. You would use the other stages for maintenance activities.

There is one other startup mode to discuss. You can open the instance in RESTRICTED mode. In this mode, the instance starts to the OPEN stage. However, only those users with the RESTRICTED SESSION system privilege will be allowed to connect to the instance. You would use this method when you want to gain access to the database for maintenance activities, but you do not want those activities to negatively impact end users.

Moving On

This chapter has discussed many facets of the Oracle architecture: files, processes, and memory structures. The information in this chapter only scratches the surface. You will want to make sure you read the *Database Concepts* guide in the Oracle documentation to add more to your knowledge.

In the next chapter, we will discuss a number of advanced options for the Oracle database. You can certainly make a career without using any of these options. The options exist to extend the functionality of the Oracle database. In many cases, the options have additional licensing costs, but can actually save your company money in the long run by saving on labor or third-party products.

CHAPTER 21

Advanced Options

In this chapter, we will discuss different advanced options for the Oracle database that you may employ in your enterprise architecture. The options exist because they extend the functionality of the core database product. In some cases, it is possible to engineer similar functionality, and in other cases, it is not possible.

Most of the options in this chapter require Oracle Enterprise Edition and, except for Enterprise Manager, come with an added cost. Most of these options are not part of your regular database license. While they do cost extra money, they can be well worth the expenditure if you need their services. As stated above, it may be possible to engineer some of the functionality an Oracle option provides, without spending actual funds by coding the functionality in your application. However, your company will still spend money in the form of labor expenses. Not only will you have to develop the functionality, you will have to maintain it going forward. If you desire to extend the functionality further, you will incur additional development time. Too many organizations that want the functionality look at the cost of the Oracle option and then decide to develop their own functionality. While this choice looks attractive, they often fail to look at it from a long-term perspective. Oracle Corporation is likely to implement the functionality much better than a home-grown solution. Lastly, the functionality from these extra options is largely application independent. The application may not even know or care if the option is in use. If you code your own functionality, you may have to deploy it to the next application, which means your functionality now needs to be maintained in multiple places. If you use Oracle's option, you do not maintain the feature and it is all in one location, the database.

Because these features are extra-cost items, Oracle Corporation will examine the usage of each with great detail during an Oracle audit. If your company is ever audited, Oracle will ask you to run a series of scripts against all databases in your enterprise. These scripts will detect if you have ever used the feature in your database. All it takes is one time for the audit script to detect the usage of that feature. If you are not licensed for that option, you will be in breach of your Oracle contract and Oracle Corporation may take legal action.

© Brian Peasland 2019
B. Peasland, *Oracle DBA Mentor*, https://doi.org/10.1007/978-1-4842-4321-3_21

If you do want to try out an option, do not use the feature in any of your development, test, and production databases. Doing so, even for a simple test, will flip that flag Oracle Corporation will find during an audit. Instead, set up a testbed and kick the tires on the feature there. After your testing is done, you can destroy the testbed. Oracle's Technology Network license will allow you to test out features of the advanced options, but you cannot perform real development work with any option until you have paid for the extra option. Put some sample data in your testbed and derive a proof of concept for your organization. Kick the tires on the feature and see what it will do and what it will not do for your project. In the first few chapters of this book, we created our own testbed, so you know how to create an area for this type of activity. Do not attempt the examples in this chapter in non-testbeds unless you have licensed the option!

As you read this chapter, do not try to become an expert in each of these options. Instead, try to determine what each option is trying to provide for you and your enterprise. In the future, you may be working on the design for some new project and then remember that an option exists which can help you. At that time, your organization can further explore the option and determine if it is worth the extra cost.

Diagnostics Pack

This is the one extra-cost option I cannot live without. The last time I interviewed for a job, I asked if they had licensed the Diagnostics Pack for their Oracle infrastructure. If they did not have the option licensed, there is a strong possibility I would have turned down any job offer based on that alone. The Diagnostics Pack is that important to me. Not everyone will agree with me.

As a senior-level DBA I am often tasked with resolving a number of performance issues. The Diag Pack is a huge, huge time saver when examining Oracle performance. While it has an added cost, and you have to license it for all of the databases you want to use it on, it is well worth the money. If I did not have this option licensed for me, my company would have to hire two or three additional database administrators. It saves me that much time. The number of extra employees mentioned is probably a conservative estimate.

The Diagnostics Pack is primarily used for database performance activities. Many times when I am working on a performance issue, I can determine the root cause of the problem within minutes because of the Diag Pack. Without it, I would spend days finding the bottleneck. If I have to compare bad performance today to good performance last month, the Diag Pack lets me do this in minutes. Without it, I might spend a week completing the comparison. It literally saves me that much time.

The Diagnostics Pack consists of the following:

- Automatic Database Diagnostic Monitor (ADDM)

- Active Session History (ASH)

- Automatic Workload Repository (AWR)

- AWR Warehouse

The best way to see the Diag Pack in action is with Oracle Enterprise Manager. You can interact with the Diag Pack through SQL statements, but EM does this for you and displays usable and informative graphs to help you understand at a glance what is going on with the database and its performance. For example, if we navigate to a database in EM, and then click Performance ➤ Performance Home, we can see a chart showing the current activity in the instance, as shown in Figure 21-1.

Figure 21-1. *EM Performance chart*

It's hard to see in Figure 21-1, but there is a red line at the top of the chart denoting this system has 16 CPU cores. When the graph goes above the red line, that is an indicator that end users are experiencing poor-performance issues. In Figure 21-1, the graph is well below the line. This does not necessarily mean that performance is fine, because we may have a few sessions that are having some difficulties, but overall, performance should be good for most users.

On the right side of the chart is a color-coded legend showing classifications where user sessions are spending their time. The graph has a predominately green color and, from the legend, we can see this represents users spending their time processing on the CPU. If we mouse over an item in the legend, it will change to a yellow highlight and the corresponding classification in the chart will change to match. This can help view some of the classifications that are not easily seen in the chart.

If we click a classification, EM will drill down into that area. Because the dominant classification is CPU, I will drill down into that area. In the graph in Figure 21-2, there is a shaded box which can be dragged from side to side.

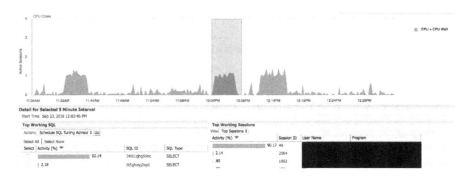

Figure 21-2. *EM drilldown into CPU usage*

We can see from Figure 21-2 that there are a few spikes in CPU utilization. If we were to drag the shaded box over one of those spikes, the Top Working SQL and Top Working Sessions would be updated to match. In this case, we can see one SQL statement from one user is taking up over 90% of the CPU during the time period represented by that shaded box. If I was working on an issue where a user called complaining of poor performance, the first chart would not have yielded much information. By drilling down in the CPU utilization, I was able to see that one user does appear to be using large amounts of CPU, and it is likely that I have very quickly found the root cause. Note that I blacked out the User Name and Program columns to obscure potentially proprietary information.

The SQL ID and Session ID columns contain hyperlinks. I can drill down quickly into the session's details and even the SQL statement. In Figure 21-3, I clicked the SQL statement to see why this was using so much CPU.

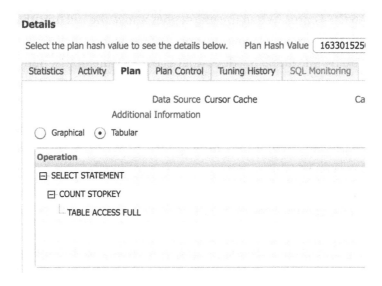

Figure 21-3. *EM SQL details execution plan*

By drilling down into the SQL statement, I can see the exact SQL text. I clicked the Plan tab and changed from a graphical execution plan to a tabular one. I can see a Full Table Access step being performed. That doesn't seem right, so I click the Statistics tab, as shown in Figure 21-4.

Execution Statistics

	Total	Per Execution	Per Row
Executions	19,974	1	1.00
Elapsed Time (sec)	31,552.31	1.58	1.58
CPU Time (sec)	30,914.45	1.55	1.55
Buffer Gets	136,662,868	6,842.04	6,842.38
Disk Reads	9,065	0.45	0.45
Direct Writes	0	0.00	0.00
Rows	19,973	1.00	1
Fetches	19,973	1.00	1.00

Figure 21-4. *EM SQL details statistics*

I can see from the statistics on this SQL statement that the SQL has been executed 19,974 times. It has generated over 136 million buffer gets. This means user sessions have read the data from the Buffer Cache over 136 million times. Reading from the Buffer Cache requires CPU. If I look in the Per Execution column, I can see that this SQL statement requires 6,842 buffer gets per execution. Looking further in that column, I can see that this SQL statement is returning one row per execution. As the database administrator, I know that the block size for the database is 8,192 bytes. Multiplying the number of buffer gets by the block size, 8,192 × 6,842, indicates that over 50MB of data is being read from the cache just to return one row! To a trained Oracle performance specialist, it is easy to diagnose that performing a full table scan is leading to the performance problem. If I could leverage an index to speed up the query, I could reduce the CPU time significantly, freeing up CPU resources for other users as well.

This problem resolution is a good example of why the Diagnostics Pack is very valuable. With a few clicks of my mouse, I was able to drill down and spot the problem query and determine why it was performing so terribly. Without this ability from the Diag Pack via Enterprise Manager, I would have needed to run multiple scripts by hand, calculate and interpret the results, and then figure out which scripts to run to lead me further down the path. EM and the Diag Pack made this process much quicker.

Another useful view in Enterprise Manager is to select Performance ➤ SQL Monitoring. In Figure 21-5, I clicked the Database Time column to sort the SQL statements in descending order so that I could view the longest-running SQL statements. Again, I blacked out sensitive information in the figure. I wanted to show real-life production performance, which meant proprietary information needed to be obscured. Subsequent figures also have blacked-out portions for that reason.

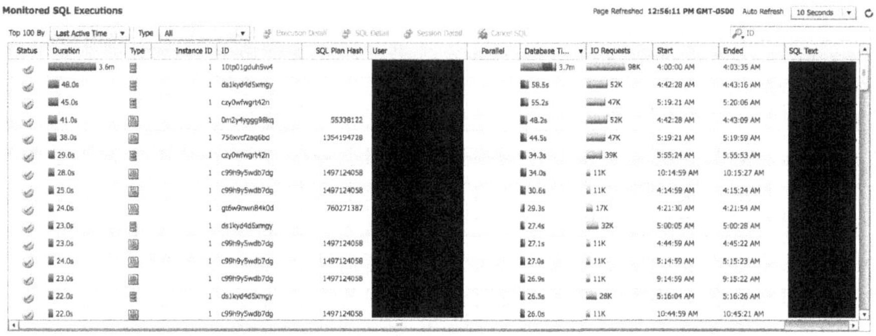

Figure 21-5. *EM SQL Monitoring*

In Figure 21-5, we can see that one SQL statement at the top is showing Database Time much larger than the rest. While no one has complained of a performance issue, we might want to spend just a few minutes and see if we can be proactive. As an aside, the database administrator should find opportunities to be more proactive with administration of their systems. Resolve problems before end users complain.

Clicking the ID for this SQL statement takes us to more details about this SQL statement, shown in Figure 21-6.

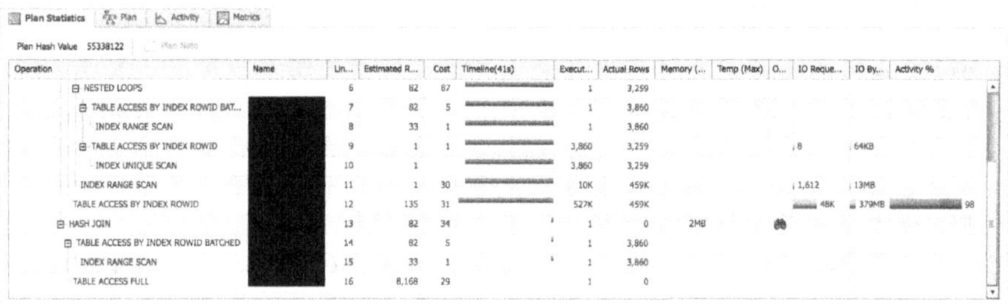

Figure 21-6. *EM SQL Plan Statistics tab*

If we look at the Plan Statistics tab for this column, the bar charts in the Activity % column can be a good indicator of where this SQL statement is spending its time. In this case, 98% of the activity for this SQL statement was spent accessing a table using an index. Maybe in this case either the index is the wrong one to use or a full table scan would be more efficient.

We will capture this information and figure out how much effort is needed to make this SQL statement more efficient. With just a few clicks in EM, leveraging the Diag Pack, we were able to quickly spot a potential issue and proactively address the problem.

The Diagnostics Pack also includes the Automatic Database Diagnostic Monitor, ADDM. ADDM will take a look at overall database performance for a period of time, usually an hour, and make recommendations on how to improve performance. It should be noted that ADDM does this automatically. We do not have to set it up.

If we look at a performance chart, EM will show a little clipboard icon below the graph, circled in Figure 21-7. We can click that icon to see the results from an ADDM run.

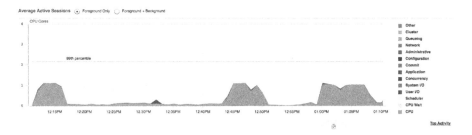

Figure 21-7. *EM ADDM run icon*

Clicking this icon will take us to the ADDM section in EM. We can see a chart showing the ADDM runs in the past 24 hours. We now see multiple clipboards. In Figure 21-8, I clicked the icon under the largest peak of activity in the graph.

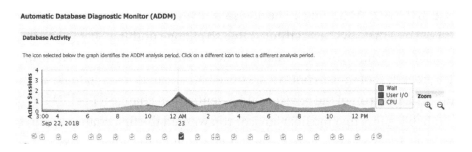

Figure 21-8. *EM ADDM screen*

When we click one of the icons to see ADDM results, the information below the chart changes to match. After clicking the clipboard icon under the largest peak in Figure 21-8, ADDM presented the findings shown in Figure 21-9.

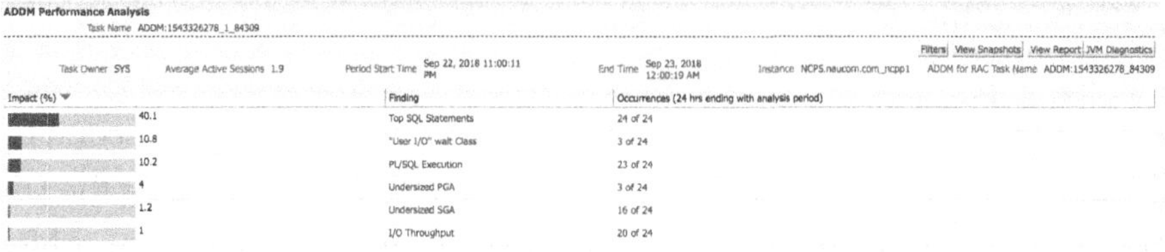

Figure 21-9. *ADDM Performance Analysis*

We can see that ADDM has determined that top SQL statements contributed 40% to the impact of overall database performance during this period. If we click the link in the Finding column, we can drill down into the top SQL statements, as shown in Figure 21-10.

Figure 21-10. *ADDM top SQL statement recommendations*

ADDM found five SQL statements. All seem to have similar impact. We can click the Schedule SQL Tuning Advisor button to have Oracle give us recommendations on how to tune the SQL statement if we choose. Clicking this button requires the optional Tuning Pack to be licensed, which is discussed in the next section.

I should make one note about advisor recommendations in general, such as what you will see in the ADDM findings. The advisors always make a recommendation. I have yet to see one that says "everything is fine so change nothing." If you are constantly looking at advisor results, you will constantly be making changes and, in return, spending a great deal of time in one area. I once had an advisor say to make a change, which I did. The next run of the advisor said essentially to change it back. Which I did. You can probably guess that the next advisor run wanted the first change again. I would have been stuck in an endless loop if I continued to follow the advice. Take advisor and other expert system recommendations with a grain of salt. Know when to stop and move on to other DBA tasks.

So far, we have seen the Diagnostics Pack in action to quickly drill down to a singular session or SQL statement experiencing performance issues. The Diag Pack also includes the Automatic Workload Repository (AWR) to capture information at the instance level. The AWR is often useful when we want to get a detailed analysis of the instance's performance. Out of the box, the AWR takes a snapshot of instance performance once per hour, but you can manually capture a snapshot on demand. Many of the metrics will be indicators of the activity since instance startup. For example, there is a metric tracking the total number of disk reads since instance startup. All of this metric collection occurs automatically. The data is stored in the SYSAUX tablespace and retained for 30 days unless you modify the retention period.

When the database administrator wants to look at overall performance, they will run an AWR report. The AWR reports asks for a beginning and ending snapshot. The report then calculates the differences and uses the time interval to generate averages. For example, in the case of disk reads, the AWR report will subtract the number of disk reads in the beginning snapshot from the number in the ending snapshot and obtain the total number of disk reads over that interval. If the snapshots were taken 60 minutes apart, the AWR report will divide the total disk reads by 3,600 to obtain an average number of disk reads per second for that report period.

To generate an AWR report, you can run the $ORACLE_HOME/rdbms/admin/awrreport.sql script in SQL*Plus, or you can navigate to Performance ➤ AWR ➤ AWR Report in Enterprise Manager, as shown in Figure 21-11.

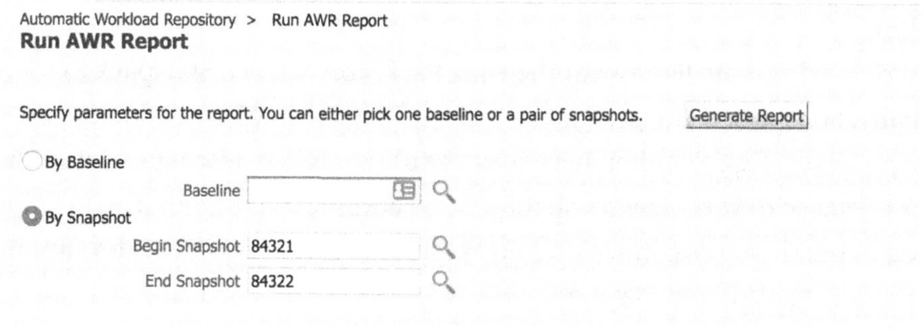

Figure 21-11. *Specifying AWR report parameters*

In the example in Figure 21-11, I selected the By Snapshot option. I clicked the magnifying glass icon to bring up a list of snapshots and chose two of them for my report period. Then I clicked the Generate Report button. After a few minutes, the report shown if Figure 21-12 was displayed in the browser. The first part of the report contains some introductory information such as hostname, database version, etc.

WORKLOAD REPOSITORY report for

DB Name	DB Id	Instance	Inst num	Startup Time	Release	RAC
▉▉▉▉▉	1543326278	▉▉▉▉▉	1	20-Sep-18 22:09	12.1.0.2.0	YES

Host Name	Platform	CPUs	Cores	Sockets	Memory (GB)
▉▉▉▉▉	Linux x86 64-bit	8	4	1	93.90

	Snap Id	Snap Time	Sessions	Cursors/Session	Instances
Begin Snap:	84321	23-Sep-18 12:00:08	175	9.0	4
End Snap:	84322	23-Sep-18 13:00:03	173	9.3	4
Elapsed:		59.93 (mins)			
DB Time:		20.99 (mins)			

Report Summary

Top ADDM Findings by Average Active Sessions

Finding Name	Avg active sessions of the task	Percent active sessions of finding	Task Name	Begin Snap Time	End Snap Time
Top SQL Statements	.35	78.86	ADDM:1543326278_1_84322	23-Sep-18 12:00	23-Sep-18 13:00
PL/SQL Execution	.35	30.89	ADDM:1543326278_1_84322	23-Sep-18 12:00	23-Sep-18 13:00

Figure 21-12. *Example AWR report*

If you have licensed the Diag Pack, you can view the pages of information found in the AWR report. Learning how to leverage the AWR report is the subject of another book. I would start by reading the *Oracle Database Performance Tuning Guide* if you want more information.

If you do not have the license for the Diag Pack, you can use Statspack to mimic the functionality. Statspack is the predecessor to the Diag Pack. With Statspack, you run some scripts to set it up. You then have to schedule a job to perform the data collection. Statspack comes with your license, so there is no additional cost, but it is no longer being developed as new features come with new versions. Oracle saves their development effort at extending AWR, not Statspack.

One of the downsides of the AWR is that the repository keeps the data for 30 days and then it is automatically purged. You can change the retention period, but then your AWR disk usage will grow, and we normally do not want that in a production system. Oracle has provided the ability to automatically migrate AWR data to an AWR Warehouse. If you have licensed the Diag Pack, you can enjoy the AWR Warehouse. In Enterprise Manager, click Performance ➤ AWR ➤ AWR Warehouse and follow the directions to set it up. You will need to create another Oracle database, and this should not be on the same server as your production databases. The AWR Warehouse configuration is shown in Figure 21-13. We can see that it was created by me, its database version is 12.1.0.2, and 75% of the disk space is currently used.

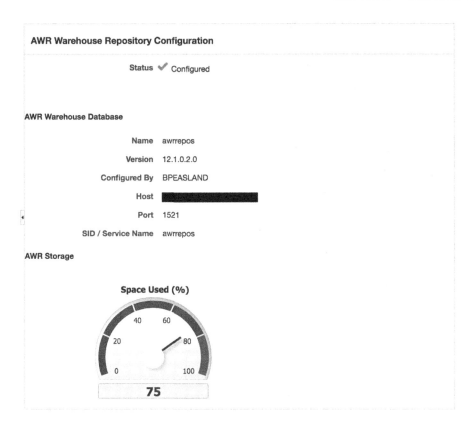

Figure 21-13. *AWR Warehouse configuration*

Figure 21-14 shows that three databases hold data in the AWR Warehouse, totaling 105GB of disk space.

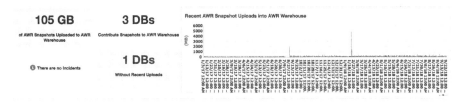

Figure 21-14. *AWR Warehouse details*

The best use of the AWR Warehouse is to be able to compare performance today with performance quite a while ago. In my AWR Warehouse, I have defined the retention period to be two years. How long you keep data in your warehouse depends on your business cycle. My business experiences ebbs and flows with the calendar. I wanted to be able to compare over slightly more than one year ago, so I chose a two-year retention period. Once the warehouse is created, I can then create an AWR report that shows the differences between two periods. The most common place for me to use this is when trying to correlate performance after an upgrade of the database or the application to the same period the year before.

Tuning Pack

The Tuning Pack is a great companion to the Diagnostics Pack. We have already seen that the ADDM in the Diag Pack gives us a button to generate a session with the Tuning Pack. This is one pack that I do use on occasion, but I am not as insistent that it be made available to me as I am the Diag Pack. The Tuning Pack consists of the following:

- Real-time SQL Monitoring

- SQL Tuning Advisor

- SQL Access Advisor

- SQL Profiles

- In-Memory Advisor

- Object Reorganization

If we return to the ADDM findings as shown in Figure 21-10, we can click the Schedule SQL Tuning Advisor button. The next screen asks us to fill out some information on how to schedule this work, as shown in Figure 21-15.

Figure 21-15. *Scheduling SQL Tuning Advisor*

In Figure 21-15, I changed the name of this advisor run to be SQL_TUNING_DBA_ MENTOR. You can use the default name if you like. The scope of the analysis is defined in the Scope section. A limited scope is much less resource intensive, but will not allow the advisor to consider all of the alternatives. If you want a more comprehensive scope and do not want to run this during peak periods of instance activity, you can schedule the execution during a quieter time and check on the results tomorrow. When everything is ready, click the Submit button. Due to my options, my advisor run will execute immediately. When I click the Submit button, I can watch the task run, as shown in Figure 21-16.

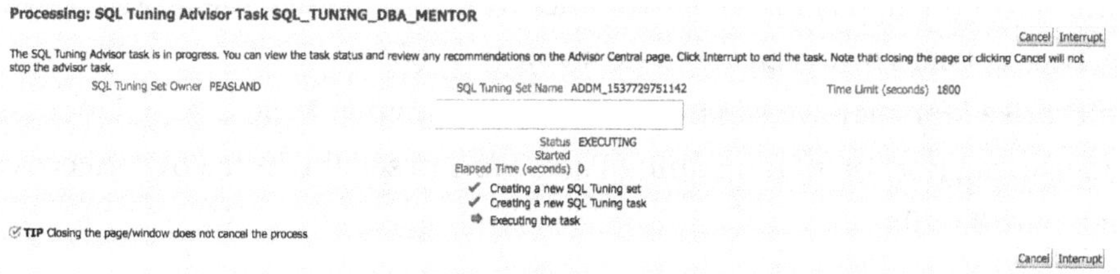

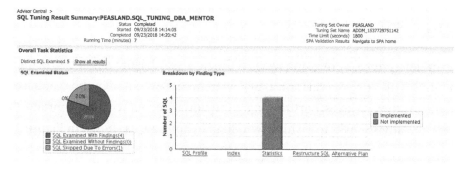

Figure 21-16. *Tuning Advisor execution*

The advisor run will eventually complete. The results can then be seen in Figure 21-17.

Figure 21-17. *Tuning Advisor overall findings*

At a glance, I can see the biggest finding type was related to statistics. If I scroll down further, I can see that a table and an index have stale statistics contributing to the problem, as shown in Figure 21-18. The object name and schema were obscured to protect proprietary information.

Statistics Finding Summary

Validate with SPA

Object Name	Object Type	Schema	Problem	References
■■■■■■	INDEX	■■■■	STALE	4
	TABLE		STALE	4

Figure 21-18. *Tuning Advisor statistics finding*

Without doing much work, I was able to leverage the Diag Pack's ADDM functionality to tell me there was a problem with some SQL statements. I then leveraged the Tuning Pack's advisor to tell me statistics were stale on a table and its index. This type of time savings will pay for itself over and over again, which makes the cost of the Diag and Tuning Packs much easier to deal with.

In Enterprise Manager, we can navigate to Performance ➤ SQL ➤ SQL Access Advisor to use that portion of the Tuning Pack. We can see the initial SQL Access Advisor screen in Figure 21-19.

Advisor Central > SQL Access Advisor: Initial Options
SQL Access Advisor: Initial Options
Select a set of initial options.   Cancel Continue

○ Verify use of access structures (indexes, materialized views, partitioning, etc) only
◉ Recommend new access structures

Overview

☐ Inherit Options from a previously saved Task or Template

The SQL Access Advisor evaluates SQL statements in a workload Source, and can suggest indexes, partitioning, materialized views and materialized view logs that will improve performance of the workload as a whole.

✓ **TIP** You are selecting the starting point for the wizard. All options can be changed from within the wizard.

Cancel Continue

Figure 21-19. *SQL Access Advisor*

In the initial options, I am going to see if the Access Advisor will recommend any new structures. This advisor will look at SQL statements executed in the database and recommend any new indexes, partitioning, or materialized views if appropriate. On the next screen, the advisor asks me which workload to analyze, as shown in Figure 21-20.

Select the source of the workload that you want to use for the analysis. The best workload is one that fully represents all the SQL statements that access the underlying tables.
◉ Current and Recent SQL Activity
   SQL will be selected from the cache.
○ Use an existing SQL Tuning Set
   SQL Tuning Set
○ Create a Hypothetical Workload from the Following Schemas and Tables
   The advisor can create a hypothetical workload if the tables contain dimension or primary/foreign key constraints.
   Schemas and Tables
                                                                         Add
   Comma-separated list
   ✓ **TIP** Enter a schema name to specify all the tables belonging to that schema.

▷ **Filter Options**

✓ **TIP** For workloads containing a large number of SQL statements, Oracle recommends using filtering to reduce analysis time.

Cancel Step 1 of 4 Next

Figure 21-20. *SQL Access Advisor workload*

I have chosen to use the current and recent SQL activity. On the next screen, I selected the type of access structures to consider. I also chose the Comprehensive scope. My options are shown in Figure 21-21.

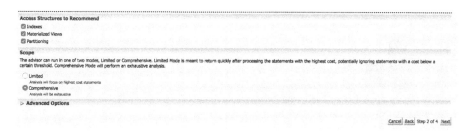

Figure 21-21. *SQL Access Advisor options*

The next screen asks for scheduling options similar to those requested by the Tuning Advisor. When ready, submit the job and the Access Advisor will go to work. The more comprehensive and the more SQL statements the advisor needs to analyze, the longer the job will take to complete. Once the analysis is complete, we can view the report similar to Figure 21-22.

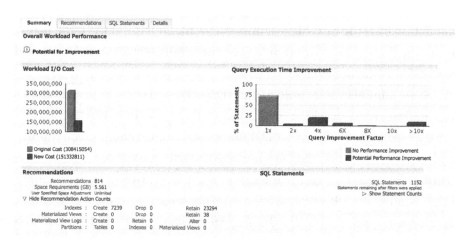

Figure 21-22. *SQL Access Advisor Summary tab*

The Summary screen shows us the original I/O cost is over 308 million I/O operations. If we implement the findings from this advisor run, the new cost will be less than half of that, about 151 million I/O operations. The advisor is recommending that we create 7,239 new indexes. I typically do not introduce that much change, so let's dig a little deeper into the findings by clicking the Recommendations tab. We can see the recommendations in Figure 21-23.

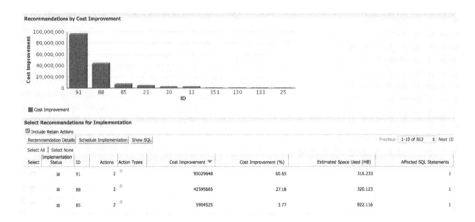

Figure 21-23. *SQL Access Advisor Recommendations tab*

The advisor has 812 recommendations. If we look at the bar chart, we can see that recommendation ID 91 will contribute almost 100 million I/O operation improvements. Recommendation 88 is the next biggest improvement. Looking at the table below the chart, we can see those two recommendations contribute 60.65% and 27.18% of the cost improvement, for a total of 87.83%.

The database administrator could go through each and every SQL statement in the system and analyze them individually or could save a ton of time with the SQL Access Advisor. This advisor run analyzed 1,152 different SQL statement in seven minutes. While the advisor was doing its work, the DBA multitasked and worked on other activities.

The Tuning Pack can be a great time saver for the DBA. However, if the application is from another vendor, the DBA typically is not responsible for tuning the SQL statements. That is the software vendor's job. The Tuning Pack is used by DBAs that need to support in-house developed applications.

Partitioning

Partitioning is an extra-cost option that lets you subdivide a table into smaller tables, called *partitions*. Transparent to the application, partitioning allows these smaller tables to function together as if they were one large table. A table is partitioned if it needs to be able to handle a very large number of rows, typically millions or more. Small tables do not normally benefit from partitioning.

The diagram in Figure 21-24 shows an ORDER_DETAILS table from a typical web-based store. As customers fill out orders, the details of the order are stored in this table.

Because this is a high-volume website that sells many products daily, the DBA has partitioned the table based on the year the order was placed. The diagram in Figure 21-24 shows four partitions for the table corresponding to the years 2016 through 2019. Prior to the year 2020, the DBA will want to add a partition for that year.

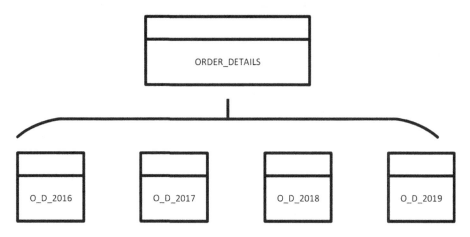

Figure 21-24. *ORDER_DETAILS partitioned table*

Users and applications do not typically reference a partition directly. Instead, they still query the ORDER_DETAILS table. The ORDER_DETAILS table does not exist on storage, only in the data dictionary. It is the partitions that are stored on disk. When a user or application queries the ORDER_DETAILS table, Oracle pulls the data from the partitions. There are two main reasons to partition the table, storage and performance.

A table is located in one and only one tablespace. However, if a table is partitioned, the partitions can be placed in different tablespaces. This lets the DBA put older, rarely used partitions on slower disk storage if desired. For example, the 2016 ORDER_ DETAILS partition can be on the "slow" disk and the 2018 and 2019 partitions on the faster disk because they are more current. The DBA does this by creating different tablespaces on different disk storage types and moving the partitions to the appropriate tablespace. Because the 2016 data will not change, the DBA can then alter that tablespace to be READ ONLY, thus letting RMAN back up it up once and skip it for subsequent backups.

A properly partitioned table can benefit from Oracle's *partition pruning*. In the example diagram in Figure 21-24, it is rare for someone to look at order details from older years. Typically, we would be querying for recent orders. The DBA could place an index on a column in the table that stores the order detail date. However, if we query on a date range that is large enough, such as order details from the previous quarter, Oracle's Optimizer may decide the index is not selective enough and perform a full table scan, reading the details going back years. This can cause terrible performance. If the table is partitioned on the detail date, Oracle will automatically remove, or prune, nonparticipating partitions from being accessed. In our example, if we are querying for all order details in the fourth quarter of 2018, Oracle would only access the 2018 partition and ignore the rest because it knows they do not have any records to satisfy the SQL statement.

When people partition an Oracle table, the biggest mistake they make is failing to look at the most common SQL statement executed against that table. You want to leverage partition pruning as much as possible. If you often query by the order detail date, then partitioning on the order ID column will not give you any partition pruning benefit. Before deciding on a partition column, make sure you know which SQL statements need to benefit from partition pruning.

Before partitioning was an Oracle option, people implemented what has been termed a "poor man's partitioning." They did this by creating multiple smaller tables and then creating a view which did a UNION ALL operation over all of the tables. While this solution does let you enjoy the same storage benefit as Oracle's Partitioning option, it does not automatically participate in partition pruning.

In Listing 21-1, we can see an example of how to partition the table from Figure 21-24.

Listing 21-1. Partition Table Example

```
CREATE TABLE ORDER_ENTRY.ORDER_DETAILS (
              ORDER_ID NUMBER(38,0) NOT NULL,
              ORDER_DETAIL_DATE_BEGIN DATE NOT NULL,
              ORDER_ITEM_ID NUMBER NOT NULL,
              ORDER_ITEM_COST NUMBER(38,2) NOT NULL,
              DATE_ITEM_SHIPPED DATE)
  TABLESPACE ORDER_ENTRY_DATA
  PARTITION BY RANGE (ORDER_DETAIL_DATE)
(PARTITION o_d_2016  VALUES LESS THAN (TO_DATE('01/01/2017 00:00:00',
'MM/DD/YYYY HH24:MI:SS')) TABLESPACE ORDER_ENTRY_DATA,
PARTITION o_d_2017  VALUES LESS THAN (TO_DATE('01/01/2018 00:00:00',
'MM/DD/YYYY HH24:MI:SS')) TABLESPACE ORDER_ENTRY_DATA,
PARTITION o_d_2018  VALUES LESS THAN (TO_DATE('01/01/2019 00:00:00',
'MM/DD/YYYY HH24:MI:SS')) TABLESPACE ORDER_ENTRY_DATA,
```

```
PARTITION o_d_2019  VALUES LESS THAN (TO_DATE('01/01/2020 00:00:00',
'MM/DD/YYYY HH24:MI:SS')) TABLESPACE ORDER_ENTRY_DATA,
PARTITION o_d_max  VALUES LESS THAN (MAXVALUE) TABLESPACE ORDER_ENTRY_DATA);
```

In the example above, the ORDER_DETAILS table is partitioned on the ORDER_
DETAIL_DATE column. The first partition, O_D_2016, contains all records where the
column's value is less than 01/01/2017. The 2017 partition contains all records with
values higher than the 2016 partition and less than 01/01/2018. The last partition is a
catch-all for any values higher than the other partitions and less than the maximum
value possible for that column. I often include this catch-all in case the DBA neglects
to add the next year's partition. Once the DBA figures out they made a mistake, they
can take corrective action during a maintenance window, but this way, the application
functionality does not break due to human error.

The example shown so far uses *range partitioning*. The partition is defined on a
specific range of values. Oracle supports the following partitioning schemes:

- *Range partitioning*: Probably the most commonly used partitioning
  method. Data is partitioned on a range of values, as we have seen in
  the previous discussion.

- *List partitioning*: The DBA defines the partition to hold a list of
  discrete values. For example, you could partition by the state or the
  country, or similar governmental boundary. In the United States,
  there would be 50 partitions, one for each state, as an example.

- *Hash partitioning*: The value is run through a hash algorithm to
  determine which partition is used.

- *Automatic-list partitioning*: Oracle will automatically extend a list-
  partitioned table for you.

- *Interval partitioning*: Very similar to range partitioning. Instead of
  defining a range on specific boundaries, we can use the interval on
  the data type. For example, on a date datatype, we can define the
  interval to be the year portion of that date.

- *Composite partitioning*: A table is partitioned by one method, then
  subpartitioned with a second method. A common example would be
  to use range partitioning based on a date, then use hash partitioning
  to further subdivide the data.

If you deal with significant volumes of data, the Partitioning option may be just what you need. Not everything should be partitioned, but this option really helps tame larger datasets.

Real Application Clusters

In the previous chapter, we examined the difference between an Oracle database and an instance. Remember that the database is the files on disk and the instance is the collection of memory and processes on the server. For many Oracle deployments, there is a one-to-one relationship between the database and the instance. This architecture has two problems. One, if the server is unavailable, no one can access the data. Two, performance is constrained to the limits of the resources on that server. Oracle Real Application Clusters (RAC) addresses these two issues. Oracle RAC is a high-availability and high-scalability solution. You do not have to pick one or the other. You can have both with Oracle RAC.

With Oracle RAC, the architecture has multiple instances, each on its own server. These instances can simultaneously access the same database, the same files on disk. With Oracle RAC, you get a many-to-one relationship between instances and the database. The diagram in Figure 21-25 illustrates an Oracle RAC system.

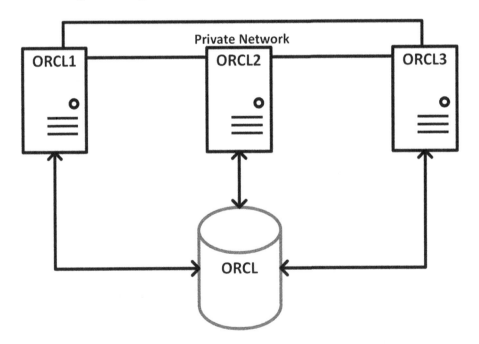

Figure 21-25. *Oracle RAC system*

We can see the database, ORCL, on disk. The disk must be shared over all systems in the configuration. As such, the disk is often Network Attached Storage (NAS) or in a Storage Area Network (SAN). To avoid single points of failure, the disk system should have built-in redundancy. Additionally, the disk needs to be accessible via multiple pathways.

A private network is created between the servers in the configuration. This network is high speed and is used for instance-to-instance communications. It is important that the network be private so that other network activity does not negatively impact Oracle RAC performance.

In the diagram in Figure 21-25, we have three servers for this Oracle RAC system. The servers form a *cluster*, meaning many machines acting together as one. The glue that makes the cluster work is Oracle software called Grid Infrastructure, which must be installed and running before an Oracle RAC database can be created.

Each server has an instance running on it. The instance name is the same as the database name but with an instance identifier appended to it. For the ORCL database, we have instances ORCL1, ORCL2, and ORCL3.

User sessions can connect to any of the instances. High availability is achieved because if a server is unavailable, another server in the cluster (called a *node*) can do the work. If the system is configured with Transparent Application Failover (TAF), a session can move from one instance to another should its instance terminate.

Scalability is achieved by adding more nodes to the cluster. Oracle RAC systems typically use lower-cost servers for the nodes in the cluster. Should more resources be needed, add another node to the configuration. Need double the resources? Double the nodes.

Keep in mind that the Oracle database software needs to be licensed on all nodes in the cluster. Oracle Real Application Clusters also needs to be licensed on all nodes. While this may sound like a lot of extra licensing, it is often cheaper than buying a larger-capacity server with enough resources to support the workload.

If you are looking for a high-availability or high-scalability solution, look at Oracle RAC. You will be able to enjoy both aspects for the one purchase.

Multitenant

Oracle Multitenant is the way of the future for Oracle databases. Multitenant brings virtualization down to the Oracle level. Earlier in this book we created a virtual machine to act as our testbed server. We used a virtual machine so that we could have our own distinct database server without requiring additional physical hardware. Wouldn't it be nice if we could create virtual databases within Oracle? That's what Multitenant provides.

Before Multitenant, the Oracle DBA could consolidate servers by running multiple instances on the same database server. Each instance has its own database, so please do not confuse this with Oracle RAC. As an example, we might have an Oracle database supporting our company's Human Resources application and another database supporting our company's Accounting system. To reduce costs, we can host both on the same physical machine. We have two databases each with their own instance. As we know from the previous chapter, when we start the instances, each requires its own SGA, its own background processes. Each brings with it a certain amount of overhead.

Oracle database administrators then tried to combine these into the same database by placing the HR tables in their own schema and the accounting tables in a different schema. This works so long as the two systems do not have the same public synonyms or the same grants to PUBLIC.

To facilitate database consolidation, Oracle provides the Multitenant option. With Multitenant, we have a container database that is mostly empty. We then plug in a database for HR and plug in another database for Accounting. All of the resources and overhead occurs in the container database. We can plug in many databases, called Pluggable Databases (PDBs), without increasing the overhead. Each PDB is segregated from the other PDBs. PDBs do not even know other PDBs exist.

Multitenant is also a great time saver for Oracle database administrators. Instead of patching each database separately, the DBA patches the container database. All of the PDBs are patched with this single operation. If the DBA is using RMAN for backups, a backup of the container will also back up all PDBs. If the DBA adds another PDB, no additional work is necessary for ensuring it is backed up.

Oracle Multitenant is transparent to the application. The application connects to the instance and can see only that PDB, no different than if this were a non-Multitenant database. Applications do not have to change one bit to work with Multitenant.

While not required, Oracle Multitenant is often deployed on top of Oracle RAC. When consolidating database servers, we may not want to put them all on one server. If that server fails, all of the PDBs would be down, causing problems for multiple applications. Also, there might be a concern that the workloads from all of these applications would be too much for one server. Oracle RAC, with its high availability and high scalability, addresses these concerns. Many customers are moving tens or over a hundred Oracle databases from individual servers to Oracle RAC clusters with Multitenant and using fewer machines. Oracle RAC and Multitenant are two different products that really have nothing to do with each other. You can use one or the other or both. Increasingly, we are seeing Oracle RAC being deployed with Multitenant.

Oracle Corporation has stated that Multitenant is the way of the future. Oracle 12*c* has deprecated the non-Multitenant Oracle database. While you can still create a non-Multitenant database, as we did in our testbed, at some point that will not be an option. You can begin using Multitenant today and in the future without incurring any additional costs so long as you limit yourself to a singular PDB. If you want a second PDB, or more, that is when you must start licensing the Multitenant option.

Data Guard

Adding to the high-availability capabilities of the Oracle database is a product called Data Guard. Oracle RAC does a great job of providing high availability for databases at your production data center. What happens if that data center is unavailable for some reason? Your business requirements may need a duplicate copy of your database running at another data center. Data Guard accomplishes this by shipping transactions from the primary site to the standby site. As a transaction modifies data in the primary database, that transaction will keep the standby database up to date. Should a failure occur at the primary data center, the DBA can open the standby database and allow applications to perform their business.

Without Data Guard, the only other option is to take a backup of your database and restore on hardware at the standby site. If the database is large enough, the amount of time to perform a restore could be more than is acceptable to the business. Additionally, if the backup is not very current, a large amount of data loss will occur. With Data Guard, there is no need to restore anything because the database is always there and available.

Data Guard can be configured for zero data loss or, for those concerned about the potential performance hit, minimal data loss. A zero data loss configuration means that when a transaction commits, it must commit in both the primary and standby databases. The lag time between the sites may cause performance issues in a zero data loss configuration. The DBA may want to configure Data Guard to have minimal data loss so that application performance will not suffer. While we never like to lose data, this is the most typical configuration for database administrators deploying Data Guard. In most configurations, the minimal data loss solution amounts to one second of data loss or less. I work with one large primary database that sees over 1TB of transactional volume per week, and the standby is at most one second behind the primary. Ideally, we would like a zero data loss solution, but the performance hit is too costly to the business. Losing one second of transactions is much more acceptable.

The diagram in Figure 21-26 shows how the Oracle architecture changes to support Data Guard.

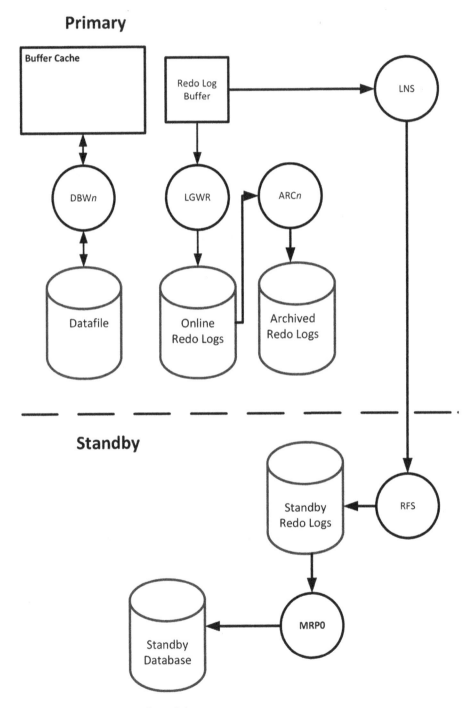

Figure 21-26. *Data Guard architecture*

The first part of the diagram was taken from the previous chapter. When Data Guard is in place, a new process named LNS will transport the redo from the primary database to the standby site. This is little different than LGWR writing redo to the online redo logs. The only thing that changes is that LNS is writing the redo to the RFS process running on the standby instance. When RFS receives the redo, it writes the redo to standby redo logs. The Managed Recovery Process (MRP0) reads the redo from the standby redo logs and updates the standby database with the transactions.

In Oracle terminology, there are two activities taking place in this diagram. First, there is redo *transport*, the act of sending redo to the standby database. Second, there is redo *apply*, the act of replaying those transactions. LNS is responsible for redo transport. MRP0 is responsible for redo apply.

With the two systems in place, the standby database just sits there, continually updating, until it gets the call to action. If the DBA performs a *switchover* operation, the two databases will reverse roles. The primary becomes the standby and vice versa. There is a short amount of downtime for the switchover. During this downtime, all committed transactions will be assured of being sent to the standby and applied there. A switchover is a zero data loss operation. Because the roles are being reversed, it should be obvious that the primary database needs to be available. If the primary database is not available, then the only option is a *failover* operation. When the DBA institutes a failover, the standby becomes the primary and the old primary is essentially a dead database, no longer part of this configuration. The amount of data loss from a failover depends on the Data Guard configuration.

Data Guard does not require an extra license. However, the standby database does need to be licensed. If you want to create a standby database, work with your Oracle Sales rep or reseller and let them know you are interested in a license specifically for a standby database. They will probably offer you a discount for this Oracle license so long as the database is only ever used as a standby database.

Oracle does have an extra-cost option called Active Data Guard. In addition to licensing the standby Oracle database, you can buy the extra Active Data Guard to provide even more capabilities. Normally the standby database just sits there applying redo. While this is great should a disaster strike, it's mostly unusable for anything of value until that time. With Active Data Guard, you can open the standby in read-only mode and use it for a reporting database, offloading resource-intensive reports to this system. While in read-only mode, Active Data Guard will also be replaying transactions, keeping the standby up to date with the primary.

Active Data Guard can detect and automatically repair block corruption in both the primary and the standby. Because the databases are transactionally consistent, a data block will contain the same data in both locations. If block corruption is detected in the primary, Active Data Guard will fetch that block's contents from the standby and replace the block in the primary. This also works the same if block corruption is detected in the standby.

Prior to Oracle 12*c*, the DBA had to choose between zero data loss or better performance. With Active Data Guard in 12*c*, the DBA can have the best of both worlds. Oracle 12*c* introduced the new Far Sync capability, which gives you zero data loss while maintaining the same level of performance.

Active Data Guard also supports rolling upgrades. This will reduce the downtime window to upgrade an Oracle database. Without Active Data Guard, upgrades will incur a larger downtime window as the primary database is upgraded and unavailable to end users.

These additional Active Data Guard features need to be weighed against the cost to determine if the product merits the additional cost. Keep in mind that Data Guard comes with your Oracle Enterprise Edition database license. Active Data Guard does not.

Lastly, Data Guard and Active Data Guard work with Multitenant and Oracle RAC. You mix and match these to meet your requirements.

Enterprise Manager

Throughout this book, we have seen some screenshots of Oracle Enterprise Manager (EM), even in this chapter. Enterprise Manager is Oracle's monitoring and management console. It will certainly handle your Oracle databases and their servers, but also web servers and many more. EM is included in your current Oracle license so, unlike the other options in this chapter, there is no extra cost.

Enterprise Manager comes in two different distributions, EM DB Express and EM Cloud Control. EM DB Express can be created with the Database Configuration Assistant and is used to manage one and only one database. If you have a second database, you need to point your web browser to a second instance of EM DB Express. The more databases you want to manage with EM, the more URLs you will have to bookmark if you use EM DB Express.

EM Cloud Control is a centralized version that can manage any number of Oracle databases. EM Cloud Control should be set up on its own server. It will also require a separate database to serve as its repository. If you use this database only for the EM Cloud Control repository, there is no extra license needed for this repository database.

This section of the chapter will focus on EM Cloud Control, and will refer to it simply as EM. If you have more than two or three Oracle databases, you may wish to use Cloud Control over EM DB Express, although that number is up for debate. Some might say you want more databases before looking at EM Cloud Control.

After you connect to EM, you will be presented with an option to choose your welcome page, as shown in Figure 21-27.

Figure 21-27. *EM home page selection*

I often choose the Summary screen, but feel free to choose the one that best suits your role. The Summary screen shows an overview of how your managed targets are doing at that given time. An example of the Summary screen is shown in Figure 21-28.

Figure 21-28. *EM Summary screen Overview section*

In Figure 21-28, I can see EM is managing 228 targets. Two of those targets are undergoing scheduled maintenance and nine have an unknown status. If the status is down or unknown, this tells me I need to investigate further. The table below the chart shows incidents that have occurred in the past seven days. This system has no incidents that need anyone's attention. Navigating to Targets ➤ Databases shows us a list of managed databases, as shown in Figure 21-29.

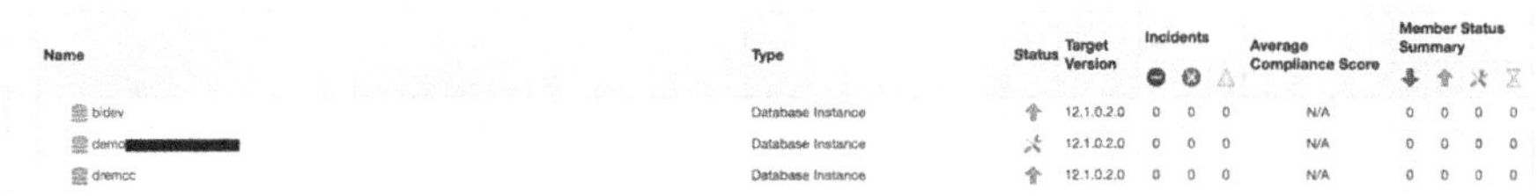

Name	Type	Status	Target Version	Incidents ⊝	⊗	⚠	Average Compliance Score	Member Status Summary ⬇	⬆	⚒	⊼
bidev	Database Instance	⬆	12.1.0.2.0	0	0	0	N/A	0	0	0	0
demo	Database Instance	⚒	12.1.0.2.0	0	0	0	N/A	0	0	0	0
dremcc	Database Instance	⬆	12.1.0.2.0	0	0	0	N/A	0	0	0	0

Figure 21-29. *EM managed databases*

Figure 21-29 shows a few of the managed databases along with their status, database version, and any open incidents. If we click one of the databases, we can obtain information and manage that target. In Figure 21-30, I clicked the bidev database to see more about that specific target.

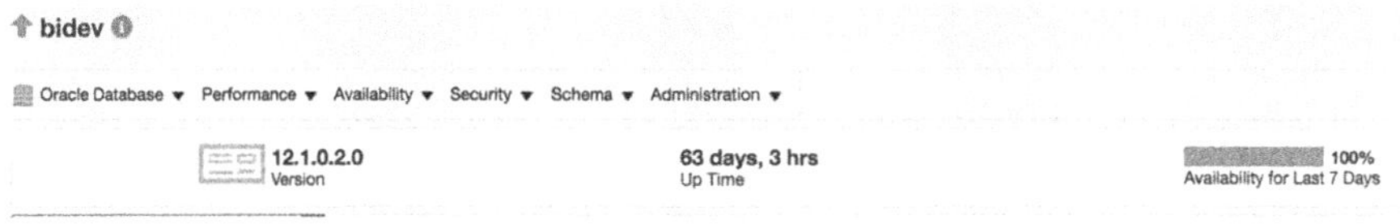

⬆ **bidev** ⓘ

Oracle Database ▾   Performance ▾   Availability ▾   Security ▾   Schema ▾   Administration ▾

| 12.1.0.2.0 Version | 63 days, 3 hrs Up Time | 100% Availability for Last 7 Days |

Figure 21-30. *EM database target*

We can see a green up arrow next to the database name indicating this instance has a status of Up. We can see the database's version and the uptime. Above the version and uptime are a number of drop-down menus that can be used to monitor and administer the database. We have already seen a number of items in the Performance menu when we discussed the Diagnostics Pack. The Availability menu lets us back up and recover a database and add a standby database to the configuration. The Security menu is where we can create users, assign privileges, and modify audit policies. The Schema menu gives us access to create database objects. The Administration menu lets us configure storage and handle scheduled jobs. There is so much more to explore here, so if you have access to EM, poke around and see what interests you.

EM will monitor your databases, servers, and other managed targets, looking for circumstances that are out of bounds with normal operating conditions. If something is not right, EM will raise an incident and can send a notification to the DBA so that they can look into the issue. The DBA has the ability to modify alert thresholds so that they are not notified if the problem is not severe enough. Should the monitored metrics out of the box be insufficient for your needs, you can create your own custom metrics.

One of the problems with EM is that it is too easy to use extra-cost options like the Diag and Tuning Packs. Simply navigating to a database's Performance Home page will require the Diag Pack to be licensed. You can see your licensing needs for a specific page by clicking Setup ➤ Management Packs ➤ Packs for This Page, as shown in Figure 21-31.

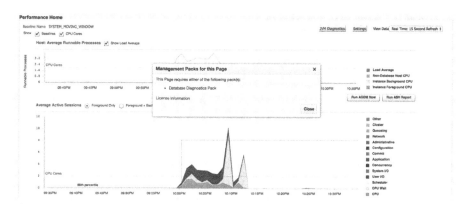

Figure 21-31.   *EM Packs for This Page*

In Figure 21-31, we can see the Performance Home page. We can also see the Database Diagnostics Pack must be licensed to use this page. The big problem from my perspective is that you cannot see what is required of this page until you land on the page. By then, you have flipped the flag that says you are using the extra-cost option. EM now lets you control the pages for these extra-cost options on a database-by-database basis. Navigate to Setup ➤ Management Packs ➤ Management Pack Access and you will see a screen similar to Figure 21-32.

Figure 21-32.   *EM pack access options*

For each managed database, you can deselect the options you are not licensed for. Unfortunately, these options are enabled by default. Make sure you uncheck the boxes you should not be using due to a lack of the license. Every database can be configured differently. With these boxes unchecked, you will not accidentally signal you have used an extra-cost option.

The Diag and Tuning Packs have their boxes grayed out because these two are controlled by the CONTROL_PACK_MANAGEMENT_ACCESS initialization parameter in each database. Valid values are NONE, DIAGNOSTIC, or DIAGNOSTIC+TUNING. In Oracle Enterprise Edition, the default is to enable both packs at the database level. Set this parameter appropriately to maintain compliance with your license agreement.

Advanced Compression

As the name implies, Advanced Compression is an optionally licensed product that lets you compress the data in your database. Compressed data requires less disk space, which can lead to savings on hardware. Compressed data can also lead to better performance because a single disk read is able to read more data than if it wasn't compressed. Applications often require fewer overall disk reads, leading to faster response times. Because the data is compressed in the data block, the Buffer Cache may not need to be as large because each block is storing more data. RMAN backup and recovery is also faster because fewer disk blocks need to be moved to and from the backup device. Lastly, Advanced Compression is transparent to the application.

Real Application Testing

One of the problems when introducing any major change to a database system is the ability to adequately test the application to ensure the change does not cause any problems. Real Application Testing (RAT) is an extra-cost option that lets the database administrator capture a real workload run against a production database. This workload can be moved to a different database and replayed on that target. RAT will then analyze the new performance against the original performance and report on any deficiencies. This is very beneficial when upgrading to a new Oracle version. Capture the production workload. Upgrade a duplicate database to the new version and replay the workload on this upgraded database. The DBA will have a good idea how well the version change affects the workload, if at all.

Moving On

This chapter has provided overviews of a number of Oracle database options. Most of them have an extra cost that you will want to understand before using the feature. In many cases, but not all, the extra cost is worth it to the business because of the time saved. I strongly recommend the Diagnostics Pack if you are not already licensed for it.

This chapter marks the end of the book. I thank you for reading it and hope you find the advice helpful in advancing your Oracle DBA career. Your journey has only begun and there is much to learn, but it should be an exciting adventure! Good luck!

Index

A

Active session history (ASH), 411
Admin file directories, 47
Administration, 229–230
Administrator's guide, 232–233
Advanced compression, 438
Agile development methodologies, 307
Alert log
 DBMS_SYSTEM package, 210
 error message, 207
 fixing control file, 207
 instance crash, 209
 instance shutdown, 208–209
 instance startup, 204–206
 missing control file, 207
 Oracle DBA, 204
 Oracle RAC, 203
 querying, 211
ALTER command, 210
ALTER SESSION command, 217–218
Application developers, 5
Archivelog mode
 database, configuration, 106
 redo log, 105, 107–108
Archiver Processes (ARCn), 398
Ask TOM website, 294
Audience, DBA, 20–22
Auditing, turn on, 126
Automatic Database Diagnostic Monitor
 (ADDM), 411

Automatic Diagnostic Repository
 Command Interpreter (ADRCI), 198
 package creation, 219
 problems, 219
 purge trace files, 220
 trace files, 219
Automatic-list partitioning, 427
Automatic memory management (AMM), 78
Automatic workload repository (AWR),
 397, 411, 416

B

Background processes, 395–396
 trace files, 213
Backup and recovery, 235
 documentation, 96
Backups, 9
Base tables
 DBA_TABLES creation, 247–248
 SYS.OBJ$ table, 246–247
 SYS.TAB$ table, 244, 246
 X$ tables, 248
Blog
 content, 289
 database administrators, 291
 memory retention, 290
 NewsBlur, 292
 problem resolutions, 290
 share information, 289
 WordPress, 289

© Brian Peasland 2019
B. Peasland, *Oracle DBA Mentor*, https://doi.org/10.1007/978-1-4842-4321-3

M

Manageability monitor (MMON), 397

Manageability monitory lite (MMNL), 397

Managed recovery process (MRP), 398

Mandatory processes

    CKPT, 397

    CLMN, 396

    CLnn, 396

    DBWn, 397

    LGWR, 397

    LREG, 397

    MMNL, 397

    MMON, 397

    PMAN, 396

    PMON, 396

    RECO, 397

    SMON, 397

Manual IP address, 180

MobaXterm, SSH, 182

MongoDB databases, 14

MOS certification

    EM results, 282

    quick links, 280

    search sections, 281

MOS dashboard, 270–271

Multiplatform work, DBA

    cheat sheet, 17

    database engines, 15

    employable skills, 18

    Oracle, 16

    relational database engines, 18

    SQL Server, 15–16

Multitenant, 429–430

My Oracle Support Community

    (MOSC), 295

My Oracle Support (MOS)

navigation tabs, 268

relative time, 282–284

sign in screen, 268

training videos, 271

N

NAT network adapter, 32

Network attached storage (NAS), 429

Network configuration assistant

    (NETCA), 197

NewsBlur, 292

Non-production areas, 23

NoSQL databases, 15

O

Object privileges, 128

Online redo logs (ORLs), 5, 49, 386

Open Database Computing (ODBC), 148

    connection, 153

    data source window, 150–151

    driver configuration, 151–152

    DSN, 150

    oracle drivers, 149

    Python, 153

Optimal flexible architecture (OFA), 43–44

Optional background processes, 398

ora12_verify_function, 118

Oracle

    client, 141

    DB software to VM, 60

    installation guide, 53

        documentation button, 54–55

        Linux links, 56

        selecting version, 55

        shared folders, 59

Printed in the United States
By Bookmasters